SO-AZE-775

A History of Russia

Also by Paul Dukes

*The Emergence of the Super-Powers: A Short
    Comparative History of the USA and the USSR*
Catherine the Great and the Russian Nobility

A History of Russia

Medieval, Modern and Contemporary

by PAUL DUKES

McGraw-Hill Book Company

New York   St. Louis   San Francisco

FERNALD LIBRARY
COLBY-SAWYER COLLEGE
NEW LONDON, N. H. 03257

DK
40
D84

9bq/ps Ekotern 11.25

Copyright © 1974 by Paul Dukes

All rights reserved.

Printed in Great Britain by Macmillan.

No part of this publication may be reproduced, stored in a retrieval
system, or transmitted, in any form or by any means, electronic,
mechanical, photocopying, recording, or otherwise, without prior
written permission of the publisher.

67353

Library of Congress Cataloging in Publication Data

Dukes, Paul, 1934–
  A history of Russia.

  1. Russia–History. I. Title.
DK40.D84   947   74–1154
ISBN 0–07–018032–6

To my brothers and sisters
and their children

Contents

Maps

Acknowledgements

Alfred G. Meyer, 'Theories of Convergence', from *Change in Communist Systems*, ed. C. Johnson, reprinted by permission of Stanford University Press; Arthur Ransome, *Six Weeks in Russia in 1919*, reprinted by permission of Mrs Arthur Ransome.

Preface

While this History of Russia does not claim to be any better than its many predecessors, it does aim at providing a distinctive interpretation, even if through change of emphasis rather than complete novelty. Its basic purposes may be placed in two main groups:

1) Since the Revolution of 1917, and particularly since the death of Stalin, Soviet historians have produced an impressive amount of useful information and interpretation, which has still to receive the recognition it deserves in works produced primarily for those who do not read Russian. While all too obviously suffering from an imperfect acquaintance with Soviet historiography, I have tried to take coverage of it at least a little further. At the same time, with similar handicaps, I have attempted to make use of pre-revolutionary Russian historical writing and of the publications of Western scholars, both old and new.

2) Economic and cultural developments are sometimes considered as appendices to the mainstream of political analysis; this book aspires to inclusion in the number of those which have achieved thematic integration. Similarly, its division into three distinct sections – medieval, modern, contemporary – has been implemented as an expression of agreement with those who hold that history has a fundamental pattern rather than constituting a disconnected series of essentially unique events. Moreover, it attempts in however modest a manner to reveal the limitations of an exclusively national approach to Russian history and to contribute to its analysis in a comparative framework. To put it briefly, my intention has been to adhere to the view of history put forward by E. H. Carr.

The errors and misunderstandings in the book are all my own work. For the rest, I have depended heavily on the published work of others, the principal debts being acknowledged in the Select Bibliography and

References. Of those who have helped directly in the writing of the book, I owe most to Barry Hollingsworth of the University of Manchester. He has made penetrating comments on the entire manuscript, and his comprehensive erudition tempered by a profound charity has been invaluable. Next I am pleased to record my gratitude to Rosie Mackay for her patient and careful reading of successive drafts which has eliminated a large number of inconsistencies and stylistic lapses. I also wish to express my thanks to Ron Grant for his incisive appraisal of most of the contemporary section, and to David Longley for giving me the benefit of his specialist understanding of the Russian Revolution. I have received a large amount of generous advice from members of the History Department and others at the University of Aberdeen. These include Roy Bridges, John Hiden, Jean Houbert, Leslie Macfarlane, George Molland and Bill Scott, and all the members of the Russian Department – Jim Forsyth, Richard Hallett, John Murray, Jo Newcombe and Cor Schwenke. Maureen Carr, Lily Findlay, Ann Gordon, Christine Macleod and Ann Murray all helped prepare the typescript for publication. The staff of King's College Library has as always been most helpful, as have associates of McGraw-Hill and Macmillan.

A more general debt is to the hundreds of students at the University of Aberdeen who have contributed to the unfinished process of my historical education. I consider myself more than lucky to have studied the subject under consideration with them in a locale which has many connections with it. Not many miles from here, an embassy from Ivan the Terrible was wrecked on the north-east coast of Scotland. Patrick Gordon and many other Russian mercenaries set sail from the local harbour. Aberdeen was a port en route from and to Petrograd during the momentous years of the Russian Revolution. There are Soviet fishing boats and timber ships at its docks today.

A few technical matters need to be touched on. The system of transliteration used is a variation of that adopted by the *Slavic Review*. Final -ii is rendered thus rather than -y, and all hard and soft signs have been omitted. Russian names are strictly transliterated on their first major appearance, but are normally given in their most usual form, particularly when they are well known. The names of Western scholars of Russian descent are given as they themselves spell them, and the authors of books and articles given as on the title page. Measurements have been made metric: those used most frequently are the hectare – just under $2\frac{1}{2}$ acres; the kilometre – just over $\frac{3}{5}$ mile; and the metric ton – a little less (36 lb) than the avoirdupois ton. Billions are American rather than British, that is a thousand million rather than a million

million. The maps drawn by Lawrence Maclean are intended to give
no more than location. For further geographical reference, the items
listed in the Select Bibliography should be consulted.

Dates from Chapter 5 to Chapter 10 inclusive are given Old Style:
eleven days behind New Style in the eighteenth century, twelve in the
nineteenth and thirteen in the twentieth.

King's College, Old Aberdeen   PAUL DUKES
December 1973

General Introduction

Everybody knows that the Russian land is vast, cold and mostly flat, with mighty rivers but little access to the sea. Like most common knowledge, this particular sample is in an important sense correct, but it also requires some modification. Taking up one-sixth of the world's land surface, the Soviet Union is by far its largest state; anybody who does not appreciate this basic fact should spend a week or so on the Trans-Siberian Railway. It is also among the coldest, as W. H. Parker tells us, with appropriate modifications:

> In winter over the USSR as a whole there is a predominance of cold polar air which often stagnates, becoming extremely cold and dry, and producing the lowest temperatures recorded on the earth outside of Antarctica. Warm maritime air no longer blows into the south-eastern region from the Pacific, but the south-western, Transcaucasian area is more fortunate and continues to receive maritime tropical air by way of the Mediterranean and Black Seas. From the west maritime temperate air, still retaining some of its original mildness and moisture, attempts – with varying success from winter to winter – to penetrate the great mass of cold air settled over the interior of the country. When it does so it too becomes increasingly cold and dry as it passes eastwards.[1]

Roughly a half of the Soviet Union is too cold for agriculture of any kind to be carried on, and a large part of Central Asia is too dry for it to be attempted without irrigation. The extraction and processing of the USSR's natural resources have been hampered by difficult problems of distance and climate.

These problems combine with a uniform geological structure and relief involving a widespread unvarying landscape to produce, in the view of many observers from at least as far back as the eighteenth century, a strongly centralised political arrangement. After each extension of the area of settlement, the government soon imposed its control. The huge Eurasian plain, with no clearly demarcated frontiers except for the rivers and part of the Urals, has been the wide stage for the continuous process of colonisation which the great pre-revolutionary historian Kliuchevskii singled out as the major theme of Russian history.[2] Towards the end of this process, it is true, the frontiersmen came up against the Arctic and Pacific Oceans to the north and east and high mountains to the south, but before the nineteenth century they were essentially plainsmen.

The flat monotony is to some extent broken up by the variation in soil and vegetation from north to south. First, there is the *tundra*, where little grows naturally except for shrubs and mosses. Then comes the *taiga*, coniferous forest for the most part, and the source of great wealth in the shape of timber and furs. Next there is the mixed forest in which deciduous trees join with the conifers. This area, which is wide in the west but tapers towards the Urals, has been the centre of Russian civilisation from Kievan days onwards, even though it provides by no means ideal conditions for agriculture. Finally, we come to the steppe, wooded to the north and desert to the south, with the grassland in between. Here is the best farmland, at least to the west of the Volga.

Cutting through these zones are the mighty rivers, most of which flow north to south, like the Volga, Don and Dnepr, or south to north, like the Dvinas west of the Urals and the Siberian rivers east of them. But the tributaries often flow laterally, as it were, thus enabling people and goods to move across the country without insuperable difficulty before the coming of the railroad.

The 'urge to the sea' that R. J. Kerner[3] and many other analysts have seen as another of the great themes of Russian history is too strong to be denied. The struggle for outlets to the Black Sea and the Baltic, then to the Pacific Ocean, occupied the attention of successive governments for many centuries. And yet the sea has not been so absolutely vital to the prosperity of Russia as it has to that of smaller states. With a whole continent to explore and develop, and then to control, governments have been obliged to look inwards at least as much as outwards. Even today, the Soviet leaders are deeply concerned with such problems as the improvement of agriculture and the development of Siberia at the same time as attending to the various aspects of international relations. Inevitably, they still have to strive to coexist with their inhospitable climate and the other problems of their immediate environment as well as attempting to put into practice their policy of 'peaceful co-existence' in the world at large. Theirs is an inheritance which comes not only from 1917 but from thousands of years before it.

In the early days of human history, the warmer regions to the south first encouraged the growth of organised tribal communities. Neither the Black nor the Caspian Sea is far from the valleys of the rivers Tigris and Euphrates, which have often been called the cradle of civilisation, and archaeological discoveries have revealed the connection between the ancient cities of the Middle East and the peoples to the north of them. Greece and Rome then colonised the Black Sea in particular; Byzantium followed in their wake, sending expeditions up the Dnepr and other rivers. As a result of such contacts as well as migration and internal evolution, tribal organisations gave way to that of an embryonic Slavonic state from the seventh to the ninth centuries. During this period, towns such as Novgorod and Kiev came into existence. In their hinterlands, settled agriculture came to be practised as the steppe and the forest receded before the plough. Foreign contacts were established not only with Byzantium but with other peoples to the east and west. Intercourse with the Islamic and Christian cultures of Central Asia and Transcaucasia was mutually beneficial, as was that with fellow Slavs, Germans and Norsemen.[4]

Of all these contacts, it is the last, with the Norsemen, Vikings or Varangians that has been the most famous or notorious in Russian history. These restless itinerants came down the rivers from the Baltic to the Black Sea not only to trade and to fight, but also to settle. As well as making good use of the commercial route to Byzantium, they hired themselves out as mercenaries to one Russian city in its struggle with another. In this manner, they probably came to furnish Novgorod and Kiev with their first well-known dynasty. But they were not complete conquerors or cultural innovators; they rather worked hand in glove with the native ruling class and became assimilated by it. The controversy still rages about the origin of the word 'Rus' and many other aspects of the birth of medieval Russia, but many Western specialists now agree with their Soviet colleagues that both 'Rus' and most of the characteristics of its civilisation were conceived on native soil rather than being a foreign insemination.[5]

Part One
Medieval Russia: Kiev to Moscow

Introduction

The myth persists that Russia was cut off from Western civilisation until the reign of Peter the Great. In fact, ties were often close with West as well as East during the early medieval period in the political, economic and cultural spheres of life. Nevertheless, the Western contacts that were established during the prosperous days of Kiev were severely curtailed during the worst days of the so-called 'Mongol yoke'. They grew again by fits and starts with the rise of Moscow.

The first chapter commences with a brief analysis of another myth – that Kievan Rus was the creation of immigrant princes rather than the culmination of a process unfolding itself during the course of several centuries. Most attention, however, is given to Kievan Rus from its construction and development in the ninth, tenth and eleventh centuries, to its collapse in the twelfth century. At its peak, Kievan Rus was not only a powerful state carrying on diplomatic and economic relations with a large number of its fellows throughout Europe and the Middle East, but also the centre of a remarkable culture. Some of its princes deserve inclusion among the ranks of the great rulers of medieval times. Nor should it be forgotten that, during the same period, a high level of civilisation was reached in the regions of some of the future Soviet republics in Transcaucasia and Central Asia.

1   Medieval Russia, 882–1645

The two centuries or so which followed the disintegration of Kiev were among the least helpful for the development of Russia. For the major part of that time, the Mongols dominated the fragments into which the state had broken, and their general influence was for the most part negative. German, Polish, Lithuanian and Swedish incursions from the West added to the problems faced by Novgorod and the other principalities. While many of the figures who passed across the national stage in the thirteenth and fourteenth centuries remain shadowy to the point of anonymity, there are individuals such as Alexander Nevsky who have come to occupy a prominent place in the pantheon of national heroes. Moreover, processes were at work leading the way towards the emergence of a new centre of political unity, Moscow, and it would also be wrong to look upon this period as one of undiluted economic depression and cultural inactivity. Some scholars, such as the émigré G. V. Vernadsky, have argued that even the Mongol influence had its positive, constructive side. His views, and those of other scholars, are discussed in Chapter 2.

Chapter 3 is devoted to the consolidation of the Russian state under Moscow. It is there argued that this was a process in broad conformity with a European pattern. The chronological termination of the chapter and of Part One comes after Moscow's collapse at the end of the six-teenth century in the Time of Troubles with its resurgence at the beginning of the seventeenth century under a new dynasty, the Romanovs.

Throughout the medieval section, the principal underlying theme is feudalism. It must be borne in mind that, while Western historians concentrate on feudalism's political aspects, their Soviet colleagues emphasise the economic aspects.[1]

1 The Construction and Collapse of Kiev, 882–1240

'Let us seek a prince who may rule over us, and judge us according to the Law', said the warring tribes of ancient Russia to each other in 860 according to the *Primary Chronicle*. And so: 'They accordingly went overseas to the Varangian Russes': these particular Varangians were known as Russes, just as some are called Swedes, and others Normans, Angles, and Goths. . . . As the old story continues, the tribes then said to Varangian Russes: 'Our whole land is great and rich, but there is no order in it. Come to rule and reign over us.'[1] Three brothers in particular were chosen, and the eldest of them, Riurik, settled in Novgorod and began the princely dynasty that was to rule over Kiev from 882 onwards. On such a foundation was developed in the eighteenth century the so-called Normanist theory of the beginning of the history of the Russian state.

The old story is colourful and persistent, but essentially Russian history no more began in 860 than British history in 1066 or American history in 1776. Moreover, the construction of Kiev could hardly be the exclusive achievement of a small group of men, as the distinguished Soviet historian B. D. Grekov strongly insists:

We reject the naive conception that a state is formed by individual heroes. We know that the formation of a state is not a sudden occurrence, but is the result of prolonged social development. We know that states appear in a period when society has already become divided into classes, when relations between them become aggravated and when the economically strongest class assumes power and subordinates the masses. Consequently in our attempts to discover the origins of the state of Ancient Rus we should discard outdated scientific conceptions and study the history of the people as a whole, rather than the activities of individuals.[2]

Following the argument of Grekov to a considerable extent, we shall also refer to the writings of his colleagues and of pre-revolutionary historians such as V. O. Kliuchevskii, as well as to those of historians who have lived abroad such as G. V. Vernadsky. We shall also attempt to make some reference to the principal sources for the history of Kiev, or 'Ancient Rus' as Grekov chooses to call it. These include the *Primary Chronicle* edited and translated by S. H. Cross, and other early indigenous documents, supported by evidence of foreign origin, particularly Byzantine and Arabic, and of domestic oral tradition, epics, songs and tales. Other disciplines, notably archaeology, which have also made additions to our knowledge and understanding of Kiev, will receive at least some mention.

While both the nature of the sources and our aspiration for objectivity will persuade us not to neglect the contributions of individuals to the construction and collapse of Kiev, we must recognise that they often stand as the embodiments or reflections of more general political, social, economic or cultural processes. Moreover, we shall see that these processes are often inter-related. For example, discussion of the basis of the Kievan economy as agriculture or commerce has important implications for the typification of its society. At the same time, the international setting of Kiev will have to be sketched in, to the east as well as to the west. Readers who start with the assumption that Kiev was backward in comparison with the rest of the European continent will have to be reminded that more than almost any other early medieval state, Kiev had contact with the greatest of contemporary Western civilisations – Byzantium, and close contact with the Arabic and Turkic cultures of the Middle East and Central Asia.

Having commenced with the argument that the part played by the rulers of the Kievan state should not be exaggerated, this introduction should properly end by escaping the opposite danger of complete anonymity. While Riurik probably did not exist, such princes as Vladimir I (980–1015), Iaroslav the Wise (1036–54) and Vladimir Monomakh (1113–25) undoubtedly made a significant personal impact on the course of the events which will be unfolded in the folllowing pages.

Political

While the *Chronicle* tells us that Riurik's successor, Prince Oleg, came down from Novgorod with an army of Varangians and Slavs to capture Kiev in or about 882, Grekov believes that the fact of the merger between the two great cities should be underlined, irrespective of its exact manner and timing. For him, the emergence of the Kievan state as the centre of ancient Rus was primarily the result of its proximity to Byzantium and to other communities adjacent to the Black and Azov seas.

Having established himself in Kiev, Oleg set about the fulfilment of three principal tasks. The first was the subjugation of those tribes which constituted centrifugal forces in the nascent feudal state. The second was the prosecution of wars against rivals for dominance to the east and west. The third was the commencement of a series of campaigns against Byzantium which, in a Soviet view, constituted the 'struggle of a young and developing barbarian state against a big centre against the successor to the civilisation of antiquity . . . a struggle to affirm its international position and strengthen economic and cultural ties with Byzantium.'³ Oleg led Kiev a considerable way towards the realisation of these three aims; the culmination of his reign was probably the expedition against Byzantium in 907, which produced treaties giving the Russians recognition and guarantees as equal partners.

Oleg died soon after this triumph and was succeeded as Grand Prince by Igor, whom Soviet historians look upon as 'the true beginner of the Russian princely line'. Late in his reign, Igor led two further attacks on Constantinople (or Tsargrad as the Russians called it), which ended by 945 if not in disaster then certainly in the reduction of the advantages gained in earlier treaties. Igor maintained his predecessor's policy of wars against rivals from the Caspian Sea to eastern Europe, using the Black Sea town of Tmutarakan as a base and invading Muslim Azerbaidzhan, for example. He necessarily continued the struggle against neighbouring tribes, too. On his way back to Kiev in 945, Igor decided to stop off to gather tribute from one of these tribes, the Drevliane. Mal, their prince, agreed with his followers that: 'If the wolf makes a habit of coming to the fold he will carry away the whole flock, unless he is killed. So will Prince Igor, too, destroy us all, unless we kill him'⁴ And so, as Igor and his small bodyguard revealed an insatiable appetite for tribute, the Drevliane attacked and killed them.

Mal made overtures to Igor's widow Olga for a marriage alliance, but Olga used her cunning to extort a cruel and ingenious revenge for her husband's death. Over 5000 Drevliane fell in a campaign which constituted the final reduction of the tribe's independence as well as a widow's vengeance. For nearly twenty years, Olga remained in power during the minority of the son she had borne Igor, Sviatoslav. A formidable ruler, Olga managed not only to hold Kievan Russia together but even to strengthen it, particularly through her substitution of a system of regular taxes on surrounding tribes in place of their regular collection of tribute that had brought about her husband's death. She almost constantly maintained full and personal contact with Byzantium, which brought about the event for which she was best remembered later and canonised by the Orthodox Church, her conversion to Christianity. But Sviatoslav remained true to the pagan faith of his fathers, and the official state acceptance of Christianity did not occur until after the accession of his son Vladimir.

The consolidation of Kievan Russia was completed during the reigns of Sviatoslav and Vladimir. Sviatoslav (962–72) made his presence felt more positively than had his predecessors theirs in both Europe and Asia. While hectic campaigns left little time for the civil aspect of government, Grekov nevertheless declared Sviatoslav to be 'a major statesman, and not merely the ringleader of a band of vagabonds intent on plunder'.[5] While certainly not uninterested in booty, Sviatoslav also took an interest in the protection of trade routes and the security of the state. He himself expressed the dual nature of his policy in a proposal to transfer his capital from the banks of the Dnepr to those of the Danube, saying: 'Here is the core of my lands, since the good things of different countries converge here: silk cloth, golden utensils, wine and fruit of various sorts from Byzantium; silver articles and fast horses from Bohemia and Hungary; and valuable furs, beeswax, honey and captive slaves from Rus.'[6] To foster such interests, Sviatoslav had carved his way in campaigns of the years 963 to 968 from the Volga to the Caspian Sea, then along the north of the Caucasus, the Azov and Black Seas to Bulgaria. And now established on the Danube after the defeat of many enemies, Sviatoslav turned his attention to his previous ally, Byzantium. Under a new and vigorous Emperor, John Zimisces, and with the help of the Bulgars, the Byzantine forces were able to defeat the Kievan Russians and to force their Grand Prince to sign a treaty in 971, renouncing all claims to Bulgaria and the Crimea. On the way back to Kiev, Sviatoslav met an end similar to that of his father. Attacked by a hostile Turkish tribe of the southern steppe, the Pechenegi, Sviatoslav was overcome and killed, his skull being made into a drinking cup for the Pecheneg prince.

Before setting off on campaign in 970, Sviatoslav had divided the trust of Kievan Russia among his three sons. After a period of fraternal strife in which two of the brothers were killed Vladimir emerged as sole ruler by 980 and remained in power until his death in 1015. Perhaps the principal concern of Vladimir's reign was the struggle against his father's murderers, the Pechenegi, although reasons of state were at least as important a part of the motive as personal retribution. To defend Kievan

Russia from the incursions of this and other tribes, he caused to be constructed along the northern banks of the rivers of the steppe five series of forts. As G. V. Vernadsky points out, Vladimir thus provided 'a model for generations of Russian rulers to come, and "fortified lines" as a protection against the nomads were still built by the Russians in south and east Russia as late as the eighteenth century and in Turkestan even in the nineteenth century.'[7] To man the forts, Vladimir brought down northerners to join the local people, and heroic tales were soon being told at banquets and in epic ballads of the deeds accomplished among them by individuals such as the brave knight Ilia Muromets.

In at attempt to stabilise the state further, Vladimir followed his father's example by sending his sons to rule the cities in his name. But precedent was followed in the negative as well as in the positive sense, for family quarrels broke out during the last years of his reign, notably with Iaroslav in Novgorod.

Like Sviatoslav, Vladimir also carried on a vigorous foreign policy throughout Asia and Europe, relations with Byzantium remaining the central concern and continuing their earlier variable course. Under a new Emperor, Basil II, Byzantium found itself under threat from both the Bulgars and internal dissidents based in Asia Minor. In desperation, Basil turned to Vladimir for assistance, apparently going so far as to hand over his sister Anna in marriage as one of the reciprocal concessions, a gesture which would be made to 'barbarians' only in the most extreme circumstances. When Vladimir moved his forces to bring relief to Basil, however, the Emperor defaulted on his agreement, and did not attempt to keep to it until Vladimir laid siege to an important Byzantine fortress in the Crimea. The story goes that Anna herself refused to marry Vladimir before he was baptised.

Vladimir's baptism, in or around the year 988, meant for him at least the official abandonment of six wives and 600 concubines, and for Russia the adoption of Christianity as the state religion. The importance of this step for the medieval and modern history of Russia is incalculable, from both spiritual and secular points of view.[8] In the materialist conception of Soviet historians, the adoption of Christianity meant that society had reached a new level of complexity for which pagan cults were no longer sufficient. (More of this below.)

After the death of St Vladimir, as the Russian Orthodox Christians know him, in 1015, it immediately became apparent that the internal Christian values had not been assimilated along with the external observances of the new religion. The fratricidal conflict which preceded the reign now followed it in a more virulent form, and the separatist forces that were to play such a large part in the dissolution of Kievan Russia were already in clear view before the process of formation was completed. To Grekov, such disintegration was a common feature of the early history of feudal states. He writes: 'New developments in the relations of production clashed with the old political system, and each component was faced with new tasks which it began to handle independently of the others. At a certain point the flimsy cohesion under Charlemagne became superfluous and even an impediment to the further growth of each part.'9 As with the Carolingian Empire, so it was with Kievan Russia 200 years later as its towns gained greater strength.

Such a socio-economic process, or at least the beginning of it, was reflected in the years following the death of Vladimir from 1015 to 1036, as his twelve sons (albeit by different mothers) struggled among themselves for the succession, finding allies wherever they could to strengthen the power bases which they had established in various cities throughout the land. Iaroslav in Novgorod emerged the ultimate victor. Married to a daughter of the King of Sweden, he had invited Varangians in to help him fight his father, but the mercenaries were slaughtered in August 1015 by the Novgorodians. In retaliation, Iaroslav killed a thousand Novgorodian warriors. With the news of the death of Vladimir reaching him immediately after these reprisals, he quickly tried to conciliate the two sides, part of the terms of reconciliation being made concrete in the first section of the *Russkaia Pravda*, or Russian Law, which will be generally examined later. As a consequence, the warriors of Novgorod fought in uneasy alliance with the Varangians to take Kiev. The struggle was by no means over, however, for the brother ousted from Kiev gained support from both the Pechenegi and the Poles, and took up the counter-attack. This particular fight was not finished until 1019, and other fraternal squabbles kept Iaroslav busy for a further fifteen years. Most of Vladimir's sons died tragically, two of them, Boris and Gleb, becoming the first martyr-saints in the Orthodox calendar.

In his years as Grand Prince from 1036 to 1054, Iaroslav the Wise, as he came to be called, made Kiev a great cultural and ecclesiastical centre, and extended its contacts with the outside world. Grekov, who argues that Russia at mid-eleventh century was 'the biggest and strongest state in Europe',10 points out that Iaroslav had diplomatic relations not only with Poland and Bohemia but also with Germany and France. Among the Grand Prince's Viking associates was Harald Hardrada, who lived at the Russian court and married a daughter of Iaroslav before going off to fight for fame and fortune in Sicily and Italy, and then to become King of Norway and then of England before losing his life at the battle of Stamford Bridge in 1066.

Nearer home, Iaroslav continued the vacillating relations with Byzantium fighting against the Emperor's forces in 1043 on the one hand, but probably cementing ecclesiastical and commercial relations with a dynastic marriage in 1052 on the other. Just before this, Iaroslav attempted to make the Russian Church independent. According to Vernadsky:

> The Russian move must have caused considerable anxiety in Constantinople, since this was a period of great tension between the Patriarch and the Pope of Rome. The Russians might be expected to profit by it and to shift their allegiance from Constantinople to Rome. In a sense, then, the move became a factor in the great schism between the Greek and Roman Church. . . . By a coincidence which seems full of inner significance, the death of Iaroslav and the final rupture between the Eastern and the Western Church occurred in the same year, A.D. 1054.[11]

Before he died, Iaroslav divided the Russian lands among his sons, giving Kiev to the eldest Iziaslav and other cities to the other four, urging them: 'Heed him as ye have heeded me, that he may take my place among you.'[12] Although Iziaslav was assigned to be senior prince, in fact a triumvirate emerged and managed to exercise an uneasy control until 1073. Then two of its members conspired against the third, Iziaslav, who fled to Poland and sought the help of both the Holy Roman Emperor and Pope Gregory VII. The death of one member of the old triumvirate, Sviatoslav, brought Iziaslav back in 1076 to ally with the other, Vsevolod, only to be killed fighting for his patrimony in 1078. From 1078 to 1093, Vsevolod ruled Kiev, surrounded by younger feuding princes. From 1093 to 1113, the son of Iziaslav, Sviatopolk, managed to retain power in Kiev while his cousin, the son of Vsevolod, Vladimir Monomakh, ruled in Chernigov, one of the cities which were increasingly emerging as rivals to Kiev.

In the second half of the eleventh century, Kiev was being weakened by internal conflict and external threat, as well as by fratricidal princely disputes. All three of these elements combined in 1068 to produce probably the largest civic disturbances that Kievan Russia experienced. With the growth of the political influence of the cities, their assemblies known as *veche* became more important. The Kievan *veche* was assembled in 1068 by the army which had just been defeated in the first full-scale invasion by the successors to the Pechenegi as southern steppe Turkish tribesmen, the Polovtsi or Cumans. The *veche* decided to raise a new army from among the common people, but Iziaslav attempted to overrule the decision. In an ensuing popular riot, Iziaslav took flight and the crowd released his imprisoned grandson, Vseslav, to be their prince. Vseslav the Sorcerer, as he was widely known, was the subject of folk epics, and was described as a grey wolf or a lynx as well as a magician. Little is known of his brief rule in Kiev, but he almost certainly encouraged a popular reversion to paganism. There was a disturbance in Novgorod, too, during the year 1068, but with Polish help, Iziaslav soon managed to restore an uneasy control.

His son, Sviatopolk, could hardly be said to have enjoyed a more secure reign from 1093 to 1113. This Grand Prince made himself personally unpopular, particularly through his assumption of a monopoly on salt. Various and devious interprincely feuding continued, although a general conference at Liubech near Chernigov in 1097 attempted to quell it. According to the *Chronicle*, the princes said to one another: 'Why do we ruin the land of Rus by our continued strife against one another? The Polovtsi harass our country in divers fashions, and rejoice that war is waged among us. Let us rather hereafter be united in spirit and watch over the land of Rus, and let each of us guard his own domain. . . .'[13] While the principle of Kievan seniority was not formally rejected at Liubech and succeeding conferences, emphasis was put on the autonomous rights of each princely branch to its inheritance. In order to preserve his own rule, Sviatopolk was not above making peace with the Polovtsi by marrying the daughter of their khan or removing a rival by blinding him, a Byzantine practice held to be unprecedented in Russia.

At the death of Sviatopolk in 1113, social tensions and princely squabbles flared up at a time when the threat from outside was still great. There was another revolt in Kiev, put to an end by the *veche*'s hurried election of Vladimir Monomakh, who had made a considerable reputation for himself by leading Russian resistance to the Polovtsi and through his comparatively honourable conduct in family feuds. Vladimir Monomakh, 1113–25, enjoys the reputation of a true knight, stern yet just, a devout Christian while keen on the manly arts of hunting and fighting. He was first married to the daughter of Harold II of England, Gyda, who had escaped to Denmark after her father's defeat at Hastings in 1066. For the sons that she bore him and possibly for his followers in general, Vladimir composed a *Testament*, in which he told of his own life and of his views on life in general.

Vladimir Monomakh's reputation at large was clearly demonstrated at his death by the unopposed succession of his eldest son Mstislav, who had previously been Prince of Novgorod. His mother was English and his wife was Swedish, and he worked to keep his Baltic connections secure, while successfully struggling to maintain order among his princely relations. His reign, from 1125 to 1132, largely achieved its aims, since Mstislav, like his father, managed to keep the support of Kiev and a sufficient number of other towns. From about the end of the first third of the twelfth century, however, the various centrifugal forces which had been in existence from the beginning now assumed strength enough to threaten Kievan Russia with complete disintegration.

To Grekov, the process of disintegration was 'primarily the result of the growth of her component parts, each of which began to follow its own policy and strive to achieve its own goals. Kiev lacked the means to further the growth of these lands, and unquestionably retarded their development by its demands for men and money.'[14] Moreover, the Polovtsi and other tribesmen continued to harry the beleaguered Russians and to hamper their communications with the outside world. Changes in this outside world were also to the detriment of Kiev, notably the creation of trade routes from Byzantium to Western Europe via Venice by sea or by way of Bohemia overland. The Crusades encouraged the growth of Italian and French cities on the Mediterranean and German cities along the Rhine to the detriment of Byzantium. The fourth Crusade in particular consisted of little more than the sack of Constantinople in 1204.

As Kiev declined, so three other important centres arose within the loose framework of the Russian state. The first of them was Novgorod, whose eclipse had never been total, and which was now benefiting from the revival of trade in the Baltic. With a huge hinterland providing furs, wax and other items to supply and supplement its handicrafts industry, Novgorod gained the resources to establish an independent republic at the end of the first third of the twelfth century. The *veche* assembly possessed the supreme power, elected its own civil and military governors and managed relations with the princes. However, Novgorod was an oligarchy rather than a democracy, for, although the *veche* consisted of all free citizens, a smaller group of boyars, as the leading nobles were called, was actually in control. Much the same might be said of Pskov, the city to the south-west of Novgorod at the foot of Lake Peipus.

A second focus of political organisation was to the north-east, with Vladimir the most important of a number of principalities. Rostov and Suzdal were more important cities earlier on, particularly during the reign of Iurii Dolgorukii, a son of Vladimir Monomakh, although he is best remembered as the founder of Moscow, first mentioned as a fortified settlement in 1147. It was during the reign of Iurii's son, Andrei Bogoliubskii, that Vladimir gained its political predominance. Andrei managed to get sufficient support from new men and new towns to establish something like an embryonic absolutism in the north-east and to conduct a successful campaign against Kiev in 1169, capturing the old capital and sacking it. But his attempt to conquer Novgorod in 1170 ended in failure, and in 1174 Andrei was assassinated by his boyar opponents. After a confused interregnum, Andrei's younger brother, Vsevolod Bolshoe Gnezdo (Big Nest – because of his fertility) took Vladimir to greater heights in a long reign lasting to 1212.

A third area to gain importance as Kiev lost it was composed of Galicia, Volynia and other principalities to the south-west. The area received a great boost from the passage through it of the new land trade route from the East, and possessed considerable strategic value because of its situation bordering on Poland and Hungary as well as Russia. A notable ruler was Roman Mstislavich of Volynia who united his own principality with Galicia at the end of the twelfth century. On the eve of the Mongol invasions then, the unstable federation of Kievan Russia was already passing the point of disintegration.

The process of disintegration could be said to have been under way already before the federation was properly set up; nevertheless, the Kievan state was, at its peak, much more than an anarchic conglomeration. If political relations between the princes often appeared to consist of nothing more than unrestrained fratricide, there were other times at which a father's testament or a brother's seniority could not be ignored. Similarly, while the day-to-day behaviour of the citizens of Kiev and the other cities was governed largely by force or custom, there were also attempts to put it on a more regular basis. The most notable example of such an endeavour was the *Russkaia Pravda*, which Kliuchevskii deemed 'a good but broken mirror of Russian law in the eleventh and twelfth centuries'.[15] From this and other imperfect sources, at least some kind of composite picture of Kievan society can be assembled.

At the apex, of course, stood the princes, supported by their *druzhina* or retinue, which came to be composed mainly of boyars. The *druzhina* comprised the commanders of the armed forces, the chief administrators and the greatest landlords. The merchant class was important in the towns, its most important members allying with the boyars to dominate the *veche*. Capital was for Kliuchevskii the most important element in the *Russkaia Pravda*. Most of the peasants and townsmen were legally free, the slaves proper constituting a comparatively small class. But the degree of freedom enjoyed by the Kievan people has sometimes been exaggerated in talk of 'good old days' which in fact never existed. Payment of extortionate taxes and recruitment to military and other severe forms of service often pushed the people towards actual if not legal servitude. Even when the legal freedom was strictly observed, there could be no guarantee of complete security for the threats of famine and epidemic, fire and war were never far away. A conflagration in Kiev in 1124, for example, was said to have destroyed 600 churches, and another in Novgorod in 1211, 15 churches and 43,000 houses.

A final word must be added here about the contemporaneous situation in Central Asia and Transcaucasia. Waves of Muslim-Turkic invaders into Central Asia merged with the older settlers there to create a number of states in the eleventh and twelfth centuries. With the reception of the Arabic language and Muslim culture, the region enjoyed a high level of civilisation, creating fine works of art and literature and making important contributions to philosophy, mathematics and the sciences. In Transcaucasia, Christian Georgia, Armenia and Muslim Azerbaidzhan had already acquired a distinctive personality by the twelfth century; again, the arts and sciences were at an advanced level of development. Thus, even the most superficial acquaintance with the early medieval history of Central Asia and Transcaucasia obliges the investigator to realise that he should not look exclusively westwards for feudal societies to compare with Kievan Russia. This realisation is thrust on his attention much more forcefully as he turns to consider the impact of the Mongol invasions.

Economic

Within the wide and loose boundaries of Kievan Russia, there were ample natural resources from which its people could extract a living – forests, arable lands, lakes, rivers and mineral deposits. However, historians have not been able to agree on how these resources were put to use.

In his 'classic' description of the early Russian economy, Kliuchevskii wrote:

The history of our society would have been substantially different, if our economy had not been for eight or nine centuries at variance with the nature of the country. In the eleventh century, the bulk of the Russian population was concentrated in the Dnepr black-earth region, and by the mid-fifteenth it moved to the Upper Volga area. It would seem that in the former area, agriculture should have been the basis of the economy while in the latter, foreign trade, forestry and other activities should have gained the upper hand. But external circumstances were such that while Rus remained in the Dnepr black-earth territory she engaged predominantly in the sale of forest products and so on and began vigorously to plough only on the loamy Upper Volga soils. As a result, both leading economic forces, land-ownership by men-at-arms and urban trade took an artificial turn and failed to develop where natural conditions were most propitious, but where they developed with success, their achievements were artificial.[16]

A categorical antithesis to Kliuchevskii's formulation was given by Grekov, who declared: 'Agriculture became the main occupation of the Eastern, as well as of the other Slavs long before the formation of the Ancient Rus state. It continued to develop in Kiev Rus, assuming new forms with the growth of the productive forces. . . . Feudal land tenure and peasant economies remained the basis of Rus life for several centuries.' [17] Grekov's argument, which also denies large-scale migration, has been so well substantiated by his own research and that of his colleagues that it can no longer be rejected by appeal to the authority of Kliuchevskii. Grekov and his colleagues would not deny the importance of trade to the Kievan economy, but they do debate the relative weight to be attached to it.

The total number of people engaged in economic pursuits of all kinds is impossible to estimate. Vernadsky tentatively suggested about 7,500,000 for the late twelfth century, with not less than a million, or about 13 per cent, living in cities, but his method of compilation was necessarily so primitive that no firm reliance can be placed on it.[18] Therefore, we cannot exactly tell how many unsung peasants were involved in farming or how many anonymous townsmen pursued commerce or industry, but can only record their activities in a proportionately representative manner.

The evidence for the argument that agriculture was from early times the way of life for the majority of Kievan Russians has been partly documentary but more archaeological; it is above all the spade that has revealed the predominance of the plough. Many remains of implements, animals and grains have been unearthed. Moreover, their disposition strongly suggests that there was an expansion of agriculture up to the twelfth century, new fields being opened up with the slash-and-burn method (*podseka*) in forested regions, with the more wasteful extensive approach (*perelog*) being adopted in the grassy steppe. By this time, the two-field and even three-field crop rotation system had come to be widely adopted in the more settled regions. The basic unit of production was the peasant commune, which was increasingly based on territory rather than on blood, according to Blum, while Vernadsky prefers to talk of the 'greater family' (smaller than the clan but larger than the nuclear family) as the norm.[19]

Superimposed upon many communes by the eleventh century were the estates of the princes, the nobility or the Church. Although they probably occupied less land than did the unattached communes, these estates are more fully described in written sources, for the obvious enough reason that nearly all such evidence was produced by or for the people who owned them. The organisation and activities of these estates, which would not be unrecognisable to anybody familiar with the Western European manor, are recorded adequately enough. However, as Grekov points out, 'the chroniclers pay very little attention to the rural population. It continued to plough. With its corn it fed itself and those who either could not or would not plough. It paid state taxes punctually and went to war, but the better service it rendered, the less mention it got. . . .'[20]

Since hunting was at least as popular with Kievan princes and boyars as it was with their Western European counterparts, we learn more about their performance at the chase than about the workaday activities of their social inferiors. Even the devout Vladimir Monomakh was proud to enumerate his active and passive experiences in his *Testament*, writing:

> At Chernigov, I even bound wild horses with my bare hands or captured ten or twenty live horses with the lasso, and besides that, while riding along the Rus, I caught these same wild horses bare-handed. Two bisons tossed me and my horse on their horns, a stag once gored me, one elk stamped upon me, while another gored me, a boar once tore my sword from my thigh, a bear on one occasion bit my kneecap, and another wild beast jumped on my flank and threw my horse with me. But God preserved me unharmed.[21]

Hunting was subject to strict regulations, since it was often part of even a nobleman's livelihood as well as his pastime. For the rank and file, particularly those to the north, hunting was a basic necessity as a source of food and clothing and, especially in the case of furs and hides, a provider of the means of paying taxes or engaging in commerce. Forest dwellers would often go in for bee-keeping, from which the honey and even more the wax could be exchanged or sold for internal or external trade. A further companion or alternative to hunting, as in later days, was fishing.

Hunting or fishing, bee-keeping or farming, Kievan Russians in the countryside often lived in a near-subsistence manner, salt and metal artefacts being among the few items of daily use that had to be purchased. Nevertheless, few rural inhabitants could be completely unconscious of the possibilities of selling surpluses for urban consumption and industry or for export, and most of them would be liable for taxes.

As for the urban population, M. N. Tikhomirov tells us that the majority consisted of craftsmen. Their work has been impressively described both by Tikhomirov and by B. A. Rybakov.[22]

The craftsmen made use of the produce of their provincial brethren, including flax and hemp, as well as of domestic iron and foreign raw materials, notably non-ferrous and precious metals, to process and fashion goods for sale at home and abroad.

Domestic trade – between forest and steppe, town and country – preceded foreign in time and probably always surpassed it in volume. Nevertheless, the foreign branch of trade is the more fully described, indeed the most widely recorded of all Kievan Russia's economic activities. This partiality is easily explained by the fact that foreign observers were usually most interested in commercial possibilities, and should not persuade us to over-emphasis in our description. But we cannot talk of humble dealings in local market places, their very frequency making them unremarkable to contemporary commentators.

So more space will be devoted here to Kiev's participation in international trade, the degree of which by early medieval standards certainly encourages special mention. The importance of Kiev's place on main routes converging on Byzantium – from the Baltic to the Black Seas and from the Orient to the West – has already been noted, as has its reduction from the end of the eleventh century with the interference of the Polovtsi, by the rise of Venice and the start of the Crusades. In the twelfth century, Kiev retained some of its commercial importance as overland trade grew through central Europe, while Novgorod prospered from trade with the Baltic. In her heyday, Kiev exported furs, honey and wax to Byzantium, with slaves in addition in earlier times and grain later. Luxury items, such as wines, silks and jewels, predominated among the imports from Byzantium. The same exports – furs, honey and wax – together with woollen fabrics were sent to the Orient to be exchanged for silks, spices, jewels, luxury metal goods and horses. In the earlier period, Kiev supplanted Novgorod as the main intermediary between the Orient and the West, but by the twelfth century, Novgorod was regaining her predominance. From Novgorod, as well as from other cities in the north-west such as Pskov and Smolensk, went not only furs, honey and wax, but vegetable and animal raw materials and semi-manufactures such as flax and hemp, tallow and hides. Such a volume of international trade took Russians abroad and brought foreigners in. This interchange had a great political and social importance, as we have seen, and a great cultural influence, as we are about to see.

In conclusion, the attempt must be made to typify the economy of Kievan Russia as a whole. Vernadsky uses the term 'commercial capitalism'[23] pointing out that the furs and cattle used in earlier times as media of exchange were replaced by gold and silver, and that credit transactions were in wide use, particularly in foreign trade. For Soviet historians, on the other hand, 'the economic basis of the social order established in Rus was feudal landed proprietorship.'[24] The implication of the foregoing description is to express agreement with the second of these two views.

Cultural

'If, before you inspect Kiev's Sophia Cathedral', Grekov advises his fellow citizens, 'you are inclined to be condescending regarding the ability of our ancestors to express the great and the beautiful, then you will be extremely astonished.' He continues: 'You no sooner cross the threshold than you come under the spell of its grandeur and magnificence: its imposing interior, its austere proportions, its ornate mosaics and frescoes captivate you by their perfection even before you have had an opportunity to examine the details and to comprehend what it was the creators of this outstanding work of architecture and painting had in mind.'[25] Foreign visitors, too, might well find themselves echoing Grekov's words, not only in Kiev but also in Novgorod, Suzdal and Vladimir. Interpretations will vary as to the exact significance of the culture of Kievan Russia, but nobody could doubt the worthiness of its inclusion at a high level of achievement in early medieval Europe as a whole.

However, in Russia as elsewhere, before the reception of Christianity, paganism flourished for several centuries, and, even after it, persisted for several more. For the common people, Christianity was as difficult to accept in the Kievan period as was materialism in Soviet times. And while paganism produced nothing on the scale of the early medieval cathedrals, it can in no way be equated with barbarism; some of the idols, jewels and decorations which have survived possess their own power and subtlety.

To an atheistic historian such as B. A. Rybakov, paganism and Christianity are not to be neatly separated, they rather merge into each other. But even he can distinguish the two enough to make the following appraisal of the sequel to the conversion of Vladimir in 988:

> The Russian church played a complex and many-sided role in the history of Rus during the 11th–13th centuries. On the one hand there was the undoubtedly progressive role of the church as an organisation that helped to consolidate the young Rus statehood in the epoch of the vigorous development of feudalism. It also undoubtedly helped in the development of Russian culture, bringing it closer to the cultural treasures of Byzantium, in the spread of education, and the creation of literary and artistic works of great value.
>
> But it must be remembered that the Russian people paid dearly for that positive contribution of the church: the poison of religious ideology penetrated (deeper than in pagan times) into all the pores of the people's life, it dulled the class struggle, revived primitive notions in a new form, and for centuries fastened in the consciousness of the people the ideas of a world beyond, of the divine origin of rulers, and providentialism, i.e., the concept that the fates of people are always governed by God's will.
>
> The Russian people were not as religious as the church historians try to make out, but religious ideology was nonetheless a hindrance on the road to a free understanding of the world.[26]

From the other side, G. P. Fedotov concludes that:

> Kievan Russia, like the golden days of childhood, was never dimmed in the memory of the Russian nation. In the pure fountain of her literary works anyone who wills can quench his religious thirst; in her venerable authors he can find his guide through the complexities of the modern world. Kievan Christianity has the same value for the Russian religious mind as Pushkin for the Russian artistic sense: that of a standard, a golden measure, a royal way.[27]

Fedotov recommends for our attention the *Confession of Faith* and the sermon entitled *On Law and Grace* by Ilarion, the only Metropolitan

of Kiev of Russian origin for over a century and 'unanimously acknowledged the best theologian and preacher of all ancient Russia, the
Muscovite period included'. He considers that in Boris and Gleb are
to be found the prototypes of a peculiarly Russian kind of saint, the
'sufferers'. He reminds us that the first European scholar to study the
Russian *Chronicles* in the eighteenth century thought that 'Nestor, the
supposed author of the ancient *Chronicles* had no rivals in the West'.
And he finds in the *Testament* of Vladimir Monomakh 'Russian lay
religion at its best'. [28] All these examples are taken from Kievan Russia
in the period of its greatest cohesion and influence. If the list of the most
outstanding works alone were extended to include the following century
and the other principalities, those who share Fedotov's outlook on life
would find ample evidence to accept his conclusions with enthusiasm.

Moreover, the list would not have to be restricted to works of religious
authorship or emphasis. For example, a prominent place would have
to be given to the famous *Slovo o Polku Igoreve*, or *Saga of Igor's
Campaign*, provided, that is, that its authenticity is taken for granted.[29]
Concerned with the vicissitudes and failure of the campaign against
the Polovtsi undertaken in the late twelfth century by Prince Igor of
Novgorod Severskii, it is a Russian equivalent to the later Viking sagas,
to the French *Song of Roland* or the German *Saga of the Nibelungen*.
Kievan Russians were interested in geography as well as history, trans-
lating works in these fields and making their own original contributions.

So far, we have been talking for the most part of the higher levels
of activity; we must now attempt to say more about the middle and
lower levels, about literacy and education, and about folk culture. With
some justification, Soviet historians assert that literacy was 'widespread,
not only among the higher classes of society, but also among the ordinary townsmen'.[30] Evidence for this is to be found in the birch-bark
documents dug out of the soil of Novgorod.[31] The written language used
in Kievan Russia increasingly became that based on the *kirillitsa* or
Cyrillic alphabet, one of the two uniform systems introduced at the
time of Christianity and replacing more primitive and disparate systems.
While the reception of the Cyrillic alphabet was obviously a progressive
step, Fedotov would not be alone in regretting the limited scale of the
move forward when he writes: 'Russian cultural aspirations, however
open and sincere, found a drawback in their Slavonic language, narrowly limiting the circle of available translated literature. This fact, be
it by contingency or destiny, explains a tragic lack in ancient Russian
culture, a complete absence of rational scientific thought, even in the
theological field.' [32] In so far as they would agree about such absence,

Soviet historians would blame neither contingency nor destiny, but the obscurantism of the Orthodox Church.

The folk culture, as has already been pointed out, would often escape the influence of the Church by remaining resolutely pre-Christian in nature. Such persistence was encouraged by the persistence of oral tradition, at the centre of which stands the songs. As Seaman says of the ancient Slavs: 'Their whole life seems to have centred round the seasonal year, and their music took the form of songs to alleviate the task of manual labour.'[33] Echoes of pagan sun worship are intermixed with Christian themes in celebrations of the sowing, harvesting and other stages in the farming cycle. Love, marriage and death also receive appropriate musical attention. And the great epic songs tell of the exploits of such peasant heroes as Ilia Muromets.

To the illiterate, the wonders of Christianity could best be conveyed by imposing buildings and powerful pictures. We have already indicated that the impact is still strong on twentieth-century atheists; its strength in the early medieval period for the religious is immeasurable. But such creations are better seen to be believed. We will therefore not attempt here to describe them in words or talk about their comparability with the contemporary creations of the West, even though there have been very interesting stylistic suggestions, such as the architecture of Vladimir and Suzdal as a 'Russian Romanesque'.[34] Let us make the simple assertion that there is less in Kievan culture to stimulate the mind than to delight the ear and to excite the outer and inner eye.

And let us remember in conclusion that the Byzantine influence that brought Kiev the icon and many other features of her Christian culture did not set her apart from the rest of the Western world. Discussing this point, Dimitri Obolensky writes:

Russia was . . . closely linked with central and western Europe, by trade, culture, and diplomacy, above all by the consciousness of belonging to one world of Christendom, where, for the most part, there was still no Hellene nor Latin, but a common culture and a common faith. It is highly significant that Russia entered the European family of nations through her conversion to Christianity, for which she is indebted to Byzantium. The heritage of East Rome was not, as it is sometimes suggested, Russia's 'mark of the beast' that isolated her from medieval Europe: it was, in fact, the main channel through which she became a European nation. Byzantium was not a wall, erected between Russia and the West: she was Russia's gateway to Europe.[35]

Accepting much of what Obolensky says, some scholars would feel that his enthusiasm carries him too far. Soviet historians, in particular, stress the indigenous roots of the culture that enabled Kievan Rus to play a significant role in the affairs of early medieval Europe and to withstand the ensuing onslaught from outside. B. A. Rybakov declares: 'The depth of the popular culture allowed Rus to survive the onerous times of the Tatar-Mongol yoke, and to conserve an inexhaustible strength for the overcoming of the consequences of foreign domination.' [36]

2 Invasion and Disunity, 1240–1462

At the beginning of the thirteenth century, the Mongols under Chingis Khan began the great conquests that brought upon the Russian principalities the much-lamented Mongol or Tatar 'yoke'. (Although strictly different, the two terms have often been used interchangeably and will be here.) According to Grekov, who follows in the tradition of many pre-revolutionary historians, Russia in the heyday of Kiev 'was ahead of many European countries which only later outstripped her when she bore the impact of the Mongolian hordes and acted as a shield to Western Europe'.[1] To Mongol historians, on the other hand, Chingis Khan is an Alexander the Great, and the empire set up by him constitutes a high point of history rather than a low. Chinese historians have also stressed the positive side of the Mongol impact, one of them, Han Ju-Lin, writing of Chingis Khan that 'his war horses broke through the iron walls of forty large and small states in which the people had become locked. As a result their peoples came to see a broader world in which they could act and become familiar with a higher culture from which they could learn.'[2] And for the 'Eurasian' school of historians, G. V. Vernadsky was an eloquent spokesman, who saw in the Mongol expansion of the thirteenth century 'one of those crucial and fateful eruptions in the history of mankind which from time to time change the destinies of the world'.[3] The views of Vernadsky will be pitted against those of other historians below.

At the same time as the 'Mongol yoke' was being imposed, other invaders – Swedes, Teutonic Knights and Lithuanians – were attacking the Russian principalities from the western side. Such an additional challenge together with a great problem of internal disunity called for heroic leaders to arise from among the Russian people. Some, such as Alexander Nevsky and Dmitrii Donskoi, did appear at critical moments. But the period as a whole is probably the most colourless of the medieval era, and the remarks of John Fennell concerning the silence of the sources on the first half of the fourteenth century tellingly echo the complaints by Kliuchevskii and other predecessors about the years preceding and following:

> No references are made to physical characteristics; there are no attempts to describe any recreational activities as hunting or drinking which might throw even a glimmer of light on personality. . . . The meagre obituaries or eulogies dutifully supplied by the chroniclers are little more than a concoction of clichés which tell us nothing of the men whose piety or goodness they extol.[4]

Thus, little can be said about the rulers or their administrations.

The central figure in the political story of Russian development at this time is not so much an individual or an institution as a principality – Moscow (as Moskva is generally called in English). Denied the opportunity to exercise his great talent for characterisation on one of its princes, Kliuchevskii turned to Moscow itself for the subject of one of his clear and convincing portraits. But here as well as elsewhere, the 'classical' picture presented by the great master has been under heavy criticism from his successors, and it can no longer be completely accepted.

Moreover, in the comparative setting to which historians are increasingly turning, analysis of Russia's disunity and subsequent unification reveals that it was by no means a completely unique experience, even though it possesses special features of which the Mongol yoke is perhaps the most important.

Political

After their conquest of Northern China and Central Asia, the Mongols fanned out to establish their control over a vast area of Western Eurasia, including Transcaucasia and the Russian principalities. An early scouting raid led to the first encounter with Russian forces in the south-east at the river Kalka in 1223, the Mongols enjoying an overwhelming victory. The death of Chingis Khan in 1227 brought a lull, but ten years later a large army under his grandson Batu Khan embarked on a more thorough campaign. Contemporary descriptions of the fall of the Russian cities were horrific in the extreme, one of them stating that:

> The prince, with his mother, wife, sons, the boyars and inhabitants, without regard to age or sex, were slaughtered with the savage cruelty

of Mongol revenge; some were impaled, or had nails or splinters of wood driven under their finger-nails. Priests were roasted alive, and nuns and maidens ravished in the churches before their relatives. No eye remained open to weep for the dead.[5]

The northern principalities fell one by one, with the exception of Novgorod; Kiev was sacked in 1240. The Mongols swept into Central Europe, collecting nine large bags of the ears of their victims after a battle in Silesia in 1241. Terror spread as far as France and the Low Countries, according to Matthew Paris.[6] Neither the Holy Roman Emperor nor the Pope could unite Christendom against the invaders, and if Batu had not turned back at the news of the death of the Great Khan in 1242, Mongol destruction might have penetrated as far as the news of it.

Meanwhile, far from coming to the aid of their fellow Christians, the Catholic Swedes and Livoninan Knights viewed the predicament of the Orthodox Russians as a perfect opportunity for their own hostile invasion. In the summer of 1240, a strong force led by the son-in-law of the King of Sweden, Earl Birger, blocked Novgorod's access route to the Baltic Sea, the river Neva, and threatened the great city itself. A determined counter-attack drove back Birger and the Swedes, and gained for the leader of the Novgorod forces, Prince Aleksandr, a title taken from the river Neva to commemorate the success – Nevskii (Alexander Nevsky). Meanwhile, the Livonian Knights, who had been called away from their attack on Pskov to help their brethren resist the Mongols, were able to return and take Pskov in 1241. Advancing on Novgorod in 1242, they were met by Alexander Nevsky's army and decisively crushed on 5 April in the battle on the ice of Lake Peipus, which was later celebrated by Eisenshtein in his famous film named after the great leader. In a Soviet evaluation, the victory 'saved the Russian people from sharing the fate of the Baltic tribes and the Slavs of the Elbe who were enslaved by the Germans'.[7] Even if this was so, pressure from the West continued to be an important feature of Russian history through the years of the more notorious infiltration from the East.

On his return to Mongolia, Batu did not manage to get himself made Great Khan or even to exert much influence at the centre of Mongol power. However, he gained some consolation from founding what came to be known later as the Golden Horde with its capital at Sarai on the Lower Volga. Batu inaugurated the custom that was to last for 200 years of the Russian princes coming to Sarai to pledge their allegiance and to pay their tribute. Emissaries from as far away as Western Europe also came to Sarai or passed through it on their way to the Great Khan, the most famous of them being Marco Polo in the late thirteenth century. To keep the Russians in subjection, the khans of the Golden Horde did not hesitate to form alliances with European princes, notably the Lithuanian, or to encourage internecine rivalry among the Russian princes themselves. Such is the broad framework in which the rise of Moscow must be examined.

But before embarking on such an examination, let us consider the nature of the Mongol impact on Russian development. While Kliuchevskii attributed little significance to the Mongols, Soviet historians emphasise only the negative aspects of the 'Tatar yoke'. Vernadsky was a skilled and moderate advocate of the 'Eurasian' view that the Muscovite state contained a considerable admixture of Mongol elements in its political, social, economic and cultural aspects. Concentrating for the moment on government and society, let us take a brief look at Vernadsky's exposition.

He asserted that if the mixed (partly monarchic, aristocratic and democratic) system of Kiev is contrasted with the absolutism of Moscow, then obviously and necessarily 'the process of the transformation of the free society into a service-bound society started during the Mongol period although it was not completed until as late as the mid-seventeenth century'.[8] The destruction of the cities which had been the main bastions of democracy and the discouragement of the boyars from forming themselves into an aristocracy meant that the way was clear for the Grand Duke of Moscow to become an autocrat.

During the period of the emergence of the Muscovite autocracy, moreover, its administration was being formed under the tutelage of the Mongols. Of the three major spheres – judicial, military and financial – the first was least affected, although capital and corporal punishment and torture became more widespread in Muscovite than in Kievan law. Western European practices as well as Mongol could be important here, it is true. Much clearer and less equivocal was the Mongol contribution to Moscow's tax arrangements and army organisation. The mere fact that the Russian word *kazna* or treasury is of Asian origin is powerful evidence of the significance of the Grand Duke's role as collector of tribute for the Golden Horde. Both the five-part division of the late medieval Muscovite army and its tactics of encirclement, as well as its universal conscription and emphasis on mobility, can all be said to possess Mongol roots. Moreover, both the service obligations of the upper class and the enserfment of the lower stemmed partly from the centuries of the 'Tatar yoke'. A significant phenomenon at the higher social level was the infiltration into the Muscovite service class of Mongol elements, which is said to have contributed later to a lower level of racial consciousness in Russia than in other expanding empires. Finally, some of the ritual of the Muscovite court and diplomatic procedures had Asian as well as Byzantine origins.

· Vernadsky concluded his work on the Mongols with the assertion that 'Autocracy and serfdom were the price the Russian people had to pay for national survival'.[9] Here, he would find himself more in general agreement with other historians than in some of his other assertions concerning the Mongol impact. Let us now turn to consider the manner in which the survival was effected, particularly through the agency of Moscow.

We have already observed that the first documentary mention of Moscow is in the year 1147, and that the founder has traditionally been named as Iurii Dolgorukii, Prince of Suzdal, who built a castle by the Moscow River, the beginning of the famous Kremlin. While the town was destroyed by the Mongols in 1238, it had recovered sufficiently by the end of the thirteenth century to be in a position to struggle for supremacy with other principalities. With Vladimir-Suzdal in decline, Moscow's chief rival was Tver, situated about a hundred miles to the north on the river Volga.

In 1304, Prince Mikhail of Tver and Prince Iurii of Moscow were rivals for the succession to the Grand Duchy of Vladimir. They both presented their claims before the Golden Horde, which decided to give its authorisation or *iarlyk* to Mikhail. Initially supported by the Church and by many boyars, Mikhail was the first to adopt the title 'Grand Duke of All Russia', and he attempted to make the title into more of a reality by asserting his authority over Novgorod and other cities in particular. But Iurii continued to oppose Mikhail's rule, and won the Tatars over to his side, marrying the khan's sister. Mikhail was executed in 1318 for resisting the decision of the Golden Horde to replace him as Grand Duke by Iurii. The reign of Iurii was troubled in turn until 1324, when he was assassinated by the son of Mikhail.

Out of the confusion, Iurii's brother Ivan emerged as Prince of Moscow, and by 1328 he had become Grand Duke of Vladimir, too. Ivan I, known as *Kalita* or Moneybag, has often been looked upon as the real founder of Moscow's power, although the case for the maintenance of such a view rests not so much upon Ivan's parsimony and skilful land purchase as upon his remunerative subservience to the Tatars. Ivan Kalita succeeded in gaining for himself their approval not only to rule as Grand Duke but also to collect tribute on their behalf from all the principalities. To counter the growth of Moscow's control, Tver and other principalities attempted to gain the support of the Lithuanians. But they were not able to muster sufficient strength to overthrow Ivan, who gained the support of the Church and the boyars as well as of the Tatars. At his death in 1341, the tomb of Ivan Kalita in Moscow became an object of veneration, a contemporary celebrating his reign as the time from which 'there descended a great calm upon the whole land'.[10]

During the reigns through the 1340s and 1350s of Ivan I's immediate successors, his sons Semen the Proud and Ivan II, Moscow's policies remained broadly the same, as did those of Tver and other rival principalities. The threat was fairly constant of Tatar intervention on the one side and of Lithuanian intervention on the other, while the princely families quarrelled among themselves about seniority and rights of succession. At the death of Ivan II in 1359, Moscow lost the ascendancy for a few years at the beginning of the reign of his son Dmitrii.

Dmitrii Ivanovich (1359–89) was to see Moscow through a further important phase of its rise to supremacy. During his early years, he was assisted, even replaced by the Metropolitan Aleksei, who came near to equating the interests of the Moscow principality with those of the Church, for which he gained canonisation in return. The struggle with Moscow was carried on by the principalities, including old rivals such as Tver and new such as Nizhnii Novgorod. Conflict with Lithuania and the Golden Horde continued as before, the most celebrated event of Dmitrii's reign being the victory over the Tatars at Kulikovo on the banks of the river Don in 1380.

For some years the power of the Golden Horde had been weakening, with various groups attempting to break away and numerous candidates putting themselves forward for the office of Khan. Irritated by a decline in the acquiescence of the Russians the Horde decided to re-establish its firm control over them by inflicting complete defeat on Moscow. Although Lithuania in alliance with the Tatars and the other principalities refused to help him, Dmitrii nevertheless managed to muster a large army. After a fierce battle in which the blood was said to flow like rain, he put the Tatars to rout, winning for himself the honorific title of Donskoi. True, after further internecine conflict, the Golden Horde was able to revenge its defeat and to reimpose a harsh tribute, but Moscow's leadership in the drive towards unification was now further established. Of course, there was some way to go before that drive was completed.

After the death of Dmitrii Donskoi, Vasilii I (1389–1425) managed to retain the Golden Horde's licence to rule. He also affected at least a fluctuating *rapprochement* with Lithuania, marrying the daughter of the Grand Duke Vitovt in 1391. Vitovt attempted to lead a crusade against the Tatars, but was defeated by them in 1399. He was nevertheless strong enough to assert his influence over Novgorod, to annex Smolensk and in 1410 to defeat the Teutonic Knights at the famous battle of Grünwald or Tannenberg. Before this time, Vasilii had broken with Vitovt and sought the support of the Tatars, themselves experiencing a great resurgence under the leadership of Timur, or Tamburlaine as he is often known. But by the time of Vasilii's death, with the centrifugal forces of the principalities, particularly Tver, constituting a severe threat, he had turned again towards Lithuania, asking Vitovt to protect his wife and his son and heir.

The first years of the reign of Vasilii II, also known as the Blind (1425–62) were disturbed by another succession struggle, the principal rival being his uncle Iurii, who could claim seniority. Supported by other disaffected princes, Iurii was able to take Moscow in 1433, but he could not hold it, and had to yield his seniority to Vasilii. The sons of Iurii were not prepared to give up the struggle immediately, however, and Tver and Novgorod showed signs of disaffection from Moscow. Moreover, after the Council of Florence in 1439, there were elements in the Church who wished to acknowledge papal supremacy. The Tatars caused great concern, too, a khan who had defected from the Golden Horde making Vasilii his prisoner in 1445. Meanwhile, one of Iurii's sons, Dmitrii Shemiaka, took advantage of the situation. By the time that Vasilii had secured his release from capture through a large ransom, Dmitrii had mustered sufficient support from princes and merchants to take Moscow, to seize his cousin and to have him blinded. Like his father, however, Dmitrii Shemiaka found it impossible to retain Moscow and was forced to free Vasilii who re-entered Moscow at the beginning of 1447, supported by the Tatars. In the last twelve years of his reign Vasilii was able to carry the process of unification further towards completion.

After this bare narrative of the early stages of the unification of Russia under Moscow, some analysis must be attempted. Let us as elsewhere start with the 'classical' account of Kliuchevskii and then note the criticisms of it made by other historians. Essentially, Kliuchevskii argued that the principalities of the north-east had much less solid social structure and cohesion than had Kiev. Their very weakness therefore made them comparatively easy prey for the one among them that was best placed to merge them into a national unit. Moscow was the successful candidate for reasons both geographical and historical. In the first place, the Moscow river, on which it stood, was connected to the Volga with its outlet on the Caspian Sea and led towards the rivers of the north-west flowing into the Baltic Sea. It was well placed to receive immigrants coming in from the south-west. Secondly, the Moscow princes did not have legal seniority and could therefore pursue their expansionist aims in a manner unrestrained by legal considerations. For example, they could ardently court the Golden Horde for the licence to rule and to gather tribute on behalf of the Tatars. When they had gained sufficient strength, however, they were able to gain further prestige by biting the hand that had fed them, so to speak, and defeating the Tatars at Kulikovo under Dmitrii Donskoi. The princes of Moscow were also assisted by the support of the Church. They made their own distinctive individual contribution by siring progeny sturdy enough to allow an unbroken line for more than a century.[11]

Some historians, finding Kliuchevskii's analysis too neat and too Moscow-centred, look for a more reliable interpretation of Moscow's rise in the work of A. E. Presniakov, who died in 1929.[12] Presniakov pointed out that unification was a dual dynastic process, that both the weakening and strengthening of principalities was going on at the same time. The fierce civil war that produced Moscow's autocracy involved many fluctuating fortunes for the princely families rather than a smooth and relentless gathering together of the Russian lands. Moreover, the 'Mongol yoke' that Kliuchevskii sees as a peripheral factor is put by Presniakov at the very centre of his explanation, giving strong emphasis to Moscow's use of the Golden Horde to gain sufficient strength to defeat it.

A British analyst, John Fennell, argues that the geographical argument falls down in face of the fact that Tver was in a better position for the task of unification than was Moscow. For him, the emergence of Moscow in the first half of the fourteenth century is explained by 'the will of the khan and, though still in a relatively embryonic stage, the support of the Church'.[13]

The most elaborate Soviet interpretation comes from L. V. Cherepnin, who, not surprisingly, stresses the economic aspects of the argument.[14] The development of agriculture, the growth of towns and the increase of commodity circulation constitute the key to his understanding of the process of unification. We will examine this argument more closely below.

Concentrating for the moment on the political and social aspects of the problem, let us take a wider comparative view, first recalling that, with the decline of Kiev, two other centres rose along with the north-east. One of them was Novgorod, which bore under Alexander Nevsky the

67353

FERNALD LIBRARY
COLBY-SAWYER COLLEGE
NEW LONDON, N. H. 03257

brunt of invasion from the west, but was also able for several centuries to make good diplomatic and commercial use of its situation near the Baltic Sea and the frontier. Although its economic hinterland was vast, and although its government was by the standards of the time efficient and progressive, it remained fundamentally a city state and was not therefore in a position to lead a nation. A second centre was Galicia-Volynia to the south-west, which by the fourteenth century became incorporated in Lithuania. A threat for the most part to the unification under Moscow, as we have seen, Lithuania has also been seen as an alternative candidate for the leadership of that process. Some analysts, such as M. K. Liubavskii, have looked upon Lithuania as a state more worthy than Moscow of being considered feudal, and the inference has therefore sometimes been drawn that a Russia led by Lithuania would have been less autocratic. Such speculation is idle, since, as Liubavskii himself pointed out, population movement is centred on Moscow.[15] Moreover, Lithuania lacked the government and the society to withstand the pressures exerted upon it during the late medieval period, when it became absorbed by Poland. Meanwhile, the Baltic peoples to the north and the Ukrainians to the south were under foreign domination, either Teutonic, Tatar or Polish, although the Cossacks were able to achieve a measure of independence in the broad southern steppe.

To the east and south of Moscow, the states of Central Asia and Transcaucasia were able to achieve something like their former status as the Mongols withdrew, but this process had not gone very far before the middle of the fifteenth century. In the case of Central Asia, it is true, the 'Mongol yoke' had more constructive features than elsewhere. During the empire of Timur in the late fourteenth century, Samarkand was transformed into a magnificent capital; in the early fifteenth century, it enjoyed a remarkable artistic and scientific flowering. But evidence such as this does not deter Soviet historians from maintaining that 'the whole Timurid dynasty played a negative role in history, not only for the countries subjugated by Timur, but for Central Asia itself whose peoples Timur deprived of all rights and subjected to ruthless exploitation'.[16]

To return in conclusion to Moscow, and to assert that its polity and society may still best be typified as frontier European rather than as Asian. This assertion will be supported by the ensuing examination of its economy and culture.

Economic

The population of Russia towards the end of the thirteenth century has been roughly calculated by Vernadsky at ten millions; possibly the town population was about half a million.[17] But the sources are no more helpful on this than those from the Kievan period, and lack of evidence is a general problem for the economic aspects of the later period as a whole.

As far as agriculture, which remained the basic activity is concerned, a thorough Soviet researcher G. E. Kochin tells us that there is a 'catastrophic gap' in the sources from the 1240s to the beginning of the fifteenth century.[18] Nevertheless, he skilfully manages to build up a composite picture from fragmentary evidence, a rough outline of which now follows. The characteristic feature of the period is the spread of arable farming in the forested non-black-earth region. The *podseka*, or slash-and-burn, stage having been largely accomplished in Kievan times, from the middle of the thirteenth to the end of the fifteenth century the fallow method was introduced with widespread adoption of the three-field system. For this transformation to take place, a somewhat improved set of farming practices had to be employed, an essential item of which was a better plough. Another necessity was manure to intensify production, and so cattle numbers had to be increased. Although progress was slow, and although the Mongol incursions delayed it, by about the end of the fourteenth century it had gone far enough in the lands of Novgorod and Pskov as well as those of the north-eastern principalities for the very terms 'village' (*derevnia*) and 'peasant' (*krestianin*) to assume more certain meaning. The villages of the period were not large, many of them consisting of no more than one or two households, but their organisation was nevertheless communal rather than individualistic, with the arable strips often subject to periodic redistribution and appurtenances such as forests and meadows usually being held in common. The basic peasant social unit remained not the nuclear family but the extended family, or even the clan based on territory as well as or even instead of blood.

Increasingly, the communes were obliged either to give their labour (*barshchina*) or their rent, usually in kind, (*obrok*) to landed proprietors, both secular and religious. Because of the large scale of their operations, the boyars and the monastic communities could go in for such activities as horse-breeding, vegetable cultivation, bee-keeping and handicrafts more readily than those peasants who were unattached. In the fifteenth century, particularly its later decades, the landlords appear to have intensified their interest in agriculture and therefore their demands on the peasants. Both labour and rent rates were raised, and restrictions on peasant movement were tightened. Domestic manufacture increased as well as arable and cattle farming. The village was becoming involved in at least the local market, and some rents began to be paid in money rather than in kind, in the Novgorod lands, for example. A further consequence was the build-up of economic links within the principalities, and between them. The foundations were laid for the unification of the principalities in one state. Far from seeing the period as one of general decline, Kochin concludes by saying:

> The second half of the thirteenth, fourteenth and fifteenth centuries were taken up by a great and powerful feat of the working people of old Russia, as a result of which huge areas of northern forest were brought into arable farming; tens of thousands of new settlements were created, villages built permanently and surely for centuries, lasting down to our own times; hundreds of thousands of well organised and by the standards of the time highly productive units of agricultural economy were created or structurally renewed.[19]

Not only Kochin, but other less economically specialist colleagues such as L. V. Cherepnin base their interpretations of the unification of Russia on economic developments. For Cherepnin, these include not only the centrally important agricultural expansion but also urban growth. Of this, he writes that throughout the fourteenth and fifteenth centuries several settlements became towns and several old towns took on new life as centres of trade and manufacture. The princes became conscious of the need to encourage these activities by freeing commercial routes, partly under the pressure of the leading merchants. However, like agriculture, manufacture and trade were subject to restrictions characteristic of feudal society elsewhere.[20]

Novgorod and its 'little brother' Pskov were the major commercial cities at the beginning of the period. Novgorod was one of the major European cities, with its own well-developed political system and cultural life as well as an energetic economic activity; exciting archaeological discoveries have revealed a considerable amount about all these aspects. Its principal contact was with Germans and Central Europeans and with the Hanseatic League, the representatives of which carried on their business under strict controls. The trade consisted mainly of the export of furs and wax, leather and hemp, and the import of woollen and other textile materials, metal goods, wines and spices.[21]

Newer towns such as Nizhnii Novgorod on the Volga and Moscow itself began to develop their economic importance round about this time. Trade with the east down the Volga and through the Tatar capital of Sarai started to grow as the Mongols stopped their interference. The

Don was also an important commercial artery, with the Genoese capital of Tana at its mouth. Sarai and Tana were both bustling, cosmopolitan centres for the exchange of oriental silks, spices, precious stones and other luxury goods with Western furs, wax, honey and caviar. The Genoese also had another colony called Sudak, or Surozh in Russian, in the Crimea. A special group of Muscovite merchants dealt with the Genoese.

We must be careful not to exaggerate the intensity of economic activity throughout the period of invasion and division. But a greater danger is to look upon it as a period of complete ruin and stagnation. Of course, feudal society was not conducive to rapid growth. Undoubtedly, the devastation brought about by the invasions of the Mongols and others, as well as the squabbling between the principalities, acted as braking forces. It would be premature in the extreme to talk of national markets or budgets. And yet, to divorce the economic aspects of Russian life from the others and not to note the part played by the extension of agriculture and the expansion of commerce in the process of unification is to omit from consideration a vital part of the explanation of that process.

Cultural

During the period of Mongol invasion and feudal division, at least the 'official' Russian culture remained in the care of the Orthodox Church. This was recognised by the princes and even by the Mongols. While churches and clergymen were at first as much the object of Mongol attack as anything and anybody else, the Church was soon exempted from tax assessment. After 1266 it was given further immunities, ostensibly under the authority of Chingis, in return for which it was expected to pray for the Great Khan's successors. As a powerful economic force and as a political intermediary between the princes, the Metropolitan and his associates by no means confined their activities to the spiritual life. With new churches and monasteries being built and the administration being extended into rural areas as well as the towns, Russian Orthodoxy was basically well prepared to take on the succession after the Council of Florence in 1439 and the fall of Byzantium in 1453. It continued to produce great works of art and architecture, of which more below. With such individuals as St Sergius of Radonezh, founder of the Trinity Monastery to the north-east of Moscow and adviser to Prince Dmitrii before the battle of Kulikovo, it produced outstanding figures deemed capable of deep piety and national leadership.

However, the Church by no means completely succeeded in carrying its message to the people. Its comparative failure was inevitable if Florinsky's assertion is correct that 'the indifference of the masses towards religion is one of the characteristics of Russia's history'.[22] Soviet historians would certainly agree with him on this point, if not on many others. But it is also the case that the rank and file of the priesthood were often incapable of their pastoral duties. Genadius, Archbishop of Novgorod in the fifteenth century, complained:

> They bring me a peasant to be ordained as a priest or deacon. I bid him read the Epistles, and he does not know how to begin. I bid him read the Psalter, he cannot take the first step. . . . I order him to be taught at least the liturgical prayers, but he is unable even to repeat the words one gives him. When told to read from the alphabet, after a short lesson he begs to leave, does not want to learn. And if I refuse to ordain him, I am told such is the world, your Holiness, we cannot find anyone versed in knowledge.[23]

The ignorance and the poverty of the ordinary or 'white' clergy were to remain problems for many centuries. So were the luxury and corruption of many church leaders and others in the 'black' monastic orders. In order to retain or regain their purity, many hermits removed themselves ever further from the great ecclesiastical centres. As a more positive response to the situation, various heretical sects arose. Among these were the *strigolniki*, who appeared in Novgorod and Pskov in the late fourteenth century and early fifteenth century respectively. Rejecting the Church hierarchy and appealing for a return to the ideals of the early apostolic church, the *strigolniki* were persecuted with severity. Their ideas would obviously bear comparison with those of Wyclif in England and Hus in Bohemia. For Soviet historians such as A. M. Sakharov, their significance lies less in their religious than in their social protest.[24]

While the Orthodox Church might often have failed in its humanitarian and spiritual duties, it certainly continued to play an outstanding part in the preservation and development of education, literature and the arts. Commerce and, to a lesser extent, government would also play their part in the maintenance and expansion of literacy, numeracy and learning, but such schools and libraries as there were would almost exclusively be found attached to the monasteries and churches. Orthodoxy also produced not only works of spiritual uplift and admonition but more records of the past as well, including the *Trinity Chronicle* destroyed by fire in 1812 but skilfully reconstructed by Soviet scholars. World history as well as national retained the interest of Russian clerics.

The outstanding artists of the period were Theophanes the Greek and Andrei Rublev. Theophanes came from Byzantium to Novgorod in the late fourteenth century, both teaching the style he brought with him and assimilating that which he now encountered. He worked in Moscow and Nizhnii Novgorod as well as in Novgorod. Among his collaborators was Andrei Rublev, who at the beginning of the fifteenth century, brought the art of icon-painting to a new level. His masterpiece is generally agreed to be the *Trinity*, dedicated to St Sergius of Radonezh and now kept in the Tretiakov Gallery in Moscow. This charms Vernadsky with 'the serene quiet of the composition and the symphony of delicate colours'[25]; and an outstanding Soviet critic V. N. Lazarev writes: 'The wonderful compositional rhythm of the icon is enhanced by the colouring, which is musical beyond all words. Amity – such would be the most appropriate terms for the colour scheme of the icon, so clear, so lucid, so transparent; for it expresses with remarkable force the amity, the harmony among the three angels.'[26] Facing such a work, one can hardly doubt that inspirations to the eye and to the mind's eye continue to be the major achievement of early Moscow as of Kiev.

This is so even though stone building was interrupted for several years by the Mongol invasions. By the middle of the fifteenth century, however, both Novgorod and Moscow were adorned with great churches as well as with their Kremlins. Moscow, it is true, had to wait for its real architectural flowering until the reign of Ivan III. And as far as European parallels are concerned, while it is possible to talk of a Russian Romanesque and a Russian Renaissance style, the great Gothic achievement finds almost no expression except in the Novgorod Kremlin.

A palace is not a church building, and a considerable amount of the cultural activity of the period under discussion was secular rather than religious in its emphasis. This remained the case with much of the folk culture, including the songs of the peasants, even though the Church attempted to adapt some of its music to the folk style. Outstanding among the creations of the time are the great epics or *byliny* lamenting the calamities wrought by the Mongols or celebrating the great deeds of Alexander Nevsky or Dmitrii Donskoi. At the same time, a certain amount of improvement in the manufacture of the materials of war and peace can also be detected – for example, in the casting of cannon and the minting of money.[27]

Russia's culture, like her political, social and economic activity, was open, from 1240 to 1462, to influences from both Asia and Europe. Vernadsky and others have rendered great service in reminding us of the Mongol impact; and yet there can be little doubt that a white race with a Slavonic language and folklore, and a considerable involvement in the Orthodox variation of the Christian world-view, must be considered fundamentally as an outpost of the West even in the severest days of the 'Mongol yoke'.

3 Consolidation under Moscow, 1462–1645

The period from the middle of the fifteenth century to the middle of the seventeenth century is known in the Western world as that of the formation of national states, of great geographical discoveries, of the Renaissance, Reformation and Counter-Reformation. Parallel developments occurring at the eastern extremity of the Western world clearly demonstrated that remoteness by no means constituted complete separation in this period any more than in its predecessors.

Under such powerful tsars as Ivan III or Great (1462–1505) and Ivan IV or Terrible (1533–84), the hold of Moscow was strengthened over much of Great Russia if by no means over the whole of the future Soviet Union. The government became somewhat better organised, and the armed forces acquitted themselves well enough against enemies to the east and west at times, although suffering painful reverses at others. Social stratification from the highest to the lowest level was more clearly demarcated, with both the service nobility and the enserfed peasantry taking on recognisable if still embryonic shape. As well as arousing the hostility of foreign powers, particularly its neighbours of which Poland–Lithuania was the most formidable, Moscow also became the centre of diplomatic blandishments proffered by European states, from England to Venice, not to mention the contacts reinforced in Asia. In order to support such rising status, the economic resources of the state had to be exploited to the full, and even beyond. Activity both internal and external was directed whenever possible towards increasing the government's wealth to the distress and even ruin of many of its subjects. Under the appalling strain, which was compounded by a dynastic crisis at the end of the sixteenth century, Moscow fell apart during the Time of Troubles. Boris Godunov (tsar from 1598 to 1605) was the most notable of a rapid series of rulers, several of whom were no more than puppets in the hands of the Poles and other invaders.

Recovery only partly occurred by the end of the reign of the first Romanov, Mikhail or Michael (1613–45).

Meanwhile, landlocked as they were for the most part, Muscovites could not hope to make much of a contribution to the exciting sea voyages of discovery during the period, but found their nearest counterparts to Columbus and Drake in such freebooters as the Cossack Ermak.[1] His passage eastwards through Siberia was assisted by Ivan the Terrible's conquest of the Kazan Tatars, and the weakness of the remnants of the Golden Horde elsewhere. But Muscovites were not the only people to cast their aggressive eyes on areas vacated by the Mongols. Persia and Turkey between them managed to subjugate most of Central Asia and Transcaucasia, and increased their importance as rival claimants for the steppe. Diplomatic and other forms of contact in the vast, amorphous frontier areas continued to necessitate the crossing of cultural as well as political barriers.

Similarly, Russia could hardly fail to become more caught up in the cultural changes occurring in the Christian West as involvement in that direction grew more intense. Michael Cherniavsky has drawn an interesting portrait of Ivan the Terrible as Renaissance prince, and Soviet historians have amplified the assertion of predecessors such as S. F. Platonov that neither the Reformation nor the Counter-Reformation left Russia untouched. Moreover, if the fall of Constantinople did not initiate the Western Renaissance, it soon served to strengthen Muscovite self-consciousness as the Orthodox Church claimed for itself the true Roman inheritance and the princes declared themselves to be Caesars or tsars. Ivan the Terrible addressed himself to Elizabeth of England in terms of by no means distant formality, while the first Romanovs set up amicable relations with the Stuarts in a similar manner. The majority of their subjects shared the tsars' view that Russian culture was more than the equal of its European counterparts.

Equally, the condescension of Western travellers to Muscovy (as the contemporary British called it) was often the result of a reciprocal insularity of viewpoint rather than of an objective estimation. For example, if Muscovy presented itself to an English visitor as a 'rude and barbarous kingdom',[2] the first ambassador to England from Ivan the Terrible could hardly have formed a more flattering picture after his shipwreck on the north-east coast of Scotland and his subsequent despoliation by, to use Hakluyt's words, 'the rude and ravenous people of the country thereunto adjoining'.[3] The problems of cultural relativity that always confront the historian using travellers' accounts as sources are compounded in the Muscovite instance by the circumstance that they are often of outstanding importance owing to the scarcity of sources in general. This predicament, which has caused Edward Keenan to wonder if the historians of any Christian country of the period other than Ethiopia are similarly handicapped,[4] is largely the consequence of fires destroying vast amounts of documents. Uncritical use of the travellers' accounts by historians of Russia both before and after the Revolution of 1917 has led to some fanciful hypotheses. From critical use of them and other extant sources, however, historians have been able to extract convincing interpretations of governmental policies and interesting portraits of the tsars themselves.

Ivan III stands in relation to Ivan IV rather as Henry VII of England stands in relation to Henry VIII, at least as far as popular conceptions are concerned. Ivan the Great comes over as a somewhat colourless but determined figure, while Ivan the Terrible exhibits not only a peculiar kind of flamboyance but also a taste for multiple matrimony. In fact, not a great amount is known about Ivan the Great, although some anecdotes about him from a near contemporary Habsburg emissary, Von Herberstein, indicate the sardonic bonhomie usually associated with Ivan the Terrible or Peter the Great. For example, Von Herberstein reports that 'he generally drank so excessively at dinner as to fall asleep, and while his guests were all struck with terror and sitting in silence, he would awake, rub his eyes and then first begin to joke and make merry with them'.[5] Ivan the Great's harsh treatment of all those who stood in the path of final unification would more than adequately explain the terror of his dinner guests. And yet, as Michael Cherniavsky argues in his discussion of Ivan the Terrible, tsarist cruelty in the sixteenth century was by no means wholly gratuitous and was usually tempered by at least a crude sense of justice. Referring to a wide range of sources including Machiavelli on this point, Cherniavsky cites the argument of a Soviet historian concerning Tsepesh of Wallachia, the original Dracula, to the effect that 'the ambivalent image of cruelty and justice was in response to men's hopes that in an age of many small feudal dragons, one great dragon would provide justice and peace'.[6] Ivan IV's sobriquet is in some respects unfortunate, since *groznyi* means less horrible than awe-inspiring. Many of the English and other visitors who described him made frequent reference to his warmth and charm, while Soviet pathologists who have examined his exhumed skeleton have argued that his apparent insane sadism might well have been less the result of an unhinged mind than of a diseased spine. Boris Godunov has also suffered somewhat from the image projected abroad, Mussorgsky's operatic adaptation of Pushkin's verse drama being far from completely fair. In Kliuchevskii's estimation, 'On the throne Boris proved as wise and cautious an administrator as he had shown himself to be when standing beside it.'[7] As for Michael Romanov, Florinsky describes him as 'an ailing, self-effacing and docile young man ... only too anxious to let others govern in his name'.[8] While Boris has sometimes received too bad a press from historians, Michael has often been given by them one that is too good.

The principal subject of this chapter, the process of consolidation, is inextricably connected with the tsars just described and with others lesser known, and with the all-conquering principality of Moscow. Yet we must also recall that the period from the middle of the fifteenth to the middle of the seventeenth centuries, during which the term 'Russia' as well as 'Russian land' and 'Russian state' come to be used, is of comparable significance for other European nations too.

Political

The history of the period from 1462 to 1645 falls into four main sections comparable in significance if not in chronological length: the reign of Ivan III; the reign of Ivan IV; the Time of Troubles; and the reign of Michael Romanov.

By the accession of Ivan III in 1462, Moscow had become the political as well as the religious centre of the Russian lands. A considerable amount of ingathering remained to be accomplished, however, before the process of the consolidation of the Muscovite state became complete. Ivan III's reign marks 'an important stage' in this process, according to Soviet historians who on this point are in agreement with Kliuchevskii and other pre-revolutionary predecessors, as well as Western colleagues, in their assertion that 'It was the period in which the basic territory of Russia was welded into a single state and completely liberated from the Tatar yoke, and in which the political foundations of that state took shape.'[9]

To take the last mentioned development first, the Boyar Duma was transformed from an advisory organisation into a more formal supreme council attended by the greatest princes and aristocrats. In the authoritative view of G. Alef, this 'oligarchic cast of the duma membership intimates that the Grand Prince succumbed to pressures benefiting a number of select families. The price was minimal, for he derived inestimable gain from long years of loyal service by the many members of these families who vied for appointments and competed for promotion.'[10] The price was not raised by the circumstance that Ivan was obliged to pursue policies broadly acceptable to the boyars and the nobility as a whole, if not to dissident or centrifugal individuals among them, since the interests of the Grand Prince and of his chief servants basically converged. While most important problems were considered by Ivan presiding over the Duma, a larger body was summoned for such supreme matters of state as his own testament or war and peace. Consisting of the Boyar Duma and the Holy Conclave of the Church, and sometimes of lower-ranking members of the nobility, too, this occasional assembly was the forerunner of the *Zemskii Sobor*, or Assembly of the Whole Land, which was to be convened in the sixteenth century. The executive functions of the central government began to be carried on by departments known as *prikazy*, while local government was continued on the basis of the *kormlenie* or 'feeding' system, by which lucrative offices were farmed out to favourites. An attempt at a uniform judicial system for central and local government was made by the *Sudebnik* of 1497, a code of laws applying for the first time to the whole of Muscovy.

These organisational and procedural changes both reflected and initiated notable socio-political adjustments. The Muscovite aristocracy and nobility, along with the leading members of the commercial class, for the most part gave their support to the Grand Prince, but some princes and boyars from the centre as well as the periphery were disaffected as their old liberties and privileges yielded before the process of centralisation. In order to regulate clashes between the various families and clans, the system of appointment to places known as *mestnichestvo* received something like its final form during the reign of Ivan III. At the same time, *mestnichestvo* received further encouragement from the tendency noted by G. Alef for more than half of the personnel of the Boyar Duma to become 'more deeply involved in ceremonial and administrative affairs'. In other words (as the Soviet historian S. O. Shmidt tells us in further detail), the bureaucratisation of the nobility discerned by historians of contemporaneous Western European states was a phenomenon of late medieval Russia, too.[11]

For this to be so, the Russian monarch, like his brethren elsewhere, had to demonstrate a new confidence in the authority of his own government. As Ferdinand and Isabella were putting together Spain, Charles VIII was consolidating France, Henry VII asserting control over England, and Maximilian I extending, possibly over-extending, the control of the Habsburgs over much of central Europe, Ivan III was celebrating his own comparable performance by assuming the title of Tsar (or Caesar). This title was derived from the first Rome by way of the second, Byzantium, the niece of the last emperor of which became Ivan's second wife in 1472. Furthermore, Ivan adapted Byzantine ritual for his own court, and took the double-headed eagle of the Palaeologoi to accompany the Kievan St George as a royal coat-of-arms.[12] The Church assisted the formation of tsarist self-confidence through the following years with its development of formal coronation, elaboration of saintly contributions to Russian history and promulgation of Moscow as the Third Rome. These innovations by no means met with universal acceptance, but it was a measure of the tsars' power that they could not be long withstood.

The principal physical extension of Ivan III's power in particular was through his continuation of the process of the ingathering of the Russian lands, a prerequisite for the more final subjugation of the Tatars. Unification still involved questions of foreign as well as of domestic policy, since the state remained somewhat amorphous. For example, in a bid to preserve the optimum measure of independence, Novgorod attempted in 1470 to exchange vassalage to Moscow for that to Poland and Lithuania. In the following year Ivan III conducted a successful campaign against Novgorod which compelled the great city to reaffirm its former oath and to sever all foreign political connections. Further factional fighting in Novgorod brought about another campaign against it in 1478, and within a year Ivan fulfilled his threat to silence the *veche* bell forever, even if its echoes were to linger on. The fall of Novgorod made the position of other principalities more precarious, and several of them, notably Tver, succumbed in the following years, those which retained any measure of independence doing so only on the sufferance of Moscow. Tension with Poland and Lithuania, heightened by the defection to Moscow of a considerable number of members of the Polish-Lithuanian nobility, led to the outbreak of a series of wars. At the peace arranged in 1503, the successes of Russian arms were marked by the recognition of Russian control over large areas to the west and south. In the same year, a treaty with the Livonian order marked the acceptance of Muscovy's right to conduct trade with the West.

Lands acquired during the ingathering process were distributed among the adherents of the tsar on the basis of conditional service tenure. In such a manner, both the loyalty of the new regions and the maintenance of the army were to be guaranteed.

The victories of the army during the reign of Ivan III indicated that Moscow was not particularly backward at this time from the military point of view. An American expert on the subject, Thomas Esper, has indicated that Russia adopted the bronze cannon and the iron cannon ball almost as soon as other European states. Foreign craftsmen, including Germans, Italians and Scots, assisted in this adoption, and some of them contributed towards the necessary modification of fortresses, including the Moscow Kremlin. But artillery was still of secondary importance, for siege and pitched warfare had yet to reach the eastern extremity of Europe, where the peculiar qualities of the steppe made mobility a primary consideration.[13]

Under Ivan III, the Russians demonstrated that they had mastered the art of fighting on the steppe. With Ivan's position strengthened by the reduction of the principalities and the Golden Horde disintegrating into mutually hostile khanates, the time was ripe for the final removal of the 'Tatar yoke'. When Khan Ahmed attempted to reunite the Golden Horde and reimpose its yoke in 1480 with the encouragement of the Poles and Lithuanians, Ivan allied with the Crimean Tatars who kept the Poles and Lithuanians busy while he himself concentrated on turning back Ahmed from Moscow. The khan was killed during his retreat in internecine conflict, and the Golden Horde soon fell apart completely. Meanwhile, Ivan was able to force Kazan to make obeisance to Moscow, and to continue his drive into Siberia, incorporating into his state a number of tribes as far over as the Ob River and the Northern Sea. Expansion to the south could not be taken to the Black Sea, since the Crimean Tatars became disillusioned by Ivan's exploitation of them and turned to Turkey for protection.

The unification and expansion of Russia was sufficient by the end of the reign to have brought her to the closer attention of other European states. Contact with Venice, Genoa, Naples and the Papacy was increased, as well as with governments nearer home in central Europe. Relations were also developed with the Orient, both the easily accessible and the remote.

During the reign of Vasilii III (1505–33), existing foreign and domestic policies were continued, the Holy Roman Empire and India being added to the number of diplomatic contacts. The fundamental ingathering of the Great Russian lands was brought to a successful conclusion after the principalities of Pskov and Riazan had been incorporated in 1510 and 1521 respectively, and a war with Lithuania from 1512 to 1522 had resulted in the acquisition of Smolensk. Expansion to the east was less to be embarked upon, for in 1521 the khan of the Crimean Tatars engineered the downfall of the pro-Muscovite khan of Kazan, and then, with the support of Lithuania, brought both hordes into an attack on Moscow, devastating large areas as he did so. Disaster threatened as several princes conspired with the enemy to attempt the separation of their lands from Muscovy. Vasilii stifled the conspiracy, but discontent lingered on in the higher circles of the aristocracy, particularly after the tsar divorced his first wife, a daughter of an old boyar family, in 1525, on the grounds that she was incapable of bearing him children. Before the discontent was stilled, Vasilii died suddenly in 1533, instructing his second wife Elena to institute her regency until their son Ivan attained his majority.

In 1534 Elena assumed power for herself, aided and abetted first by her uncle and then by her lover. Elena and her associates soon found themselves assailed from all quarters, by the Tatars and Lithuanians from without, by dissident boyars and hard-pressed peasants from within. A revolt in 1537 by the inhabitants of Moscow on behalf of the claims to the throne of a younger brother of Vasilii III was crushed, but then in 1538 Elena died as suddenly as had her husband, probably poisoned by the boyars. Two groups of them, the Shuiskiis and the Belskiis, now struggled for power in a ding-dong manner, each in turn sharing out the spoils among their followers and making some attempt to secure the support of other social strata such as the service nobles. The attempt was in vain for by 1547 a sufficient number of service nobles had joined with a quorum of boyars to promote the cause of the Grand Prince. Ivan's coronation as tsar in January of that year, followed by his marriage to his first wife Anastasia in February, is usually said to mark the beginning of the independent reign of Ivan the Terrible, although he had already demonstrated a precocious independence, notably in his instigation of the assassination of one of the Shuiskii princes in 1543.

The reign continued according to a pattern already well established, in violence. The summer of 1547 brought the greatest town revolt of the sixteenth century as a resurgence of popular dissatisfaction was intensified by a severe drought followed by a 'Great Fire'. Ivan fled from the capital as his mother's kinsmen, who were his own advisers, were blamed for the 'Great Fire' and made the chief object of the crowd's attack. Flames both real and metaphorical arose throughout Moscow.

Regaining a grasp on the situation after one of his many bouts of religious melancholia and a public confession of his sins, Ivan moved towards reform with the advice and support of a different entourage, the 'chosen council'. This was a confidential circle of advisers including Metropolitan Makarii, the tsar's tutor, Father Silvestr, the tsar's confessor, and Aleksei Adashev, one of his boyhood friends, along with his wife's relations, the Zakharin family.[14]

At the beginning of 1549, new policies were announced by Ivan himself, first to the Boyar Duma and Holy Conclave in joint session, and then to officials and nobles summoned to Moscow for what appears to have been the first *Zemskii Sobor*. In his declaration, Ivan preached and promised social peace and the restoration of law. Practical steps towards such an end were taken later in the same year with decrees regulating relations between the various strata of the ruling class and the commencement of preparation of a new code of laws or *Sudebnik* to replace that of 1497. Promulgated in 1550 and approved by a *Zemskii Sobor*, the *Sudebnik* attempted to bring further stability into relations not only between the individuals and groups who composed the ruling class, but also between the class as a whole and the peasantry, whose legal freedoms became restricted. At the same time, the *Sudebnik* gave heavier emphasis to the power of the *prikazy* of the central administration and reduced the power and influence of the leading officials in local government. The former steps were carried out in conjunction with a further extension and bureaucratisation of the Boyar Duma, while the latter move may generally be seen not only as part of the completion of the unfication process, but also as a reflection of the government's awareness of the wastefulness of the *kormlenie* or 'feeding' system at a time when the meagre resources of the country had yet again to be exploited for the purpose of making war.

The national resolve strengthened by a reform in the Church, which we will examine later, the government soon moved towards more down-to-earth military preparation with a sweeping army reform. The Service Regulations of 1556 encouraged the merger of hereditary and service land tenure and thus furthered the tendency for all members of the upper class to serve in return for estate ownership. The contribution in men, horses and material was more precisely fixed according to estate size. At about the same time, Ivan organised a new standing force of *streltsy* (musketeers, or more precisely *harquebusiers*) to carry out police duties as well as to supplement the irregular levies. As the structure of the army was remoulded, its strategy was adapted too, with more emphasis being given to the fortified line and to the artillery, which was now supported by an ammunitions industry not greatly inferior to that of many European states. Although by no means invincible, the Russian army enjoyed a number of considerable successes during the 1550s.[15]

The most important and permanent of these were to the east, and included the final reduction of the khanates of Kazan and Astrakhan, as well as the extension of Russian control over the Middle and Lower Volga regions. Despite a flank attack from the Crimean Tatars urged on by the Turks, the Russian forces were able to lay a carefully prepared siege to the town of Kazan in 1552, bombarding and starving the citadel into submission. Soon afterwards, the fertile lands of the Volga and its many peoples – including the Chuvashes and Bashkirs as well as Tatars – were obliged to pledge their loyalty to the tsar, and the town of Astra-khan at the mouth of the Volga fell in 1556. Although the Tatars had now been neutralised on the eastern flank from Kazan to the Caspian Sea, their brethren in the Crimea Khanate remained an irritating thorn in Moscow's southern side.

War to the west broke out in 1558. The ostensible reason was Livonia's non-fulfilment of the obligations of its treaty with Ivan III and the underlying cause was the problem of Moscow's access to the Baltic Sea. Initial Russian success meant a setback for both the Livonian Order and its Polish and Lithuanian allies. However, Russian acquisi-tions of the important port of Narva and other footholds on the Baltic provoked the alarm of Western European states as well as of those near the littoral. Poland and Lithuania, formally brought together by the Union of Liublin in 1569, worked with Sweden and Denmark through-out the 1560s at pushing the Muscovite forces back in the Baltic region. The English, while solidifying their access to Moscow via the Northern Cape route (first accidentally discovered by Richard Chancellor in 1553 while searching for the North-East Passage to the Indies), held back from full alliance.

With some, if by no means total, justification, Ivan the Terrible blamed the reverses of the 1560s on the opposition to the war of many boyars and the defection of Prince Andrei Kurbskii, who had been prominent in the siege of Kazan and then commander of the Baltic army. The tsar decided that the moment had come for a new internal policy involving a break with the boyars and even with his erstwhile close advisers. Suspecting Silvestr and Adashev of implication in a plot to poison his first wife Anastasia Zakharina, who died suddenly in 1560 never to be adequately replaced by her six successors, he banished them. Metropolitan Makarii died in 1564, by which time the Zakharin family was losing its favour and Ivan therefore losing the last of his nearest entourage. After striking out, not for the first time, at suspected boyar opposition Ivan decided at the end of 1564 to go into a seclusion that threatened to become monastic. Having in such a dramatic manner blackmailed people of all classes to petition for his return – an episode most graphically if not accurately represented in Eisenshtein's famous film, *Ivan the Terrible* – he then persuaded them to confirm his introduc-tion of the *oprichnina* (or lands apart).

This notorious institution divided the whole country into two halves – the *oprichnina* and the *zemshchina* (or national lands) – even the town of Moscow itself being split in this manner. Some of the boyars and service nobles were incorporated into the administration of the *oprich-nina*, the rest were put into the *zemshchina* supposedly administered under the tsar by the *Zemskii Sobor*, which was convened in 1566 to give its support to the prosecution of the Livonian War. Opposition expressed there and elsewhere to the *oprichnina* decided Ivan in favour of an intensification of his peculiar institution and the introduction of terror. From 1566 to 1572, the black-cloaked *oprichniki* rode amok throughout the land, their 'gnawing' and 'sweeping' symbolised by the dog's head and broom fixed to the saddles of their black horses. Ivan himself participated in the tortures and executions, the rapes and orgies, alternating such bouts of sadism with contrite hangovers of sackcloth and ashes. Yet for all its horrific drama, the impact of the *oprichnina* must not be exaggerated. A careful Soviet scholar, R. G. Skrynnikov, has calculated that one of the most notorious incidents, the sack of Novgorod, accounted for no more than two thousand lives and that the *oprichnina* as a whole for less than double that number. In like manner, Skrynnikov has argued that neither the short-term nor long-term consequences of the *oprichnina* should be exaggerated.[16]

With most of the opposition – aristocratic, ecclesiastical and commoner – both real and imagined, having been purged by the beginning of the 1570s, and with the whole country threatened by Crimean Tatar incursions culminating in the ravage of Moscow itself, and by the renewal of the Livonian War, not to mention harvest failure, famine and plague, Ivan decided in late 1572 to bring the *oprichnina* to an end, strictly prohibiting any future mention of the term itself. A united army had by this time pushed back the Tatars from Moscow, but the Livonian War proved to be a much stiffer proposition. Although the Russian army met with some successes in the 1570s and early 1580s, these were more than outweighed by the reverses suffered, particularly when the forces of Poland–Lithuania and Sweden engaged them on two fronts. Treaties of the early 1580s resulted in a net loss of territory for Russia. A high price, both economic and social, had been paid for small returns. Nevertheless, Soviet historians argue that the Livonian War was by no means completely negative in its effect from the Russian point of view: the Livonian Order had been crushed; the way ahead was cleared for Ivan's successors culminating in Peter the Great; and the 'anti-feudal friendship' of the Russian and Baltic peoples was firmly established.[17]

Although the *oprichnina* was over, Ivan's behaviour in the last decade or so of his reign did not lose its apparent eccentricities. In 1575, he not only resumed executions, but put on the throne for a short time a converted Tatar prince, Simeon Bekbulatovich. And then in 1581, either accidentally or on purpose, he killed his son Ivan during a quarrel. According to some interpretations, this last incident, added to the bloody experiences of his youth and adulthood and the death of his first and favourite wife Anastasia, took him over the brink into a painful madness from which he had not recovered by his death in 1584.

Both the personality of Ivan the Terrible and the significance of his reign continue to arouse a lively debate. Possibly, the one is best seen as the reflection of the other. Thus, the 'madness' of Ivan is to be looked upon as an indicator of the great difficulty of putting Muscovite absolutism upon a certain foundation at a time when the symptoms of dissolution which were to show themselves clearly in the Time of Troubles were already more than dimly apparent. He himself appears to have been often convinced of the insuperability of the obstacles in his path, revealing his despair, either in suggestions to Elizabeth of England for mutual asylum or in his bouts of religious melancholia and bloody sadism. However, as has already been pointed out, at least part of Ivan's passive and active frenzy might have been caused by a painful disease of the spine. Moreover, as Cherniavsky has argued, there may have been more than a little Machiavellian method in Ivan's madness. An extreme and influential version of such an interpretation was put by J. V. Stalin to the actor N. K. Cherkasov (who took the part of Ivan in Eisenshtein's film). Cherkasov reported the Soviet leader as saying, not only that the *oprichnina* played a 'progressive role', but also that Ivan's greatest error was not to have taken his purges far enough, an omission which led to the Time of Troubles.[18]

Since the death of Stalin, Soviet historians have largely abandoned glorification of Ivan in favour of an attempt at a more balanced evaluation, centring a considerable amount of their discussion around the problem of the social orientation of his policies. While still inconclusive, the discussion has at least demonstrated the limitations of any too clearcut distinction between the interests of the boyars and other upper-ranking nobles on the one hand and those of the service nobility at large on the other. At the same time, the confluence of noble interests as opposed to those of the peasants has been vigorously propounded. Examining the reign in a wider focus, some historians have attempted to compare the Russian type of absolutism with that of other European states. While much work remains to be done in this very difficult area, and while it is already apparent that there are significant specific differences as well as similarities between, say the *Zemskii Sobor* and its European counterparts, there can nevertheless be little doubt that the process of the formation of states throughout the continent conforms to a basic general pattern.[19]

Fedor Ivanovich, or Theodore (1584–98), was not very strong either physically or mentally and left most of the business of government to his advisers, particularly to his brother-in-law, the boyar Boris Godunov. Apart from some important economic and ecclestiastical developments, which will be considered below, the reign was primarily significant for its wars and for its expansion of the national territories.

Peace was maintained with Poland so that the Russian army in the west could be directed principally against Sweden. Between 1590 and 1595, the foothold on the Baltic was regained, although Narva was not. As Russia's international prestige was raised by the establishment of a Russian Patriarchate in 1589, diplomatic contacts were being broadened with western and central European countries. To the south, the Crimean Tatars were pushed back and Russian control was extended as far as the Caucasus, a protective alliance being arranged with Transcaucasian Georgia in 1587.

Even greater penetration was achieved to the east. A Cossack party under the patronage of the commercial Stroganov family and the swash-buckling leadership of Ermak had already succeeded by 1582 in reducing the Tatars of Western Siberia through a combination of bravado and firearms. Although Ermak himself was killed in 1585, both the Stroganovs and the government continued to send expeditions to the region, confirming the Russian hold on it. Yet Western Siberia was looked upon as an outpost of the nation rather than as a constituent part of it; by the end of the sixteenth century, Moscow was composed essentially of five parts, two inner and three outer. At the centre were the regions surrounding the towns of Moscow and Novgorod. To the north, there was the seaboard and its hinterland, to the south-east the Middle and Lower Volga and to the south there was the steppe. This basic structure was still in a condition too new and incomplete to be firmly established when it was struck by the catastrophe of the Time of Troubles.

In his *Of the Russe Commonwealth*, published in London in 1591, Giles Fletcher had predicted that the 'wicked and tyrannous practice' of the *oprichnina* had filled the country 'so full of grudge and mortal hatred ever since, that it will not be quenched (as it seemeth now) till it burn into a civil flame', and that the military despotism of the tsar and his entourage 'maketh the people for the most part to wish for some foreign invasion, which they suppose to be the only means to rid them of the heavy yoke of this tyrannous government'.[20] Both the 'civil flame' and

the 'foreign invasion' were to strike Moscow more severely than anybody could have predicted or hoped in the fifteen years following the
death of Fedor Ivanovich in 1598. Not that the *oprichnina* and tsarist
tyranny were wholly to blame; the reasons for the Time of Troubles can
clearly and comprehensively be seen in the nature of the three stages
into which the great historian Platonov divided it.[21] Firstly, from 1598
to 1606, there was dynastic confusion, as the Godunovs, Shuiskiis and
Romanovs bickered among themselves for the succession along with
the first 'False Dmitrii'. Secondly, from 1606 to 1610, there was social
struggle, as the Cossacks became the focus of the discontent of the lower
classes against a background of further impersonation of the Tsarevich
Dmitrii. And thirdly, from 1611 to 1613, there was the fight for nation-
hood, as foreign intervention, notably from Sweden and Poland–Lithuania, brought about a suppression of personal and collective rivalries in
a flush of patriotism concentrated to drive the alien from the Russian
soil. Such patriotism is far from ignored by Soviet historians, who
nevertheless give more emphasis than does Platonov to the social
struggle.

After a *Zemskii Sobor* had elected him tsar in 1598, Boris Godunov
found it more difficult to rule in his own right than to rule in fact behind
the legal façade of the tsardom of Fedor Ivanovich. Although he almost
certainly had not instigated the murder of Fedor's step-brother, Dmitrii
Ivanovitch, the ghost of the tsarevich rose up to torment him metaphorically if not literally. For at the beginning of the seventeenth century, the
news spread that the young son of Ivan the Terrible had been spared,
and had appealed to the Polish nobility and King Sigismund himself for
support in gaining his rightful inheritance. With the connivance if not the
active assistance of Sigismund and the fervent encouragement of the
Jesuits, the Polish nobility canvassed the candidacy of the first 'False
Dmitrii' and prepared for invasion as the expectant rumour became disseminated among the ranks of the Cossacks and the peasantry. In the
spring of 1605, Boris Godunov died unexpectedly, perhaps through self-
administered poison, and the boyars took the army over to the side of the
pretender and his sponsors. In June, after Godunov's wife and son had
been murdered by the boyars, the invading forces entered Moscow in
triumphant procession. In order to secure his position, however, 'False
Dmitrii' had to make concessions to the desire of his protectors for the
acquisition of land and the spread of their faith. The xenophobia of the
Russians was inflamed to fever pitch during the preparations in Spring
1606 for the pretender's marriage to the daughter of a Polish landowner,

thousands of Poles coming to Moscow and beginning a round of celebrations which arrogantly flouted local custom and prejudice. And so without great difficulty, Vasilii Shuiskii was able to rise above Romanov and other rivals to lead both boyars and people against the heathen. 'False Dmitrii' was killed, the Poles were driven out, and Shuiskii had himself declared tsar by a 'popular acclamation' specially arranged in Red Square.

The Cossacks and other provincial dwellers who had been excited by their ideal vision of the Tsarevich Dmitrii and had not seen the sordid reality of the Polish occupation of Moscow were alarmed by the news of the accession of Shuiskii, whom they rightly suspected of promoting policies to the principal benefit of his fellow boyars. It was not long before a new and more powerful wave of discontent was swollen into a revolt great enough for Soviet historians to deem it the first in a series of 'peasant wars'. Led by Ivan Bolotnikov, a courageous, shrewd and well-travelled Cossack, the insurgents were joined by several members of the nobility, and a formidable force moved from the Ukraine towards Moscow, gathering supporters en route. However, as the capital was laid to siege and the peasant war spread throughout the whole country, the ideological weaknesses of the movement became apparent, particularly its 'naive monarchism'. Many nobles defected to Shuiskii, who also gathered support from the west and north, and the 'boyar tsar' was able to inflict a cruel and crushing defeat on Bolotnikov and his forces by the autumn of 1607. At his surrender, a promise was given to Bolotnikov that his life would be spared, but, after he had been exiled to the north, he was first blinded and then drowned. Meanwhile, the Polish nobility had finally succeeded in finding a second 'False Dmitrii', and laid siege to Moscow from the summer of 1608 onwards, gaining support from various sections of the Russian community. In desperation, Shuiskii appealed to the Swedes to intervene on his behalf. The raising of the siege and the death of the second 'False Dmitrii' angered Sigismund of Poland, who sent his own troops to assist those of the Polish nobility. As the Poles threatened Moscow again, the boyars ousted Shuiskii as a sop to the lower orders and concluded an agreement to put the Polish king's son on the throne on his place. And so the second phase of the Time of Troubles came to an end with the Poles in occupation of Moscow and several other towns, while the Swedish presence was also being fully felt.

Although several attempts were being made to drive out the invaders, the national fortunes had fallen to their lowest ebb by the summer of 1611. But then a new popular force was formed at Nizhnii Novgorod at the instigation of a town elder, Kuzma Minin, and under the leadership of Prince Dmitrii Pozharskii. A renewed attack on Moscow, succeeded by the autumn of 1612 in partly fighting, partly starving the Polish invaders into submission. And then at the beginning of 1613, in a turbulent atmosphere full of factional squabbling and the threat of more pretenders, a *Zemskii Sobor* elected as tsar a young member of an old boyar family, Mikhail Fedorovich Romanov. With their unity still sufficiently intact, the national forces were able to pursue the task of driving the foreigners from the Russian land. By 1617, the Stolbovo Treaty brought peace with the Swedes who gave up Novgorod, but maintained their control of the coastal regions and thus cut Moscow off from the Baltic. In 1618 the armistice of Deulino with the Poles, which was to last for fourteen years, involved their more complete withdrawal. In other words, the principal aim of the national resurgence had been imperfectly achieved to the north-west and west, but the new dynasty could now turn its attention to the maintenance of domestic stability in a difficult but no longer desperate situation.

In 1613 Tsar Michael was sixteen years old, in poor health and of by no means strong character. These very inadequacies assisted his election, according to Platonov, who saw him as 'the single figure around whom both sides of the still not finally reconciled segments of Muscovite society – the service class of the countryside and the Cossacks – could unite'.[22] The early years were by no means easy for 'Romanov the Cossack Tsar' as disgruntled opponents called him, but centrifugal social forces had been weakened by the Times of Troubles and the spirit of united nationalism continued to reveal itself in the buttress of Michael's power constituted by the *Zemskii Sobor*. Great personal strength accrued to Michael in 1619 with the return from Polish exile of his father, the Patriarch Filaret, who became virtual ruler of Moscow until his death in 1633, while sharing the title of 'Great Sovereign'.

John Keep has clearly described the manner in which Filaret exercised strong control over all parts of the administration and worked against what he saw as dangerous innovations. In Keep's words, 'Filaret was a medieval figure, for whom stability was the *summum bonum*. He idealised the past and saw himself not as a reformer but as a restorer.'[23] And so the *prikaz* apparatus of the central government was maintained as much as possible, although in local government, a new leading representative of the tsar's power, the *voevoda*, had to be introduced. At the same time, Filaret made minimum use of the Boyar Duma and the *Zemskii Sobor*, depending for his social support on the leaders of the army, who came mostly from the service nobility.

As the national resources were put into strengthening and modernising the army, with the restoration of Moscow's armaments and munitions industry and increased use of foreign mercenaries, attention could now be given to the major tasks of foreign policy. Filaret's main aim was to revive the struggle against Poland for Smolensk and other western lands; significant secondary purposes were to make secure the southern steppe frontier and to extend Russian interests elsewhere in Europe and Asia. In 1632 the fourteen-year armistice of Deulino came to an end, and war broke out with Poland, Smolensk being the main bone of contention. Peace was arranged in 1634 (after the death of Filaret) through the Treaty of Polianov, by which Poland retained Smolensk. Meanwhile, much effort was being expended on the construction of the Belgorod fortified line to keep out the Tatars and to keep in peasants tempted to run away to join the Cossacks. In 1637 the Don Cossacks took the Turkish fortress on the sea of Azov, but the government had no desire to become embroiled in a war with Turkey and so encouraged the Cossacks to withdraw. At the same time as preparing for war with Poland, Filaret had attempted to weaken it through support of Sweden. Encouragement and subsidies were given to Gustavus Adolphus to consolidate his move into the German lands and thus to arouse Polish fears of a partial Swedish encirclement. Russian diplomats also entered into negotiations for a Pan-Christian anti-Turkish crusade, and maintained a close interest in developments throughout Europe and Asia. For example, at the death of Michael in 1645, the government was watching as closely as possible the intensification of the English Revolution.

Economic

By the mid-seventeenth century, according to Vernadsky, the Russian population numbered about ten million people, with the urban population totalling just over half a million. In other words, the demographic situation had not radically changed since the end of the thirteenth century, even though the Russian lands had increased enormously in size. Such an assertion, however, must be strongly qualified. In the first place, the figures remain the broadest of approximations calculated on the basis of inadequate data. Secondly, natural disasters such as famine and epidemics and man-made reductions such as wars often meant a decline in population for which there would have to be a compensating rise. Thirdly, on no account should these figures be taken to suggest that the economic picture as a whole was unchanging.[24] In fact, as well as witnessing important political and social adjustments, the two centuries before the mid-seventeenth century also saw significant developments in agriculture and commerce; indeed, to Soviet historians especially, these developments were an indispensable accompaniment to the whole process of consolidation under Moscow.

Agriculture was still the predominant way of life for the vast majority of the Russian people. While the technical level of farming does not appear to have risen significantly, its organisation went through a considerable alteration as many of the large estates of the old boyar aristocracy were broken up and given to the new service nobility, the *dvorianstvo*. Students of English history will be familiar with the problems associated with the investigation of 'the rise of the gentry', and will therefore be reluctant to accept without good evidence the assertion of such a transformation of the pattern of landholding. So far, the necessary detailed analysis does not appear to have been carried out by Soviet historians, and it may well be impossible. With somewhat more confidence, we may posit the incorporation of an increasing number of peasant communes in the estates of noble landlords and the adoption by the *dvorianstvo* of lands newly brought into the Russian state.

The first of these two processes is inextricably connected with the process of the enserfment of the peasantry which was taking place throughout the period of Muscovite consolidation. Not only the peasants attached to the noble landlords, but also those dependent on the Church or the court, found their right of transfer restricted more and more. For example, the *Sudebnik* or code of laws of 1497 finalised a tendency that had been spreading for some time in its general restriction of peasant movement to the week before and after St George's Day. At the same time, and continuing later, the two basic systems of the exploitation of the peasantry, the labour *barschchina* and the rent *obrok*, were being intensified, with payments in money rather than in kind becoming a more widespread form of *obrok*.

The second of the two clearly discernible processes, the adoption by the *dvorianstvo* of the newly acquired lands of Novgorod and elsewhere, coincided with the spread of a new form of tenure, the service *pomest'e*, in place of the former hereditary *votchina*. In such a manner the socio-political and economic aims of the consolidating government could be more fully realised, as well as those of the *dvorianstvo*. Meanwhile, at the old centre of Moscow, many of the great estates, both secular and ecclesiastical, remained relatively unscathed. With the defeat of Kazan and the penetration into Siberia, the state acquired a vast amount of largely unpopulated territory, into only a small part of which, notably along the Volga, new noble landlords had introduced their system of farming by the middle of the seventeenth century.

During the two centuries under discussion, the commercial life of Moscow took on a different shape, both internally and internationally. From the sixteenth century onwards, industry began clearly to separate from agriculture. The extraction and processing of metals, particularly iron, and the manufacture of pottery, textiles, wooden and leather goods, all became more subject to specialisation, even though many peasants at the same time still aimed at subsistence. Separate areas in the towns were set aside for craftsmen and for traders. The latter found themselves not only dealing in the wares of their neighbours, but also travelling to other towns to buy and sell there as well. Regions as well as individuals became involved in specialisation, for example, flax and hemp becoming a prime concern for the north-west towns of Novgorod, Pskov and Smolensk, while grain occupied much of the attention of the towns along the Volga. Tula was an early centre for the iron industry. Moscow itself was the focal point of the internal trade, although it is still too early to talk of a national unified market.

It is certainly not too early to talk of an extended international trade, both to west and east. While access to the Black Sea was interrupted after the fall of Constantinople in 1453 and to the Baltic with the rise of Sweden at the end of the sixteenth century, the curtailment of Russia's trade with the rest of Europe was neither severe nor permanent. Regular trade with England was established after Richard Chancellor, in an attempt to find the North-East Passage to India with the encouragement and advice of Sebastian Cabot, came to the White Sea and then to Moscow in 1553. The Russia Company was chartered in the following year to follow up and exploit the contacts made by Chancellor. The Dutch as well as the English were keen to develop commercial relations with Moscow during the next hundred years, and in the seventeenth century surpassed their rivals. Russia's principal exports to the West continued to be such items as furs and leather, wax, tallow, flax and hemp, with weapons and luxury goods prominent among the imports.

Luxury goods – silks, spices and jewels – were still among the important imports from the East, with Russian exports in that direction following the pattern of those westwards to some extent but including a higher proportion of manufactured goods. Sometimes, the Tatars interfered with the oriental trade, but they could mediate sometimes, too. Russian merchants penetrated deep into Asia and Asia Minor, one of them, Afanasii Nikitin, making a journey to India more than twenty years before the more celebrated voyage there from Portugal of Vasco da Gama.

Involved as it was both through trade and war with powerful neighbours such as Turkey, Poland and Sweden, Muscovite Russia found it necessary to devote a large amount of its energy to building up the strength to be able to coexist with them. At the end of the sixteenth century and beginning of the seventeenth, as we have seen, the attempt became almost too demanding, and the nascent state came near to falling apart in the Time of Troubles. Even at more settled times, there could be little relaxation or lowering of the guard, and before the official introduction of serfdom in its complete form, the peasants who constituted the vast majority of its scanty population were very conscious of the taxation and service demands made upon them by their immediate landlords and by the more remote government. Their task was made all the harder by Russia's involvement in European monetary and other economic fluctuations of the sixteenth and seventeenth centuries.[25]

Cultural

'The development of Russian culture in the late fifteenth and sixteenth centuries was closely bound up with the process of the unification of Russia in a single state', declares a Soviet textbook.[26] Regional divergences from the national norm were already under threat. So were some of the bequests from the past. For example, the Orthodox faith which was superimposed upon pagan belief now found itself challenged by the spirit of the Renaissance, Reformation and Counter-Reformation. But all these movements were weaker at the eastern extremity of the continent than in many other areas of Europe; indeed, some historians would deny their presence in Moscow. And so the old was more powerful than the new, and the first two components of Russian culture, mixed together in the heathen–Christian 'double faith', had barely begun to lose their dominance by the middle of the seventeenth century.

This would very much be the case with the mass of the people, particularly rural inhabitants. Their songs and stories, proverbs and superstitions, handed down from generation to generation, carried around and improvised upon by strolling players and sometimes inscribed in woodcuts, vigorously resisted the discouragements and prohibitions of the Church. Nevertheless, even at the popular level, the persistence of tradition did not mean complete absence of change. Some Soviet historians maintain that at the end of the fifteenth and beginning of the sixteenth century considerable progress occurred. Russian peasants deepened the recognition of themselves, not as the slaves of God, but as real people living on earth. The *bylina* epic began to comment more on the conditions of the people and to acquire a new popular estimate of the strength of Russia. And so old subjects took on new details: for example, Ilia Muromets, while liberating Tsargrad or Constantinople, now saves the Emperor Constantine.

Even members of the upper classes were neither able nor wished to remain completely aloof from the culture of their Slavonic ancestors, but publicly at least they acknowledged the supremacy of the 'official' culture. By the middle of the fifteenth century, Orthodox Christianity was of sufficiently long standing in Russia for it to have evolved into maturity, and to be able to stand on its own feet after the Council of Florence of 1439 and the fall of Byzantium in 1453. The Council of Florence appeared to be reconciling East and West, but in fact officialised the schism between them. As for the fall of Byzantium, it was first understood as a prelude to the end of the world, which was calculated to occur in 1492, the year believed to mark 7000 years from the creation. In 1492, as everybody knows, a new world was discovered rather than an old world lost. The leaders of Russian Orthodoxy were by now more confidently seeing themselves as the leaders of the Eastern Church in general, and could concentrate on the legitimisation of their assumption of the Byzantine inheritance. They accepted the view expressed by a Pskovian monk Filofei in a famous letter to Vasilii III written in 1570:

The Church of old Rome fell for its heresy; the gates of the second Rome, Constantinople, were hewn down by the axes of the infidel Turks; but the Church of Moscow, the new Rome, shines brighter than the sun over the whole universe. Thou art the ecumenical sovereign, thou shouldst hold the reins of government in awe of God; fear Him who has committed them to thee. Two Romes have fallen, but the third stands fast; a fourth there cannot be. Thy Christian Kingdom shall not be given to any other ruler.'[27]

For Nicholas Zernov, an Eastern Orthodox historian, the first Rome gave Christendom 'law, order and discipline' and the concept of universality, while the second Rome offered 'intellectual leadership', doing much 'to formulate creeds and combat heresies'. Moscow – the Third Rome – 'expressed the conviction that the entire corporate life of a nation should be inspired by the Holy Spirit'.[28] For Soviet and some other secular historians, on the other hand, the adoption of the new ideology was an integral part of the contribution of the Church to the unification of Russia, for which the Church in return received protection against its opponents.

Whichever point of view we adopt, we cannot help observing that there was no shortage of opponents, both from within and without. The central internal dispute was between the 'possessors' and 'non-possessors', led respectively by Joseph of Volotsk and Nil Sorskii. As their name probably suggests, the 'possessors' believed in the secular as well as the spiritual power of the Church, making no real distinction between them. They supported the authority of the Grand Prince, accepting that it should extend as far as the administration of the Church. They advocated strict ritual and ruthless eradication of dissent. For their part, the 'non-possessors' argued for more complete absorption in the world of God and less in that of Caesar. The clergy, particularly the 'black' clergy of the monastic orders, should not own great lands or other wealth, but concentrate on simple labour and spirituality. The Word of God rather than ritual should be sacrosanct, and dissent overcome by dissuasion rather than persecution. While both Joseph of Volotsk and Nil Sorskii were canonised after their deaths, their beliefs could not be held in equal reverence or even for long coexist. While there was some hint of secular support for an early 'dissolution of the monasteries', the state gave its support to decisions taken in favour of the 'possessors' by Church councils throughout the sixteenth century. The Church responded, as it were, by creating a considerable number of Russian saints and accepting a genealogy which also connected the princes with the Roman inheritance. At the *Stoglav* or Hundred Chapter Council of 1551 and others, the Church attempted to keep its organisation efficient and its doctrines pure, tackling such problems as the profound ignorance of many of the rank-and-file members of the 'white' clergy or parish priests, and the corruption of many of their superiors.

The establishment of the Moscow Patriarchate in 1589 meant that the Russian Church had been sufficiently successful in the eyes of its Eastern Orthodox peers for it to be acknowledged by them as worthy of entrance into the highest rank.

Meanwhile, however, the Russian Church was under external threat as well as internal, particularly after the Liublin Union of Poland and Lithuania in 1569. This strengthened Roman Catholicism, with the Jesuits and other orders moving eastwards in increased numbers, reaching as far as Moscow itself during the Time of Troubles. A considerable number of Lithuanians and Ukranians became Uniates, that is Orthodox acknowledging the supremacy of the first Rome rather than the third, the Pope rather than the Patriarch. Moreover, Protestanism encroached as far as the Russian borders, too, especially as a consequence of the extension of Swedish power in the Baltic. The Russian Church was able to withstand the onslaught for the most part, the attitude of most of those who heard of the Reformation being well expressed in the reported words of Ivan the Terrible to a visiting pastor, 'Go to the devil with your Luther'.[29] And yet Soviet historians have been able to devote considerable attention to what they call the 'reformation movements' of the period.[30] They take as their point of departure the assertion of Engels that such movements and the struggle connected with them were no more than the repeated attempts of the bourgeoisie, the urban plebeians and the peasants – becoming revolutionary with them – to adapt the old theoretical outlook to the changing economic conditions and the position of the new class. They go on to examine such heretical movements as the Judaisers in the late fifteenth century and such individuals as Feodosii Kosoi and Matvei Bashkin in the mid-sixteenth century, and Ivan Khvorostinin in the early seventeenth century, and to look for evidence of the desire to bring into the Bible words in ordinary usage and to introduce a new humanism. While the bourgeoisie was not yet strong enough in Moscow for 'reformation movements' to make such an impact as elsewhere, there is a sufficient basis for the authoritative D. S. Likhachev to talk broadly of 'a crisis of the medieval manner of the representation of man occurring at the beginning of the seventeenth century'.[31]

This crisis would express itself in learning, literature and the arts as well as religion, although it is an indication of the distance that the secular spirit had to travel that religion was still a powerful influence on all other branches of cultural activity. The career of the cosmopolitan scholar, Maxim the Greek, in Moscow after 1516 is an illustrative example, giving Russians, in the words of Nicholas Zernov, 'a unique opportunity of enlarging their mental and spiritual horizon by linking their cultural life with the Renaissance in Italy'.[32] Maxim soon ran into difficulties and finished up with twenty years in prison. On the other hand, Michael Cherniavsky's plausible attempt to portray Ivan the Terrible as Renaissance prince includes a comparison of the writings of Ivan Peresvetov with those of Machiavelli. Educated Russians knew Latin and Greek, and read the ancient authors. From the fifteenth century onwards, Russians went more often abroad and foreigners more often visited Russia. Ideas were exchanged, albeit in a tightly restricted manner.

The general degree of literacy and intellectual awareness during the period has been placed by Soviet historians at a somewhat higher level than many of their Western colleagues would be prepared to accept. Printing made its appearance in Moscow by the mid-sixteenth century, enabling literature to develop, albeit in conditions of strict censorship. Thus the first recorded printed book was the *Apostle* in 1564, and it was followed by about twenty others mainly of a religious nature in the rest of the sixteenth century. There were other works on such subjects as arithmetic, history and geography, although these were rarely printed, and the *Domostroi* or *Household Management*, which gave authoritarian instructions for the arrangement of the lives of upper-class families. At least the beginnings of a lay literature can be detected by the mid-seventeenth century. Even for those who could not read, experiences such as the invasion by foreigners during the Time of Troubles could not help but be educational.

As in earlier periods, it is in painting and even more in architecture that the cultural achievement of Moscow makes its most striking impact on us. Its seclusion from the Roman Catholic world meant that the spirit of Byzantine tradition would be stronger than that of the Renaissance, but a number of Italian masters invited in by Ivan III – Fioravanti, Ruffo, Solari and Alevisio – were able to adapt their styles to local taste in the cathedrals, palaces and walls of the Moscow Kremlin. A more exclusively Russian hand was at work in the construction of the church outside Moscow at Kolomenskoe and in Moscow of the famous, fantastic Cathedral of St Basil in Red Square. The icon-painting tradition was carried on at a high level and somewhat adapted by the artist Dionisii and his sons. By the middle of the seventeenth century, Moscow had been transformed into one of the most celebrated of European cities, thus standing as a symbol of the development generally achieved within the course of some two centuries. While her basically Orthodox 'official' culture and Slavonic 'unofficial' culture somewhat set her apart, Russia had nevertheless undergone a process of national consolidation in many ways comparable to that of many of the other states in Europe.

Part Two
Modern Russia: The Tsarist Empire

Introduction

Pre-revolutionary historians placed the commencement of modern Russian history at the end of the Time of Troubles soon after the beginning of the seventeenth century. Kliuchevskii gave four reasons for such a choice: the arrival on the throne of a new dynasty, the Romanovs; the extension and consolidation of the boundaries of the state, a process continued during the following two centuries or so; the emergence of a new nobility, the *dvorianstvo*; and new economic developments, particularly the enserfment of the peasantry and the appearance of industry. Soviet historians would not disagree completely with such an argument, although they would virtually dismiss the first of Kliuchevskii's reasons and place heavy emphasis on the fourth. For them, above all, the story of modern Russia consists of the rise and fall of capitalism. As a convenient point of departure, they have chosen the middle of the seventeenth century. Here, with some concession to the traditional view of the matter, but also with misleading exactitude, 1645 (the date of the accession of Aleksei Mikhailovich, or Alexis) has been selected.

Within the basic framework of their discipline laid down by Marx and Lenin, Soviet historians argue keenly among themselves about the nature of Russian capitalism and of the absolutist state which accompanied it. For the modern section of this book, and making adjustments

North
Sea

Arctic

Rhine

Baltic Sea
FINLAND

Nystadt

White Sea

Tallin
Narva
Vyborg
Riga
St.
Petersburg
Archangel

POLAND

Dvina

Novgorod

Danube

Dvina

Dnestr
Prut

Smolensk

Dnepr

Moscow

Oka

Jassy
Kiev
Tula
Andrusovo
Nizhnii Novgorod

Kishinev
Krivoi Rog
Kazan

Kuchuk
Odessa
Voronezh

Kainardzhi
Kharkov
Poltava
Simbirsk

San
Stefano
Kherson
Bakhchisarai
Saratov

Sevastopol
Don
Volga

Constantinople
Black
Sea
Astrakhan
Ural

R U S S I A N

Ob

Irtysh

OTTOMAN
EMPIRE

GEORGIA
Tiflis
Aral
Sea

ARMENIA
Erevan
Baku
Lake
Balkhash

Caspian Sea
Khiva

AZERBAIDZHAN
Bukhara
Kokand

IRAQ
Samarkand

PERSIA
CHINA

AFGHANISTAN
Kabul

INDIA

Persian Gulf

2 Modern

Russia, 1645–1917

to retain the chronological divisions by the reigns of the Romanovs and to accommodate the views of pre-revolutionary and Western writing, I have adopted from the Soviet discussion the following broadly accepted six phases of development: 1645–98; 1698–1762; 1762–1801; 1801–55; 1855–94; and 1894–1917. The first phase contains the birth of absolutism and the foundation of the Empire. The second is dominated by Peter the Great's vigorous attempt to consolidate and enlarge upon the work started under his predecessors, and the third, the period of 'enlightened absolutism', sees a continuation and variation of his work by Catherine the Great. Up until now in some ways progressive, absolutism takes a more clearly reactionary turn in its fourth phase under Alexander I and Nicholas I as it strives to retain the increasingly outmoded serf order within a nationalist framework. But, by the fifth, the pressure is too strong and a step is reluctantly and incompletely taken by Alexander II towards a transformation of absolutism into constitutional monarchy, with the emancipation of the serfs and other measures, although Alexander III tries to move in the opposite direction. In the sixth and final phase capitalism reaches a level sufficient for it to make at least a partial entry into its highest stage, that of imperialism. Tsarism is forced to take further steps towards constitutional monarchy, but cannot adapt itself sufficiently under Nicholas II to avert revolution. Accompanying these economic and political trends throughout the six phases is the less perceptible but equally significant gradual assertion of a secular culture. Moreover, far from taking place in its own remote enclosure, Russian modernisation is intimately connected with the same phenomenon taking place at different speeds in other societies. Indeed, the key to an understanding of Russian modernisation may be found in its relative tempo.

Baldly presented as above, our schema is crude in the extreme, for all historical periodisation entails inconsistency and distortion. In the present case, there were elements of 'enlightened absolutism' in the policy of Alexander I while that of his father Paul before 1801 was largely reactionary. Crudest of all is the proposition that modern Russian history begins and medieval Russian history ends in 1645. There are strong feudal elements (particularly in the economic and cultural senses) in the Russia that succumbed to revolution in 1917; some of the characteristics of absolutism may be detected in the reign of Ivan the Terrible, or even earlier. The choice of 1645 for the dawn of the modern age approximates not only to Soviet but also to widespread Western convention, although some Western historians would be reluctant to include Moscow in that dawn. Our reasons for doing so are elaborated during the course of Chapter 4.

4   The Foundation of the Russian Empire, 1645–1698

Arguments concerning the beginning of modern European history, like arguments concerning the origin of the universe, fall into two broad categories, 'the big bang' and evolution. The 'big bang' consists of the 'general crisis' thesis, which maintains that in the years around 1650 the continent of Europe was subject to a series of political, economic and cultural shocks which gave birth to absolutism, capitalism and the secular outlook.[1] Moscow was both the taker and giver of such blows, as we shall see. The core of the evolutionary process is described by E. N. Williams in the following manner: '. . . absolute monarchy arose out of the need for internal and external security which made a standing army as a royal monopoly essential. This army required higher revenues; the revenues required economic growth; they all required the formation of a royal bureaucracy to eliminate, or push aside, the manifestations of the corporate state'.[2] Generally speaking, Moscow conforms to such a pattern, although it also possesses peculiar features. Among these is the enserfment of the peasantry, a phenomenon occurring throughout much of central and eastern Europe at a time when the western part of the continent was developing a freer form of society.

In its formative days, then, the Russian Empire exhibited two principal features, absolutism and serfdom. Both these institutions took on something like definite shape during the last half of the seventeenth century. The period also saw a great expansion with the takeover of a large part of the Ukraine and the infiltration of most of Siberia. This enlarged area was loosely interlocked by trade, kept in rough order by the army and subject to the administration of a somewhat improved central bureaucracy. Orthodoxy provided a cohesive influence, and the first glimmerings of a secular rationale for empire are discernible. By the end of the century, Russia had reached a stage sufficiently advanced for Peter the Great to build the imperial superstructure on a fairly firm foundation.

Peter's predecessors on the throne were undistinguished enough for the laying of the foundation to be an exercise which transcended royal personality. Nevertheless, their proclivities and distinguishing characteristics gave a special flavour to society at the top level, and even in the passive mode, their lives distilled the spirit of the times even if they did not infuse it.

Aleksei Mikhailovich, or Alexis (1645–76) was sixteen years old at the time of his accession. In a welter of threats from pretenders and rumours about his own authenticity, the young tsar was more than ready to turn for support to his tutor, the boyar B. I. Morozov, who became the ruler of the country in fact. According to a foreign contemporary, Morozov was driven by a thirst for gold as great as other Muscovites' thirst for drink. He was also a master of court intrigue, consolidating his power by marrying the tsar's sister-in-law, a member of the Miloslavskii family. Alexis withdrew from the business of government into the rituals of church and court. Although he gained a reputation for gentle piety, little of such a quality is to be found in the policies to which he gave his name. He had some literary aspirations, and allowed foreign music and theatricals, as well as furniture into the tsar's palace for the first time. In this he may well have been partly under the influence of his second wife, who had been brought up in the Westernised household of another favourite, Artamon Matveev, whose own wife was from the Scottish Hamilton family. In a more traditional manner, Alexis kept around him a bunch of beggars and idiots, venerated by the Orthodox as holy fools. The favour of Alexis was bestowed on A. Ordin-Nashchokin and the Patriarch Nikon, as well as on Morozov and Matveev. But favour could also be withdrawn, as we shall see.

Alexis died suddenly in 1676 and was succeeded by his ailing fourteen-year-old son, Fedor Alekseevich, or Theodore (1676–82). The great families struggled for power, the Miloslavskii related to the late tsar's first wife squabbling with the Naryshkins related to his second wife and with the Matveevs. As the favourites disposed of each other, outsiders managed to grasp the best positions, while Theodore, whose literary aspirations were greater than those of his father, retired to the sickroom to indulge them. He married twice, but without lasting issue, thus leaving behind him a tricky situation at his death in 1682.

The temporary victress in the bloody crisis which followed the death of Theodore was his elder sister Sofia Alekseevna, or Sophie, who was installed as Regent (1682–9) in the name of her younger brother Ivan and half-brother Petr or Peter, who were declared joint tsars. Not unintelligent but ugly, and, according to some descriptions, bearded, Sophie nursed a great passion for V. V. Golitsyn, one of Theodore's more capable advisers, and her struggle for power has been seen as an attempt to secure reciprocity of this passion through Golitsyn's advancement. Although Sophie fell from power in 1689 after a coup in favour of Peter, Peter did not become sole ruler in law until 1696 and was not secure in power in fact until two years later.

Political

During the first two years of the reign of Alexis, the boyar Morozov built up a network of power in the central bureaucracy, at the time alienating the functionaries of the *prikazy* and the *streltsy* musketeers. To these two dissatisfied groups were added the nobility of the capital and of the provinces, who protested about unjust judges and inadequate arrangements for the recapture of runaway peasants. Readjustment of the taxation system led to a more general malaise which soon broke out into positive action.

After some minor disturbances to the north and south and in Siberia, a revolt broke out in Moscow in June 1648. Townspeople annoyed by exactions and encroachments upon their privileges joined with provincial nobles to petition the tsar, and the loyalty of the *streltsy* was soon in question. Alexis himself, icon in hand, made an appeal to the insurgents and then delivered up to them as a sop to their unabated anger some of his chief advisers, although he successfully pleaded for the life of Morozov. Land and higher payments were given to the nobles, money was handed out to the *streltsy*, presents distributed to the people at large, and negotiations carried on between the government and the town leaders, while the dignitaries of the Church preached peace and Morozov was sent to a monastic exile.

A wave of revolts with similar origins broke out in 1648 throughout European Russia. A *Zemskii Sobor* was summoned to satisfy some of the demands being made everywhere, and after some stormy elections it met in Moscow from September 1648 to January 1649. The representation heavily favoured the nobility and to a lesser extent the burghers; the people as a whole had no voice at all. Petitions from the two dominant groups strongly influenced the formulation of the Code of 1649: the landed and other privileges of the nobility were guaranteed, while serfdom received fuller definition; exemptions from urban taxation were reduced, and a fairer division of such burdens was therefore achieved. However, the burghers were not given the control over trade and industry that they had been hoping for. As for the poor townsfolk and the peasants, they gained nothing from the Code, which was to remain in legal force until the nineteenth century. However, serfdom was imposed upon the communal structure rather than destroying it.

Meanwhile Morozov returned to power, only to be confronted with another wave of town revolts in 1650. This time the largest outbreaks, which were compounded by poor harvests and regional as well as class conflict, were in Pskov and Novgorod. Moscow did not escape entirely, but in the capital a much larger disturbance took place in 1662. The long war with Poland concerning the Ukraine had physically weakened the inhabitants of the capital, and they had suffered from an epidemic of smallpox in the mid-1650s. Its financial difficulties if anything greater than usual, the government went beyond harsh taxation to debasement of the silver coinage by copper. The corruption of officials at all levels was a further aggravation. In July 1662 a mob of about 5000 confronted Alexis at his home in the suburb of Kolomenskoe, and demanded that those guilty of fraud – including the tsar's father-in-law – be brought to justice. As Kliuchevskii described the further actions of the insurgents and the response of the government:

> Some of them held the tsar by the buttons of his kaftan, while he was made to take an oath that he would deal with the matter himself, and he was forced to shake hands on it. However, the first mob was joined by a second from Moscow, and both boisterously began to demand that the tsar hand over the traitors to them; if he did not they would be taken by force. Tsar Alexis called on the *streltsy* and his courtiers for assistance, and an indiscriminate slaughter ensued, followed by tortures and executions. Hundreds were drowned in the River Moskva, and whole families were exiled permanently to Siberia.[3]

The government was shaken enough to bring back silver in 1663, but was now generally more confident than before of the support of the service nobility, which was coalescing into a distinct class and becoming the chief bastion of absolutism, at the same time as the boyar aristocracy was in decline.

The policies of the government at the time clearly revealed that it knew where its main support was to be found. The concessions given to the nobility in the Code of 1649 were extended in subsequent legislation. The nobles banded together to make sure that the residual rights of their peasants were much reduced and persuaded the government that it had the duty to catch runaways. The government also conducted a generous

land policy towards the nobility, particularly in the aftermath of successful wars which both encouraged the tsar to reward his servants and
acquired for him the land to use as a reward. The burghers also received
state encouragement in the years following 1649. The administration of
the towns was reorganised in the years 1649–52, internal customs were
regularised in 1653 and again in 1667, and the New Commercial Regulations of 1667, as we shall see, boosted the position of Russian merchants in relation to their foreign counterparts. At the same time, we
must remember that neither the nobility nor the bourgeoisie were as yet
completely formed as classes in the socio-economic sense, even less in
the juridical, and so the relations between them and the government
were not as clearly consistent as this summary account makes them
appear.

However, as with the two top classes so with tsarism itself, a relatively
more articulated structure was evolving during the middle years of the
seventeenth century. Although the relations between the tsar and his
subjects could sometimes be informally direct, as they were during the
town revolts, the ceremonies and processions in which the tsar normally
took part were attended with great pomp and elaborate ritual, which
made a deep impression on both reverential populace and visiting
foreigners. Samuel Collins, the tsar's physician, believed of Alexis that
'As for his Treasure of Jewels, I think no Prince does exceed him', and
the secretary of an English embassy to him in 1664 wrote that 'The Tsar,
like a sparkling sun . . . darted forth most sumptuous rays, being most
magnificently placed upon his throne'.[4] Behind this splendid façade,
which had not changed significantly for some time, the real strength of
the tsarist apparatus was achieving a new degree of consolidation. The
Zemskii Sobor was crushed, and central and local government were both
made somewhat less inefficient. The *Zemskii Sobor* continued to meet
after the middle of the century, but by then had lost any independence it
had ever possessed. Something similar might be said about the Boyar
Duma; although the Duma was not yet a cipher, the *prikaz* of Secret
Affairs replaced it as the tsar's privy council during the latter part of the
reign of Alexis. The *prikaz* of Accounts was created in the attempt to
bring order into financial affairs, and there was a more general attempt
to rationalise the *prikazy*, both as to sphere of competence and to geographical area of jurisdiction. The key figure in local government was
the *voevoda*, who ruled his province in a manner as absolute as the tsar
ruled the state. Local peasant officials were powerless before the *voevoda*
and the army detachments which supported him.

Neither the control of the central government nor that of the local government was complete enough to avert passive and active resistance, of which the most common symptoms were peasant flight and banditry. Occasionally, there were large-scale outbreaks of violence in the provinces as there were in Moscow and other towns. The biggest of these was the second of the peasant wars, as Soviet historians know it, or the Razin Revolt as it is more traditionally called. Having gained a wide reputation through bold piratic adventures along the Caspian Sea, Stenka Razin moved against Moscow in 1670. Having achieved great success in the Volga region, where he attracted a large following from the peasantry, Razin was crushed by regular army units near Simbirsk and fell back to the Don, where the Cossack leaders handed him over to the authorities. He was executed in Red Square, Moscow, in June 1671. The reasons for the failure of the Razin Revolt are isolated by a Soviet historian V. I. Buganov as: 'spontaneity, localism, disorganisation of the movement, the absence of a clear political programme, poor armaments. The heterogeneity of the composition of the insurgents led to disagreements in their midst.' Nevertheless, he asserts that 'The Second Peasant War was distinguished by a clear polarisation of the class forces'.[5] Razin had been executed, but his name lived on in song and legend. The descendants of his followers were to move in support of Bulavin and Pugachev in the peasant wars of the eighteenth century, still exhibiting the naïve monarchism that could see no wrong in the tsar and believing that peace and justice would come to the Russian land after the eradication of its lesser lords, the nobility.

After the death of Alexis in 1676, there was no radical change in governmental policy, rather a move several stages further forward for the policy already inaugurated. Thus, in the reign of Theodore (1676–82), serfdom was further entrenched and more land distributed to the nobility. The solidity of the ruling class was at the same time encouraged by the convergence between different types of landholding, and by the continued reduction of the boyars. The process was brought an important stage forward by the abolition in 1682 of the system of *mestnichestvo* by which upper-class families had been awarded places in the government hierarchy according to their birth. This last measure contributed to the further improvement in the structure of the central government, which was also encouraged by more rearrangement of the central *prikazy*. The administration of the provinces was improved by the introduction of the household as a new tax unit.

The period between the death of Alexis and the consolidation of the power of Peter the Great showed continuity not only in the tsarist policies but also in the opposition to them. The acquisition of the Regency by Sophie in 1682 was attended by civil disturbance demonstrating the dissatisfaction of several groups, particularly the *streltsy*, and the same might be said about her loss of it in 1689. A third and more violent outbreak by the *streltsy* occurred in 1698 while Peter was away on his first visit to Western Europe. Loyal troops under the leadership of the Scottish General, Patrick Gordon, suppressed the *streltsy* for the final time, and Peter came back hastily not only with ideas for progressive reform but also with the burning desire for torture and execution of a more traditional Muscovite nature.

The reduction of the *streltsy* was a significant step in a late Muscovite development of enormous importance not only for internal stability but also for imperial expansion and foreign wars – the regularisation of the army. Peter the Great, who has often been given the credit for this measure, himself accorded the honour to his father, pointing out that in 1647 Alexis began to use regular forces on the basis of the military manual published in that year. In fact, the process was more gradual, having been inaugurated in the reign of Michael, but a tremendous growth in the proportion of the new order occurred by the early 1660s when, according to Thomas Esper: 'The army was not only larger (how much larger depends upon how many Cossacks and *streltsy* one counts), it was also completely different in organisation. Seventy-nine per cent of the army (about 77,000 men) was composed of what were called 'foreign' units – cavalry, dragoons, hussars, infantry. This was the core of the new army, trained and to some extent officered by foreign mercenaries'.

Esper also tells us that Russia was by this time self-sufficient in the production of cannon and gunpowder, if not of handguns.[6] These developments, which were in rough parallel with military changes elsewhere in Europe, had important social consequences in Moscow as well as in foreign states. During the transitional period they included the decline and fall not only of the *streltsy* but also of what Richard Hellie calls the 'middle service class'.[7] By the end of the century, the consolidation of the service nobility, or *dvorianstvo*, as the officer caste was nearer to completion, although mercenaries still made an important contribution, and the rank and file was largely recruited on a regimental rather than a militia basis.

The army was improved in response to the challenge facing Moscow as it became consolidated as the Russian Empire. First of all, there was the task of maintaining order in the more settled central regions. Then, the frontiers had to be protected against Tatar and other incursions, a problem which increased in complexity as the frontiers expanded.

During the later seventeenth century, infiltration of Siberia went as far as the Kamchatka peninsula and the Amur river valley, where a clash with China forced Russia to make the concessions of the Treaty of Nerchinsk of 1689. The Church lent the weight of its authority to the Cossack and other units, which were carrying out the penetration for the exploitation of fur and other resources. For their part, the natives did not always appreciate the privileges of paying tribute, undergoing conversion and being subjected to imperial control, and such tribes as the Kalmyks and the Bashkirs resisted their assimilation as forcibly as they could.

The most demanding task imposed upon the reformed army was the engagement of the state's external foes principally the Poles, the Turks and the Swedes. The war of 1654–67 against the Poles succeeded in achieving aims similar to those which had been frustrated in the 1630s, the acquisition of Smolensk and Left-Bank Ukraine including Kiev. The new success was due partly to the increased relative strength of the Muscovite forces, but mainly to the alliance between them and the Ukrainian Cossacks, who rose up in 1648 in a great war of liberation under the leadership of Bogdan Khmelnitskii. Having inflicted considerable defeats on the Poles, which won for him the recognition of Oliver Cromwell and other Western Europeans, Khmelnitskii led the Ukrainians into union with Russia in 1654. War with Poland inevitably broke out again, and continued with intervals until the Treaty of Andrusovo in 1667.

At several points, the war took on a more complicated international character as the Turks and the Swedes joined in. For example, Russia fought against Sweden from 1656 to 1658 to protect the gains which had been made and to seek the long-desired outlet to the Baltic. And then, in the aftermath of the war, the Turks with their allies forced the Muscovite government to promise to pay an annual tribute to the khan of the Crimean Tatars at the armistice of Bakhchisarai (1681). Vasilii Golitsyn, the favourite of the Regent Sophie, conducted two unsuccessful campaigns against the Crimea in the late 1680s, partly as a contribution to a Pan-Christian campaign inaugurated by King Jan Sobieski of Poland against the Turkic Muslims after their siege of Vienna in 1683. Soviet historians criticise Golitsyn's priorities and give their approval rather to such statesmen as A. L. Ordin-Nashchokin who usually placed the complete defeat of Poland at the top of their list of aims. But even Peter the Great began his military career in the 1690s with campaigns against the Black Sea fortress of Azov.

At the beginning of the seventeenth century, Moscow had shrunk to the size of a principality; by the century's end, it grew into the largest state in Europe, with encroachments not only into the Polish sphere of influence but also deep into Asia. Closer diplomatic relations had been established with a whole range of states from France to China (though the Treaty of Nerchinsk of 1689 made a temporary halt to Russian expansion into the Amur valley). Not only was the nascent Empire more of a force to be reckoned with in the international relations of all these states, its expansion had exerted an effect throughout Eurasia. For example, the assimilation of the Ukraine, leading to the weakening of Poland, had in turn made less secure the eastern flank of the Habsburg Empire, and thus the rise of Moscow generally received a warm welcome from the enemies of the Habsburgs throughout Europe. Already playing an important part in the dénouement of the Thirty Years War and the continental crisis which followed it,[8] the Russian Empire was poised by the dawn of the eighteenth century for an even greater appearance on the international stage. Of course, the impact was mutual, and many analysts would argue that the changes undergone by Moscow as a result of her widened contact with other states were far more profound than those she inflicted on them. To take again the example of the Ukraine, Russian political strength, economic growth and cultural progress all received a considerable and lasting boost from the reunion of Moscow with Kiev.

Economic

Soviet historians dutifully follow the lead of Lenin, who wrote that

> Only the modern period of Russian history (approximately from the seventeenth century) is characterised by the actual amalgamation of all . . . regions, lands and principalities into one whole. This amalgamation . . . was brought about by the increasing exchange among regions, the gradually growing circulation of commodities, and the concentration of the small local markets into a single, all-Russian market. Since the leaders and masters of this process were the merchant capitalists, the creation of these national ties was nothing else than the creation of bourgeois ties.[9]

While Western historians have tended to dismiss this picture, their Soviet colleagues have provided enough detail for Lenin's outline to appear reasonably accurate.

It is still virtually impossible to say anything definite about the size of the population in the late seventeenth century, although it is probable that earlier losses had been made up and that the total was now approaching fifteen millions. Certain tendencies may be more positively observed in the various branches of the economy, even though here too it is difficult to talk with any confidence in a quantified manner. In agriculture, the various groups comprising the nobility retained a preponderant share of the populated land, making good use of the enserfment of the peasantry. According to the assessment of 1678–9 which roughly covered the European part of the state, the tsar possessed about 9 per cent of a total of 812,000 households; townspeople and state peasants, something more than 10 per cent; the Church, just over 13 per cent; and the feudal lords, around 67 per cent. Towards the end of the 1640s, the top boyar B. I. Morozov owned more than 30,000 serfs living in more than 300 different places. Noble landlords moved into the southern Oka and Volga regions, cultivated new fields in the centre and occasionally raised the technical level of farming, although the spread of agriculture was more normally extensive than intensive. While the spread of the area under cultivation was to some degree a political and social phenomenon, it also reflected increasing possibilities for marketing produce, themselves partly the result and partly the cause of the incorporation into the state of the Ukraine, Volga and Ural territories. The growth in commercial agricultural activity was also revealed in the increased specialisation of, for example, the southern black-earth region, where labour on the land was the usual kind of peasant service, and the central non-black-earth region, where the serfs often spent some of their time in manufacturing enterprises. The same process was at work in the sharper distinction becoming apparent between town and country, although even in Moscow itself townspeople sometimes still farmed.

Specialisation may also be seen in manufacturing and industry. Textiles were made in several districts to the north-east of Moscow, and iron was produced in the south of the capital at Tula, where the Dutchman A. Vinius had set up a works in 1632. By the 1660s, there were 119 people, nearly half of them foreigners, employed at seven works in the Tula region. By the end of the century metallurgical activity was also started in the north-west and in the Urals. Enterprises included at least a dozen large armaments works. Although the transfer from domestic production to the blast furnaces meant more quantity and higher quality, wind and water remained the sources of power and ore was usually mined on or near the spot. Raw materials were not always so acquired for industrial enterprises, however. For example, the hides for the tanneries of Kazan were brought from many different places, including the distant Urals. As far as the necessary entrepreneurial initiative for these various industrial activities was concerned, it came largely from the state, but also from nobles, monks, merchants and peasants. Such families as the Stroganovs were already prominent. Various groups were involved in producing not only textiles, metals and leather, but other items such as salt, potash and pitch too.

The beginnings of the all-Russian market could be seen mostly in the grain rather than the industrial goods trade. State needs for distillation purposes, for the supply of some districts in Siberia and for the export market were a major stimulus. Sometimes large contracts were given for the supply of grain, and the middleman flourished. Peasants were important suppliers, but Morozov and other landlords were also interested in the business. The unification of markets could be seen as local centres merged into a larger system of regions formed on the basis of the grain trade. Smolensk was a focal point in the west, Voronezh another in the south. Flax was grown commercially in the north-western territories with Pskov as an *entrepôt*, and animal products, particularly leather and lard, were bought and sold in Archangel. The fur trade was on a huge scale in Siberia and elsewhere.[10]

Goods were usually transported by routes which coincided with the great river networks, most of them converging on the Sukhona–Northern Dvina route which led to Archangel, Moscow's only sea port. In 1653, goods to a value of just over one million roubles (one rouble of the period being equal to seventeen roubles of the early twentieth century) were exported from Archangel, including furs, potash, leather, lard and cloth and more than a million bushels of grain. Imported through Archangel in 1671 were a wide range of items including diamonds, gold and silver goods, paper, hats, pins and needles, wine, ginger, pepper, herring, apothecary materials and arms. The principal foreign intermediaries for most of the century were the Dutch, followed by the British.

Northern markets were linked with the Volga region, where the most important commercial centres were Nizhnii Novgorod, Kazan and Astrakhan, and with Siberia. The Oka River and its upper tributaries served as a link with the Ukraine, and in the south and south-west, the Dnepr and Western Dvina systems were much used, with Smolensk at the cross-roads. Through Smolensk, as well as through the declining towns of Pskov and Novgorod, commercial land routes made their way to the rest of Europe, and a not insignificant trade was carried on through the Baltic by Swedish and other intermediaries.

The centre of the growing all-Russian market was, of course, the town of Moscow, with nearly all the trade routes leading to it and contacts established with more than 150 other towns. Here were to be found Ukrainians, Tatars, Mordvinians and representatives of many of the other peoples of the nascent Empire. All sorts of foreign intermediaries lived in Moscow, too, confined from 1652 onwards in their so-called German settlement. (All foreigners were Germans as far as the masses were concerned, the word *nemets* meaning German or foreigner coming from *nemoi* meaning dumb, that is unable to speak Russian.) A wide variety of goods from all parts of Eurasia were to be bought in the capital and at the great fairs such as that of St Macarius near Nizhnii Novgorod.

Large mercantile fortunes were being made in the late seventeenth century. Huge profits accrued from import, export and some internal trade. The state patronised the rich merchants, particularly the so-called 'guests', favoured in return for special services with this title, leases and contracts. There were not many 'guests', about thirty only in Moscow, for example, but they possessed great influence as well as riches. The most outstanding of them was G. L. Nikitinov, who dealt in wool cloth, salt and fish, plied a fleet of ships down the Volga as far as Astrakhan, and owned one quarter of the total capital of all the other Moscow 'guests', many of whom were worth up to 100,000 roubles themselves. Another 'guest', M. Gurev, claimed to have spent 200,000 roubles on the construction of a town at the mouth of the river Iaik which bore his name and protected his fishing interests. The size of state contracts can be seen from the example of one Fedor Silin living near Moscow, who sold more than 60,000 metres of cloth to one of the government departments in 1676, as well as being a supplier of salt and iron.[11] At a lower level than the 'guests' were a growing number of middlemen or *skupshchiki*, travelling far and wide to buy and sell. Although a lot of manufacture and trade was still local, there were few Russians, from the tsar and the boyars down to the meanest peasants, who were not affected in a direct or indirect manner by the commercial network.

A preponderant part in late Muscovite economic change was played by the state. Its taxation policies, stemming from a constant extreme need for money, were severe enough to produce serious revolts. Its commercial policies could either restrict or aggrandise Russian merchants. For example, the latter tendency was encouraged by the New Commercial Regulations of 1667, which forbade foreign merchants to involve themselves in retail trade and imposed high tariffs on foreign goods. Moreover, the tsar and his entourage formed by far the largest commercial concern, retaining several monopolies for themselves.

Samuel Collins called Alexis 'The chief Merchant in all the Empire'.[12] Some observers have selected this circumstance as the major reason for the weak development of Russian capitalism, although the part played by the state elsewhere in Europe may have been as great. Others have wondered if this backwardness might not have some connection with the absence from Russia of Protestantism and the failure of the Old Believer movement to provide an adequate alternative.[13]

Undoubtedly, Moscow was in some measure economically backward in the late seventeenth century. Her remoteness from the major trade routes of burgeoning Western capitalism made this so, although the importance of the Muscovite trade to this process was by no means negligible. The institution of serfdom was in part the response of a less advanced region to a region that was beginning to move quickly forward, although we must not forget that the commercial revolution of the Western European world could not have taken place without the institution of Negro slavery.

The degree of Moscow's backwardness in the seventeenth century might well never be exactly calculated because of the paucity and unreliability of statistics. What can certainly be said is that it was not always apparent to contemporary visitors to Moscow. One of the outstanding foreign descriptions, that by Olearius in the 1630s, notes the bustle of Russian markets and says that the people's 'cleverness and shrewdness are manifested in their commerce, among other activities'. Olearius considers that the merchants 'are shrewd and eager for profit' and that the artisans have learned foreign techniques quickly, and 'with technological improvement, they sell their manufactured goods at higher prices than before'.[14] Beyond this, it appears reasonably certain that about three-tenths of the manufacturing enterprises of the eighteenth century were founded in the seventeenth century. And so, there is a strong if not incontrovertible case for concluding that the great leap forward in the economy associated with Peter the Great was in fact the culmination of a more gradual process and that Lenin was broadly correct in dating the growth of Russian capitalism 'approximately from the seventeenth century'.

Cultural

During the seventeenth century, the process of secularisation gradually infiltrated Europe as churches lost influence to encroaching state authority and a humanistic element firmly forced its way into a still predominantly religious culture. The struggle between the old outlook and the new in Moscow was fought against the background of the Schism in Orthodoxy.

In the city of Moscow in the 1640s there was formed a revivalist group called the Zealots of Piety, aimed at the purging from the Church of impurities and deviations. The leader of the group was the tsar's confessor, and its members included the two future protagonists of the Schism, Nikon and Avvakum. Both born near Nizhnii Novgorod – Nikon the son of a peasant, Avvakum the son of a priest – they were both men of great intellect, powerful character and tremendous self-righteousness. Each was a firm believer in the power of miracles, and each was a strict ritualist. Fierce fanatics, they had no mercy for their opponents, who came to include each other. And both of them came to a disastrous end.

Nikon became Patriarch in 1652, after a career which took him from priest to monk to archimandrite to Metropolitan of Novgorod. His elevation to the highest power was attended with much ceremony, which entailed Alexis prostrating himself on behalf of the people before Nikon, who asked for and received full authority to purify the Church and to reform it. Such a policy involved changes in the number of alleluias and genuflections made at certain moments of the service and in the number of fingers used in making the sign of the cross, as well as emendations in the holy texts on the basis of Greek models. Such alterations were certainly important for a Church which believed very much in ceremony and ritual, but their implications went considerably further. To put it bluntly, Nikon was making an attempt at the establishment of his complete authority over the 'Third Rome' and even hoping that he might lead it to a predominant position throughout the whole Orthodox world. With such aims Nikon drew on the historic Byzantine tradition and the more recent example of Filaret.

For both religious and political reasons, if the two can be separated in seventeenth-century Moscow, Nikon soon ran into opposition. He alienated most of his friends among the Zealots of Piety, who began to look upon him as a wolf in sheep's clothing. At first trying to conciliate the two parties in the dispute, Alexis broke with Nikon in 1658. By this time, the tsar had grown tired of the Patriarch's overweening manner, and he took advantage of Nikon's resignation in a fit of pique to accept him at his word. A long period of jockeying for position ensued, at the end of which in 1666 a Church Council was summoned with the Patriarchs of Alexandria and Antioch in attendance to put Nikon to trial. After some stormy sessions, the Council condemned a defiant Nikon to be reduced to the clerical ranks and exiled to a remote monastery. Nikon was disgraced, but his policy was continued in most aspects except the most important – the reduction of the Patriarch was a significant step towards the final subjection of the Church to the state.

Meanwhile, Avvakum, whom Nikon had sent into exile, was emerging as the leader of those who would not accept the Church reform. These, the Old Believers, were condemned by the same Council as broke Nikon. From *The Life of Archpriest Avvakum by Himself*, we learn much of the trials and tribulations of the schismatics: the unspeakable hardships of exile in Siberia and in the Arctic North; and the circumstances which brought it about, the religious and to a lesser extent the secular. Emphasis on the former came from both sides of the continuing struggle in the pre-revolutionary period, while populist historians of the nineteenth century anticipated their Soviet counterparts by stressing the latter. For Robert O. Crummey, Old Belief after 1667 was 'an indistinguishable blend of opposition to the liturgical reforms, foreign cultural influence, bureaucratic centralism, and social injustice. Antichrist was the symbol of all that was new and oppressive in Muscovite society. His power had to be resisted'.[15] Soviet historians show most interest in the movement's social variation (the aristocrat Prince Khovanskii being one of its first leaders and the *streltsy* providing many of its most stubborn adherents) and in the contradictoriness of its aims and methods (the lack of agreement about whether to commit suicide or to rise up in protest).

Avvakum himself was burnt at the stake in 1681, and between 1675 and 1695, up to 20,000 Old Believers threw themselves into the flames in expectation of the imminent end of the world. At the same time there were Old Believer revolts against the reform, those of the *streltsy* being at least partly definable thus, and the monks at the Solovetskii Monastery on the White Sea waged a long battle against the government from 1667 to 1676.

At the beginning of the revolt, when the news of the Nikonian reform first reached the Solovetskii Monastery, the monks are reported to have said: 'Brothers! Brothers! Alas, alas! Woe, woe! The faith of Christ has fallen in Russia, just as in other lands . . . .'[16] The monks were referring to the decline of Orthodoxy elsewhere, but one may be at least permitted to speculate if they did not also have in mind the great religious upheavals of non-Orthodox Europe. Certainly, later historians have put forward the hypothesis that the Old Believer movement could well have been part of a Pan-European phenomenon, France and to a lesser extent Scotland both being cited as states where parallel developments took place.[17] Throughout the continent, the established Church made a compromise with the state while sectarian groups sacrificed themselves in the vain attempt to adhere to what they believed to be former standards of pure devotion.

If religious currents were able to cross the frontiers of localism and prejudices as the old culture started to disintegrate, the more liberated spirit of the new culture could well be expected to flow through them too. And so it proved, although the numbers directly affected by it in each state was small, and although even they had not yet made the clear distinction between the world of God and of man. In Russia, for example, contemporary petitions and other documents show that many members of the upper classes and even some ordinary townspeople and peasants had at least crossed that first important threshold and mastered the art of making their own signature. However, the first printed grammar of 1634 left no doubt that the main aim of primary education was to enable people to understand Holy Writ.

At a somewhat higher level, an education was being acquired from private tutors and, before the end of the century, in a small number of institutions. Simeon Polotskii from the Kiev Academy, an important percolator of advanced ideas, was engaged by Alexis to teach his children, and boyars and other prominent members of society soon followed the tsar's example. Polotskii was put in charge of a theological school in Moscow in 1666, and, although its activities were soon curtailed, another school fashioned after the Kiev Academy was opened under one of Polotskii's pupils in 1682. This school, in which the basic emphasis was on Latinism, was soon merged with another founded at about the same time as the Moscow printing press, where Hellenism was the predominant influence, to form the Slavono-Graeco-Latin Academy. From the mid-1680s onwards, the Academy was not only an institution of higher learning but also the guardian of educational respectability. New subjects such as foreign languages or philosophy and physics were undertaken in conditions of strict security and only with sworn professions of Orthodoxy by both teachers and students. Emerging from these oppressive conditions before the end of the century were men like A. L. Ordin-Nashchokin, A. S. Matveev and V. V. Golitsyn, whose libraries reveal them to have been men of considerable breadth conversant with works not only in Russian, Greek and Latin but also in Polish, German and other foreign languages. Poland was the most important conveyor of the new culture.[18]

And so a new humanism was apparent, even in icon-painting. Some specialists in architecture talk of a Russian baroque. Parallel developments have been noted in verse and prose.[19] At a lower social level, too, popular tales began to concern themselves with such mundane subjects as the corruption of judges and other day-to-day vicissitudes of ordinary life.

Perhaps the arrival of the new as well as the persistence of the old are best represented in the example of a single person. Kliuchevskii said that many of the ideas of Peter the Great were anticipated by Ordin-Nashchokin. Much the same may be said about V. V. Golitsyn, of whom a French visitor of the late seventeenth century, Foy de la Neuville, wrote, albeit not completely accurately:

He had built a very magnificent stone College, invited a score of doctors in from Greece, as well as a quantity of good books, exhorting the great men to educate their children, and permitting them to send their children to Latin Colleges in Poland while advising that Polish tutors should be brought in for the others. He accorded to foreigners the entry to and exit from the realm, which had never been practised before him. He also wanted the nobility to travel and learn how to make war in foreign countries, since his design was to change into good soldiers those legions of peasants whose land remained uncultivated when they were led to war. And instead of such service which was useless for the state, he wanted to impose on each head a reasonable sum, to maintain Ministers in the principal courts of Europe, and to allow liberty of conscience in the country.[20]

This same Golitsyn usually slept in an old wooden bed and ate from wooden plates, even though he had a magnificent bedroom and silverware to show off to his guests. In this and many of the other features of his outlook as reported by the French visitor he resembled Peter the Great. Peter was distinguished by his wholehearted submission to a wider range of foreign influences first in Moscow's German Settlement and then in Western Europe, and above all by the tireless authority which he commanded for over a quarter of a century and used in the attempt to shake all his fellow-countrymen out of that Muscovite exclusiveness and suspicion from which only a few Russians had fully emerged before the consolidation of his power in 1698.

5 The Completion of the Structure, 1698–1761

In 1698, Peter I hastily returned from his first visit to Western Europe determined to crush the *streltsy* and to put into practice his new ideas for the transformation of Russia. As well as cutting off the heads of the *streltsy*, he cut off the beards of his courtiers, the outward symbols of their adherence to Muscovite tradition. From 1 January 1700, Russia moved closer to the West by adopting the Julian calendar and starting to record time from the birth of Christ rather than from the dawn of creation. Later on in that year, Russia suffered a great defeat in the battle of Narva at the beginning of the Great Northern War against Sweden, and the long journey which then began back to reconstruction of the armed forces, complete victory and a secure foothold on the Baltic has often been seen as the major theme of Peter the Great's reign. As Pushkin put it, Russia entered the ranks of the great powers with the knock of hammers and the roar of cannon.

In adulthood, Peter was nasty, brutish and extremely tall. He liked sick jokes, and since he was an Emperor, could make them come to life. The well-organised centre of his merry pranks was 'The Most Drunken Council of Fools and Jesters', dedicated to the worship of Venus and Bacchus, and specialising in the elaborate ridicule of church and court ceremony.[1] Citing Reinhard Wittram's argument that such antics developed a 'rational political purpose' – the debasement of the Patriarch's dignity and the thawing of Byzantine tsarist ritual, James Cracraft believes that they should primarily be seen as the reflection of a 'possibly tragic flaw', of a persistent and insensitive tendency 'to regard those who were thereby offended as obstinate children who would not see that most things western or new were better than most things Russian or old, that in Russia radical reform had become urgently necessary'.[2]

Peter's own childhood had been very disturbed, and this circumstance probably explains much of his bizarre temperament. For example, at the age of ten, he was obliged to witness the execution of two uncles and several other kinsmen. For reasons such as this, his childhood games of soldiers were attended by a precocious element of seriousness, and his irregular education at the hands of Scots and other foreigners in the German Settlement possessed from the first an unusually practical element. His upset youth also made him into something of a nervous wreck with frequent convulsions of the head and acute insomnia. His health was probably further undermined in later life by syphilis. Before his final collapse, however, constantly on the move, shaking people at all levels of society into action with his oak club, Peter stormed throughout Russia and Europe as like a colossus as anybody else in history.

It is little wonder, therefore, that such a man has been a subject of great fascination for historians for more than two hundred years. The Soviet evaluation is positive, in the tradition of Frederick Engels, who called Peter 'a really great man'.[3] In his day, Stalin singled him out for special mention, and fruitful if anachronistic analogies may be made between the contributions of these two personalities to the consolidation of modern and contemporary Russia in turn. Soviet historians in the post-Stalin years praise Peter for the progressive character of his reforms, but censure him for the exploitation of the popular masses. They admire him for his tremendous will-power, but condemn his neglect of the individual and his cruelty, which included the torture and execution of his own son, the Tsarevich Alexis.

L. G. Beskrovnyi and B. B. Kafengauz see Peter as:

. . . one of the greatest ideologues of absolutism. Together with his assistants he gave it a theoretical basis. . . . Peter I considered autocracy to be 'the bastion of justice'. The state was seen by him as a most powerful force, capable of transforming society on the basis of reason. The people must subject itself to laws which were issued in the interests of the 'general good', by which were meant the interests of the ruling class. Together with the theory of the divine origin of power was instilled the secular basis of absolutism – rationalism and the propositions of natural law.[4]

Voltaire, who in the history of her father first commissioned by the Empress Elizabeth was one of the first analysts to see Peter as an early version of the enlightened absolutist, wrote that his work was carried on after his death by four women, 'who have maintained, in full vigour, all the great designs he accomplished, and completed those which he had begun'.[5] The fourth of these women, Catherine II or Great, was remarkable for her reign to be considered separately in the next chapter. Here, we will attempt to sketch the other three, less remarkable women, Catherine I, Anna and Elizabeth, as well as the men whom Voltaire neglected to mention.

At Peter's death in 1725, the succession was unsettled. In 1722, he had issued a decree giving the tsar the right to appoint his successor, but he did not act upon the decree until too late, his last decipherable words being 'Give all . . . .' But to whom nobody was sure, and so his widow was declared Empress by a group of officials supported by the Guards. Ekaterina or Catherine I (1725–7) had been a good companion and second wife for her husband, but by herself was capable of nothing more than the continuation and extension of their drunken debaucheries. The real ruler quickly became Peter's close associate Menshikov. To encourage the support of other men in high places, Menshikov was forced to accept the establishment of a new organ of central government, the Supreme Privy Council. At Catherine's death in 1727, Menshikov and the others declared that the throne would go to Peter, the son of the son of Peter the Great, the Tsarevich Alexis. The eleven-year-old Peter II was affianced to Maria Menshikov and her father appeared to be within reach of new heights of power. But then the fall of Menshikov was engineered by the Dolgorukii family who supplanted him as the protectors and prospective in-laws of the young Emperor.[6] On the day appointed for his wedding, however, Peter II died of smallpox, and the male line of the Romanovs died with him.

In the confusion which followed his death in 1730, the Supreme Privy Council haggled among themselves, finally deciding to offer the crown to Anna Duchess of Courland, a daughter of Peter the Great's sometime co-ruler, Ivan V. Their offer was attended by certain 'Conditions', but Anna succeeded in tearing them up, overwhelming the Supreme Privy Council and introducing a new establishment, largely but not wholly of German origin, which formed her Cabinet.[7] The most outstanding favourite was named Biron, and so her reign (1730–40) has often been called the *Bironovshchina*, although such a title neglects the importance of other individuals in Anna's establishment, including some Russians. The Empress was a passionate huntswoman, and was at least as fond of weird entertainments as Peter the Great. She had a particular taste for freaks and dwarfs; one of her greatest entertainments was the marriage of one of her jesters in a palace made of ice on the frozen river Neva. An interesting case study in the psychopathology of Russian monarchs, she did not herself make much impact on the government's policies, and need not therefore detain us any longer.

On her deathbed in 1740, Anna declared that Biron should be regent during the minority of her niece's son, who was to become Ivan VI. After her death, Biron was ousted and the niece herself, Anna Leopoldovna, assumed the regency. The Germans along with some Russians continued to squabble among themselves until a coup was staged by the Guards on behalf of the daughter of Peter the Great, Elizaveta or Elizabeth. She herself preferred guardsmen to power, but would probably have lost the first if she did not gain the second, and then have been confined in a nunnery. For her this would have been a fate worse than death, and so she allowed herself to be made Empress. As Empress, Elizabeth (1740–61) was able to indulge her insatiable liking for clothes, both men's and women's, hardly ever wearing the same outfit twice and leaving about fifteen thousand dresses at her death. Like her father, she was always worried about her security, and for this reason was often afraid to sleep, ordering her ladies to talk to her while tickling the soles of her feet to keep her awake. She paid more attention to the business of government than had Anna before her, but still left most of it to her favourites. Towards the end of her reign, a Conference was formed to replace the defunct Cabinet, and formed a convenient focus for the confluence and clash of the interests of the favourites.

While none of the monarchs between 1725 and 1761 had anything like Peter the Great's drive and acumen, some of their ministers were capable enough to continue his work, which itself was a culmination of a process inaugurated before his effective reign. Absolutism remained progressive during its ascendant phase which lasted in Russia approximately down to the end of the eighteenth century. Granted that Peter's contribution to the completion of the structure of the Empire was far greater than that of most of his predecessors and successors, it is nevertheless surely misleading to persist with any variation of the idea summarised in a Russian pastiche of Alexander Pope's epitaph on Sir Isaac Newton:

> Russia for many years lay hid in night,
> God said, Let Peter be! and all was light.[8]

Political

The neat row of buildings, first constructed for Peter's bureaucrats and now part of Leningrad University, give the impression of an order and probity which in fact were at least as lacking in the Russian administration as in any other in Europe during the eighteenth century. People were not intrinsically more inefficient or corrupt at this time than in later periods of history, but were influenced by the social circumstances in which they found themselves. In the Russian case, the salient features of the situation were a huge enserfed peasantry, a small and weak bourgeoisie, and a small but strong nobility. Hence, as the state became more unified, its government took the form of a bureaucracy responsive to the wishes of the nobility and prone to be a clumsy tool of class oppression as well as a focus for the interplay of personal rivalries and individual ambitions. On such a foundation, Peter superimposed an edifice constructed according to contemporary theoretical principles. Although in many respects, the edifice was to survive until the Revolution of 1917, the tension between it and its unstable underpinning resulted in cracks soon appearing both literally in the marshes of St Petersburg and metaphorically in the great swamp of the Russian Empire.

Peter's reforms in government as elsewhere were improvised rather than carefully planned, particularly in the beginning. The first of them were tinkerings with the *prikaz* and *voevoda* system bequeathed to him by his Romanov forebears, and need not detain us here. The first of the comprehensive reforms, which was introduced in the years 1708 to 1710, aimed at the improvement of social good order and financial efficiency. The whole country was divided into eight large provinces: Moscow, Ingermanland (later St Petersburg), Kiev, Smolensk, Kazan, Archangel, Azov and Siberia. All of these, except Moscow, contained part of the Empire's troublesome frontiers, and they were all entrusted to governors from among Peter's close associates. Into the governor's hands was entrusted the judicial, administrative, police and financial power of the huge area under his jurisdiction. The *prikazy* were struck a mortal blow, but the *voevoda* gained new strength at the expense of the municipalities and other provincial officials below the level of governor.

Meanwhile, at the centre, the Boyar Duma was virtually dead on its feet, and the Privy Council, manned by eight of Peter's trusted underlings, was handling the most important business of state although legally subordinated to the Duma. And then in 1711, while the tsar was away on the campaign of the Prut, the Senate was set up to take care of business. At first envisaged as a temporary replacement for the sovereign, the Senate was entrusted with those tasks currently occupying Peter's attention. Thus it was instructed to consider some leases for the sale of salt, trade with China, the attraction of young nobles into service, and so on. Gradually, however, deliberations about the service of young nobles led to a general supervision of the army and navy, concern for the Chinese trade grew into management of trade in general, and activity connected with one aspect of the tsar's income soon became the control of all the state's finances. In such a manner, the Senate became a permanent body and its nine members came officially to be the most important government functionaries. However, none of the members was a close henchman of Peter, and all of them, like everybody else in the land, were kept under close scrutiny by a network of supervisory officials known as fiscals.

With the introduction of the Senate and the fiscals, the first period of Peter's political reforms came to an end; the second consisted of the creation of the colleges and some new officials, and a further reform of local administration. The idea of the institution of colleges had been with Peter for some years before its final implementation; they were widely accepted in Europe as the best available bureaucratic system. Foreign experts were consulted, and many recruited to come to St Petersburg either to help with the planning of the colleges or to man them. They came into existence on paper in 1717, but by 1718 only the top three, War, Admiralty and Foreign Affairs, were in actual operation. By 1720, the six others had been created, three dealing with finance, and three dealing with industry and trade. None of them functioned for long on the co-operative collegial principle, however. The most important of the new officials was the procurator-general, at first Pavel Iaguzhin-skii, whom Peter considered to be his own private eye and Russians at large believed to be the second most important man in the Empire. The procurator-general was to be in charge of the secret police and to supervise the government, including the Senate, to which in Peter's later years were added a number of offices, notably the herald-master's. The reform of the local administration from 1718 onwards, like the new arrangement of town government in 1721, was too elaborate to be transplanted from Western European soil to the vast spaces of the Russian Empire. The personnel were just not available to fulfil the aims projected.

Soon after Peter's death, decrees of 1727 and 1728 restored a simplified control of fifty provinces by governor and *voevoda*. Together with local army units, and a growing number of nobles living locally, this system worked reasonably well for the time being. Central government, as already noted, experienced a number of sudden changes after 1725, with fluctuations in the fortunes of the Senate and other parts of the machinery, and the creation of a succession of advisory bodies to the sovereign. A point of greater importance, according to some contemporary observers and later analysts alike, was the nature of the personnel in the entourages of the various sovereigns. For this reason, the palace revolutions of the period take on no small significance.

The most interesting of them was that which brought Anna to the throne in 1730. The traditional interpretation of the succession crisis following the death of Peter II is that the members of the Supreme Privy Council, particularly D. M. Golitsyn, presented Anna with restrictive conditions, because they sought to introduce an oligarchic form of government into Russia. But the mass of the nobility, preferring the rule of one too many, persuaded Anna to tear up the 'Conditions' and were at least in the short run content to see the restoration of autocracy. Several reservations must be made to this traditional interpretation. Firstly, it is doubtful that Golitsyn ever had the constitutional dreams that have been attributed to him; at least none of them is known to be in existence on paper.[9] Secondly, the opponents of the councillors included some nobles of very high rank who had previously been in office, and so the clash should be seen less as an ideological clash than as a simple struggle between 'ins' and 'outs' who agreed on the basic forms that the government should take. As Lenin said of 1730 and the other coups of the eighteenth century, they 'were ludicrously easy, when it was a question of taking power from one clique of nobles of feudal lords and handing it over to another'.[10] The whole process was assisted by the greater cohesion achieved by the nobility in the eighteenth century, a circumstance that stands out in stark relief when we contrast its coups with the bloody struggles of the seventeenth century. This is not to say that the structure of the *dvorianstvo* did not contain strains and weaknesses, but they were obviously of a less profound nature than the tensions between the upper and lower classes.

These revealed themselves in a number of revolts, the greatest of which was the third peasant war under the leadership of Kondraty Bulavin. This broke out soon after the first large-scale incident of civil disturbance in the eighteenth century, the revolt of 1705 centred on the town of Astrakhan at the mouth of the Volga and involving *streltsy* and soldiers many of whom were Old Believers. In 1707, the major conflict erupted on the Don, where the Cossacks were aggrieved at encroachments on their freedom by the centralising government. Under the leadership of Bulavin, a local hetman, or commander, Cossacks from the Don and the Dnepr joined with peasants from a large number of places, and prepared to go 'to Rus to kill the boyars'. Negotiations were carried on with various tribesmen and with Turkey, and some vain attempt was made to reach accommodation with the tsar. Bulavin was assassinated in the summer of 1708 by some dissident Cossacks, but it was early 1709 before the revolt was brought to an end. Cruel reprisals followed, and the people were cowed into passivity. Bulavin's revolt, we are told by V. V. Mavrodin resembles the other three peasant wars 'in such traits as the leading forces . . . (above all the peasantry, the Cossack rank and file, the poor townspeople), its anti-serf ideology, its aspiration to a struggle for power, the wide territory seized by the incursions of the insurgents, the existence of a general centre for the movement'.[11] Until the fourth peasant war under the leadership of E. I. Pugachev in the 1770s, there was no revolt of comparable size, although the serfs of the field and the factory and the tribesmen were by no means completely quiescent. For example, at the end of the 1750s and beginning of the 1760s, there were more than sixty violent outbreaks on noble and monastic estates. In 1755 there was a culmination of much unrest in a large-scale rising of the Bashkirs and other tribesmen along the Volga. Small-scale brigandage and flight were problems of great concern to the authorities and their supporters at all times.

The reasons for such troubles are not hard to find; social and racial inequalities were perpetuated and even aggravated by a government primarily responsive to the property-owning classes. Peter's policy, which was continued under his successors, strengthened the bonds of serfdom and intensified the process of the incorporation and russification of the nationalities, while contributing to the cohesion and strength of the bourgeoisie and particularly of the nobility. Not only did Peter recruit a vast number of peasants for his army and navy: the construction of St Petersburg and the improvement of canals also made great demands on the Empire's manpower, 120,000 workers being requisitioned for the new capital during each of several years following 1704. A further considerable quantity of peasants were given away to the tsar's favourites. The introduction of the poll tax in 1718 and of compulsory internal passports in 1724 were only two of a whole series of decrees burdening and restricting the peasantry at large. A sample decree from the post-Petrine era was that of 1760 permitting landlords to send their serfs into Siberian exile. Such laws were more likely to be implemented than that of 1721 condemning the break-up of families and the piecemeal sale of peasants 'like cattle'.

Meanwhile, the embryonic bourgeoisie was nurtured by the government, although not to the extent recommended by such spokesmen as Ivan Pososhkov, a passionate mercantilist who wanted his class to receive, among other concessions, exclusive rights to commerce. Legislation encouraging gilds and municipal government constituted a graft which could not find suitable Russian roots, but merchants and manufacturers certainly received material subsidies from the government, enough to achieve a level of prosperity at which many of them could aspire to membership of the nobility.

Undoubtedly, the nobility received the greatest wedge of the national cake, although the slices were by no means equitably distributed among the individual members of the class, the poorest of which were miserable clients aspiring to nothing more than a few crumbs given to them by their richer brethren. The cohesion of the *dvorianstvo*, already encouraged by such networks of patronage in the armed forces and the civil service, was increased in a statutory manner, notably by the introduction of the Table of Ranks in 1722. Deriving partly from earlier Muscovite evolution and prepared also by a thorough study of the arrangement of other nobilities, particularly the German and Scandinavian, the Table guaranteed ennoblement, hereditary or personal, to those reaching certain levels in the hierarchy. The principle of rank as a reward for service was to remain a basic element of the Russian imperial state until its overthrow. However, an attempt made in 1714 to introduce from abroad the concept of single succession in estate ownership was never really accepted and had fallen into disuse long before its repeal in 1730.

Entry to the nobility could also still be achieved by the personal grant of the monarch or through the translation of non-Russian ranks. One of the first to go through the former procedure was the industrialist N. I. Demidov; several of those to take the latter route came from the upper class of the peripheral nationalities. During the first half of the eighteenth century, not only Ukrainians and Balts but also representatives of the Bashkir and other peoples along the Volga and beyond were adopted in such a manner, thus assisting the russifying drive of the central government. Future candidates for such assimilation would come from the Caspian littoral, Transcaucasia and Central Asia, into all of which areas the Russian influence was penetrating during the period, as indeed it was into Siberia too.

The demands made on the armed forces for the support of such expansion, the maintenance of domestic security and the prosecution of foreign wars were even greater than before and demanded a higher degree of modernisation than that achieved by the first Romanovs. Peter discovered in his Azov campaigns and even more at the disaster of Narva that the forces at his disposal were insufficient for the tasks that he wished to pursue, and he therefore introduced a more developed recruitment system as well as widening the regimental structure and publishing new regulations. The army reached a size of 100,000 with between 200,000 and 300,000 men being called to take their turn with the colours during the first ten years of the war against Sweden. Meanwhile, the navy was created out of virtually nothing, some 800 ships being manned by nigh on 30,000 sailors by the end of Peter's reign. After the death of

Peter, the navy virtually returned to non-existence, but the army was larger during the Seven Years War than during the Great Northern War, and probably by then the largest in Europe.[12]

Such changes were partly the consequence of changes in the priorities of foreign policy, a shift of emphasis to the sea and then back again to land. At the beginning of his reign, Peter concentrated his energies against the Turks, attempting vainly to revive a Christian coalition during his first trip abroad. However, he did succeed in reaching agreement with the Poles for a joint attack on Sweden, and from 1700 until 1721, the struggle for a firm foothold on the Baltic became his major preoccupation. The Great Northern War developed ramifications throughout Europe. Polish and other support was fitful; Britain, alarmed at the self-assertion of what she previously considered to be something of a client state, generally supported Sweden against Russia. For his part, Peter often became embroiled in the petty dynastic affairs of German princes, as well as having to fight the Turks at the same time as the Swedes. Having recouped much of the morale lost at Narva in the victory of Poltava in 1709, Peter believed it necessary to pursue Charles XII of Sweden and his Ukrainian henchman, the hetman Mazepa, down into the Turkish domains, where he found himself surrounded on the river Prut by the Turks. He was forced to return Azov and make other concessions to the Turks in the treaty of 1711. In the end, after further victories on land and sea, Russia acquired a large part of the Baltic littoral and the grudging recognition of Europe through the Treaty of Nystadt of 1721. By the end of Peter's reign, then, the window on the West was firmly established, with extremely important consequences for Russia and for the whole continent.

In the 1730s wars against Persia and Turkey deprived Russia of the shore of the Caspian, but regained for her the possession of Azov, albeit with the fortress destroyed, and a large amount of southern Russia. Throughout the period after 1725, relations with the rest of Europe were usually uneasy as the power balance was upset not only by the more positive assertion of Russian interests but also by the rise of Prussia. Already revealing itself in wars concerning the Polish and Austrian succession and against Sweden, this latter development was the central circumstance leading to the outbreak in 1756 of the Seven Years War. The struggle between Great Britain and France for overseas dominance was another major theme of the war, the British supporting Frederick II and the Prussians against the French and their Austrian and Russian allies. Kaplan, following up a suggestion of Herbert Butterfield, has argued that the continental initiative for the war came from Russia, with the Empress Elizabeth herself showing an unusual amount of interest in it.[13] If this was so, although his arguments are far from conclusive, it was all the more surprising when, after a series of victories over the Prussian army leading to a brief occupation of Berlin itself, the Russian troops found themselves at the death of Elizabeth in late 1761 not only withdrawn from the war against Frederick by Peter III but put back into it on Frederick's side. This *volte-face* has normally been seen as a clear example of Peter III's insane Prussophilia. However, there is at least the common-sense argument in favour of it that a completely dismembered Prussia would have been almost as dangerous for Russia as a Prussia all-powerful. The historic struggle between Germany and Russia for a balance of interests in central and eastern Europe undoubtedly reached a new intensity as a consequence of the Seven Years War, with serious implications for the states separating them, particularly Poland.

Economic

Before the reign of Peter the Great, there was no adequate estimate of the Russian population, and even the eighteenth-century censuses were probably unreliable. From the first census begun in 1719, a total may be inferred of just over $15\frac{1}{2}$ millions, with the most thickly peopled regions being the centre around Moscow, and then, a long way behind, the Left-Bank Ukraine, the Middle Volga and the north-west focused on St Petersburg. By the second census, begun in 1744, the total had risen to nearly $18\frac{1}{4}$ millions, the steepest rise having occurred in peripheral areas such as the Lower Volga, the Northern Urals and Left-Bank Ukraine.

Some of this rise would betoken an extension of the basic economic pursuit, agriculture, although as before this was not accompanied by much intensification. The three-field strip system still predominated, particularly in the centre, and a simple plough with only the share made of iron continued to make shallow furrows, while harrows usually consisting of a wooden frame with pegs or even a bunch of branches lashed together barely scratched the surface. Under Peter and to a lesser extent his successors, attempts were made to increase fertilisation, to introduce better ploughs and harrows and to discourage sickles in favour of scythes, and to encourage the cultivation of crops that could boost exports or reduce imports such as flax, hemp and tobacco. The silk industry was fostered by the government, with experts being persuaded to come for this purpose from Italy. Silesian and Spanish strains of sheep were imported to improve the domestic flocks, which were to be found mostly in the south and the Ukraine, and special military stud-farms were developed at Kazan, Kiev and Azov. The government also made attempts to protect Russia's timber resources and to promote bee-keeping.

For all such attempts at change and progress, rye remained the predominant crop and traditional farming methods persisted. The flavour of rural life is caught by the instruction for the estate of the Dutch family Vinius near Moscow. In February the steward was to see to it that brushwood was put down on the arable land, so that it would be dry and be ready for burning by spring. In March manuring should be carried out as well, and by May ploughing and sowing were to be in progress. The steward was to make sure that the peasants did not steal seed, to check that stones were placed on the harrows so that they would bite deeper, and to stop time being wasted, since late sowings in previous years had meant harvests spoiled by frost. Work for the landlord was naturally made a priority, the peasants being allowed two days for themselves. Disobedient peasants were to be beaten with rods or receive other corporal punishment. In August, after the harvest, seed had to be collected from the peasantry in return for what had been lent them in the spring. Vegetables and berries were to be collected too. In the autumn and winter months buildings were to be repaired, flax processed, and the peasants given yarn so that they could produce cloth.

The Vinius peasants worked on the *barshchina* corvée labour basis rather than making *obrok* quitrent payments to their landlords. Roughly speaking, *barshchina* was to be found in the black-earth region and *obrok* in the centre and the north where the land was less fertile. While about half the peasants belonged to the nobility, about a quarter were the property of the Church and most of the remainder in the charge of the state. In each category of peasant, there were those who managed to achieve a comparatively high level of prosperity, at least in good times, as well as some in the depths of poverty, particularly in bad.

With the extension of agriculture in the first half of the eighteenth century went a growth of petty manufacturing. This could include iron-working, as well as the smithery of silver and gold, but textiles of various kinds would be more typical products. Furriers, shoemakers, soap manufacturers, tailors and carpenters were in business in most towns of any size, while luxury specialists producing such goods as wigs, chairs, carriages and gowns were to be found primarily in the capitals. In Moscow there were about 2500 such petty manufacturers and in St Petersburg around 7000 of them, about half of whom in both cases were of peasant origin, a not insignificant number of foreign extraction, and the majority self-employed. In other towns there would be fewer foreigners and more peasants. Government policy towards this sector of the economy wavered, on the whole aiming at the encouragement of gilds and higher standards. For example, the width of certain kinds of cloth was regulated, and the use of tar in shoemaking forbidden. But it was very difficult to enforce such policy.

Large-scale industry, as is well known, flourished with official support during the reign of Peter the Great. It is rather less well known, although clearly demonstrated by Arcadius Kahan of Chicago as well as Soviet scholars, that it continued to flourish after his death. Now, however, there was less active state participation, fewer public works programmes, and not so many imaginative gestures such as Peter's invitation to the Chinese government to send over some experts in bridge building. The grand total of large-scale enterprises from the death of Peter the Great to the accession of Catherine the Great, which has been variously estimated according to definitions used, probably rose from something approaching 200 to nearly 700.[14] Families such as the Stroganovs and Demidovs were making vast industrial fortunes during the period.

While the extent of Russia's industrialisation during the early eighteenth century must not be exaggerated, it was already sufficient to make an international impact, a British writer of the period fearing that: '. . . the sound of the Forge in the next Generation will not be heard or known among us. We need not call in the *Americans* to their Assistance; the *Swedes* and *Russians* alone are sufficiently able to subdue the British Woods and Iron-works.'[15] In other words, Russia was by about 1725 already exporting a not insignificant amount of iron, as well as a considerable amount of linen, along with hemp and flax, leather and naval stores. Her major imports at this time were woollen goods, dyestuffs and wines. The balance of trade was in her favour, and the government's trading policy protectionist. The major trading partner in the west was Britain, followed by Holland; the eastern trade was with a number of places from Persia to China, silk being the most important single item. In commerce as well as industry, there was both growth and an essential continuity after Peter's death, although Soviet historians condemn Anna's government for its treaty of 1734 which gave Britain most favoured nation privileges with regard to the Persian silk trade and made other concessions.[16] Throughout the period, the government attempted to adhere to its own version of mercantilist principles, although even Peter's energy was not enough to create a Russian mercantile marine. In 1757 protectionist tariffs were raised on many items to a higher level than in Peter's list of 1724.

The growth of domestic trade was most clearly reflected in the abolition of internal customs in 1753 for all regions except Siberia. The all-Russian market was now taking on a firmer shape around such centres as St Petersburg, Novgorod and the fair of St Macarius near Nizhnii Novgorod, as B. B. Kafengauz has clearly demonstrated.[17] Links with the Ukraine and other peripheral regions were strengthened.

Quite naturally, the government was interested not only in promoting the expansion of the economy, but also in extracting from whatever prosperity there was as large a share as possible. 'Money is the artery of war', wrote Peter the Great to his Senate, and even after the end of the Great Northern War nearly 75 per cent of state expenditure went on the army and navy. By this time, over half the state's income came from the poll tax levied on all males in the common populace, and a further third came from the indirect sources of the state trade in vodka and salt and the levies on trade in general. Debasements of the coinage were a much-used traditional method of increasing revenues, and resulted in a loss of half the purchasing power of the rouble during Peter's reign. But even this was not enough to keep the artery pumping properly, and further stimulants had to be applied, including all sorts of ingenious taxes thought up by a group of 'profit-makers', such as those on boots, watermelons and blue eyes. Of course, in Peter's reign and after it, a vast amount of state money went into the pockets of corrupt officials. In the later period there were some half-hearted attempts to reduce government expenditure, but also some great rises in it, during the Seven Years War, for example. The distinct social bias in the financial system became if anything more apparent with the institution in 1754 of a State Bank which lent money primarily to members of the nobility.

Cultural

The reign of Peter the Great marked a significant step forward of a Russian secular culture. The first lay education institutions were set up, the Church was brought firmly under state control, and language, literature and the arts and sciences began to focus their attention more on earth and less on heaven.

By a decree of early 1701, a School of Mathematics and Navigation was set up, staffed by Henry Farquharson of Marischal College, Aberdeen, and two youthful graduates of the Royal Mathematical School at Christ's Hospital, London, on which the Moscow School was largely modelled. The curriculum was to include arithmetic, geometry, trigonometry, navigation, astronomy, fencing, reading and writing. The inaugural years were very difficult, because teachers and pupils could not understand each other, there were no Russian textbooks, and the preparatory education of the students had often been inadequate. The situation improved after a Russian mathematician, L. Magnitskii, joined the organisation, and soon the School was producing not only navigators but also civil servants and teachers, artillerymen and engineers, topographers, hydrographers and architects. In 1715 a Naval Academy was opened in St Petersburg, and other navigation schools were set up in several towns. Specialist schools were also set up for Artillery (1701), Engineering (1712) and Medicine (1707). A different kind of school was the Glück Gymnasium opened in Moscow in 1705, and specialising in such subjects as languages, philosophy and politics, and 'compliments in the French and German manner'. Before its closure ten years later, the Gynasium had succeeded in sending out into the world some 250 graduates, including bureaucrats and diplomats as well as soldiers and sailors.

An attempt at the introduction of a general network of primary schools was made with the creation in 1714 of the cipher or mathematical schools. The decree projected two such schools for each province, with a simple curriculum of reading, writing, arithmetic, geometry and trigonometry. In fact, by 1716 only 12 such schools had been opened, and by 1722 only 30 more. By 1744, a mere 8 were still in existence, and only the 3 largest of them were retained, merged with garrison schools. These, a second type of general school, were just starting in Peter's reign and were expanded in the 1730s. A third category, the most successful, were the diocesan schools. There were nearly 50 of them with about 3000 students by 1727, at Novgorod, in the Ukraine, and elsewhere. These and other church schools were often plundered for their students by ailing secular educational institutions.

.   This was so with the Academy of Sciences, founded in 1724 as a repository and propagator of higher learning and opened in 1725 by Peter the Great's widow, the illiterate Catherine I. European savants such as Leibniz and Wolff made a considerable contribution to the St Petersburg Academy, as did several of their lesser-known colleagues in the university and gymnasium attached to it. The great ideas of Newton and others were received, while the work of the Academicians became known abroad.[18] But the teaching side of the Academy's activities did not prosper and had virtually ceased before the opening of Moscow University in 1755. Soviet historians stress the participation in this project of Mikhail Lomonosov, while the initial impetus appears to have come from one of Elizabeth's favourites, Ivan Shuvalov. Another institution of some importance was the Noble Military Academy, founded in St Petersburg in 1731. Here, most obviously, the ever-present element of class discrimination in education was apparent, although it could be argued that young nobles were given the best facilities because of the key role that they were expected to play in the armed forces and in the bureaucracy.

Nobles and commoners alike often received some kind of education at the hands of private tutors, and many young Russians were sent abroad for training of various kinds, the emphasis being practical under Peter the Great, less so under his predecessors. Many of the tutors were themselves barely educated, and were often appointed solely on the basis that they were German or French and could therefore teach their own language. At least one of the Russian tutors was a widow who could not read, but recited passages that she had learned by heart from church books for her pupils to make of what they could. As for the journey to Western Europe, the young Russians were at first terrified at the prospect, and then naïvely impressionable when they actually arrived at their destination. Gradually, the visitors from Eastern Europe came to take a deeper interest in aspects of Western European life although not many Frenchmen would have agreed with the appraisal made of Louis XIV's France by one of the visitors, who could see only order and the absence of arbitrary government.[19] Ignorance and misunderstanding were mutual, of course, and many foreigners were hopelessly inaccurate in their observation of eighteenth-century Russia.

The gap between the two extremities of the continent must not be exaggerated, for a broad conformity to a general pattern of cultural development may be discerned in Russia. This is so with regard to education and to the church, about which Miliukov wrote: 'The entire ecclesiastical policy of Peter can be summarized as a consistent development of two ideas: the elimination of the Patriarch, who could become a Russian Pope . . . and the subordination of the Church to the reigning monarch.'[20] In 1700, the Patriarch Adrian died, and Peter did not hurry to appoint a successor. The *locum tenens* Stepan Iavorskii soon embroiled himself in controversy with the tsar, and thus contributed to the abolition of the Patriarchate. And then, in 1721, the Ecclesiastical Regulation was introduced, setting up the Holy Synod as the basic governor of the Russian Church, with a layman as its chief procurator keeping it in order. Peter himself had a soldier's bluff faith, which encouraged him to concentrate on the morality and loyalty of his subjects rather than on niceties of doctrine. For this reason, he considered it necessary to subject the Church itself to the discipline of his all-pervasive bureaucratic state, as James Cracraft has clearly indicated. For example, a decree on a seminary's daily routine stated that: 'like soldiers at the beat of a drum, the seminarists will, at the sound of a bell, proceed to the performance of whatever is appointed for that hour.'[21] Historians of the Russian Church are divided in their interpretation of the effect of Peter's reform, some seeing it as a liberation for clerics who could now concentrate exclusively on spiritual matters, while others look upon it as a victory for encroaching secularism. Either way, ecclesiastical matters will henceforth be of smaller concern up to 1917.

The second of these two directions is certainly more apparent in the linguistic and literary developments of the period. During the reign of Peter the Great, when a large amount of translation was carried out particularly of technical books, the written language based on Church Slavonic had to be adapted to the needs of the new age. This task, which was reputed to have driven at least one translator to attempt suicide on several occasions, prepared the way for the poets and prose writers of the period after his death. While popular tales and ballads similar to those of the seventeenth century continued to be composed in the eighteenth, the more ordered world of the ode and the drama was establishing itself. This involved the transplantation to Russian soil of Western verse forms and classical models. The work was carried out by such men as A. D. Kantemir, V. K. Trediakovskii, A. P. Sumarokov and M. V. Lomonosov.

Lomonosov was a man of many parts, producing scientific and historical treatises as well as poetry. Another historian of note was V. N. Tatishchev, who also produced a mature piece of political thought at the time of the constitutional crisis of 1730, a rational defence of autocracy as the most suitable form of government for the Russian Empire. Scientific voyages of discovery through Siberia and over to North America were made by such individuals as Vitus Bering and Aleksei Chirikov.

Before the accession of Catherine the Great, then, the way had been prepared for the cultural flowering usually associated with her name, not only in literature and the sciences but also in the arts. The reign of Elizabeth was a clear precursor as the dominant foreign influence turned from German to French. Painters such as I. Ia. Vishniakov and A. P. Andropov, and architects such as I. F. Michurin and D. V. Ukhtomskii received Elizabeth's patronage, which was also given to the portraitist François Tocqué and the Paris-born creator of the Hermitage Palace, Bartolomeo Francesco Rastrelli.

Thanks to Peter the Great, and if not to his successors, then at least to many of their advisers, Russia by 1761 had in all three principal areas under our consideration – political, economic, cultural – made the effort to adapt to herself the most advanced ideas of Europe, and had thus effected the completion of much of the structure of the Russian Empire on the foundation laid during the second half of the seventeenth century.

6   Enlightened Absolutism, 1761–1801

'Peter gave Russians bodies, and Catherine – souls', declared a contemporary poet, thereby expressing in a personalised manner some of the differences between the two phases of absolutism.[1] Peter's emphasis was indeed on the practical and Catherine's on the intellectual. The two phases may also be separated according to the major Western influences on them: Peter was struck mainly by the scientific movement and the rationalism of the late seventeenth century, while Catherine was more receptive to the somewhat more rarefied arguments of the eighteenth-century *philosophes*. At the same time, there was more than a little continuity between the two phases, as there was between the sources of their inspiration and between the problems that they aimed at overcoming.

Along with Ekaterina, Catherine II – or Catherine the Great (1762–96) as she is more normally known – we must consider her husband Petr or Peter III and her son Pavel or Paul I. Peter III reigned for little more that six months, yet this period saw quite an amount of legislative action which has been the subject of considerable discussion among historians. A not insignificant feature of the discussion is the personality of Peter himself. Born in Kiel in 1728, Peter had arrived in Russia from Germany soon after the accession of his aunt Elizabeth. He was declared the heir of Elizabeth after being received into the Orthodox Church. Catherine came from Germany in 1745 to be married to him, and, although the young couple soon decided that they did not care much for each other, they both agreed to find consolation elsewhere and were able to enter into something like a stable state of peaceful co-existence. Unfortunately for Peter, however, one of the major sources of information concerning him is the *Memoirs* of Catherine, in which she showed much more devotion to self-justification than to objective truth. Other sources suggest that Peter was not the childish imbecile, not the 'permanent patch upon a very beautiful face' that Catherine made him out to be.[2] He spoke three languages – in ascending order of fluency Russian, French and German – although he wrote them all rather incorrectly. He liked his large library, and was probably no less an intellectual than many of his predecessors, if not the equal of his wife. His passion for playing the violin, which he did badly, and for coarse merry-making, at which he was an accomplished master, again hardly set him far apart from most of his forebears. While some analysts have found the key to an understanding of his policy in his psychological make-up, others have discovered it in his great admiration for Frederick the Great of Prussia. Certainly he had a taste for drill which might be called Prussophile, as he forced even high-ranking officers to turn out on the parade ground, and changed army regulations and uniforms according to Prussian models. Undoubtedly too, he did have great personal respect for Frederick the Great. But as we shall see below, to explain his short reign exclusively by the quirks of his personality would be to exaggerate his importance and to under-estimate the part played by other individuals.

Sophia Augusta, an obscure German princess born in 1729, was about sixteen years old when she came to Russia to marry Peter, and became Catherine with her conversion to Orthodoxy.[3] The major influences on her early life are considered to have been her father and her governess: from the former she acquired a serious interest in politics as well as a certain tomboyish masculinity; from the latter she gained a great curiosity if not so much the means of satisfying it. These traits were to stand her in good stead during the frustrating years from 1745 to 1762, as she read widely and imbibed a considerable amount of ancient and modern wisdom. Her correspondence with Voltaire and most of the other great men of the age shows her to be well-informed and lively if not profound or original. Allowing her to lead her notorious private life in her off-duty hours, we shall give our primary attention here to her public policies.

Catherine has not received from posterity anything like the adulation that she received from flatterers while she was alive. Pushkin called her a Tartuffe in skirts, and her vainglorious hypocrisy has come under attack from many other quarters. A more balanced appraisal came from Kliuchevskii, who wrote that, after the failure of an early liberal idealism, she consoled herself with the thought that 'after me they will follow my principles', and concentrated on educational and propagandist activity. Making herself a famous personage of Europe, she also assisted some members of society to feel a new self-confidence: 'From Peter, hardly daring to consider themselves people and still not considering themselves proper Europeans, Russians under Catherine felt themselves to be not only people, but almost the first people of Europe.' For this reason, they forgave her for the mistakes of her foreign policy and for her persecution of various internal foes, for her profligacy and perpetuation of social injustice.[4]

Kliuchevskii omits from his definition of the 'people' the rank and file of the peasantry who made up the bulk of the population and many of whom showed what they thought of Catherine by joining in the Pugachev Revolt. In such a tradition was the dismissal of her worth by Marx and Engels. Moreover, neither the fact that she was born a foreigner nor that revolutionary thought first arose towards the end of her reign helped to acquire for her anything more than the coolest of receptions from Soviet historians. However, her particular brand of enlightened despotism is now seen by at least some of them as a move towards the formation of a bourgeois ideology, and her personal qualities have also been given some recognition. I. A. Fedosov writes, 'Without doubt Catherine was one of the oustanding figures on the Russian throne – clever, and educated, and capable, and successful.'[5]

Her son has received a greater measure of rehabilitation. It is true that Fedosov considers Paul I to have been a crazy despot who 'threatened to discredit the very idea of absolutism'. On the other hand, a few pre-revolutionary historians argued that he could be called some kind of enlightened absolutist; and some Soviet historians believe that he was at least in some respects progressive. Undoubtedly, the fact that he came to power soon after the most radical phase of the French Revolution gave his reign many of its ambiguous features.[6]

Paul was born in 1754. Some doubt that his father was Peter III, but certain physical and psychological resemblances give support to the evidence that he was born in grand-ducal wedlock. He spoke the same languages as his father and spelled them as badly, and like Peter was fond of his large library. Like Peter too, he admired Prussia and disliked Catherine. His education under the supervision of Nikita Panin, one of Catherine's chief advisers, appears to have been sound, but he was kept well away from actual business of government. He paid two visits to Western Europe, one of them after the death of his first wife, a German princess; during this second visit, he found another to be his second wife. He then settled down on the Gatchina estate near St Petersburg. He was a solicitous landlord and a good if disciplinarian garrison commander. His relations with his second wife were clouded, however, by one of her ladies-in-waiting, who developed a close if chaste connection with the future Emperor and encouraged the mysticism which had already been kindled by an earlier acquaintance with Freemasonry. Around Paul gathered an entourage which was to take full advantage of the opportunity offered to it in 1796 at the death of Catherine.

During the last decades of the eighteenth century, Roger Portal asserts, 'the Russia of Catherine II, by virtue of the number of its factories and work-shops, the volume of its production and the part it played in European trade, took its place among the great economic powers.'[7] The Empire consolidated itself on the Black Sea and swallowed a large slice of Poland. Its army won great victories in Eastern and Western Europe, its navy triumphantly asserted a presence in the Mediterranean. Europe gained the impression that Russia had become one of the great laboratories of the Enlightenment. All this was achieved at enormous social cost, and led to the outbreak of the Pugachev Revolt, the fourth, last and largest of the peasant wars. And then, with the impact of that even greater civil disturbance, the French Revolution, absolutism became unenlightened and reactionary. Having at least to some degree assisted the development of the Russian Empire in the first century or so of its existence, tsarism now became, to be sure not without some echoes of liberalism, a dead weight on progress in all the major sectors of the national life.

Political

Although the reign of Peter III has often been looked upon as a crazy six months unconnected with very much that went before or came after, it may in fact be considered as a busy transitional period. To take its most celebrated decree, the so-called Emancipation of the Nobility of 18 February 1762, research has revealed a close connection with ideas put forward in the later years of Elizabeth's reign. And of course the implementation and significance of the decree depended on Catherine. In such a light, the Emancipation does not stand out as a radical alteration in the service prescriptions of Peter the Great, but rather appears as a modification of their rigours. Kliuchevskii rightly observed: 'The law said: be so good, serve and teach your children, and nevertheless, he who does neither the one nor the other will be driven from society.' More generally in the informed words of Marc Raeff: 'In no sense was the legislation radical, nor did it introduce any notions and practices that were alien to the Russian polity of the eighteenth century.'[8] The question therefore naturally arises, why was the reign of Peter III so brief? Again to follow the interpretation of Raeff, an important reason was that Peter chose a new entourage which threatened to form an exclusive government, demeaning the Senate and other parts of the administration as it did so. In this respect as well as in others, the reign of Peter was in the tradition of Anna and Elizabeth, and so some weight must be given to the traditional verdict that one of Peter's greatest mistakes was the alienation of the Guards, whom Anna and Elizabeth had been careful to patronise.

Catherine II seized the supreme power in the summer of 1762. Her current lover, Grigorii Orlov, and his brothers were sufficiently popular among the Guards to gain sufficient support for the removal of Peter III and the installation of his wife, soon, if none too soon for her, to be his widow. While Peter and other threats to Catherine's position were eliminated, the Orlovs and their associates received considerable rewards for their endeavours. In the 1770s, another Grigorii, Potemkin, became Catherine's first favourite and, like his predecessors and successors, made large material if not moral gains. Potemkin continued to influence the policies of the Empress even when he became a less frequent visitor to her bed. Of her later lovers, only Platon Zubov, the last of the long line, enjoyed any political significance; no other affair of the heart can really be called an affair of state. In an informal manner, both her favourites and her advisers in general were broadly responsive to the class from which most of them sprang, the nobility. This tacit alliance between the autocrat and the ruling class became more marked as the reign wore on, particularly after such disturbing events as the Pugachev Revolt and the French Revolution. Catherine's policies concerning both local and central government clearly reflected such a social background.

From soon after her accession onwards, Catherine was presented with a series of memoranda on the subject of local government. A suggestion contained in many of them, for the introduction of an elective noble element, was repeated many times by assemblies of nobles in their instructions to deputies at the Legislative Commission of 1767. Although Catherine did not read all the instructions, the message got through to her. And then she was impressed by her reading in French translation of Sir William Blackstone and her consequent understanding of the English system of local government, especially the part played in it by the J.P.s. Further reports of the methods of administration employed in the Baltic provinces, where officials elected by the nobility were dominant, also struck forcibly. The Pugachev Revolt of 1773–5 probably clinched the reform and accelerated its completion.

The decree of 1775 implementing the reform lamented the disorder of Russian local government and hoped to replace it with efficiency through the following four changes: increase in the number of provinces, making them less unwieldy; decentralisation of several important powers concerning police, justice and finance; division of these powers among separate agencies; and introduction of officials elected by various classes, with the nobility predominant. Although the reform was imperfectly carried out, it put the seal on the control of the provinces by the nobility that had been developing since the death of Peter the Great: at the top there were such governors as Potemkin, near the bottom many less notable but still important district captains of police supervising the affairs of commoners. The fifty or so provinces in existence at the end of the eighteenth century were thus considerably prepared for the important reform of local government which was to take place in the 1860s.

Meanwhile, during the reign of Catherine, the government's bureaucracy grew larger and partly changed its nature. In 1763 there were about 16,500 officials on the establishment, all given a salary increase to encourage efficiency and reduce corruption. With the reform of 1775, up to 18,000 men now staffed the civil service and nearly a tenth of the total expenditure of the state went on its upkeep. At first encouraging a limited democratisation of the bureaucracy by facilitating the rise from the lower to the higher ranks in the table, Catherine reverted in her later reactionary mood to the aristocratic exclusiveness of earlier times, now reinforced by the introduction of the elective element. This restriction eliminated even some of the lesser members of the *dvorianstvo* from the civil service, particularly after the Charter of the Nobility of 1785, which allowed only landed proprietors to vote, and only those of them with the rank of commissioned officer and an income of not less than 100 roubles to be elected to office. Thus, at the end of Catherine's reign, the civil service was dominated by the upper and middle nobility, which looked upon the income derived from its state service as a supplement to that from its estates – a governor-general could earn as much as 6000 roubles per annum in this manner, a middle-ranking councillor from 200 to 600 roubles. The lower echelons of the provincial bureaucracy were staffed by nobles who also depended on their salaries to make up the deficiencies of their income as landlords, and there was of course a whole ever-growing stratum of professional bureaucrats helping to swell the volume of paper in the governmental archives.

Apart from the reform of 1775, there were some other significant changes made by Catherine in the formal structure of government. First, a State Council was inaugurated in 1769, manned by an inner circle of officials who had worked as a less formal advisory group since the beginning of her reign. Although the Council was given a more defined constitutional position in the reign of Alexander I, the earlier version appears to have functioned well enough as an intermediary power between the Empress and the Senate. At the same time, it would certainly be wrong to see either in the formation of the State Council or in the preliminaries to it an aristocratic threat to the formal status of the autocrat. Second, the Senate itself was reorganised in 1763, neither for much better nor much worse as far as can be judged. With the reform of 1775, the Senate retained its administrative and judicial control of the provinces, but its ancillary Colleges were largely atrophied with the decentralisation of functions that the reform had entailed, and were soon abolished, except for the Colleges of Foreign Affairs, the Army and Navy which were directly responsible to the autocrat. Third, the office of procurator-general, which had lost much of its importance during the years before 1764, regained all that had been lost in the person of Prince Alexander Viazemskii, who was an important assistant to Catherine from 1764 to 1792. His hands were on the purse strings, his thumb firmly on the network of secret police, and he had a finger in everything of importance. Fourth, along with the Charter of the Nobility of 1785, there was a Charter of the Towns and an unpublished charter for the state peasants. Neither of these schemes got far off the ground, possibly because they were too far from it. Catherine's dreams of a self-reliant peasantry and a flourishing middle class never approached realisation.

A few words must be said about Catherine's other shattered dreams. At first a pupil of Montesquieu, Beccaria and the *philosophes*, later of Blackstone, the Empress did not succeed in adapting the ideas of Western Europe into any coherent rationale of absolutism. In the first few years of her reign, however, she made a considerable effort, with her Legislative Commission of 1767 and her *Instruction* for it, to give her adopted country a new enlightened code of laws. Although the Commission failed to provide a code, it did give the Empress a clearer picture of what needed to be done to reform the Empire. The *Instruction*, which was banned in France and severely restricted in circulation in Russia, gives us an impression of the theoretical framework in which such a process would be carried out. The political philosophy that emerges from it is a modification of the balance-of-power concept of Montesquieu coupled with the German cameralist idea of social welfare achieved within the framework of the bureaucratic state. Catherine rejected Montesquieu's libertarian views and could not even accept the independent role that he suggests for the nobility, but she did agree with him that the separation of the legislative, executive and judicial powers subordinate to the monarch would prevent her absolutism from becoming despotism. Restrained from excesses by this and other measures adapted from Montesquieu, her government would address itself to the protection and prosperity of her people in the Christian cameralist manner suggested by such writers as Baron de Bielefeld. Those who still broke the law would be punished in the humane manner recommended by Beccaria. Such an exercise in self-justification was not without ingenuity, but Catherine's essential philosophy of government was expressed in a more succinct and accurate manner at the time of the Pugachev Revolt. Writing to the Kazan nobility, she declared herself to be a 'proprietress of Kazan' and emphasised that the security and well-being of the nobility were indivisible with her own and her Empire's.[9] Such a belief became more fervent with the onset of the French Revolution.

Paul's political vision, characterised by Florinsky as 'a thoroughly disciplined polity over which a wise absolute monarch exercised a quasi-paternalistic rule within the framework of the law', did not differ substantially from Catherine's.[10] At the same time, he gave more emphasis to service than to privilege, and threatened dissident nobles with corporal punishment. The local elective governmental functions of the nobility were suppressed, and centralist control was asserted in a simplified provincial administration. The central government itself was largely unaltered, although a beginning was made towards the replacement of the colleges by ministries.

While the general tendency of Paul's governmental policy was to reverse the centrifugal trend of his mother's, his policy towards the nationalities inclined towards a reversal of her centripetal russification. For example, he restored the local rights and privileges of the Ukraine, Poland, the Baltic provinces and Finland that she had taken away. Near the beginning of her reign, Catherine wrote to her newly appointed procurator-general that the Ukraine and the Baltic provinces 'should be gently reduced to a condition where they can be russified and no longer, like wolves, look to the woods'.[11] Some twenty years later, with the application of the 1775 local government reform to these areas, this gentle reduction was brought to its culmination, the Ukrainian and Baltic nobilities being reconciled by their adoption into the *dvorianstvo* – with all the attendant opportunities for advancement in the service – and by the introduction into their regions of the institution of serfdom. Similar treatment was extended to Finland without significant opposition. The Poles, brought into the Empire by a series of partitions, were russified less but protested more, notably in the late sixties and early nineties. The extension of Russian influence in other directions brought even greater problems. The occupation of the Crimea and establishment of a protectorate over Georgia in 1783 contributed to further wars against Turkey,[12] and infiltration into Central Asia stimulated rebellions in Kazakhstan in 1783 and 1797. The consolidation of Russian interests in Siberia was attended with less violence, and the Empire's involvement in Alaska was marked by the formation in 1799 of the Russian-American Company.

Catherine's policy of the firm incorporation of the outlying provinces and of their russification was one of the major reasons for the greatest outbreak of civil disturbance of the eighteenth century, the Pugachev Revolt, or fourth and last peasant war, of 1773–5. Dissident Cossacks rising on the Iaik River were joined by tribesmen and factory-workers as the movement spread to the Urals. While the main band was led by Emelian Pugachev, a Don Cossack claiming to be Peter III, other detachments and groups wrought havoc throughout a wide area. Having suffered several reverses, Pugachev was able to recover sufficiently to take Kazan except for its Kremlin. Defeated again, Pugachev swept down into the Volga region, where more than sixty peasant armed companies were formed. The threat to Moscow and St Petersburg seemed real enough to Catherine for a month or so, but then, overcome yet again by government forces, Pugachev took flight, only to be betrayed by some of his erstwhile supporters and handed over to the authorities. Taken to Moscow, Pugachev was executed there in January 1775. Stern reprisals were taken against all participants in his movement, and the government attempted literally to erase its memory by changing the name of its place of origin from the Iaik to the Ural river. While Soviet historians concede the weaknesses of the ideology and organisation of the insurgents, they also adduce an impressive amount of evidence to show that these weaknesses can be exaggerated and to indicate that the fourth peasant war was the most worthy of the name. At least one of the Western historians who have lately turned their attention to the event is reluctant to typify it as much more than a 'frontier jacquerie'.[13]

Certainly, the Pugachev Revolt and some of the other civil disturbances of the period, such as the widespread peasant movement of 1796–8 which flared up in more than thirty provinces, would not have posed such a serious threat if the government had not been engaged in a busy period of international relations. At the beginning of her reign Catherine had to arrange Russia's final withdrawal from the Seven Years War after Peter III had taken his troops from the anti-Prussian side to the pro-Prussian. The argument that there was some *raison d'état* in this *volte-face* draws support from Catherine's continuance of friendly relations with Frederick the Great, encouraged by her chief adviser Nikita Panin. The royal pair set about carving up Poland between them after some initial self-restraint, but the suspicion of Austria and France was aroused and the enmity of Turkey provoked.

Strongly aroused in addition by Russian probes towards the Black Sea and the Balkans, Turkey opened hostilities in 1768. The resulting war brought mixed results on land, and some famous victories on sea, where Russia asserted a firm presence in the Mediterranean, notably at the battle of Chesme off the Anatolian coast in 1770. The Pugachev Revolt brought the war to a somewhat hurried conclusion, the Treaty of Kuchuk-Kainardzhi of 1774 giving Russia parts of the Crimea and of the Black Sea littoral, the right of free passage through the Straits for her merchantmen, and an ill-defined protection over Turkey's Christian subjects.

Meanwhile, the first partition of Poland in 1772 guaranteed the continued suspicion of Turkey and her European supporters. After a Russian Declaration of Armed Neutrality in 1780 had made no small impact on the American War of Independence,[14] Catherine was encouraged to think again of expansion, Potemkin's 'Greek Project' involving nothing less than the revival of the Byzantine Empire. Her occupation of the Crimea and infiltration into Transcaucasia goaded Turkey into action, and a second Russo-Turkish war broke out in 1787. This war brought about the triumphant assertion of the power and skill of the Russian forces, particularly the army under Suvorov[15] and the navy under Greig and Ushakov. It was also very complicated in its international ramifications. At first an ally of Russia's, Austria was persuaded in 1790 to leave the war by Prussia and Britain, who had also instigated a Swedish attack on Russia in 1788, brought to an end in 1790 with a recognition of the *status quo ante bellum*. For its part, the Russo-Turkish War was concluded by the Treaty of Jassy at the end of 1791; the terms of Kuchuk-Kainardzhi were confirmed, and more Black Sea littoral, notably between the rivers Bug and Dnestr, ceded to Russia. Later plans for revival and extension of the 'Greek Project' under Catherine's last lover, Platon Zubov, who wanted to move towards India as well as Constantinople, were abandoned at Catherine's death in 1796.

Before then, the outbreak and intensification of the French Revolution had brought about *rapprochement* with Austria, Prussia and Sweden, as well as good cover for the further dismemberment of Poland. The Poles took advantage of Russia's Turkish preoccupations and Prussian encouragement to adopt a new constitution in the spring of 1791, only to bring upon themselves the second partition of 1793, in which Russia and Prussia joined together, using as an excuse their fear that the spirit of the French Revolution was threatening Poland. Proof that such a fear was justified came in 1794 with the outbreak of a radical insurrection led by Tadeusz Kosciuszko, who had participated in the American Revolution and was imbued with many of the ideas of the French. The revolt was crushed, and was followed by the third partition, finally agreed between Russia, Prussia and Austria in early 1797. The Russian share consisted largely of White Russia, Lithuania and other provinces, enabling Soviet historians to call it a reunion rather than a robbery, while condemning Catherine for her acceptance of the division of Poland proper between Prussia and Austria.[16]

Paul's foreign policy included such eccentric moments as the Emperor's adoption of the knights of Malta[17] and some brilliant campaigns by Suvorov, including a rapid crossing of the Alps. These and other moves were in the shadow of the rise of Napoleon, who was to constitute Russia's primary problem of international relations during the first decade and a half of the nineteenth century. Paul also formally annexed Georgia in 1801, and was preparing a grandiose campaign for the conquest of India at the time of his assassination in the same year.

The second half of the eighteenth century produced a foreign policy at least as glorious and successful for tsarism as that of the first. Although the cost was crippling, such a policy could hardly have been undertaken at all if the Russian Empire had not been able to command an impressive amount of men and materials by the standards of the century. As Russia fell behind the rate of development of other nations in the nineteenth century, so her foreign policy became less successful, declining from the tremendous triumph over Napoleon to the humiliating disaster of the Crimean War.

Economic

At the beginning of her reign, Catherine was a keen proponent of economic progress. For example, she encouraged in 1765 *The Institution of the Free Economic Society for the Encouragement of Agriculture and Good Husbandry*. In the first number of the Society's *Works*, the editor announced that everything possible would be done to improve Russian farming, which he looked upon as the basis of the Empire's prosperity. In the same year, the Society announced a Prize Essay Competition on the advisability of allowing the peasants to own property. The attitude of the bulk of the landlords to the question was possibly expressed by an entry which declared that the abolition of serfdom would be possible when:

Russia becomes as populous as the kingdom of Holland, when our priests are as literate as foreign priests, the nobles such sharp-witted fellows as the English and the French, the peasants know their ABC and are consequently honest and obey more the wrath of God and go to church more often than to the drinking houses, do not starve in the barges on the Volga, and our rabble has a better understanding of foreign crafts, and becomes more intelligent.

The message of the winning entry, which proposed the grant to the peasants of a token amount of property, was summarised in its observation that 'It is a pleasure to see your dog following you everywhere . . . can it be compared with the burdensome labour of leading a bear?' Even such unexceptionable remarks as these were published only after the intercession of the Empress,[18] who also made some remarks which were very guarded – even more so after her advisers had expressed their shock – about the limitation of serfdom in her *Instruction* to the Legislative Commission of 1767. At the same time she spoke out more openly for the improvement of agriculture as well as of industry and trade. Enacting what she preached, she issued decrees in the first five years of her reign promoting the immigration of foreign colonists, the cultivation of potatoes and the execution of a general survey; weakening gild control and allowing people of every rank to engage in various kinds of manufacturing enterprise; and fostering trade with Great Britain and other foreign customers. While such policies as these certainly advanced the interests of the bourgeoisie, they were not necessarily to the detriment of the nobility, whose support Catherine always recognised as fundamental to the maintenance of her own power. Such a priority may be even more clearly observed through the rest of her reign.

Although her personal and legislative contribution was small, Catherine was pleased to see the rise in the population from about $23\frac{1}{4}$ millions in 1762 to nearly $37\frac{1}{2}$ millions in 1795. This steep climb was partly natural and partly the consequence of imperial expansion. The incorporation of Lithuania and White Russia brought in more than 5 million people and that of the Right-Bank Ukraine nearly $3\frac{1}{2}$ millions. Peripheral areas became much more populous as the Empire became consolidated, New Russia tripling its numbers to well over a million and the Lower Volga nearly doubling them to just under a million. The more settled central provinces also grew demographically, and altogether by the end of her reign, Catherine might have been wondering if what had appeared to be a dearth at the beginning of it had now become an excess, at least in the heart of the Empire.

The social division of the Russian people remained roughly the same at the end of the eighteenth century as it had been at the middle, although perhaps with more local variations. That is, more than 90 per cent of them were peasants, and about 50 per cent of the peasants were the serfs of the nobility. The percentage of town dwellers has been placed variously from 3·6 per cent to 8·3 per cent, depending on the definitions and figures used. The clergy, armed forces and nobility accounted for most of the rest of the population. Quite obviously, a Siberian tribesman, a New Russian peasant and a Baltic factory-worker would have much to differentiate them as well as the designation of peasant and a fundamental class interest to keep them together.

Another link would be agriculture for, as in most of the world at that time, even those not engaged in farming would never be far from it. This sector of the economy was slow to change as well as all-pervasive. In spite of all the efforts of the Free Economic Society and government decree, for example, 'earth apples' or potatoes were still rarely grown. Another comparatively new crop, wheat, spread more rapidly, with Ukrainian and other southern farmers beginning to realise its market possibilities as their colleagues in the Baltic provinces and the north-west increased their profits from the more traditional cultivation of flax and hemp. Technical improvements such as improved ploughs or harrows were mostly to be found on the estates of the noble landlords, to whom also went the lion's share of the new lands and redistributed peasants. But merchants and peasants were also taking some of the fresh fields; for example, officially, peasant homesteaders were each allowed just over 60 hectares (about 160 acres) in some of the southern regions, unofficially, they were often procuring more and even securing the services of some of their poorer fellows. Such incidents have encouraged some Soviet historians to discuss the stratification of the peasantry and the emergence from among them of a rural bourgeoisie and proletariat, but others have issued words of warning about the antedating of capitalism and pointed out the persistence of the basic, feudal three-field strip system in many provinces.[19]

Such words of warning must be borne in mind as we turn to consider the contemporary situation in industry and trade. Between the middle and the end of the eighteenth century, the number of factories and plants doubled from over 600 according to some accounts, tripled from a higher figure according to others. Iron production rose from something over 30,000 metric tons in 1750 to more than 160,000 in 1800, so one estimate suggests. The Urals had undoubtedly become the most important metallurgical centre, with local tribesmen used as labour along with Russian peasants. Textile production also appears to have climbed steeply, with other areas removing some of Moscow's earlier predominance and hired workers forming an embryonic industrial proletariat.

The importance of Russian metals, textiles and other goods to Britain, still the major trading partner, was described by Mr Foster, the agent of the Russia Company, in the following manner at the House of Commons in 1774:

> The articles we bring from Russia, our hemp, our iron, our flax, are so indispensably necessary to us for every purpose of agriculture and of commerce, that, had we no export trade, it would be very expedient we should attentively cultivate the friendship of Russia on account of our import trade only . . . without them our navy, our commerce, our agriculture, are at end; without them, where would be our wealth, where our naval honours? . . . You will never, Sir, think that trade a prejudicial one, which brings home the materials, without which commerce could neither be undertaken nor protected.

Mr Foster also said that Russia's linen exports to Britain, although not of good quality, were much used by the poor, and 'the want of them could not be supplied by our home manufacturers'.[20] As far away as the United States, Russian exports, particularly hemp, were in considerable demand before the end of the eighteenth century.[21] Imports continued to consist largely of sugar, cloth of various kinds, dyestuffs and luxury items such as coffee, wines and fruits. St Petersburg was by far the most important port, but the foundation of Odessa in 1794 helped the Black Sea trade well on its way, while Astrakhan retained its importance in the trade with the Orient. The tariff of 1766 was moderate, in line with the liberal trend of Catherine's early economic policies; an increase came in 1782, and then the rates were raised to a formidably high level in the mid-1790s. Although the general direction was towards protectionism, foreign trade almost quadrupled in total value between 1759 and 1798. To some extent, such growth was a reflection of the expansion and consolidation of the internal market.

Economic advance gave the state the opportunity to extract more money from its subjects, and the state income rose from just over 24 million roubles in 1769 to 56 millions in 1795, a formidable increase even when allowance has been made for the inflation that set in towards the end of the century. As before and after, the bulk of the burden fell upon the peasantry, who paid most of the direct poll-tax and the indirect taxes on salt and vodka. Expenditure began to exceed income, and the paper assignats issued to cover the deficit accounted for much of the inflation. Between a third and a half of the expenditure went on the armed forces, and from a quarter to a third of it on administration. The court consumed 10 per cent or more of the total, while less than 1.5 per cent was invested in education and welfare. Banking policy continued to favour the nobility, branches of the state bank being set up in the provinces most severely struck by the Pugachev Revolt in 1775, for example.

Although the Emperor Paul attempted to tax the landed estates of the nobility and to suggest a three-day limit on the *barshchina* services, the people were no more happy with his economic policies than with his mother's. And after a wave of revolts second only in seriousness to the Pugachev Revolt had broken out in the first year or so of his short reign, Paul ordered ruthless suppression. In such conditions, the rank-and-file peasants could hardly be under the impression that enlightened absolutism had percolated down to their level.

Cultural

During the reign of Catherine, there comes to an end that period which Miliukov calls 'the official triumph of critical elements'.[22] In other words, absolutism ceases to be enlightened, and the torch of progressive thought is handed to members of the nascent intelligentsia. For most Soviet historians, absolutism had never really held the torch at any time.

At the beginning of her reign, Catherine was very keen to see the spread of education, proclaiming in her *Instruction*: 'order it so, that the *Light of Knowledge* may be *diffused* among the People'. But reports from all provinces, with the partial exception of the Ukraine and the Baltic area, revealed a very gloomy school situation at the time of the Legislative Commission of 1767. And Catherine's educational reforms in her first few years had been mostly piecemeal rather than wholesale, along lines partly suggested by Peter III's legislation in the field and partly elaborated by I. I. Betskoi, a collaborator with a broad cosmopolitan outlook. Catherine and Betskoi projected development in two directions in their decree of 12 March 1764: towards the rearrangement and enlargement of special schools in St Petersburg and Moscow; and towards the introduction into the Empire as a whole of a modern system of general schools. Understandably enough, more progress was made with the first and easier aim. The cadet and other military schools in the capitals were reorganised, with their curricula made less specialised; schools for girls and for orphans were created. As far as the second aim was concerned, several skeletal projects such as that drawn up on the basis of the British educational system were formulated, several good principles such as reduction of corporal punishment were enunciated, and even some dreams such as the creation of a 'new man' were indulged. But not one positive practical step was taken.[23]

Miliukov wrote: 'Influenced by the theories of enlightenment, full of enthusiasm, the Catherine of the sixties could dream of the creation of this new race. Cooled down by experience of life and disappointed, the Catherine of the eighties could see how insufficient for the execution of this grand scheme were the means within her hands'.[24] For her second bout of educational 'legimania', then, Catherine concentrated not so much on the universal diffusion of light as on the narrower inculcation of some sound ethical concepts and a basic primary and secondary education. For several years a new collaborator, F. I. Yankovich de Mirievo, a Serbian graduate of the University of Vienna who had assisted in the establishment of schools of a Prussian type in Hungary, worked on the project with several associates. And then, on 5 August 1786, a Statute of Popular Schools was promulgated. Drawing on foreign models and adapting several special texts, the Statute proposed the institution of two main kinds of school: major or secondary, and minor or primary. The models included Prussia and Austria, while the texts included such unexceptionable statements as 'In each rank it is possible to be happy. People often think that tsars, princes, nobles and aristocratic individuals alone have a happy life; but this, however, is incorrect.' Just after Catherine's death, there were 7001 students with 269 teachers in 49 major schools and 15,209 students with 491 teachers in 239 minor schools. Although these figures are minute, they compare favourably with the 2000 figure for attendance at the cipher schools just after the death of Peter the Great. Schools run by the Church and the army had a student population of over 20,000 and 12,000 respectively towards the end of the eighteenth century, and the special schools of the capitals and private schools mainly for the nobility accounted for several thousand more. The grand total was nearly 62,000 students in nearly 549 institutions. To that must be added the large numbers of nobles and other ranks who received some kind of education from private tutors or even from waiting at their masters' tables.[25]

While Russian figures pale before others such as the 8000 elementary schools in contemporary France or the 250,000 students in attendance at the English Sunday schools of the period, there were enough culturally aware Russians for it to be possible to talk of an intelligentsia drawn from the nobility, from the middle class and even from the peasantry. The third of these was probably the smallest, and certainly least is known about it. Most of the peasants would gain their world view from songs, proverbs and legends, all strongly intermixed with Orthodox teaching and Slavonic superstition. A clear political attitude is discernible in the Razin and Pugachev legends and in the following piece of popular verse:

> The ox did not want to be an ox
> And so he became a butcher.
> When the butcher went to hit him on the head,
> He knocked the blow aside with his horns,
> And the butcher fell down.
> Then the ox managed to snatch the axe from him,
> Cut off his arms and hung him up by his legs,
> And started to pull out the guts and lights.[26]

Common sense rather than concrete evidence tells us that there were at least a handful of peasants with some awareness of more advanced thought in politics and other fields. As far as the middle-class or democratic (as Soviet historians – notably M. M. Shtrange [27] – call it) intelligentsia is concerned, such men as M. V. Lomonosov and S. E. Desnitskii were highly educated and in some senses critical of the tsarist establishment, although it is too early to talk of groups of them.

Even the noble intelligentsia was composed less of organised cells than of bold individuals. Outstanding among them was A. N. Radishchev, who in his *A Journey from St. Petersburg to Moscow* laid bare the wretchedness of the peasantry. Through what Allen McConnell has called his 'sensitive moral vision',[28] Radischev saw clearly the inequity of an Empire based upon such an institution as serfdom. Radischev incurred Catherine's deep displeasure, as did N. I. Novikov, satirist and publicist. The first Russian journals had been published during the earlier phase of absolutism, but the early 1770s saw the first real wave of them. Catherine and Novikov both had their own vehicles of satirical comment, but while the Empress concentrated on evil in the abstract, Novikov's barbs were more pointed. A Freemason, like many other members of the intelligentsia, Novikov later devoted himself to good works and general publishing activities. A critic of the Empress from the right was Prince M. M. Shcherbatov, who in his best-known work, *On the Corruption of Morals in Russia*, accused Catherine of undermining the rigorous governmental system set up by Peter the Great and in particular of bringing to ruin the backbone of society, the nobility.[29]

The ideas of the Enlightenment were disseminated by such men and by such translations as that of some five hundred articles from Diderot's

Encyclopedia. Even the provincial nobles gained a veneer of Voltairism, and would bear comparison with their foreign peers. At the same time at the highest level, without being as critical as Radishchev, Novikov and Shcherbatov, a few Russians were making considerable contributions to literature and learning. G. R. Derzhavin was the finest lyric poet, and D. I. Fonvizin wrote two good lightly satirical comedies, *The Brigadier* and *The Minor*. A. P. Sumarokov created some less memorable pseudo-classical tragedies, while N. M. Karamzin was active as publicist, historian and prose writer.[30] Most of these, particularly Karamzin, made contributions to the formation of the Russian literary language, and to international movements such as neo-classicism and sentimentalism. Meanwhile, students from Russia continued to go abroad for the completion of their education and Russian scientists and savants were in increasing touch with their counterparts throughout the Western world. If the foreign names Leonhard Euler and Petr Pallas are the most celebrated, their indigenous colleagues included such worthy men as Lomonosov, whose experiments in atmospheric electricity parallelled those of Franklin,[31] the naturalists I. Lepekhin and N. Ozeretskovskii, the astronomer S. Rumovskii, the mineralogist V. Severgin and the mathematician S. Kotelnikov. A contemporary Scot wrote: 'The Russians, hitherto, have made but an inconsiderable appearance in the republic of letters; but the great encouragement given by their sovereigns of late, in the institution of academies, and other literary boards, has produced sufficient proofs, that they are in no way deficient as to intellectual abilities. The papers exhibited by them, at their academic meetings, have been favourably received all over Europe.'[32] Several academic expeditions were sent to Siberia and the Pacific during the period. Historiography was advanced by I. Boltin as well as by Shcherbatov and Karamzin. Russian artists such as F. Rokotov, D. Levitskii and V. Borikovskii produced fine portraits, while architects such as V. Bazhenov and M. Kazakov extended the Kremlin and constructed new buildings in Moscow, doing for the old capital what the Italian G. Quarenghi, the Scot C. Cameron and the Russian I. Starov did for the palaces of Petersburg.

In literature, science and art, Catherine was patron and often participant. But most of the cosmopolitan enlightenment had gone from Russian absolutism by the time of her death. Although at the beginning of her reign she had carried through the secularisation of the monastic estates, she increasingly leant on the Church as a preacher of imperial peace and cohesion. Even the toleration that she extended to Old Believers and Muslims could be the cover for their assimilation.[33] And then, under the impact of the French Revolution, both Catherine and Paul after her turned towards the conservative ideology of the nineteenth century – Orthodoxy, autocracy and nationality (i.e. Great Russian patriotism.)[34]

7 Russian Nationalism, 1801–1855

To Soviet historians, the first half of the nineteenth century marked the ripening of the crisis of the serf order. A weakening feudalism and strengthening capitalism faced each other; measures were taken to boost the old order, but the industrial revolution was nevertheless in full spring flow. Contradictions abounded. Imperial expansion was continued to shore up the weakening power of the nobility, but also served to accentuate internal social divisions through such results as the free peasant colonisation of the new regions. Moreover, the nationalities in the Empire began to get together as they carried on their mutual anti-tsarist struggle, assisted by the closer links which were now established with the people of Great Russia. Similarly, while the great victory over Napoleon in 1812 gave a great boost to nationalism and fostered the belief that the army was invincible, it also intensified the motivation of the members of the intelligentsia, particularly the Decembrists, or first revolutionaries. Increasing its influence throughout Europe and Asia, tsarism found itself helping the national-liberation movement in Germany, the Balkans and the Caucasus, and accelerating the disintegration of the outdated Turkish Empire, but also promoting reaction in the Holy Alliance. Not only the tsars found friends abroad, so did the radicals of the post-Decembrist phase such as A. I. Gertsen or Herzen and V. G. Belinskii. As a Soviet view has it: 'The role of Russia in world history grew as the elements of the revolutionary situation in it ripened. The more actively tsarism showed itself as the gendarme of Europe and its own country, the greater the international significance obtained by the liberation struggle of the Russian people and the other peoples of Russia.'[1] Even before the shocks of the 1848 revolutions and the Crimean War, the gendarme strove rigorously to censor and control the creativity of its writers and artists. Such obstacles nothwithstanding, Russia made its first outstanding contributions to modern world literature through such persons as Pushkin, Lermontov and Gogol.

To many Western historians, the principal emphasis should be given
not to the revolutionary movement which was still small, but to the
mainstream of tsarist activities which may be subsumed under the
general heading of the growth of the Russian species of that general
nineteenth-century European genus, nationalism. The distinguishing
characteristics of the species are formed during the reigns of Aleksandr
or Alexander I (1801–25) and Nikolai or Nicholas I (1825–55), both
tsars making a significant personal contribution. Catherine the Great
wanted her eldest grandson Alexander, who was born in 1777, to be
educated according to Rousseau's principles of reason and nature, and
took him away from his father Paul for the purpose, entrusting him to
a very talkative Swiss liberal named La Harpe. Combined with the
influence of this tutor and some other Russian tutors was the impact of
weekly visits to his father at Gatchina, where the atmosphere was that
of the barrack room rather than that of the classroom. Further confusion
was brought upon Alexander by his marriage at the age of fifteen to a
German princess, Louise of Baden (Elizaveta or Elizabeth as she became
called in Orthodox Russia). Since the marriage occurred at a time when
the principles inculcated into him in childhood were producing the
French Revolution, it did not make his development any easier. And
if all this was not enough to create a personality of some complexity,
the manner of his elevation to the throne, through the assassination of
his father, added yet another dimension to the enigma. To Allen Mc-
Connell, a searching Western analyst, Alexander did not want Paul
killed and felt himself betrayed by his trusted associates who carried out
the deed. And so it was partly because those who had murdered his
father favoured a constitution that Alexander rejected it. He became a
strict paternalist because he could trust neither the Russians at the top
of society nor those at the bottom of it.[2]

While Alexander had a tendency towards daydreaming, mysticism
and infatuation, Nicholas was more down to earth and practical. This
was partly because he was not at first expected to become tsar, since
another brother Konstantin or Constantine was his senior. The manner
of his accession is intimately connected with the Decembrist movement,
and will therefore be considered below. Nicholas had been born in 1796
and married to a German princess, Charlotte of Prussia, later Alek-
sandra or Alexandra after her removal to Russia. Kliuchevskii believed
that his cast of mind and the sum total of his early impressions led
Nicholas to the conviction that it was not enough to have a plan, the
plan had to be fulfilled in detail. Whereas Alexander had looked at the
state from above, Nicholas viewed it from below. He was therefore

interested in improvement rather than innovation, revision rather than reform, systematisation of laws rather than legislation.[3] Engels said that Nicholas had the outlook of a company commander, and, enlarging upon such an observation, N. M. Druzhinin has written that:

> The political wisdom of Nicholas I amounted to the ideal of an autocratic monarch, who was guided by 'the descendants of the ancient nobility' and paternally concerned himself with the welfare of his humble subjects; the army, schooled by the disciplinary cane, and the bureaucracy, fettered by the feeling of service duty, had to serve as the weapons of a powerful authority watching over the people.

Such a philosophy, points out Druzhinin, was a variation of the 'patriarchal-feudal absolutism' which Marx and Engels saw dominating Eastern Europe until the middle of the nineteenth century. To Druzhinin and his colleagues, it is more profitabe to consider Alexander in such a light rather than as the crowned Hamlet of some of the more romantic Western biographies. Like his younger brother, Alexander was a thoroughgoing autocrat and a lover of military order, a 'paradomaniac'. Both of them could therefore readily assist in the formation of that feudal-military nationalism which was to provide a rationale for tsarism down to the end of its existence.[4]

Political

At his accession, the twenty-three-year-old Alexander proclaimed that he would rule 'according to the heart and the laws' of Catherine II.[5] Since such a sentiment was vague and Alexander had no great liking for his grandmother, his policy was not immediately clear, but the frenzied activity of the first few months of his reign soon revealed its main drift. As well as liberal measures releasing from exile or jail thousands of citizens who had been arrested without trial under Paul, abolishing the Secret Chancellery and restoring the right to publish freely, Alexander's early actions also included the reaffirmation of the 1785 Charter of the Nobility. Such support for the *dvorianstvo* was to be a much more lasting theme than respect for the rights of the individual, and long before Alexander's death in 1825, arbitrary police activity and the censorship were back in full swing. In fact, the Emperor was as much an absolutist as his successor, and equally interested in the maintenance of noble support for his throne.

And so, although a Permanent Council was set up in 1801 to replace the State Council instituted by Catherine in 1769 and to discuss and confirm with the sovereign decisions regarding state affairs, it in fact enjoyed little freedom of deliberation. An attempt to restore the Senate to its previous high position ended in failure. Similarly, although the tsar's 'unofficial committee' enabled him to use much of the language he had learned from La Harpe about the rights of man, he agreed with his eloquent friends that such a step as the emancipation of the serfs must be considered only as a remote possibility. The committee dissolved in a flood of meaningless chat, and even such a measure as the 1803 law on free farmers (of which more below) arose from a private project via the Permanent Council.[6] The reactionary Arakcheev, who had begun his career under Paul, returned to a position of prominent power in the important War Ministry, and the comparatively liberal Speransky, who devised an ingenious constitution and promoted other progressive measures, incurred the enmity of the nobility and the displeasure of the tsar, and was sent into exile in 1812.

Mikhail Speranskii or Michael Speransky (the subject of a scholarly biography by Marc Raeff[7]) was the son of an ordinary village priest. His outstanding abilities secured him an early transfer from an ecclesiastical to a bureaucratic career. He then demonstrated considerable administrative talent and capacity for hard work, and by 1809 rose to become the tsar's right-hand man. He had already in 1803 produced a draft of constitutional reform during a period when the great task of law codification, which had been unsuccessfully attempted several times during the eighteenth century, was under consideration. And then in 1809, after a request from Alexander himself, he presented a general plan for constitutional reform, including the separation of powers – legislative, executive and judicial – under the Supreme Power, and the election of a State Duma. Franchise was to be restricted by a property qualification, and no provision was made for the eventual enfranchisement of the working people. In the context of its time and place, however, Speransky's plan was forward-looking, and not surprisingly it got nowhere. In the rearrangement of the central government carried out in 1810–11, there were no more than distant and distorted echoes of Speransky's proposals: a State Council, appointed by the tsar to help him with legislation and substituting for the Permanent Council of 1801; and a group of ministries, their number increased and their functions rationalised in comparison with their first arrangement in 1802, when they were first introduced to replace Catherine's colleges.

Little can confidently be said about the improvement of standards of administration resulting from the reforms of 1810–11. In conjunction with another of Speransky's brain-children – a decree of 1809 which laid down that civil service promotions above a certain rank should be by examination or through the possession of a university degree – they perhaps made for the procedural improvements noted by some pre-revolutionary constitutional historians. Certainly, they did not present such a threat to the privileges of the nobility and the prerogative of the tsar as some contemporaries believed, clamouring in their dismay for Speransky's removal. Alexander's own suspicion of Speransky grew, and he was more than ready to drop his pilot by 1812.

Meanwhile, Arakcheev was in the ascendancy. Powerful enough during the preceding years, he was in virtual control of the government from 1815 to 1825. As he himself put it, 'I am the friend of the tsar and complaints about me can be made only to God.'[8] The situation of the people was unhappier than usual after the departure from Russia of Napoleon. A. A. Bestuzhev, later active in the Decembrist Revolt, wrote at this time that: 'Negroes on the plantations are happier than many of the landlords' peasants.'[9] Disturbances were frequent if mostly local, and discontent was also to be found in the army, even in the Guards. In 1820 the Semenovskii Regiment mutinied against a cruel commander, and in the Preobrazhenskii Regiment a leaflet was circulated expressing sentiments against both the tsar and the nobility. Arakcheev's formula for the maintenance of the peace was rigid control. In 1815 a decree was issued which forbade peasants to seek their freedom, and another of 1822 assured to the landlords the right to send serfs to Siberia without trial. In 1823 the monopolistic right of the nobles to serf ownership was confirmed, and the government continued to reinforce it by the distribu-bution of land and serfs.

In more than any other measure the general tenor of Arakcheev's policy was expressed by the extension from 1816 onwards of the institu-tion of military colonies, even though the project appears to have been first conceived by Alexander rather than by his minister, who was at first opposed to it. The basic idea was to combine farming with soldier-ing in a manner that would improve the lot of the rank and file; in fact, the close supervision considered necessary made things far worse for them. To carry on agriculture by numbers and with spit and polish – as one commentator put it 'for both soldier and cow, one and the same exact schedule for their daily routine' – rendered the life of the colonists an over-regimented hell on earth.[10] By the end of Alexander's reign, there were about 375,000 unfortunates, roughly one-third of the peace-time army, in such settlements, mostly in the peripheral provinces of St Petersburg, Novgorod, Kherson and Kharkov. Worst off of all were the peasants on Arakcheev's own estate Gruzino near Novgorod, where the master required the women to produce at least one child a year each and ordered all cats to be hanged because he liked nightingales. Assessing the significance of such a system, A. P. Bazhova and A. V. Fadeev comment:

> It would be incorrect to think that the drill and the canes were the consequence of some kind of pathological cruelty of Arakcheev or some other individual military commander. No, the Arakcheev regime in the army was the expression of a definite political line, consciously created by the tsarist government with the support of the higher aristocracy and the military bureaucracy.[11]

If this was so, then something like the Decembrist Revolt was bound to happen, for those members of the nobility who had hoped that Alexander would bring reform to Russia could only become alienated from the system as a whole when they realised that his early promise was not to be fulfilled. The roots of the Decembrist movement may be traced back to the late eighteenth century, when the first noble members of the intelligentsia aspired to apply the ideas of the Enlightenment and the French Revolution (and to a lesser extent the American Revolution) to their own fatherland. Strong elements are also to be found in it of Freemasonry and mysticism, and of early nineteenth-century German idealistic philosophy and French utopian socialism. The Decembrist movement was not then apart from the mainstream of European development but very much in it; parallels are to be found in the German *Tugenbund*, the Italian *Carbonari*, and the Spanish liberal organisations.[12] These opposition groups (as well as those supporting the government) may be best seen as reflections of the age of nationalism which followed the end of the Napoleonic era in 1815. Looking back, one may see the Decembrists as the last purely noble movement and the distant heirs to D. M. Golitsyn and other projectors of the eighteenth century.

In 1816 in St Petersburg the Society of True and Faithful Sons of the Fatherland, or the Union of Salvation, was founded. Formed by Guards officers returning from abroad and other members of the nobility, the Union aimed at the emancipation of the peasants and the introduction of a constitutional monarchy. Already divisions were apparent between those who wanted a wide or narrow membership, and between those who were for moral propaganda or political, even revolutionary action.

By and large, these divisions were reflected in the two principal groups to emerge out of the ashes of the Union of Welfare, which had replaced the Union for Salvation in 1818, only to collapse itself by 1821. The Southern Society was led by Colonel Pavel (or Paul) Pestel, whose ideas were expressed in his *Russian Justice*, written between the years 1821 and 1825 as 'the obligations to be imposed upon the Provisional Government'. Pestel wanted Russia to be a unified, one-class republican state. Everybody would own a plot of land, although some land would also be retained by the state for its own support and profit. A Provisional Supreme Administration would gradually introduce a system of representative government, Pestel declaring that 'The fear that the so-called populace will shake the state if it participates in the elections is completely unnecessary and groundless.' To win over the people to their cause, an associate of Pestel's in the Southern Society produced an 'Orthodox Catechism' which included the following question and answer: 'Why are the Russian people and army unhappy? Because the Tsars robbed them of their freedom.'[13] Meanwhile, the Northern Society developed a more moderate programme, Nikita Muravev drawing up a plan for constitutional monarchy, not republicanism, for the abolition of serfdom, but no mass hand-over of land, for civil liberties and voting rights, but limited by property qualifications.

The two societies and their allies attempted to use the occasion of the sudden death of Alexander I to carry out their revolt. Tsarism itself experienced a moment's hesitation as it was not clear who would succeed to the throne; Constantine had secretly given up his right to the succession, but even Nicholas was not at first certain that the imperial inheritance was his. But the Decembrists themselves were hesitant and disorganised, and their movement soon collapsed. Five leaders were executed, and became martyrs to the revolutionary cause. The Soviet attitude is certainly that the Revolt was progressive, but that its leaders were a long way from the people. The link between the revolutionary intelligentsia and the proletariat would not be formed before 1890.[14]

With the accession of Nicholas, little change could have been expected in tsarist policy. Indeed, during the aftermath of the Decembrist Revolt, if there was any change, it was for the worse. A considerable number of peasant disturbances ensued, particularly in the Right-Bank Ukraine and central industrial provinces, and in 1826, out of 178 such incidents, 104 involved considerable numbers and 54 were put down by military force.[15] Some of the insurgents appear to have misunderstood the Decembrist Revolt, believing that it stemmed from the nobility's outrage at Constantine's wish to give the serfs freedom, and several impostors purported to be Constantine or his emissary. Being under no illusion about the implication of such developments, Nicholas moved energetically to quell them.

Trusting nobody, he tried to do everything of importance himself. He personally supervised the investigation of the Decembrists. Learning from that experience, if he was not already sufficiently aware of the fact, that some rearrangement of the Empire's affairs was long overdue, he instigated a series of political discussions among a circle of close advisers. Among the contributors was Speransky, who had returned from exile towards the end of Alexander's reign and played a leading part in the prosecution of the Decembrists. His modest ideas of representative government abandoned, Speransky now suggested that the best means of maintaining law and order was through a reinforcement of the existing class hierarchy, as well as through continued technical readjustments of the administration.

The suggestions of Speransky and his colleagues on class hierarchy were to some extent followed up. The *dvorianstvo*, which Nicholas called the first support of the throne, was shored up by making it more exclusive. A decree of 1831 disqualified those with less than five serfs or 400 acres of land from voting in the provincial assemblies, and restricted the rights of all but the top members of the class. From 1845 onwards, hereditary nobility was to be reserved for army staff officers and civil officials in the highest five ranks, and prominent noble families were again encouraged to entail their estates. In 1832 a rank of 'honorary citizen' was introduced to help keep the *dvorianstvo* free from bourgeois infiltration and to boost the official middle class. A further move in this direction was the decree of 1846 on the government of St Petersburg, with the top stratum of town society being reserved for hereditary nobles, and the second being composed of personal nobles (or life peers) and 'honorary citizens'.

As far as technical readjustments of the administration were concerned, Speransky was still keen on the division, if not of powers, then at least of functions. He wanted the State Council to concentrate on legislation and the Senate on executive and judicial business, while a comparable arrangement was to be worked out for the lower echelons of government, where there were also to be a certain number of elective officials. Almost nothing came of these proposals, but Speransky was able to find an outlet for his talents and energy in an enterprise that amounted to something more than technical readjustment, the collection and codification of the laws. It will be remembered that such a task had defeated several commissions and committees in the eighteenth and early nineteenth centuries, and that the Code of 1649 was still in whatever operation a law code could be in such a lawless society. In 1833 Speransky and his aides produced fifty-one volumes of the *Complete Collection of Laws of the Russian Empire* – in fact not quite complete, and fifteen volumes of a systematic *Code of Laws of the Russian Empire* – supposedly of those still in operation. This work was followed by the promulgation of a new Criminal Code in 1845, and the extension through the early 1840s of the Russian Code to the Polish, White Russian and Ukrainian provinces of the west and south-west.

Changes in the official governmental structure and judicial framework meant less than usual during the reign of Nicholas since his rule was so personal. This did not mean that he could dispense with the traditional bureaucracy which was becoming more of a self-perpetuating professional caste during the first half of the nineteenth century, with its upper echelons firmly ensconced in the nobility. But the regular processes of the bureaucracy were cumbersome and corrupt, as Hans-Joachim Törke has made clear.[16] And so the most important day-to-day work of administering the Empire was done not by the State Council or Senate but by His Majesty's Own Chancery, an all-pervasive web, stretching out to envelop all His Majesty' subjects. Chief spider was at first General Benckendorff, in charge of the Chancery's notorious Third Section. Supposedly dealing with important police matters, the Third Section under Benckendorff interpreted its brief broadly to include everything under the sun and moon, and the general himself was more than a prime minister, although keeping himself in the background. With Nicholas taking a close personal interest in the Section's activities, it sweated to amass a vast heap of paper for his scrutiny. More sinisterly, it also produced for him a considerable amount of his often innocent subjects' tears and blood.[17]

Although Benckendorff's gendarme looked for trouble where there was none and often found it, they also had plenty of real trouble to busy themselves with. At least 400 disturbances occurred among the peasants during each five-year period following 1826, and from 1844 to 1849 the number rose to 605. None of these was on a large scale, but accompanied by mass flight to the frontier and other forms of passive resistance, they were enough to alarm the tsar and his associates. Nor was Russia's growing industry without its problems. Recognising these, the government issued in 1835 a decree to regulate relations between workers and their employers, and another in 1845 sought to restrict the night work of minors. Such paternalistic gestures did little to improve the conditions of the factory labourers, who sought to redress their grievances by collective complaint, mass refusal to work, insubordination and violence.

During and after an incident at a metalworks in the Urals in 1841, 33 people were killed, 50 heavily wounded and 300 corporally punished. Such an event was rare, and yet N. M. Druzhinin declares that 'the disturbances of the workers of Russia achieved the significance of a serious social factor, undermining the bases of feudal-serf relations and simultaneously creating conditions for the class struggle of the industrial proletariat against the capitalists which developed after the abolition of serfdom.'[18]

Of further concern to Russia's gendarmerie was the circumstance that its most busy periods of activity tended to coincide with those of its brother organisations abroad, in 1830–31 and 1848–9. True, domestic circumstances such as harvest failure and cholera were of importance at these critical times, and so was the nature of serfdom, but the international revolutionary movement was a cause of at least as much concern, and possibly more. The tsar himself wrote the famous manifesto of 14–26 March 1848, in which he lamented that rebellion and lawlessness were rampant in Prussia and Austria and menacing 'our holy Russia'. He summoned the people to arouse themselves for 'faith, tsar and country', assuring them that God was with them. An army of 400,000 was drawn up at the borders, and Nicholas intended to march it to the Rhine, a move which would no doubt have alarmed the monarchs of Europe more than the words and actions of their domestic revolutionaries. Nicholas contented himself with acceptance of an Austrian invitation to help suppress the nationalist Kossuth and his followers in Hungary.[19] The success of this measure in 1849 no doubt enabled Nicholas to breathe more easily, at least for a short time. No doubt too, some of the forces that had been unleashed in 1848 and described by Marx and Engels in their *Communist Manifesto* were beyond his comprehension. To the last, nevertheless, he worked at his command, hoping to make his garrison state impregnable against threats both domestic and foreign.

For such a purpose he needed an efficient army, and personally spent much time and effort trying to drill his forces into the proper shape. Unfortunately for him, the commanders he chose to help him in his task were nonentities. More fundamentally, Russia's social system was inadaquate for the provision of an army fit to fight the battles of the nineteenth century. Among the insoluble problems was that of providing an adequate reserve in conditions of serfdom. Although the military colonies lingered on until 1857, Nicholas himself admitted right at the beginning of his reign after a tour of them that they presented 'a most distressing picture', and that they could not fulfil the purpose for which they had been set up. On the other hand, a serf who entered the army became a free man, and so universal service would have completely upset the social system. Even the reduction of the length of service from twenty-five to fifteen years was anathema to many landowners and officers from the nobility. A general referred to by Curtiss feared that the result would be that the Russian villages would be 'filled with people without work and without means for livelihood, from which we may expect great disorders'.[20]

All such problems notwithstanding, a large army was kept up throughout the first half of the nineteenth century not only to counter subversive influences at home and abroad, but also to extend the peripheral regions of the Empire and to keep them quiet, as well as playing its more normal part in international war. Finland was taken in 1809 after war with Sweden, and then given some autonomy as a grand duchy. Georgia was finally incorporated into the Empire in the first decade of the century, much to the annoyance of the Persians and the Turks, with both of whom war broke out. As a consequence, Russia made further gains in the Transcaucasian regions of Azerbaidzhan and Armenia, and at the west end of the Black Sea – first Bessarabia and later Moldavia and Wallachia. In the twenties, thirties and forties, the tsarist forces moved into Central Asia, beginning to encounter the British thrust up from India. For Soviet historians, the Russian assimilation of the Middle East and Central Asia saved the local peoples from feudal disunity and dismemberment at the predatory hands of Turkey and Persia. Economic and cultural benefits accrued, too, although these were restricted by the nature of the tsarist establishment.[21] At the same time, Siberia was infiltrated further and the island of Sakhalin off its Pacific coast was gradually acquired. Reforms of the Siberian government in 1822 and 1827 improved its administration and the arrangements for collecting taxes there. Russian settlers increased in number, but were still very few for such a huge area.[22]

While Siberia posed few problems to the maintenance of good order, other peripheral regions were seldom trouble-free, by no means all of their inhabitants believing in the benefits of imperial incorporation. The tribesmen of Central Asia were seldom completely at peace, and Muslim resistance in the Caucasus led by the legendary Imam Shamil did not die out until the early 1860s. In Belorussia and the Ukraine there were peasant disturbances in the twenties and thirties, and similar outbreaks occurred in the Baltic provinces in the early forties. An intellectual nationalist movement in the Ukraine centred round the Kiev Brotherhood of Cyril and Methodius caused alarm in the later forties and several of its more radical leaders, including the artist and poet Shevchenko,

were arrested and punished. The biggest single source of trouble, however, was Poland, which rose against Russian domination in 1830 only
to find itself made 'an indivisible part' of the Empire in 1832 after the
uprising had been crushed.[23] Russification was applied here as elsewhere through such agencies as the Russian language and the Orthodox
Church.

Poland was of capital importance to tsarism as a barrier against the
potentially hostile powers of central and western Europe. The retention
of its loyalty was therefore a necessary aim in the conduct of foreign
policy, as was the satisfactory settlement of what came to be known as
the Eastern Question. During the reigns of Alexander I and Nicholas I,
the central events were the great triumph of the defeat of Napoleon and
the great disaster of the failure to win the Crimean War.

War with France appeared remote when Alexander and Napoleon
made their unexpected accommodation at Tilsit in 1807, but the agreement was not popular with the Russian nobility, who saw in Napoleon
the child of the French Revolution and a threat to the existence of serfdom. Merchants and nobles were worried by the adherence of Russia to
the French Continental System, which crippled international trade and
thus curtailed their grain exports. Influential members of society wanted
to retain Poland and acquire the Dardanelles. Napoleon, for his part,
recognised the vital importance of both Poland and the Dardanelles as
well as understanding that the Continental System had to be enforced if
his plans for the domination of Europe were to succeed.[24] He believed
that he would achieve mastery of the universe if he could defeat Russia
in one good battle. His chance came at Borodino, after the Russians
had avoided head-on collision following earlier disasters.

Just as it would be wrong to ascribe the beginning of the War of 1812
to the personal rivalry of the French and Russian Emperors, so it would
be over-simplifying the battle of Borodino to see it as a showdown between Napoleon and Kutuzov. Even the cool strategical account of
Clausewitz declares that: 'Kutuzov, it is certain, would not have fought
at Borodino where he obviously did not expect to win. But the voice of
the Court, of the Army, of all Russia, forced his hand.'[25] The truth of
this statement may be seen reflected in the size of the casualties at
Borodino, both the French and their allies on the one hand and the
Russians on the other losing more than 50,000 killed and wounded. The
same kind of spirit of national resistance saw Russia through the evacuation of Moscow and the burning of the capital, which were carried out
with the connivance, even the encouragement of the governor, Count
Rostopchin. And when Napoleon and his forces set out on the long

retreat they were harried not only by the weather but by the Russian regular forces and by partisans. The fears of the nobility that the serfs would be enticed by French offers of emancipation turned out to be false. Undoubtedly, the War of 1812 was a great patriotic war, even though it is sometimes still celebrated in too intoxicated a fashion by Soviet historians, as Barry Hollingsworth has shown.[26]

The defeat of Napoleon and the arrival of Russian troops in Paris made Alexander one of the principal arbiters of Europe at the Congress of Vienna. Under the mystical banner of his Holy Alliance, his chief minister Count Nesselrode strove to protect the interests of Russia in particular and of absolutism in general.[27] On the whole this was not a great problem, although there were points of tension between the Russians and their fellow-absolutists, the Austrians, guided by Metternich. The most tricky question arose when the Greek War of Independence broke out in the early 1820s. If Alexander followed his religious affiliation, he would support the Greeks, but this would weaken the Turks and upset the Balkan equilibrium, at the same time alarming the Austrians and others with the threat of the expansion of Russian infiltration into the area.

Alexander's death in 1825 occurred at a time when the Eastern Question was no more than posed for Russia and the other powers. Nicholas had to attempt to solve it in the least painful manner possible, with the continued dutiful assistance of Nesselrode. He took a more positive interest in Greece than had his brother, partly through fear that the British would become the major influence in the region if the Russians did not. In 1827, a combined Anglo-Franco-Russian naval force destroyed a Turkish fleet at Navarino off the Greek coast. This led Russia into a war with Turkey, which lasted from 1828 to 1829 and enabled Nicholas by the Treaty of Adrianople to acquire the mouth of the Danube and further influence in its hinterland, as well as passage for Russian merchant ships through the Dardanelles. But Turkey's loss was not completely to Russia's advantage, for Egypt now followed Greece in seeking its independence, and the problem of the 'sick bear' of Europe as Nicholas called it arose in threatening clarity. The Treaty of Unkiar-Skelessi of 1833 sealed the friendship of Turkey and Russia, but the other great powers were suspicious, and the Treaty of London of 1840 and the Straits Convention of 1841 brought Britain, France, Prussia and Austria together with Russia to protect the Dardanelles. It was from this situation that the Crimean War arose.

To describe in all their complexity the negotiations and the misunderstandings leading up to that fateful war would be an impossible task here, although it would be wrong to accept without qualification the assertion of a Soviet textbook by N. S. Kiniapina that: 'The Crimean War was brought about by the aggravation of class conflicts inside European states and the intensification of the struggle for external markets, linked with the development of capitalism.'[28] All we can say here is that the personality weaknesses of such people as Nicholas I and Palmerston certainly played their part as immediate reasons for the outbreak of hostilities, and that such underlying circumstances as the British desire for a protected route to India and the Russian wish for an outlet for her grain were important too.

The war itself was as full of error as the period leading up to it. 'Folly and blunder' was by no means the monopoly of the British Light Brigade. Although the Russian defence of Sevastopol moved an artillery officer there named Leo Tolstoy to write about 'The Sevastopol epic, the hero of which was the Russian people',[29] the Russian troops found themselves armed with smooth-bore muskets while their enemies had rifles, and the Russian sailing ships confronted hostile steamers. Railway and other communications were so poor that the home forces were at least as badly supplied as the foreign invaders. And so the Crimean War revealed to an ailing Nicholas I that his reign was ending in failure and probably accelerated his death. Alexander II came to the throne with the immediate necessity of accepting the humiliating Treaty of Paris (1856) by which Russia was forced to withdraw from the mouth of tne Danube, to cease to protect the Orthodox under Turkish rule, and even to give up its fleet and fortresses on the Black Sea. For the next fifteen years or so, Russia aimed at the revision of the Treaty of Paris.[30] The failures of the war also impressed upon Alexander II the necessity of introducing long-overdue reforms into the Russian Empire itself.

Economic

From the economic point of view, the first half of the nineteenth century may be looked upon in two principal ways. On the one hand, this is the period when, slowed down by such institutional features as serfdom and such environmental features as the maldistribution of natural resources, one of the leading powers of the late eighteenth century fell behind the growth rate of most of its European neighbours. On the other hand, in some senses one may agree with William L. Blackwell that, to quote the title and major theme of his impressive book, the period marked *The Beginnings of Russian Industrialization*. As Blackwell says, 'Many economists have noted that periods of quick and massive industrial development are usually preceded by longer periods of preparation, of slower, less dynamic, less comprehensive change.'[31] Certainly, some adaptation was necessary before the great spurt ahead could take place towards the end of the nineteenth century. In the all-important iron industry, for example, the Russia which had led the world when smelting was performed with the aid of charcoal had to lose its primacy before it could start to catch up again making use of coking coal.

Most Western and Soviet analysts would also agree that it was necessary for serfdom to be undermined before a properly modernised economy could start to grow. However, a minority group of Western historians imply that servile labour was not necessarily a serious deterrent to industrialisation, and that the institutional reason for the slow progress of the reigns of Alexander I and Nicholas I is therefore principally to be found in government policy, which tended to be based on the idea of Russia's national apartness based on peasant agriculture.

Certainly, there was no shortage of peasants, as the population continued to rise with the proportions remaining much as before. From a total of 37·5 millions in 1795, the population climbed to 61·5 millions in 1838 and 69 millions in 1851. The greatest areas of growth were the central agricultural region, New Russia and the Lower Volga to the south and the Northern and Southern Urals to the east, but nowhere was there not an increase of some kind. The peasants in private hands numbered more than 22 millions by the middle of the century and those under state control more than 20 millions. Crown peasants accounted for 1·5 millions and free peasants less than 0·5 million. The urban population was well above 5 millions and approached 10 per cent of the total. St Petersburg topped the half million mark and Moscow approached it, with Odessa, Kishinev, Saratov and Riga a long way behind in that order. Registered urban categories amounted to something over 3·5 millions, and the balance of the urban population would be made up of itinerant peasants and the nobles, clergymen and other non-taxable citizens who also went to make up the balance of the population as a whole. Broadly speaking, Russians were almost twice as numerous as Frenchmen and thrice as numerous as the British and Americans. At the same time, while about 55 per cent of Frenchmen, 22 per cent of the British and 65 per cent of Americans were engaged in agriculture, the equivalent Russian figure approached 90 per cent.

Russian labour was generally more extensive than that of other nations, and the pressures for its more frugal exploitation would not be felt nearly as strongly as in, say, Britain. Nevertheless, the arrival of the new order was signalled by an increasing realisation of the market possibilities of agriculture and by the expansion of industry to the point of a thorough-going industrial revolution. Landlords, to take them first, were attracted by the trade in grain for internal and external consumption. There were many more mouths to feed in the Empire, particularly in the towns. The demand from abroad increased in size, especially from Britain after the repeal of the Corn Laws in 1846. The average annual export of grain rose, not without considerable fluctuations, from about 325,000 metric tons at the beginning of the 1830s to nearly 1,140,000 metric tons by the end of the 1850s, when it amounted to almost a tenth of total production and a third of all exports. Ports such as St Petersburg, Riga and Odessa flourished, agricultural societies expanded and exhibitions were held. New implements were put to use, if not enough, and the cultivation spread of non-traditional crops such as sugar beet, tobacco and potatoes, if slowly. An important social reflection of these changes was that in the mid-fifties in 33 provinces there were 270,000 landowners among the state peasants farming a total of a million or so hectares (about 3 million acres), and in the same decade there were 300,000 peasants for hire in the Southern Ukraine, 150,000 in the Volga region, 120,000 in the Baltic provinces and up to 150,000 elsewhere. Most peasants would still be in the middle category, tending towards neither bourgeoisie nor proletariat, but this majority would not be completely untouched by the sturdy growth of the money economy, even when they were still enserfed, mostly farming by traditional methods or increasingly subject to *barshchina* services. The resultant contradictions led to a real crisis of the old order, even if it did not yet approach revolutionary intensity.

Agricultural progress would probably have been most noticeable near the Baltic and in the Ukraine, around Moscow and St Petersburg. These also were the centres of the industrial revolution, indicated by a threefold increase in the number of both enterprises and workers between the mid-twenties and late fifties. In 1825, according to one scale of measurement, there were some 5000 units of production with a total work force of about 200,000; by 1860, these figures had risen to about 15,000 and more than 550,000 respectively. During the same period, the production of cast-iron nearly doubled to reach a total of over a quarter of a million tons. The relative backwardness of Russia's iron industry by this time is reflected in the calculation that while Britain produced nearly 140 kilograms of iron per head and Belgium something over 70 kilograms, the Empire managed a *per capita* rate of hardly more than 4 kilograms. The iron industry was still largely based on the Urals and serf labour, although by 1860 about a fifth of the workers were hired. Four-fifths was the equivalent proportion in light manufacturing, which was situated in the regions listed above and consisted primarily of textiles, although sugar and vodka were also important items of production. The captains of Russia's growing industry were mainly from the middle class, but included many nobles and some rich peasants. The most forward-looking among them were becoming aware of the advantages of mechanisation.

Mechanisation was creeping into transport and communications too; with some reluctant help being given by the government, there were in existence by the end of the reign of Nicholas more than 5000 kilometres of highway and 1500 kilometres of railroad. The tsar himself was something of a supporter of the iron horse, deciding that the prosperity of his subjects would gain most from it if the first line were constructed from St Petersburg to his palace at Tsarskoe Selo. This was finished by 1837, and the next line, from St Petersburg to Moscow, was completed in 1851. According to unsubstantiated anecdote, Nicholas took a hand in this line as well, fixing its route with a bold stroke on the map. Some of his advisers were less enthusiastic railwaymen, one of them, Kankrin, arguing that trains endangered 'public morals' through their encourage-ment of 'the restless spirit of our age'. Later lines from Warsaw to Vienna and Warsaw to St Petersburg were begun largely for reasons of security and strategy. State support was useful in the necessary collection of large amounts of capital, and foreigners contributed not only some of the money but not a little of the engineering skill. River transport was improved during the period; by 1860 there were about 400 steamboats in the Empire, mostly on the Volga.

The growing land and water network assisted the expansion of domestic trade, which rose to a value of about 900 million roubles by the end of the period. Only 10 per cent was in manufactured goods, the main items being grain, foodstuffs, lumber and cattle. In the mid-forties, Russia's external trade was about one quarter the size of the domestic, the Empire occupying sixth place among the trading nations of the world. Grain was still the most important export, followed by hemp and animal fats; cotton thread and dyes were the most important imports, followed by luxury goods and footstuffs. While tariffs were high, pro-hibitions and restrictions were gradually lifted, and Russia became more involved in the commerce of the world, principally with Britain and the continent of Europe, but also with Asia and the U.S.A.

Generally speaking, the attitude of the government to the changes that were going on was one of reluctant adaptation rather than of enthusiastic promotion. Such an attitude was personified by Count

Kankrin, who believed above all in a stable fiscal situation.[32] Hence, little money was spent on the advancement of agriculture or industry, while very much, as always, was spent on the army and navy, the bureaucracy and the court. The financial reform of 1839–43, which reduced the influence of paper money and phased out the assignats which had been introduced by Catherine II, helped to achieve the desired balance. Financial policy as a whole, however, was strained by the necessity of aiding the nobility, which had mortgaged two-thirds of its serfs for 425 million silver roubles by 1859.

This central problem of serfdom was only partly tackled by a series of measures ranging from the free farmer law of 1803 to the measures associated with the name of Kiselev. The law of 1803 allowed landlords to make arrangements for the liberation of individual serfs, but very little use was made of it. Between 1816 and 1819, peasants in the Baltic provinces were emancipated, but without land. General P. D. Kiselev, in charge of a new Ministry of State Lands from 1837 onwards, attempted to give the state peasants a reasonable amount of land and to protect them with a far-reaching welfare scheme, but he allowed them very little initiative or freedom of movement. Much of the scheme remained on paper, as did the decree of 1842 on 'obligated' peasants, which bore some resemblance to the decree of 1803. For all their ineffectiveness, or restricted application such pieces of legislation were looked upon by many landlords as writing on the wall of great danger to their continued possession of the serfs.[33]

Cultural

The first half of the nineteenth century is a period of considerable progress in the development of Russian culture, but also of deep contradictions. Thus, there was a numerical expansion in education and great achievement at the highest academic level, but attended by too little financial support and too much bureaucratic control. Russian literature experienced its golden age and Russian music first began to make an international impact, but in conditions of harsh censorship and restriction. Revolutionary ideology came nearer to formation with the emergence of socialism, but tsarism also developed the political philosophy that was to see it through to the end of its existence, continuing to make great use of Orthodoxy.

To consider each of these cultural spheres in turn, we begin with the question of the schools. At the end of the eighteenth century, it will be recalled, there were about 60,000 students; by 1856 the total had grown to nearly 400,000. Just after the beginning of the reign of Alexander I, a Ministry of Education was set up in 1802, and soon announced plans in 1803 for a network of universities, and schools at the provincial, county and parish level throughout a Russia divided into six regions. Three new universities were necessary to supplement those developing on old foundations, a Russian in Moscow, a Polish in Vilno and a German in Dorpat. Universities were duly founded in Kazan, Kharkov and St Petersburg, the last named starting its new life as a teachers' training college. The universities were theoretically autonomous, but in fact increasingly brought under governmental control to make sure that bad ideas, particularly political, were not fostered and that good ideas, particularly religious, were. Many of the professors were foreign and lectured in Latin, which many of their students could not properly understand. By the end of the reign there were 1700 university students in the Empire proper (that is excluding Poland and Finland), nearly half of them at Moscow. A large proportion of the graduates probably went into the civil service, encouraged by the decree of 1809 which offered regular promotion prospects to entrants with a university degree. The grand total for state education by the end of the reign was 2118 institutions with 263,223 students, the military schools accounting for over 100,000 of them and the rest shared by schools under the Ministry of Education (or Public Instruction as it was officially called) and special and technical schools. As before, many of the nobles would go to private schools or be educated by tutors, and various commoners would learn in an informal manner at least to read and write.

The restrictions on education introduced towards the end of the reign of Alexander I were extended during that of Nicholas I, both in theory and in practice. Whereas the reform of 1803 aimed at the progress of the individual student throughout the hierarchy from parish school to university, at least in theory, each type of school was now specifically aimed at the satisfaction of the needs of that social group from which it expected to attract most of its students. Decrees of 1828 and 1835 spelled out the new theoretical approach in some detail. Among other reforms, streaming was introduced into the provincial schools or gymnasia, with those intending to go on to university being given a strong dose of classical languages. The administration of the schools was adapted to their new separation. Numerically, there was growth in the second quarter of the nineteenth century as there had been in the first quarter. The university population increased to 3659 by 1855, that of state schools in general to about 400,000. Moreover, in Riasanovsky's considered view, 'the government of Nicholas I made some significant contributions to the development of education in Russia'. Count S. S. Uvarov, Minister of Education from 1833 to 1849 and coiner of Russian nationalism's slogan 'Orthodoxy, autocracy and nationality', applied himself energetically to this task.[34]

Not only this, at the highest level Russian academic life was producing scholars of world stature. Outstanding among these was the mathematician N. I. Lobachevskii, who taught mathematics at the University of Kazan and who devised a non-Euclidean geometry. Moreover, according to Smirnov:

> In physics, especially electricity, some important discoveries were made – Vasilii Petrov (the electric arc and electrolysis) and Emilii Lentz (conversion of heat into electric power). Russia was also well to the fore in chemistry and biology – N. Zinin obtained aniline dye from benzole; K. Behr and K. Ruye stipulated the evolutionary development of the animal kingdom before Darwin's works were published.[35]

R. E. McGrew tells us that one fortunate result of the great cholera outbreaks was an advance in medical training.[36]

However, in case this is presenting too bright a picture of Russian education and its achievements, we should remember that the schools cultivated monarchist and religious ideas. 'The schools are crushed by supervisors and priests', Herzen complained. The University Charter of 1835 was an attempt to institute military discipline into the universities; a similar system was introduced into the newly founded railway and forestry institutes. Half-educated generals were appointed as supervisors of schools districts. 'I do not need educated people, I need loyal subjects', Nicholas I is reputed to have said. Benckendorff, the head of the Third Section, wrote that 'there must not be too much of a hurry with enlightenment, lest the people come to the level of understanding of monarchs and thus encroach upon their power'. Because of the dangers inherent in the subjects, the teaching of philosophy, natural law and political economy in the universities was brought to a halt.[37]

So it was also in literature, which experienced a golden age in spite of the clumsy censorship and foolish restrictions. (One censor said that, according to the law of 1826, the Lord's prayer would be under suspicion as a revolutionary document.) While the most familiar names internationally speaking are Pushkin, Lermontov and Gogol, others such as Griboedov and Krylov are among the great figures of literature to Russians and quotations from them are household sayings in the Soviet

Union. And then there is a whole host of writers at least known to most Russians who have never even been heard of by Western students of literature. This would be even more the case with the national bards and story-tellers of the non-Russian-speaking regions, who will be completely unsung and unrelated here.

Even the great giant of the first half of the nineteenth century, Alexander Pushkin, has diminished in stature somewhat when exported. This is partly because of the cultural egocentricity of other nations, partly because the poetry which forms such a significant amount of his work does not translate at all easily. Marshak had done something creative with Burns, and Pasternak with Shakespeare, but no Western poet has really got to grips with Pushkin. Vladimir Nabokov has made one of the bravest of attempts with his rendering of *Evgenii Onegin*. Through the international language of music, foreigners have been able to achieve some sort of an appreciation not only of the narrative verse of *Evgenii Onegin* and the evocative prose of the short story of *Queen of Spades* in the operas of Tchaikovsky, but also of the poetic drama *Boris Godunov* in the opera of Mussorgsky. Whether applying himself to great historical and philosophical themes as in the long poems *Poltava* and *The Bronze Horseman*, or revealing a more private world in his love lyrics, Pushkin exerts great power through his complete use of the inflexions and nuances of the language which he brought to a new peak of expression.

Like Pushkin, Mikhail Lermontov excelled in prose and poetry as well as, like him, being killed in a duel. His most accessible work is probably the short novel *A Hero of Our Time*, which some critics consider to be a better social and individual analysis than Pushkin's *The Captain's Daughter*. To call Lermontov as many have done 'the Russian Byron' is probably either to elevate Byron or demean Lermontov in the appraisal of readers of the English language, but there is no doubt a lowering spirit of romantic doom in his tales as well as his poems. He was also capable of a penetrating directness and simplicity; since he was only twenty-six at the time of his death, however, his development was cut short before it could take him towards a more mature realism.

Nikolai Gogol breaks through the language barrier best, even though his Russian is more difficult to read than that of Pushkin or Lermontov. His satirical play, *The Inspector General*, has often been successfully done on the Western stage and even been made into an entertaining Hollywood film with Danny Kaye, himself of Russian descent, as the hero, a simpleton mistaken for a government inspector in a remote provincial town. And the novel *Dead Souls*, which tells of the purchase of the records of dead serfs to be used as surety for a mortgage, has caught the attention of many foreign readers who do not begin to understand the legal complexities of the story, but who immediately appreciate the grotesque denizens of remoter parts of European Russia so well etched by Gogol. To communicate his living power to Soviet citizens today, one need only refer to items in the Soviet press referring to latter-day recreations of Gogol's classic situations in a railway buffet, where a bewildered traveller was given the red-carpet, several-course treatment laid on for a visiting inspector, and on a Moscow construction project, where an enterprising 'foreman' managed to draw the wages for a non-existent shift. (This is not to say that today's Russia is like that of Nicholas I, any more than today's United States is like that of President Polk.) Other works of great interest by Gogol include *Taras Bulba* about the Ukrainian Cossacks, and a number of short stories of which the most important is *The Overcoat*, which tells of an obscure government clerk's shattered dreams and which was considered by Dostoevsky to be the source of all later Russian fiction.

Griboedov's play *Woe from Wit*, a social satire, became a standard part of the Russian classical repertory, Krylov wrote colourful fables full of homely wisdom, and writers such as Zhukovskii, the romantic poet, are among many of whom much could be said. There is no such problem with contemporary exponents of the pictorial and plastic arts, who do not appear to merit much discussion, for most of the exhortations and attempts to found a national style produced either a stilted mock-heroism or a cumbersome monumentality. But there were individual fine buildings such as the Admiralty in St Petersburg by A. Zakharov and a few excellent paintings such as *The Last Day of Pompeii* by Karl Büllow. In music, however, the distinctive voice of Russia was widely heard in a formal structure for the first time. The great name is Mikhail or Michael Glinka, whose *Ivan Susanin* (renamed *A Life for the Tsar* at the censor's request) founded the national school of Russian operas and whose musical adaptation of Pushkin's *Ruslan and Liudmila* inaugurated a long line of operas based on rustic magical tales. His arrangement of folk tunes is best typified by his symphonic piece *Kamarinskaia*, which might be said to do for Russian music what Gogol's *The Overcoat* did for Russian literature; indeed, Tchaikovsky called it the acorn from which the oak of Russian music grew. Aleksandr Dargomyzhskii (Dargomyzhsky) also made use of popular themes in his operas, and attempted to put stress on words as well as music. Mussorgsky called him 'a great teacher of musical truth'.

By the end of the reign of Nicholas I, without much positive contribution by him or his elder brother, a Russian national style had asserted itself in literature and the arts. All kinds of cultural cross-currents moved across Europe and Asia in a complex manner which it would take a multilingual critic of uncanny perception to describe properly. All that can be said here with confidence is that at the beginning of its golden age, Russian culture was giving as good as it got, so to speak, and had arrived at a new level of maturity.

A problem of comparable complexity faces us as we move on to consider the third theme of this section, the ideological developments of the first half of the nineteenth century. Again we are confronted with elusive questions of originality and borrowing of ideas, of the main flow of concepts across continents finding their concrete expression within the national context. Broadly speaking, it may be said that the period before the death of Alexander I in 1825 was the seedtime, and the period after it contained the flowering. This change of season was undoubtedly affected by domestic developments, but was also intimately connected with events abroad such as the revolutionary outbreaks of 1830–1 and 1848–9.

Much of the thought of the preparatory period is connected with the Decembrists, and the gap between them and Radishchev was bridged in an undistinguished manner which was at least partly the result of the preoccupation of many thinking people with the impact of Napoleon. After the Decembrists, whom we have discussed above, radical thought was kept alive by various circles formed mainly at the universities of Moscow and St Petersburg. The students attempted little action, but talked at great length under the influence of German idealistic philosophers from Schelling to Hegel and French utopian socialists from Saint-Simon to Louis Blanc. It was from these circles that the principal radical figures of the thirties and forties sprang, notably Alexander Herzen (Aleksandr Gertsen) and Vissarion Belinskii. Herzen was sent into exile after graduation, Belinskii sent down before graduation. Herzen left Russia, while Belinskii stayed at home. Herzen is best remembered for his autobiography *My Past and Thoughts* and for his editorship of the *émigré* journal *The Bell*, while the best-known example of Belinskii's wide-ranging critical journalism is his denunciatory letter to Gogol, lamenting the conversion of a realistic writer to religious conformity. Herzen, like his associate N. P. Ogarev, came from the nobility; Belinskii is one of the first radicals to spring from the *raznochintsy* or third element, the commoners of the intelligentsia.[38] While their origins and careers are somewhat different, Soviet observers put them together as socialists who were non-scientific, although they were familiar with

Marx's earlier writings. They did not appreciate the part that would have to be played by the urban proletariat, and believed that the main force for change in Russia would be the peasant commune. Nevertheless, they realised the importance of the class struggle and saw the necessity of revolution. Such extremism separated them from the liberal group broadly known as the Westerners, who placed their emphasis on constitutional government and peaceful development towards capitalism. An eccentric version of the negative part of their argument was put by Petr Chaadaev, who saw the root of Russia's predicament in its reception of the cultural influence of 'decadent Byzantium'. Further to the right were the Slavophiles, whose doctrine was a strange mixture of progressive and reactionary ideas. In favour of the gradual emancipation of the serfs, they also extolled the virtues of the village commune. In favour of free speech and the re-assembly of the *Zemskii Sobor*, they also gloried in the apartness of Russian history, in Orthodoxy, autocracy and nationality, if by no means in the same way as Uvarov and the 'official nationalist' apologists for Nicholas I. They often incurred the displeasure of the censor and the police, and have been praised by E. L. Rudnitskaia for their 'great and fruitful work' on 'the Russian national culture, way of life and creativity of the people' which 'objectively encouraged the growth of the democratic tendency in the development of cultural life'.[39]

The 1848 revolutions brought a new intensification of the development of the revolutionary movement. Fifteen members of a discussion circle, the Petrashevsky group (which included Dostoevsky) were condemned to death for nothing more than 'a conspiracy of ideas'. Although these sentences were commuted at the last moment, the gendarmes were obviously becoming more alarmed. Even Uvarov, who had contributed so much to the formation of the ideology of Russian nationalism, found it necessary to resign in protest at their excesses.

8 The Emancipation, and After, 1855–1894

On 19 February 1861 the emancipation of the serfs was announced. In common with their fellows throughout Russia, the peasants of the Spassk region not far from Kazan looked for somebody to interpret the manifesto for them. In the nearby village of Bezdna, they found Anton Petrov, a barely literate Old Believer. According to his own account, Petrov mysteriously misinterpreted the figure '0.0.' to mean that freedom had been given to everybody, and then fabricated further details in order 'to attract the peasants to my side, reasoning that the more peasants there were, the sooner I should gain freedom'. He told them that the landlords would retain only one-third of the land, that they themselves would no longer have to give labour services or money payments. Petrov's imagination fired his oratory, as may be seen in the following report of one of his speeches:

> You will have true liberty only if you defend the man who finds it for you. . . . Young men and old will come to you; do not let them reach me; do not hand me over to them. They will cheat you by saying that they have come from the Tsar; do not believe them. The old men will come with smiles; middle-aged men will come; both bald and hairy men will come; and every kind of official; but you must not hand me over. And in due time, a young man will come here sent by the Tsar. He will be seventeen years old, and on his right shoulder he will have a gold medal and on his left shoulder a silver one. Believe him, and hand me over to him. They will threaten you with soldiers, but do not be afraid; no one will dare to beat the Russian, Christian people without orders from the Tsar. And if the nobles buy them, and they fire at you, then destroy with your axes these rebels against the will of the Tsar.[1]

Such eloquence did much to build up a movement around him, but could do little to protect him when the troops did come. After the revolt at Bezdna was put down, Petrov was tried by a military tribunal and then shot. But his name lived on, and legends grew up about him among the peasants to such an extent that the nobles of Kazan feared a new Pugachev. Herzen described the revolt fully in *The Bell*, and A. P. Shchapov, Professor of Russian History at Kazan University made a speech about it at the requiem mass organised by the students of the University and the Theological Academy. Addressing those who had fallen, Shchapov declared:

> Friends killed for the people. . . . In Russia for about a hundred and fifty years there have begun to appear among the bitterly suffering dark masses of the people, among you, peasants, your own Christs – the democratic conspirators. From the middle of the last century they have been considered prophets, and the people has believed in them as atoners, emancipators. Here again has been such an atone-ment, and you friends are the first to fall at its summons as sacrifices to despotism expiating the freedom long expected by the whole people. You are the first to destroy our sleep, you have destroyed by your initiative our unjust doubt about our people not being capable of initiative in political movements. . . . The land, which you worked, with the fruits of which you have fed us, which now you wanted to obtain as your property and which has accepted you as its martyrs into its bowels – this land summons the People to revolt and freedom. . . . Peace to your dust and eternal historical remembrance to your self-sacrificing deed. Long live the democratic constitution.[2]

Shchapov's speech may be looked upon as one of the first steps towards the foundation of the populist movement which was to prosper for most of the rest of the reign of Alexander II, and then to split up after his assassination in 1881 in two principal directions, towards liberalism on the one hand and Marxism on the other. About the time of the death of Alexander III in 1894, the emergence of the proletarian phase in the revolutionary movement may be discerned. The stages in the growth of the opposition to tsarism thus neatly coincide with the reigns of Alexander II (1855–81) and Alexander III (1881–94), a coincidence to some extent reflected in the personalities and outlooks of the respective monarchs.

Alexander II was born in 1818, the eldest son of the future Nicholas I and his Prussian wife. Not surprisingly, Alexander grew up with that love for most things military shared by the majority of his predecessors, although like them he found the spit and polish of the parade more to his taste than the blood and filth of actual war. The tsarevich was not much of a student, and his tutors complained of his lack of attention. Alexander preferred the open air to stuffy classrooms, and soon developed a lasting passion for hunting. He nevertheless managed to pick up several languages, and was able to put them into practice on a grand tour of Europe which followed a progress around the Russian Empire in the late 1830s. His German helped him in Darmstadt to fall in love with the Princess Mary, the fifteen-year-old daughter of the local duke. 'She is the woman of my dreams,' he told his companions, 'I will never marry anyone but her.' Although one of the objects of Alexander's grand tour had been to find a wife, Princess Mary was far from the ideal choice since, while recognised by the duke as his lawful daughter, she had in fact been sired by another man, even by a commoner. But Alexander insisted that he would rather give up the throne than Mary, and Nicholas finally acquiesced. In 1841 Alexander Nicholaevich married his Maria Alexandrovna, as she had now become according to Orthodox custom, and they were happy, if not for ever after, for at least a dozen years or so. Then, in the inevitable welter of court intrigue, Alexander took a mistress. On the whole, however, he would rather chase bears than princesses, and was a good father if not an exemplary husband.[3]

As tsar, Alexander II was idle rather than tolerant, weak-willed more than liberal. He admired his father's system of government, but lacked the energy and persistence to maintain it. Undoubtedly, the situation bequeathed to Alexander was already deteriorating, and the difficulty of the choice between resistance and accommodation explains much of the waywardness of his character. The fact that he did show exceptional determination in the great debate on emancipation could indicate not only a flash of the same personality trait that had gained him his wife but also the narrowness of his choice on this occasion. The general indecision of the Emperor was to some extent the reflection of the contradictory advice that he received from conservatives like D. A. Tolstoi and K. I. Palen on the one hand and comparative liberals like D. A. Miliutin and P. A. Valuev on the other.

If the crisis after the Crimean War called for concessions to the demands of the people, that after the assassination of Alexander II invited reaction. Alexander III responded to this challenge with enthusiasm, making no secret of his belief in autocracy and of his distrust of foreign forms of government. To him, that of France was 'vile', that of the United Kingdom was 'hardly a monarchy'[4] – Queen Victoria would not have been amused. Such crude ideas as these received intellectual support from the tsar's advisers, notably K. P. Pobedonostsev, officially Procurator of the Holy Synod, unofficially 'vice-emperor'; Count Dimitry A. Tolstoi (Tolstoy), Minister of Internal Affairs from 1882 until his death in 1889; and M. N. Katkov, editor of the establishment newspaper *Moscow News*, whose foremost reader was the Tsar himself. Although such a trio should have been united, it was in fact rent by differences of opinion and mutual suspicion, recalling to at least one contemporary's mind the fable of the swan, the pike and the crab, who could never agree on how to get the cart that they were supposed to be pulling in motion. Where he could not find solid support from his three closest adherents, however, the Emperor found it in the three main principles of his grandfather – Orthodoxy, autocracy and nationality.

Stern, even cruel with his people at large, the 'little father' was at home a corpulent, jovial family man, with none of his father's irregularities in his private life. He had married a Danish Princess called Maria Fedorovna in Russia, and their five children included the future Nicholas II. Alexander was born in 1845, the second son of Alexander II, and was not therefore thought of as tsarevich until the death of his older brother Nicholas twenty years later. As a result, his education had been somewhat neglected, and he himself had certainly not pursued it with any enthusiasm. His spelling was deficient, and so was his grammar. Such faults did not deter him from doing his job conscientiously, and he wrote dutiful annotations on reams of state papers, but he did increasingly prefer to spend his time away from the capital in rural retreat at his estate, Gatchina. There perhaps was the safest place to make a stand against the changes symbolised by the emancipation, changes which sufficiently impressed Engels for him to write in 1883: 'Russia, this is the France of our century. To her rightly and properly belongs the initiative of the new socialist reconstruction.'[5]

Political

The reign of Alexander II, like that of his father, Nicholas I, began and ended in crisis; nor was it exactly plain sailing in the middle. For too long, Nicholas had kept to his policy of 'holding on to everything', and now, to use the oldest of historical clichés, it was perhaps too late to right the ship of state. Not all Western historians have been so pessimistic, some of them considering that the Great Reform could have been the beginning of a relatively painless process of modernisation.

Among the more cautious of them, W. E. Mosse has written that a wiser, more liberal course of action in the latter part of Alexander II's reign '*might*, if adopted, have led Russia along the road of peaceful constitutional development'. [6] Other such 'optimists' have put forward an argument like this for a period as late as that following 1905. For their part, looking at society from the lower levels upwards, many Soviet historians have wondered why the situations at the beginning and end of the reign were not ripe enough for completely successful revolutions to take place. They, like Western historians, argue among themselves about the emphasis to be placed on their fundamental assertion.

As far as the years following the end of the Crimean War are concerned, M. V. Nechkina has declared that 'What happened in Russia at the end of the fifties and the beginning of the sixties was only a part of the great world-historical movement of democratic character.' [7] Unrest in Poland, an upsurge throughout the whole continent of Europe, the Taiping Rebellion in China and the end of Negro slavery in the United States were the other principal parts of this movement. Far from being a reform from above, then, the emancipation of the serfs was forced on a reluctant government by an irresistible progressive wave of global proportions, taking the form in Russia of widespread peasant unrest.

In 1858, a year in which considerable progress was made towards reform, 378 peasant disturbances took place according to Soviet calculation, and in the first four months of 1861, before and after the emancipation decree of 19 February, there were 1340 disturbances. Such figures are impressive, yet even some Soviet scholars criticise the exaggeratedly statistical approach of their colleagues. Only forty-six of the total for 1858 are sufficiently documented for the numbers of their participants to be known. Sometimes, a very small incident such as illegal tree-felling is included along with more serious occurrences such as the murder of landlords. And the disturbances of 1861 came too late to influence the nature of the emancipation itself. P. A. Zaionchkovskii points out that the military needed to be used to suppress the peasants in no more than 4 per cent of the villages of Russia during the critical years, and that the Bezdna uprising led by Anton Petrov was most exceptional. Hence, taking a different line of approach from Nechkina, he argues that the government was moved more by the fear of what might happen than by the threat of what actually did happen. Moreover, the fear of what the peasants might do had to be weighed against the necessity of maintaining the support of sufficient numbers of the landlords. Thus, there was neither a strong-enough will on the part of the oppressed nor a weak-enough will on the part of their oppressors for the situation to be truly revolutionary.[8]

The contradictory nature of Alexander II's policy, which his Minister of the Interior, P. A. Valuev, characterised as 'a system of impossible diagonals',[9] revealed itself not only in the emancipation but also in the reforms which formed its sequel. Leaving the emancipation for later discussion, we turn now to look at the measures which followed it. Although the conservative 'planters' were in the ascendant after 1861, a further series of troubles soon helped to swing the pendulum in the 'liberal' direction. At the very beginning of 1864 a local government reform was introduced, the first such reform to be comprehensive since that of Catherine II in 1775. Now assemblies and boards were to be elected at various levels of local administration by three major categories of voters: landowners; town property-owners; and peasants in communes. These new *zemstvo* organisations were to deal with a wide range of local problems including health and education, roads and famine relief. But police and administrative control were to remain with the central government, and the *zemstvo* was given only extremely limited rights to tax. While commentators such as George Fischer and S. F. Starr have argued that the experience of the *zemstvo* helped to create politicians ready for action in later years, Lenin took a dimmer view, declaring that 'the *zemstvo* was doomed from the first to be the fifth wheel on the cart of the Russian state administration, a wheel *allowed* by the bureaucracy only as long as its exclusive power was not destroyed, and the role of the deputies from the people was limited in actual practice to the simple technical execution of a sphere of tasks drawn up by the bureaucracy itself.'[10] Certainly, the nobility dominated the *zemstvo* from the first: in 1866, out of 1180 officials in thirty-three provinces, 854 were *dvoriane*. Moreover, for good or ill, the reform was applied first to the provinces of Russia proper, leaving out the borderlands.

A new system of local government had been made necessary by the emancipation. Some assemblies of the nobility believed that the time had come for the reform of the central government, too, the Tver group asking for the convocation of a constituent assembly in 1862, and the Moscow *dvorianstvo* voting by 270 votes to 36 for the summons of a general duma in 1863. Such appeals met with little response from Alexander II and his advisers. They did, however, take another important step beyond the introduction of the *zemstvo*, with the reform of the judicial system, which had also been made necessary by the emancipation. Many nobles felt that if labour were now to be free, legality would have to be ensured, and Valuev echoed such sentiments in a memorandum to the tsar at the end of 1861, declaring that it was necessary 'to intensify activity and to encourage enterprise in all branches of industry. The essential obstacle to this has long been recognised in the shortcomings of our court system and judicial process'.[11] Drawn up by a group of learned enthusiasts, the reform borrowed heavily on Western theory and practice. Such principles as the independence of the judiciary, equality of all before the law and the right to trial by jury for criminal offences were proclaimed in the statute of 20 November 1864. A reorganised Senate was to be at the apex of a unified system of courts, and lawyers, previously little employed in Russia, were to play a much bigger part in court proceedings. While the new arrangements were undoubtedly superior to the old, and the expressed wishes of Valuev and the nobility largely fulfilled, Riasanovsky's verdict on the reform, that 'almost overnight it transformed the Russian judiciary from one of the worst to one of the best', is perhaps too enthusiastic.[12] Some peasant courts, church courts and military courts were still to maintain their competence. The reform was introduced into peripheral regions of the Empire in an incomplete and slow manner, not being implemented in the Caucasus before 1871, for example, and then only partially. The social situation being what it was, in a system of classless courts some classes would be effaced less than others.

For the greatest possible success of the administrative changes of the early 1860s, there were at least two prerequisites: a sufficient number of trained personnel; and the continued enthusiasm of tsarist ministers. The first desideratum was to a considerable extent fulfilled. While in 1840 as few as 6 of the hundred or so of the top secretarial staff of the St Petersburg branch of the Senate had enjoyed higher education, by 1850 50 out of the 80 of these in the judicial sections had studied at such institutions as the universities, the School of Jurisprudence (founded in 1835), and the Lycée at Tsarskoe Selo. In 1856 more than 200 of the 300 chancellery officials in the judicial sections of the St Petersburg and Moscow branches of the Senate had been educated in such a manner. There was, then, no shortage of competent civil servants in at least some parts of the central bureaucracy. But there was a lack of leadership. By the middle 1860s the failures of the Crimean War and the threats of the ensuing years seemed remote. The Polish Insurrection of 1863 had been quelled. And so, when the ex-student Dmitrii Karakozov made an unsuccessful attempt on Alexander II's life on 4 April 1866, the advisers in favour of reaction and the dismissal of liberal ministers did not find it difficult to catch the tsar's ear. A contemporary anecdote had it that if Karakozov's bullet missed the tsar, it hit several of those around him, for ministers did indeed now find themselves dismissed. A new head of the Third Section, P. A. Shuvalov, moved to take control of the situation. Provincial governors were empowered to close private societies or clubs if they appeared to constitute any danger to the state. In 1867 the *zemstva* were forbidden inter-provincial organisation, and prohibited from publishing their decisions or accounts without the permission of the governor. The judicial arrangements of 1864 were changed, too, judges being subordinated to the governors in 1866. Count K. I. Palen, who became Minister of Justice in 1867, made no secret of his support for such measures, going so far in 1871 as to suggest to the tsar the radical alteration of the 1864 reform. Alexander is reported to have replied: 'You have not understood me, I instructed you only to discuss changes for the conduct of political cases.'[13] As before, then, some of his advisers were prepared to go further than the tsar himself wanted to.

This is not to imply that Alexander was a frustrated liberal, but there were comparatively progressive pressures on him as well as reactionary even after the 'massacre' of 1866, and some further reforms were introduced in the 1870s. A new form of city government was announced in 1870, for example, doing for the town roughly what the *zemstvo* had done for the country. Municipal councils were to be elected, although voters were to be divided into three groups according to the amount of taxes that they paid. As it was applied in Moscow, this system meant that two-thirds of the council were elected by 13 per cent of the taxpayers. An advance on the previous arrangement nevertheless, the reform was gradually brought into the whole of the Empire by the end of the 1870s, with the exception of Poland and Finland, which retained their own form of municipal government.

The most important reform of the 1870s, and arguably second only to the emancipation for the whole reign, was the universal military service law of 1874. All Russians were now bound to serve from six to seven years, although reductions and exemptions could be obtained through educational qualifications or family commitment. In theory at least, the so-called emancipation of the nobility of 1762 was now rescinded, and the conditions were created for a professional rather than a class-ridden army. The architect of the law of 1874, Dmitrii Miliutin, was Minister of War from 1861 to 1881 and was responsible during that period for a whole series of measures, which have been listed by Peter Von Wahlde as

the abolition of corporal punishment of soldiers, the realignment of the local and central military administration, the erection of a net-

work of military districts, the improvement of army housing, health,
education and training, the rearmament of the military forces, the
build-up of military factories, the recasting of army service and combat regulations, . . . and the modification of the military courts system
in line with the civil judicial reforms of 1864.[14]

Miliutin skilfully adapted Prussian innovations to Russian soil. He was
also a diplomatic and strategic thinker of some distinction, and his
memoir of 1878–9, which forcefully argued the case for defence rather
than attack should war break out in the West, remained the basis of
Russian thought on the subject down to the First World War. More than
any other individual, Miliutin helped the Russian army to recover its
confidence and efficiency after the fiasco of the Crimean War. Its performance in the Russo-Turkish War of 1877–8 was by no means great
but already an improvement. Ironically, it is arguable that Miliutin did
his job too well, since Russian generals obviously had too much confidence in their army in the years leading up to 1914, or at least up to the
disastrous encounter with Japan in 1904. Praising the Miliutin reforms
as a whole, Florinsky writes that 'it was in the army, that stronghold of
tradition and conservatism, that Russian democracy scored one of its
first modest, yet real, successes'. Forrestt Miller writes enthusiastically
of Miliutin as 'among the greatest statesmen of the Russian Empire'.[15]
On the other hand, Lenin had no more time for these reforms than for
the *zemstvo*, calling even the reformed army 'a school of wilfulness and
violence'.[16]

   The ebb and flow of reform and reaction were still very much in
evidence at the end of Alexander's reign, the years of the second 'revolutionary situation' of 1878 to 1882. Zaionchkovskii, who has devoted a
major work to this crisis, again sees it as a crisis of leadership rather than
as an all-Russian confrontation embracing every class. In so far as it
went beyond a loss of confidence on the part of the government, the
threat could certainly be discerned in popular disturbances in town and
country, but was centred mainly on the revolutionary Land and Freedom Movement and Party of the People's Will. Inaugurated by the
shooting of the military governor of St Petersburg, General Trepov, by
Vera Zasulich in 1878, a wave of terrorism brought a vigorous reaction
from the government but also some serious soul-searching, particularly
when large sections of the public made no secret of their pleasure at the
acquittal of Zasulich and, albeit to a lesser extent, of their sympathy for
the actions which followed hers. A liberal, Count M. T. Loris-Melikov,
who had been governor-general of Kharkov province, was in February

1880 placed at the head of a Supreme Executive Commission, which was entrusted with the task of putting an end to the civil upsets. An optimist, Loris-Melikov took his appointment as an excuse to further his previously expressed preference for 'measures, which would facilitate the soothing of the trustworthy elements of society, and, defending their lawful interests, revive their weakened trust in authority'.[17] Little came from the Commission, although some unpopular ministers were dismissed and the notorious Third Section was dissolved. So was the Commission itself soon after, and Loris-Melikov now took control of an enlarged Ministry of Internal Affairs, to which was subordinated a new police department. As well as making a few further concessions, Loris-Melikov also devised a project for reform which rejected both Western and old Russian models of government as too dangerous. Rather he proposed a convocation of representatives from the *zemstva* and larger municipalities to give advice on legislative measures before they were passed on to the State Council. Such a 'constitution' found some favour with Alexander II, who asked for it to be discussed by his ministers just a few hours before the People's Will succeeded (after at least seven failures) in assassinating him.

Although Alexander III and his advisers were manifestly shaken, it was rather the revolutionaries who wilted, having exhausted themselves with the assassination. And so the Loris-Melikov project was abandoned by the Council of Ministers, one of whom, Count S. G. Stroganov, declared that it would have transferred power 'from the hands of the autocratic monarch, who is now absolutely necessary for Russia, into the hands of various good-for nothings'.[18] The new tsar himself agreed with Stroganov that the acceptance of the project would be the first step towards a constitution. While some later analysts have tended to dismiss the project as not likely to have made a significant impact even if accepted, we have the authoritative opinion of Zaionchkovskii that while it 'did not violate the principle of autocratic power, . . . in the conditions of an increasingly complex situation it might, given the specific inter-relation of forces, have been the beginning of the establishment of a parliamentary system in Russia'.[19] Here Zaionchkovskii comes near to the evaluation of Mosse and other Western scholars.[20] If a constitution was what the government most feared, it was probably well-advised to reject the proposals of Loris-Melikov and to proclaim the confirmation of autocracy in the manifesto of 29 April 1881, which was written by Pobedonostsev and M. N. Katkov. Loris-Melikov and Miliutin went into retirement, and the new administration set about restoring order according to its own recipe.

The new Minister of Internal Affairs was N. P. Ignatev, dubbed by Lenin 'a diplomat with the assignment of covering the retreat of the government to complete reaction'.[21] A 'Statute on reinforced and extraordinary security' of 14 August 1881 gave the government powers which according to the French observer A. Leroy-Beaulieu were appropriate for the commander-in-chief in an enemy country, and which according to Lenin formed 'the Russian constitution in fact'.[22] Brought in originally for three years, the Statute was still in effect at the time of the fall of the monarchy. It allowed, for example, the arrest of suspects and the sequestration of their property in an extra-judicial manner, and the sentence of five years' exile without trial.

Against such a background, there were not likely to be many reforms, before or after the crisis had passed. The most immediate legislation, however, did attempt to do something to relieve the plight of the peasants. In 1881 arrangements were made for many peasants to be included in the redemption payment network with the rates scaled down. In 1882 a Peasant Land Bank was set up, although its charges were higher than those of the open market and the Bank was therefore of little use. In the same year a beginning was made to the final abolition of the poll-tax, the process being completed by 1 January 1887. To crown such work, Ignatev, who was closely connected with the Moscow Slavophiles, pressed for the summons of the *Zemskii Sobor* to mark the coronation of Alexander III set for 1883. Pobedonostsev said that this would lead to 'revolution, the ruin of government and the ruin of Russia', and his fellow-reactionary M. N. Katkov said that it would mean 'the triumph of sedition'.[23] The suggestion was unanimously rejected at a meeting of the tsar's advisers, and Ignatev was sent into retirement.

His successor as Minister of the Interior, Count D. A. Tolstoy, became known as the 'Minister of Conflict', a nickname earned by dint of opposition to progress and energetic prosecution of the interests of the landlords, who included himself. 'Your ancestors created Russia', he said to the tsar, 'but they created it with our hands.'[24] To strengthen these hands, a Land Bank was set up for the nobility in 1885, with a lower rate of interest and therefore about six times more business than the Peasant Land Bank. In 1886 the dissolution of peasant households was made more difficult, and in 1893, restrictions were placed on the re-partition of peasant lands. In 1889 a new noble official, the *zemskii nachalnik* or land captain, was introduced to consolidate the provincial grasp of the *dvorianstvo*. He was to appoint local judges, and the decisions of the peasant assemblies were to be submitted to him for approval. He was empowered to levy fines or imprison suspects without trial. In brief, as Florinsky puts it, 'nothing pertaining to the financial, economic, social, and cultural welfare of the rural community escaped the jurisdiction of the land captains'.[25] Although Tolstoy died in 1889, his spirit lived after him as the property qualifications for voting in zemstvo and municipality elections were raised in decrees of 1890 and 1892.

A note or two of paternalist concern can be detected in some of the legislation of Alexander III's reign as the labour question posed itself more clearly. For example, a law of 1882 forbade the industrial labour of most minors under the age of twelve and another of 1885 prohibited female nightwork. But more in the mainstream of the tsar's policy was the decree of 1886 which set punishments for refusal to work and disallowed complaints. Moreover, in 1890, deterioration in the industrial sector was recognised, and some exceptions which had been made to the earlier protective decrees on a temporary basis were now declared permanent. Generally speaking, the difference between the domestic policies of Alexander II and III is that, while the father had some notions which were at least partly liberal, the son had none.

Such a difference may be considerably explained by personal characteristics, as we have seen, and by the changing nature of the economic and political situation. It must also be taken into account that the world was shrinking and becoming more interdependent throughout the nineteenth century, and that Russia's attempts at imperial expansion and self-assertion were bound to bring repercussions at home and abroad. Fears for domestic stability could thus dissuade the government from too heavy an involvement in foreign problems which did not directly affect tsarist interests.

In any case, Russian patriots did not for the most part envisage their flag being carried overseas. Since the huge mass of the Empire stretched half-way round the world and the sun already hardly ever set on it, there seemed to be no need for seaborne extensions. Indeed, there was a certain amount of seaborne contraction. In 1867 the government folded up its American colony with the sale of Alaska to the United States for $7,200,000. And then, in 1875, Russia exchanged its Kurile Islands with Japan for the southern part of the island of Sakhalin. On mainland Asia, however, far from weakening, the drive for more territory and consolidation became more intense. In the Far East Count Nikolai Muravev, the governor-general there from 1847 to 1861, brought the two-headed eagle into the valleys of the Amur and Ussuri rivers. China, weakened by foreign incursions and the Taiping Rebellion, was forced to accept these losses in the Treaty of Aigun of 1858 and the Treaty of

Peking of 1860.[26] Russian expansion in the Far East was far from con-trolled and some of Muravev's lieutenants exceeded their orders to near the point of court-martial. But the government needed consolidation for the failures of the Crimean War, the losses to China of the Treaty of Nerchinsk in 1689 had been more than recovered, and so, instead of being chastised for the over-enthusiasm of his men, the governor-general was awarded the title of Muravev-Amurskii in 1858. A new city founded by the Russians near the southern extremity of their new possessions left little doubt about their intentions in the area. Its name was Vladivostok, which means 'Rule over the East'.

Further slices of land were later taken from China in Central Asia, where Russian generals such as Kaufmann and Skobelev found plenty of room for the realisation of their ambitions. Before the end of the reign of Alexander II, the khanates of Kokand, Bukhara and Khiva had been taken and the eastern shore of the Caspian annexed. As in the Far East, the men on the spot by no means listened carefully to every word of command from St Petersburg. As David Mackenzie puts it,

> The saga of Russian expansion in Central Asia during the mid-1860s reveals that the advances, initiated by government decisions, greatly exceeded its plans or intentions. The Foreign and Finance ministries envisioned cautious, limited expansion largely to promote commerce with the Orient and promote Russia's security. Their public opposi-tion to unchecked imperialism was sincere, but they proved impotent against the generals and their supporters.

In Mackenzie's evaluation, 'What eventually set limits to Russian expan-sion in Central Asia were not ministerial resolutions but mountain bar-riers and British power.'[27]

Consolidating Caucasian areas previously annexed, Prince Aleksandr Bariatinskii finally succeeded in 1859 in capturing the legendary Shamil, who had been leading Muslim resistance to the infidel invader for twenty-five years. It was nearly all over now, even if the Caucasus never became completely tame. Conversion in the Caucasus was not as forced as in other colonial cases, in which some tribesmen found the Orthodox Church extremely enthusiastic about the salvation of their souls, particularly during the reign of Alexander III. In the so-called Multanskoe case, which ran from 1892 to 1896, a group of Udmurty were accused of sacrificing human victims to heathen gods. While not condoning such behaviour, some observers saw the trial as part of a ruthless attempt to introduce rigid standardisation. Soviet historians, examining this and other elements of Russian imperial policy, make a distinction between the actions of tsarist administration at the top and the sympathetic development lower down of the 'friendship of peoples'. However, such groups as the Jews could well be forgiven for denying that the hand of friendship was extended towards them at any level.

At the time, the general line of his government's policy was vigorously defended by Chancellor Gorchakov, who compared it in 1864 to that of other expanding powers. He declared: 'The United States in America, France in Africa, Holland in her colonies, England in India, were all forced to take the road of expansion dictated by necessity rather than ambition, a road on which the chief difficulty is to know where to stop.'[28] Russification, then, was considered no worse than Americanisation or Anglicisation. Indeed, in the nineteenth century, Russians thought it was far better, many of them clothing their beliefs in the ideas of Panslavism, which had its heyday during the period under discussion. It could be used to excuse the suppression of other Slavonic cultures such as the Ukrainian and the Polish, most notably after the failure of the Polish insurrection of 1863.[29] Panslavism also gave impetus to Russian efforts to expand in the Balkans, where the humiliation of the Crimean War had to be found compensation. Neither their fellow Slavs in Bulgaria and elsewhere nor their uneasy allies, the Habsburgs, were completely happy with Russian attempts to solve the Eastern Question, and, of course, the Turks were very much alarmed. War could not be far away.

The Panslavists' chance came when revolts against Turkish rule broke out in the Balkans in 1875 and 1876. International attempts were made to avert hostilities between the major powers, but finally met with failure as Turkey rejected a Russian ultimatum. In the war of 1877–8 the forces of the tsar were in the end successful, but not before several reverses had been inflicted upon them by the troops of the Porte, notably at the important fortress of Plevna. The Treaty of San Stefano in the spring of 1878 made Bulgaria virtually independent and extended freedom widely throughout the Balkans. But fears for the balance of power were raised throughout Europe, and the Congress of Berlin in the summer of 1878 produced a revised Treaty which reduced the independence of Bulgaria and the gains of the Slavs in general. Russian nationalist crusaders were disappointed that Constantinople had not been taken and that the Empire was obliged to be content with Bessarabia and more minor acquisitions. Bulgarians and others wondered if their qualified release from the thrall of the Turk was going to be limited further by increased control exerted by their big brother. Smirnov comments: 'Although the tsarist government pursued expansionist aims in the fight against Turkey and the burden of the war was borne entirely by the people of Russia, the war nevertheless played an important part in liberating the Balkan peoples from the Turkish yoke.'[30]

The war of 1877–8 also brought tension with the Habsburgs. Rivalry with Austria combined with anxiety at the rise of Germany to make the Three Emperors' League a fragile and mostly ineffective alliance of the reactionary crowned heads of Europe against change and progress. In the pursuit of security, Russia found it necessary to seek a new ally in France. Her fresh course was marked by a diplomatic agreement of 1894, when a military convention of 1892 was also ratified. Expressly though secretly directed against the Triple Alliance of Germany, Austria and Italy, which had first been set up in 1882, the Franco-Russian accord marked a further step towards the diplomatic alignment of the period leading up to the First World War.

Economic

In the stages of the development of capitalism, Russia might be said to have reached the mercantile by the middle of the seventeenth century, the manufacturing by soon after the middle of the eighteenth century, and the industrial in the years following the emancipation of 1861. By no means all economic historians would accept such a scheme, and even those who would accept it might well disagree among themselves about its exact chronological application. 1830 has been preferred to 1861 as the third transitional date by some Soviet historians, while Western experts have tended to favour the 1880s or even later. In the broad sweep of the centuries, perhaps, fifty years is not such a long time, particularly when the subject under discussion cannot be exactly defined. In such a perspective, Russia's notorious backwardness does not appear so great. But, in the short run, the timing of Russian change was all-important in comparison with, say, German or American. Russia's apartness may be clearly seen not only in the slow pace of her capitalist development but also in the persistence of socio-economic features antipathetic to it. In other words, the Russian Prometheus was less unbound than his counterparts in the other modernising nations.

This circumstance is plainly on view in the event which is often said to launch imperial Russia on the path of industrialisation, the emancipation of 1861. Alexander II showed his awareness of the situation in his famous speech in 1856 to a section of the nobility, 'the mainstay of the throne'. The tsar declared: 'It is better to abolish serfdom from above than to wait for the time when it will begin to abolish itself spontaneously from below.'[31] Throughout the long discussions preparatory to the decrees of 1861, the ministers were conscious of the twin calls of progress and reaction. And when the announcement finally came, the illiterate peasants at Bezdna and elsewhere were able to read enough between the lines to understand that they had been cheated, while the conservative 'planters' believed that the floodgates of anarchy had been opened and that the downfall of the throne and its mainstay was now inevitable. The contradiction continues clearly visible through the wording of the 'Great Reform' and the sequel to it.

The aspiration of the emancipation edict of 1861 was that the peasants 'should understand that by acquiring property and greater freedom to dispose of their possessions, they have an obligation to society and to themselves to live up to the letter of the new law by a loyal and judicious use of the rights which are now granted to them'.[32] The serfs were to be personally free, that is not only to acquire property rights, but also to marry without the lord's permission, to engage in trade or litigation. While newly created agencies relieved the lords of most of their supervisory functions, they were nevertheless charged with the duty of preparing during the course of the following year inventories of the lands, services and payments of their former charges. After a further year, the peasants were to be 'temporarily obligated' according to these inventories until redemption payments were agreed with the lords. (Redemption agreements, the option for which was to be more with the former masters, did not become compulsory until 1883, and would still not have been completely paid off by 1950 if the whole system had not been recognised as entirely broken down by 1905.) After agreement had been reached, the landlords were to receive from the state interest-bearing securities amounting to between 75 per cent and 80 per cent of the total cost of the redemption debt, which was calculated on the basis of the serfs' previous dues. The peasants were to have paid back the redemption debt with interest over forty-nine years.

For such a system to have worked, the peasants would have needed a sufficient amount of land or unrestricted opportunities to make money in non-agricultural employment. Neither desideratum was attained. While maximum and minimum norms were established for different zones, they were not always realised or adequate in all cases even when they were realised. The peasants often lost land, particularly in the black-earth region – in Saratov and Samara more than 40 per cent of what they had previously worked. In such provinces, they were often forced by economic circumstances if not by law to continue working for their masters (*otrabotka* replacing *barshchina* in technical terms). In less fertile regions near the centre and in the north, it is true, they often gained land, but here the *obrok* form of payment had long been more profitable for the landlords than labour services, and therefore land was not as important to the erstwhile masters as cash. In European Russia as a whole, over 5,700,000 hectares were cut off from the lands previously used by the peasants. Moreover, by the retention of the commune, its incorporation into a new unit of local administration, the township or *volost*, and the continued exercise of a large amount of their power by the landlords, made it very difficult for the enterprising peasants to make their way in the world at large.

Arrangements were somewhat different for other categories of peasant such as those previously attached to the state and for other areas such as the Transcaucasian and Western provinces. Such complications make it very difficult to give with any accuracy a brief description of the emancipation, or to evaluate its impact on society. But its significance is not to be found only in the small print of the twenty or so decrees which put it in the statute book, since emancipation was very much a world-wide phenomenon in the middle of the nineteenth century. In theory, the ideas of Adam Smith and others had been widely discussed for fifty years or more, and now the intellectual movement within Russia which had started with the Prize Essay Competition of Catherine II almost a century before could be said to have borne its fruit. In practice, the awareness that serfdom was incompatible with an industrialising economy was gradually forced upon a reluctant government. Just possibly, this was a false awareness. Closer examination of the profitability of the peculiar institution might show what some experts have claimed it demonstrates for the American South that slavery is not necessary unprofitable in an expanding capitalist economy. Such an exercise would put in bolder relief the environmental features of Russia's comparative backwardness. The climate and quality of the soil, the vast distances and remoteness from the major commercial centres kept the Russian economy in their thrall almost as much after the emancipation as before it. The further exercise of comparing the Russian emancipation to the American 'day of Jubilo' would no doubt clearly show that both 'black' peoples were robbed of what they believed to be their due, but that capitalism in both economies received something of a boost. The peculiarities of the Russian case, where unrestrained industrialisation was anathema to tsarism, are described by N. M. Druzhinin in the following manner: 'the task of the government and the class of landlords standing behind its back was . . . by means of the reform to direct the economic life of the country by the peaceful path of gradual agro-capitalist development, favourable for the nobility, but tormenting for the working mass of the peasantry'.[33]

Even if the government and its supporters had wanted to force the pace, their power to goad the mass of the peasantry into action would have been too limited. Harry Willetts points out that the latter

> had a static and archaic view of their calling. Where land was plentiful they tilled part of it to near exhaustion, then moved on to long-fallow soil. Elsewhere, they observed a three-field rotation, leaving one field fallow, scratching the others with their wooden ploughs, and planting then, for the most part, with 'grey' cereals – rye and oats. Between the short, back-breaking periods of ploughing, sowing and reaping, their preference was to wait God's will in patient lethargy. These primitive procedures, wasteful enough at any time, were suicidal in the decades of rapid population increase and growing land-hunger. Peasants from the more advanced Western provinces might comment caustically on the 'lordly' mentality of their Russian brothers, those 'gentlemen at the plough' who, short as they were of land, kept a third of it permanently 'on holiday'.

As Willetts goes on to say, only 'generous help and patient indoctrination', which would have included a greater share of the land and advice on how to use it, could have brought a real change to the time-honoured practices of the *muzhiks*.[34]

Not that all agriculture was stagnant when a large amount of grain was sold abroad. Between the 1850s and the end of the century the average annual amount of exports of wheat and other grain rose from over a million to over seven million metric tons. The greatest increase occurred in the 1880s, even though this decade was in the middle of a period of depression in the world grain market, with prices at the time being nearly halved. The government laid great stress on grain exports to help Russia's international trade and credit balance, and such a policy certainly made a contribution to the Empire's growing reputation as Europe's granary. Most of the outward flow went westwards from the Ukraine through the Black Sea, although nine-tenths of the cultivation in European Russia as a whole was of grain. But no more than a fifth of the total grain production went abroad; most of it was produced either for the home market, national and local, or for subsistence purposes.

On the whole, the larger landlords, including many from the nobility, had their eyes on the export market, while the focus of the smaller farmer tended to be nearer home, where with industry growing demand was often high. The stratification of the peasantry was intensified by this expanding commerce. While the majority of them were as unenterprising as in Willetts' description, a small but growing number were taking advantage of the changing situation. Opportunities for them were greater in the periphery, where Russia was taking the American or freer road to capitalism in agriculture, than in the centre, where the Prussian or *Junker*-dominated mode was more in evidence. In the outer regions, too, some cultivators were being caught up in the new developments, wines and fruits going to the urban markets from Transcaucasia, and beet grown in the Ukraine helping to make the manufacture of sugar second in importance only to that of textiles, whose cotton spindles were increasingly fed by Turkestan.

By the end of the century there were more cotton spindles active in Russia than in France and not many fewer than in Germany. In the thirty years following the emancipation, cotton-goods production centred mainly around Moscow increased fourfold. Heavy industry, as might be said to befit it, moved forward at a more deliberate pace. Having fallen steeply from the supremacy that they had enjoyed in the late eighteenth century, Russian metalworks produced only 4 per cent of the world's cast iron in 1860 and an even smaller 2·5 per cent in 1880. In the late 1870s, however, a British immigrant named Hughes opened up the Donbass, where a town – Iuzovka – was named in his honour, and most of Russia's coal was soon produced there in a region not far from Krivoi Rog, where iron deposits were at last beginning to be properly exploited. Ukrainian smelting was now twice as important as that in the older Urals metalworks, and by the end of the nineteenth century, Russian iron production had risen to 7 per cent of the world's total. By this time, not only Mr Hughes but many other foreigners had invested in Russia's growing industry. Among other contributions, they helped with the much-needed mechanisation, which resulted in a threefold growth of machines in use in the 1890s, a half of them admittedly in trains and ships, and a 25 per cent increase in industrial productivity during the same decade. To conclude a paragraph full of statistics, which are much beloved by the Soviet historians who have supplied most of them, a further indication of the increasing mechanisation of industry is that, whereas in the 1880s there was in Russia little more than 0·09 horsepower of steam for each industrial worker, by the end of the 1890s the figure had risen to 0·65.

The establishment of industrial capitalism goes hand in hand with an improvement in communications. Metal makes the iron road and its rolling stock, the trains burning coal transport minerals and other goods more quickly and efficiently than has been previously possible. By 1871 railway lines had been completed from Moscow to Nizhnii Novgorod, to Voronezh, to Kharkov and to Brest via Smolensk and Minsk. The last of these joined Russia by rail to Europe, even though the change of gauge that was necessary en route detracted somewhat from the journey's smoothness. By 1871, too, there were rail connections from the centre to both Black and Baltic Seas. At the end of the decade, however, the war with Turkey gave the Russian railway system an examination which it failed. Partly for this reason, partly because the government-assisted state companies were profligate and corrupt, the state decided to take over. In 1880, only 4 per cent of the railroad belonged to the state, by 1900, more than 60 per cent. Meanwhile, in the 1890s, nearly 30,000 kilometres (20,000 miles) of track were added to the approximately 30,000 kilometres (20,000 miles) already in existence. Transcaucasia, the Donets Basin, the Urals and Siberia were now penetrated. During the later years of the nineteenth century, water traffic also remained important, particularly along the Volga. The number of steamboats on that and other rivers and canals grew two and a half times in the 1860s and 1870s, and by the same amount again in the 1880s and 1890s. By the end of the century, about 70 per cent of the Empire's internal transport was handled by trains, 30 per cent by boat. Roads remained primitive, carriages and carts finding them impassable except in summer. During the same period, the government-controlled postal and telegraph services were expanding. Stamps were introduced for internal deliveries in 1857 and for foreign in 1864. Nearly two million letters were handled by the end of the 1870s. Between the years 1855 and 1880, the telegraph network's size grew from over 2000 kilometres (1300 miles) to nearly 80,000 kilometres (50,000 miles). Four years before the Atlantic cable was laid in 1869, an American group sought to join North America and Russia with a cable across the Bering Strait. One of the proponents of the project declared. 'Thus the commerce of the world will find its path across this continent, awakened into life by a new power; for the telegraph is to precede all, rapidly and cheaply we press it forward as the swift-running courier. First the adventurous merchant seeks the channel opened by this messenger; then the stately ship, soon to make way for the more rapid steamer; finally the iron way joins the circle, and girds the world with steam and electricity.'[35] Neither the narrower hopes for the Bering Strait nor the wider ones for the world in general were to be realised as quickly as the group believed possible, particularly when faced by the intractability of the climate, size and government of the Russian Empire.

And as always, Russian merchantmen fared abroad but little; less than a fifth of the ships in Russian ports were of indigenous origin during the second half of the nineteenth century, by 1900 little more than a tenth of them. Nevertheless Russia was able to acquire a share of the rapidly expanding international trade of the period. In millions of gold roubles, the value of her exports rose from something over 225 in 1861 to more than 620 in 1895, while that of her imports climbed from about 205 to around 460. As before, the major exports were grains and raw materials, while machines constituted an important part of the imports. A significant change in the foreign trading pattern was the replacement of Britain as the major partner by Germany. It is also noteworthy that after a liberal tariff policy in the 1850s and 1860s, there was a return to stringent protectionism in the 1870s and 1880s.

This reversion was encouraged by the war with Turkey, which also made difficult the attempts being made by the government to stabilise the currency and to balance the budget. Most of the state's income continued to come from indirect taxation, particularly the excise on spirits which replaced the previous farming-out system in 1863, while the most important direct tax was the poll-tax until its abolition in the mid-1880s. But there was not enough money to pay for the heavy expenditures on the army and navy, and the national debt rose from 2180 million gold roubles in the late 1850s to 6046 million in 1881 and 7070 million in 1892.

Successive ministers made strenuous efforts to clean up the financial mess, and to adjust the economic administration of the Empire as a whole to the arrival of industrial capitalism which followed in the wake of the emancipation of the serfs. The most comprehensive of these efforts was made by Sergei Witte after the accession of Nicholas II in 1894. By this time, factories and mines were well on their way to superimposing themselves on the vast Russian landscape, even though its spaces were so vast that they almost swallowed up the appurtenances of modern civilisation. But the social consequences of the change – a larger urban population, a more stratified arrangement of the classes – were clearly revealed in the census of 1897, which will be subjected to analysis in the next chapter, when we shall consider Russian industrial capitalism at its highest stage, that of imperialism.

Cultural

The emancipation of the serfs and the development of industrial capitalism exerted considerable influence on the various spheres of Russian cultural life during the reigns of Alexander II and Alexander III. Neither tsar made any significant impact himself, although Alexander III had something of a taste for the theatre and music, and sometimes played the trombone. It was rather such trends as the growth of the city that affected education, literary and other forms of creation, and the revolutionary movement. A widespread phenomenon throughout the industrialising world, urbanisation in Russia was marked by the decline of the nobility-dominated culture and the rise of the part played by the *raznochintsy*, people of various ranks who formed an intelligentsia of middle-class origin. Held back by upper-class prejudice, the censor and an obscurantist Church led by such reactionaries as Pobedonostsev, progressive creativity could not be stifled, whether in the shape of a peasant teaching himself to read or a university-trained intellectual forming an idea of his revolutionary duty. At the end of the period under discussion, the all-important proletarian consciousness began to show clear signs of formation.

To begin with the most simple indicator of modern cultural advance, the growth of literacy. While in the 1860s, the ratio of literates to illiterates was about 1:15, by 1897 it had risen to nearer 1:5, for the age groups ten to thirty-nine to 1:4 or even 1:3. The urban population was about two and a half times more literate than the rural, and men more literate than women by nearly the same amount. There was regional variation as well, with no more than 12 per cent of the people being able to read and write in the Caucasus and Siberia, and 5 per cent in Central Asia.[36]

Some, but not all, of the growth of literacy was attributable to the advance in elementary education, in Sunday schools and other establishments run by the Church, and in state institutions in which the Church also had considerable influence. Proponents of secular enlightenment were in constant conflict with the ecclesiastical authorities, the clerics being in the ascendancy, particularly during the reign of Alexander III, and progressive pedagogic thinkers such as K. D. Ushinskii achieving little immediate impact. Class prejudice was running at a high level then, too, as was graphically indicated in the notorious circular sent out in 1887 by the Minister of Education, Count Delianov, who ordered candidates for admission to gymnasia to be carefully examined for social and financial adequacy. The effect of gymnasium education on 'the children of coachmen, footmen, cooks, laundresses, small shopkeepers and other similar people' was 'contempt for parents, dissatisfaction with their own station, and bitterness towards the existing order and, in the nature of things, inevitable inequality in the financial position of various social groups'.[37] Such prejudice combined with financial pressure to restrict somewhat severely the movement from elementary to secondary education. At the upper level, too, the dead hand of obscurantism applied its baleful pressure, as in the so-called 'Greco-Roman bondage' to which Count D. A. Tolstoy, Minister of Education from 1866 to 1880, subjected the gymnasia. Through Tolstoy's influence, study of the classics was intensified at the expense of such subjects as history and geography, literature and even Russian. Emphasis on the classics was, of course, a phenomenon common to all Europe at this time, rather than Tolstoy's eccentricity. Moreover, Allen Sinel has made a spirited defence of Tolstoy's record in such fields as peasant education and teacher training, asserting his contribution to the advance taking place through the reigns in question.[38] The number of boys in gymnasia and progymnasia rose by nearly three times up to 70,000, and by the 1890s, their number in secondary education as a whole, that is including those at technical, commercial, military and church schools at this level, exceeded 150,000. By the same decade, about half that number of girls were in their gymnasia and other middle-level schools. These figures derive from a base in 1896 of about 3,500,000, the number of boys and girls in 65,000 primary schools, of which more than half were church schools.

Meanwhile, the number of students at universities and other institutions of higher learning slowly increased, while the conditions in which they did so fluctuated according to the political situation. At the beginning of Alexander II's reign, for example, they were treated rather liberally: the uniforms enforced by Nicholas I were no longer obligatory; freedom to travel was restored; and certain prohibited courses such as philosophy and European constitutional law were allowed back into the curriculum. But then, just after the emancipation, there were disturbances which led to the temporary closure of St Petersburg University and to trouble at the universities of Moscow, Kiev, Kharkov and particularly Kazan. A new university charter of 1863 was comparatively enlightened, but the attempt on the life of Alexander II by the ex-student Karakozov in 1866 led to a further reaction. And so on, with reaction more in evidence than progress, the number of students rising to approximately 14,000 in ten universities by the mid-1890s, and to 29,000 in the sixty or so institutions of higher learning in general. 4 per cent of the 29,000 were women, whose acceptance by the universities in particular was slow and impeded by arguments such as that their presence would have 'a pernicious effect upon the studies of young men'. Commoners tended to be excluded as well as females, Katkov arguing that higher education should be reserved for 'the upper class which decides the fate of the nation and charts its future'.[39] Nevertheless, there was some democratisation in the social as well as the sexual, if not the racial, directions. While special arrangements were made for women to complete their education at St Petersburg, Moscow, Kazan and Kiev before the end of the nineteenth century, in the late 1890s a third of the students at St Petersburg University and three-fifths of them at Kharkov came from outside the upper class. At the same time, however, quota restrictions were imposed at the higher and secondary levels on Jews.

In spite of the difficulties with which it confronted them, Russia was producing scholars and scientists of the first world rank during the second half of the nineteenth century, such as the historians S. M. Solovev and V. O. Kliuchevskii, the chemists A. M. Butlerov and D. I. Mendeleev, the botanist K. A. Timiriazev, the biologist I. I. Mechnikov and the physiologist I. P. Pavlov. Such savants joined young people escaping from their Greco-Roman bondage, self-taught workers and peasants, to help form a quickly growing reading public. Although the censorship and other forms of restrictions were more rigorous in Russia than in most modernising countries, there were still some 350 periodicals in existence by the 1870s and more than 1000 of them by the end of the century. Bookshops multiplied sixfold from the 1860s to the 1890s, and many libraries were opened during these decades.

At its most enduring level, Russian literature of the period was the equal, and arguably the superior, of any other. In Turgenev, Tolstoi (Tolstoy) and Dostoevskii (Dostoevsky), it produced three masterly writers of prose fiction. For some Dostoevsky is the greatest, with his profound psychological insight and heights of emotional frenzy. For others, the breadth of Tolstoy's world, particularly in *War and Peace* and *Anna Karenina*, has greater attraction. Yet others would argue that Turgenev is at least as remarkable as his two contemporaries for his closely analytical descriptions of a society rent by the generation gap and social divisions. Certainly, what Lenin said of Tolstoy, that he was the 'mirror of the Russian revolution', has been a label equally not only for Turgenev and Dostoevsky, but also for Goncharov, whose *Oblomov* became a synonym for 'feudal parasitism, passivity and stagnation', and to Saltykov-Shchedrin, who in *The Golovlev Family* and other works 'exposed the autocracy, the serf-owners, the predatory capitalist profit hunters and the thick-skulled and wilful civil servants'.[40]

In an age of realism, poetry could not flourish as prose did: N. A. Nekrasov came nearest to capturing the predominant spirit of the times in verse, while Fedor Tiutchev and particularly Afanasii Fet pointed the way forward towards the flourishing of the 'art for art's sake' movement at the turn of the century. Meanwhile, the drama prospered, although the works of the greatest playwright of the period, Aleksandr Ostrovskii, have not translated well. The more direct and international language of music, on the other hand, has permitted due recognition to the remarkable composers produced by Russia in the second half of the nineteenth century. In the sixties and seventies, the *Kuchka* or Group including Balakirev, Borodin, Kiui, Musorgskii or Mussorgsky and Rimskii – or Rimsky-Korsakov was more active in its attempts to follow in the footsteps of Glinka and Dargomyzhsky and bridge the gap between folk legends and songs and the more ordered world of the opera and the symphony. The most powerful result was Mussorgsky's *Boris Godunov*, the most colourful either Borodin's *Prince Igor* or one of Rimsky-Korsakov's *opéras fantastiques*. Mussorgsky's use of the *leitmotiv* and of folksong was to influence Stravinsky and many other composers. Not so successful in the symphonic sphere, although such works as Borodin's Second Symphony have undoubted impact, the Group was clearly surpassed here by P. I. Chaikovskii or Tchaikovsky, whose genius survives without difficulty the charges of self-indulgent sentimentalism levelled at it by his detractors. Tchaikovsky's music for ballet and his operas have also deserved their lasting, world-wide popularity.

With another means of international communication, that of the graphic and plastic arts, Imperial Russia under Alexander II and III made a far less effective impression. Although several of them broke away from the pseudo-classicism of the Academy in 1863 to pursue nationally and socially conscious aims, artists did not for the most part achieve a high level of expression. The best known of them, I. E. Repin, perhaps makes his greatest impact in such historical portraits as *Ivan the Terrible*. The epic canvasses of V. I. Surikov and V. V. Vereshchagin can also hardly fail to catch the eye in the Tretiakov Gallery in Moscow and elsewhere. The sculpture of the period is less memorable than the graphic art, and the prevalent Imperial style of architecture more monumentally tedious than its counterparts elsewhere. This is not to say that the sculptors and architects fully deserve the lack of mention that they receive here. This would also be the case with the writers and artists of the national regions, whom linguistic and cultural barriers have consigned to local fame.

Similarly, as we turn to consider the history of revolutionary and other forms of political ideology, we shall be able to consider only the most outstanding figures and the most salient of their ideas. Without too much distortion, the development of the revolutionary movement after the emancipation until the consolidation of industrial capitalism may be equated with the rise and fall of populism. From the late 1850s until the middle 1860s, the chief vehicle of progressive ideas was *The Bell*, published in London by Alexander Herzen with the collaboration of N. P. Ogarev. At first hailing the emancipation as a great step forward and Alexander II as the tsar-liberator, *The Bell* soon became disillusioned with both, and declared that the people had yet to be granted their greatest needs, 'land and freedom'. With the curtailment of universities activities towards the end of 1861, students were urged to take themselves 'to the people'.

But *The Bell* was by no means the only voice to call to anti-tsarist dissidents. During the 1860s and early 1870s, ideas for action were put forward by several outstanding individuals, most notably perhaps by Mikhail Bakunin, Petr Lavrov, Sergei Nechaev, Petr Tkachev and Nikolai Chernyshevskii. Like Herzen and Ogarev, these were all moving, albeit in widely different ways, from the influence of German idealistic philosophy to something more materialistic, thus to some degree acting out the roles of the younger generation in Turgenev's *Fathers and Sons*. Bakunin, more than anybody else the creator of revolutionary anarchism, forcefully argued his case against the more disciplined views of Marx in the First International. Expelled from it in 1872 during the great debate which followed the fall of the Paris Commune, he nevertheless exerted a large influence on later revolutionaries, continually proclaiming his belief in the readiness of the masses to rise and of the peasants in particular to play an important part in any upheaval. Lavrov put forward his mature views in the *Historical Letters*, published first in 1868–9. These talked of the obligations to society as a whole of that small group of people who are capable of critical analysis of their environment. If properly aware, they can be the principal engine of historical progress, influencing the rest of society through their propaganda. Nechaev was a fanatical preacher of strict organisation and political terror, prepared to go to the length of murder to preserve party discipline. His ruthlessness alienated Marx and Bakunin, but attracted others. Those who plotted the assassination of Alexander II were spurred on by Nechaev, who rejected their alternative plan of assisting his own break from jail. Tkachev followed Blanqui, the nineteenth-century French revolutionary, in his belief that the government could be overthrown by the determined conspiracy of a small group; for which reason Tkachev has been called a Jacobin and even a Bolshevik. Chernyshevskii was most influential through his political novel, *What Is To Be Done?*, written in the Peter and Paul Fortress during the years 1862–4. Believing that tsarism should be overthrown, and that the peasants could make an important contribution to this overthrow, he argued that conditions in Russia would lead to the immediate establishment there of socialism based on the commune without the intervening stage of capitalism.[41]

Such beliefs were shared by most members of the amorphous populist movement which gathered momentum in the late sixties and early seventies. But there were many debates among them about the best means of achieving their ends. How long would the revolution process take to mature, and how if at all could it best be accelerated? These important questions were hotly discussed, with the works of Chernyshevskii and the others frequently cited in support of the views put forward. Actions varied as well as words. While Karakozov made his celebrated attempt on the tsar's life in 1866, unsung idealists were attempting to put their ideas across on the grass-roots. Soon, according to R. E. Zelnik, they were operating at the factory-floor level too, making contact with factory-workers by 1870.[42] Proselytisation reached a climax in the 'crazy' summer of 1874, when thousands of crusaders attempted to take the message to the people, often dressing as peasants and attempting to clothe their arguments in similarly homespun garb. But the people were not receptive, and the authorities moved in to suppress the agitation before it could become dangerous. All but the most dedicated populists lost their enthusiasm.[43]

From the hard core sprang a new group, organising itself in 1876 and reviving the name Land and Freedom. The members could not agree on the methods to be adopted to reach their eponymous objectives, and the group split in 1879 into two, the People's Will and Black Partition. Terrorism preoccupied those who sought to express what they believed to be the tacit desire of their fellow countrymen, and they met with their greatest but final success by the assassination of Alexander II. Pressure for distribution of all the land to the peasants, or 'black' people, was the major concern of the other splinter group, one of whose leaders was Georgii Plekhanov. This group too was soon dissolved, and Plekhanov took a new path along with other former members of Black Partition, such as P. Akselrod and Vera Zasulich. In 1883 they brought about the formation in Geneva of the Marxist Liberation of Labour organisation. Meanwhile, the workers were beginning to form their own unions, and the strike at the Morozov Cotton Mills near Moscow in 1885 compelled even reactionary newspapers to admit that the 'labour question' had arrived in Russia. The connection between Marxist intellectuals and progressive workers, however, was not made until the mid-1890s.[44]

By no means all disillusioned populists followed such an extreme course as Plekhanov. Rather more of them probably preferred to cultivate liberal ideals, pressing at the time of the crisis at the end of the seventies as they had during that of the early sixties for freedom of the press and other forms of expression of a public opinion. Such views were politely put forward by a few *zemstva*, and in 1879 a secret congress of liberals made an abortive attempt to form a united movement.[45] The dominant voice in the *zemstva*, however, was the same as that in respectable society at large, conservative, even reactionary. Pobedonostsev, with his rejection of the 'parliamentary sham', defence of autocracy and assertion of Orthodoxy, articulated the unspoken assumptions of all those who saw in the government of Alexander III not the worst in Europe but the best.[46]

While its opponents cried out in desperation from jail or exile, the supporters of tsarism declaimed their triumph over the populists and early Marxists. But appearances were deceptive. Zaionchkovskii sums up the period thus:

> The political reaction of the eighties and the beginning of the nineties, directed at the conservation and strengthening of the remains of serf feudalism, held back to a considerable degree the development of social life in the country as it brought about a series of reactionary laws and the massive arbitrariness of the administration and police. However it could not change the general process of socio-economic development, could not hold back the development of Russian progressive social thought, in spite of the repressions of the censor and other reactionary measures.
>
> However, the long period of reaction, characterised by the persecution of everything progressive, and also by massive political arbitrariness, aroused in the social organism such reserves of hatred for autocracy that could only spill out in a revolutionary outburst.
>
> The period of reaction also clearly brought about a crisis in the system of the autocratic order, the decomposition of its upper stratum, from the imperial family right down to some representatives of local authority.
>
> Thus, the political reaction of the eighties and beginning of the nineties was one of the reasons for the revolutionary events of 1905 to 1907.[47]

9 Russian Imperialism, 1894–1917

At the end of the nineteenth century, wars throughout the world clearly showed the desire of the advanced industrial nations to extend or consolidate their overseas empires. In 1898 the United States fought Spain to protect its predominance in the Caribbean and to establish more firmly its influence in the Pacific. A year later in South Africa, Britain commenced a bitter struggle with the Boers for the retention of some of the finest jewels, both literal and metaphorical, of its great Empire. Then, in 1900, the U.S.A., Britain, Germany, France, Austria–Hungary, Italy, Japan and Russia sent their troops into China to crush the Boxer Rebellion, thus guaranteeing their continued influence there.

While the struggle for colonial and other forms of control throughout the world is usually known as imperialism, Lenin and others also applied the term to the underlying reasons for this rivalry among the industrialising powers. To him, 'Imperialism is capitalism at that level of development, when the dominance of monopolies and finance capital is established, in which the export of capital has acquired pronounced importance, in which the division of the world by the international trusts has begun, in which the division of all the territories of the globe by the biggest capitalist powers has been completed.'[1] The understanding of the final period of tsarist history in Soviet works is firmly based upon such an understanding, while many non-Soviet analysts tend to ignore it.

In the Soviet view, Russia possessed some of the general characteristics of imperialism, but was also weighed down by less advanced economic features often characterised as oriental. Like other advanced countries, Russia moved into the monopoly-capitalist phase of development at the beginning of the twentieth century, and then, after 1914 until 1917, into military state monopoly-capitalism. The next stage of development was to be socialist. In the Russian case, however, the great banks and industrial monopolies coexisted with a backward agriculture and near serfdom. Russian imperialism was distinguished from most other varieties of the genus by its military-feudal nature and its application in areas contiguous to the metropolis rather than overseas. The bourgeoisie was still held back by a government more responsive to the interests of the powerful landed nobility, and thus was still carrying on the struggle for complete emancipation long after this had been achieved elsewhere. Its first task was therefore the overthrow of autocracy and the semi-feudal system of land possession which supported it.

The Revolution of 1905 did something towards the achievement of this priority. With land reforms, Russia took more positively the Prussian road to capitalism in agriculture. With the establishment of the Duma, tsarism took a further step towards transformation into a bourgeois monarchy. But such progress intensified rather than diminished the contradictions inherent in the peculiarities of Russian imperialism. The bourgeoisie found itself forced into an alliance with the landed aristocracy, and thus contributed to the maintenance of the system that it was attempting to overthrow. The alliance, in any case uneasy, was the sole focus of the rising revolutionary attack which had brought it about. Granted some respite at the beginning of the dénouement of world imperialism, the First World War, the ruling classes were then subject to a new and more vigorous onslaught from those whom they exploited. With the downfall of tsarism in February/March 1917, the weak bourgeoisie was soon virtually deserted by its expiring partner, the *dvorianstvo*, and was now at the mercy of the other class produced by industrialisation, the proletariat. The threat posed by the proletariat was all the greater because of Russia's geographical situation and late development, which presented the industrial working class with two firm allies in the shape of the oppressed nationalities and the downtrodden peasantry. Nevertheless, this new progressive combination against the bourgeoisie would not have been successful in the October Revolution and might not even have been formed in a few months of the year 1917 had it not been for the galvanising effect of the Bolsheviks, themselves dependent on the theoretical insights and strategic skill of Lenin. Such, briefly, is the Soviet historians' view.[2]

To a large group of non-Soviet historians, on the other hand, the reign of the last tsar is of greatest interest not as the final stage in the relentless march towards revolution but as a period when there were many opportunities for the old régime to reform itself by peaceful means and thus to avert destruction at the hand of fanatical opponents. The downfall of Nicholas II is seen as a tragedy, the overthrow of President Kerensky in October as a disaster. As already mentioned, those who think that there were chances for non-violent transformation have been called the 'optimists', those who take the opposite side in the debate without agreeing with the Soviet interpretation – the 'pessimists'.[3] From the 'optimist' point of view, there were several routes to salvation open to tsarism in its last years: reforms introduced by Witte and Stolypin might have succeeded; a Duma ministry might have been formed in 1906 or 1915; entry into the First World War might have been avoided; the conquest of illiteracy might have produced a more responsible people. These and other crucial questions will be examined below.

Central to most of them stands the tsar, Nicholas II. Some of the 'optimists' think that if he had been cast in a sterner mould, one of the safety routes would have been taken. To them, he was a good family man, but not the stuff that tsars should have been made of.[4] At the other end of the spectrum of interpretation, Trotsky argues that Nicholas II possessed the same fundamental characteristics as Charles I of England and Louis XVI of France, and with a wife as unsuitable for the situation as Henrietta-Maria and Marie-Antoinette. More than coincidence, these similarities revealed, not that a stronger man than Nicholas was neces- sary to suppress the Revolution, but rather that the Revolution was so relentless that the man attempting to stem it was bound to appear weak.[5]

Nicholas was born the eldest son of Alexander III in 1868. Tutors educated him, and he learned several languages. Before his accession in 1894, he travelled widely within Russia and around the world, but was given little practical training for the position he came to occupy at the age of twenty-six. Here we will not indulge in any attempt at character analysis, mostly because the exercise has become one of the most fami- liar themes of Russian history through book and film. Everybody knows about the closeness of the royal couple, Nicholas and Alexandra; about the evil influence of Rasputin brought about by the haemophilia of the tsarevich: about the final execution of the whole family, and the disputes surrounding it. Suffice it here to note that sentimentality and romantic nostalgia have often been taken too far, and that to many contempor- aries, the last of the Romanovs were by no means completely lovable. To quote one of the most distinguished members of the opposition, Leo Tolstoy, Nicholas II was to him as Nicholas I had been to Herzen, 'Chingis Khan with the telegraph'.[6] More succinctly, from the Revolu- tion of 1905 onwards, people at large thought of their tsar less as the 'little father' and more as 'Bloody Nicholas'.

About a year after the outbreak of the war, 'Nikky' left his 'Sunny' to go to the front to take up the duty of leading the armies in the field. 'Sunny' or 'Alix' now began to assert her views about the government even more confidently than before, listening ever more closely to the 'mad monk' (in fact, Rasputin was neither mad nor a monk).[7] On her role at this time, the Empress made the revealing remark, 'I am wearing invisible trousers'.[8] It would not be long before the workers and their comrades would see that the Empress and her husband, like the emperor in the fairy tale, wore no clothes at all.

Political

The reign of Nicholas II began quietly enough; right from the start, however, he made clear what his attitude would be to any question of reform. In a famous address to a meeting of deputies from the *zemstva* and municipalities at the beginning of 1895, he declared that all hopes for their participation in central government were 'senseless dreams', and that he would protect 'the principles of autocracy' as firmly and consistently as had his father.[9] He soon showed clearly what this policy would involve by expressing openly his support for those who had shot some troublesome workers in Iaroslavl, and by attending a ball after his coronation in 1896 even though over a thousand people had just died in a panic which followed the collapse of a viewing stand. The influence on Nicholas of his father and also of his tutor, Pobedonostsev, revealed itself in the further limitations which were placed on the *zemstva* and municipalities; the continued russification of the nationalities, including bloody suppression of such disturbances as the Central Asia Andijan Rising of 1898; the vigorous retention of the 'temporary regulations' of 1881; and the persecution of religious minorities, particularly the Jews, and of dangerous individuals, such as revolutionary radicals and other outsiders, notably Leo Tolstoy, who was excommunicated in 1901.

During this first half of the reign of Nicholas II, the *dvorianstvo* remained the most powerful political class, for all the efforts of Count Witte, Minister of Finance from 1892 to 1903, to develop the industrial economy and thus the bourgeoisie. Foreign policy, like domestic policy, was therefore most responsive to the needs of the landlords and the generals. While maintaining the alliance with France and aiming for peace, or at least rules of war, at the First Hague Conference which he instigated in 1899, Nicholas was also striving for the protection and extension of tsarist interests in the Balkans, the Middle East and Far East. Fearful after the Boxer Rebellion that Japan was gaining too much in the scramble for China with its seizure of Korea and infiltration of Manchuria, Nicholas moved his troops along the nearly completed Trans-Siberian Railway. They arrived just in time to be involved in the war which followed a sneak attack by the 'yellow monkeys' on Port Arthur in February 1904. While the bitter battle of Mukden in February 1905, which involved more than half a million men, ended in defeat for Russia, there was no rout on the land and the real humiliation came on the sea. The Pacific fleet, weakened by the unexpected Japanese descent on Port Arthur, was virtually annihilated while trying to break through to Vladivostok in late July 1904. Worse was to come when the powerful Baltic fleet set out to circumnavigate the world in a quest for vengeance. Nearly provoking war with Britain after mistaking fishing vessels in the North Sea for its Japanese enemies, it met the real thing at the Straits of Tsushima in May 1905 and was totally crushed.[10]

By this time, the débâcle of the war had combined with the unrest of the workers, peasants and nationalities to produce the first Russian Revolution. Ironically, Pleve, the Minister of the Interior, had at first welcomed the conflict with Japan, saying, 'To hold back the revolution, we need a small victorious war.'[11] Ironically too, the middle class, whose spokesmen had been pressing for representative government throughout 1904, soon discovered that the revolution that they had done more than a little to foment, went much further than they would have wished. Before the situation returned to something like normal in early 1906, the Revolution had spread wide enough and deep enough to fully justify Lenin's appraisal of it as a 'dress rehearsal' for the second and third Revolutions of February and October 1917.[12]

The first Revolution of 1905 broke out on 9 January with the notorious incident remembered as 'Bloody Sunday'. A peaceful procession of strikers from the Putilov Works and sympathisers was marching to the Winter Palace under the leadership of a priest, Father Gapon, in order to petition the tsar for 'justice and protection'.[13] The crowd, which numbered about 150,000 and included women and children, carried icons and portraits of the tsar. Suddenly, tsarist troops opened fire, killing more than a hundred and wounding more than a thousand. The impact of the mass murder was great and immediate. By evening barricades were up in many parts of St Petersburg. Strikes of sympathy were soon organised in Moscow and other towns. The peasants, their traditional faith in the 'little father' strongly shaken, increased the scale of revolt already in progress, the unrest reaching as far as the border provinces. A climax was reached in the summer with the celebrated insurrection on the battleship *Potemkin* in the Black Sea. The government, which had made a number of concessions and announcements, issued a manifesto on 6 August outlining the arrangements for elections to the State Duma which had first been promised in February. The public was far from ecstatic in the reception that it gave to the manifesto, nor was it happy with the terms of the Treaty of Portsmouth ending the war with Japan published in the same month. Witte's able diplomacy and Theodore Roosevelt's moderation had overcome the Japanese demands for indemnity, but Russia was forced nevertheless to acknowledge the supremacy of Japanese interests in Korea and to hand over to the 'yellow monkeys' Port Arthur and the peninsula on which it stood as well as the southern half of the island of Sakhalin.

More labour troubles led to a nationwide general strike from 7 to 12 October. Smirnov comments that it was 'on a truly gigantic scale with about two million people participating; it was the greatest mass strike that had ever taken place in Russia, or, for that matter, anywhere in the world. The military and police forces of the tsarist government were, to a certain extent, paralysed'.[14] Soviets, or Councils, of workers were organised in St Petersburg and elsewhere, and started to publish their own journal, *Izvestiia* or *News*. In the face of such opposition, persuaded by Witte that the alternatives were a constitution or a military dictatorship, Nicholas issued a manifesto which set Russia on the former course.[15]

The October Manifesto met with a mixed reception. The extreme right was appalled and became even more determined to smash all Jews and other such 'traitors' with its terroristic 'Black Hundred' gangs. The extreme left was completely unimpressed, Trotsky declaring that it was a 'scrap of paper' which could be torn up by the government as easily as by him.[16] The attitude of those in between varied from guarded suspicion to wild enthusiasm. Most certainly, the Revolution was not yet over. There were more strikes in the towns, culminating in an armed uprising in Moscow in December, which lasted for about ten days and resulted in nearly a thousand fatalities. Renewed outbreaks of violence broke out among the peasants in European Russia and the Baltic Provinces. The Finns and the Poles pushed their grievances, the Finns receiving considerable redress, the Poles none. There was more trouble in the armed forces, with a navy lieutenant named Schmidt leading the largest revolt at Sevastopol and soldiers from the defeated army of the Far East taking over a large section of the Trans-Siberian Railway for almost three months.

By the beginning of 1906, the tsarist government had restored order, Trotsky commenting 'la révolution est morte, vive la révolution'. Trotsky's wish was to be granted. As John Keep says, 'It is difficult to appreciate the extent of the psychological shock administered by the events of 1905 to men brought up on a diet of pious maxims and ancient superstitions'. He describes a political meeting which took place at Kazan University, where the speech of a Bolshevik propagandist was interrupted by an old worker shouting, 'How simple all this is! Why, brethren, did we not work this out for ourselves?' The others shouted in reply that it was because they were always drunk, but the point had got home, and at the end of the meeting, a cab-driver who belonged to the Old Believer sect called for a holy war against capital. According to Keep, the impact of the Revolution was similar in other towns, as well as among the peasants and national minorities. Its influence spread beyond the boundaries of the Empire, too.[17]

The Revolution of 1905 gave much encouragement to political parties on the left and at the centre. Of those on the left, the Bolsheviks have since become the most celebrated, but at the time they were one faction among many. The Russian Social Democratic Labour Party was formed in 1898 out of a number of groups started up in previous years in the capitals and other towns. But government interference sent some of its members to prison and some into exile, and the Party did not take on much shape before the celebrated split at the London Congress of 1903. Disagreements over the extent to which revolution should be immediately pursued and membership narrowly restricted led to the rift between the 'extremist' Bolsheviks and the 'moderate' Mensheviks. Legends have developed about these early historic moments and are encouraged in Soviet popular history. But the documentary record appears to show that at the beginning of the twentieth century affiliation to either wing of the R.S.D.L.P. did not necessarily mean complete adherence to its principles. Organisation and doctrine were both often weak and confused. To recognise such circumstances does not demean the historic achievement of Lenin and the Bolsheviks, but rather enhances it. Similarly, the Socialist Revolutionary Party, founded in 1901 with Viktor Chernov as its best-remembered leader, was neither neatly constituted in membership or programme. Broadly speaking, we may say that the S.R.s were the heirs of the populists, but they differed among themselves about the emphasis to be placed on terrorism and the degree to which they should concentrate on the peasant problem. Undoubtedly, S.D.s and S.R.s alike gained considerably from their first experience under fire in 1905.

The left-wing radicals were not the only busy politicians in the aftermath of revolution. Before the end of 1905, the two principal middle-class parties had been founded, and had prepared themselves for their self-appointed task of leading Russia along a peaceful road to constitutional monarchy. The Constitutional Democratic, or Cadet (after the initials Ka and De, not to be confused with army cadets) Party, was led by the historian Pavel Miliukov and became the main hope of Russian liberals. The Union of 17 October, or Octobrist Party, proclaimed its belief in the principles of the October Manifesto and was led by the businessman A. I. Guchkov. It was to the right of the Cadet Party, whose avowed beliefs in land expropriation were too much for landlords such as M. V. Rodzianko. Cadets and Octobrists came together with other deputies, such as those from the Trudovik or Labour Group (mainly peasants, left-wing but anti-revolutionary), the nationalities representatives and a few left-wing and right-wing radicals.[18]

The First Duma was convened in St Petersburg in April 1906. Elected on a suffrage which divided a restricted number of electors into four groups – landowners, townspeople, peasants and workers – and was then weighted in favour of the nobility and bourgeoisie, boycotted by the Bolsheviks and others on the left, the Duma was made even less dangerous by the Fundamental State Laws announced just before its first session. These retained for Nicholas the title of autocrat and complete control over the armed forces and foreign policy, which between them accounted for 40 per cent of the state budget. The State Council, which now became the upper legislative chamber, was to be half chosen by the tsar and half by various groups selected mainly from the nobility and bourgeoisie. If these limitations were not enough to render the Duma innocuous, Nicholas retained the power of veto over legislation and the right to issue emergency decrees when the Duma was not in session, although such decrees supposedly had to be confirmed during the first two months of the next session of the Duma, which was to meet every year.

The First Duma lasted just over seventy days. Its main party, the Cadets, attacked the Fundamental Laws and insisted on the implementation of its land policy, which included compensated expropriation of the landlords. While asking for an amnesty to be extended to political prisoners, the Cadets refused to condemn terrorism. In such circumstances, the failure to form a party-based ministry and the dissolution of the Duma came as a surprise to nobody.[19] Soon afterwards, about two hundred of its deputies, mostly Cadets, met at Vyborg in Finland to attack the government and call on the people to resist its requests for army recruits and taxes until the Duma was reconvened. The signatories of the Vyborg Manifesto were given three-month jail sentences and excluded from participation in the new elections.

The composition of the Second Duma, which convened in March 1907, was to the left of the First. The S.D.s and S.R.s did not boycott the elections and gained some representation, along with a reduced number of Cadets, more Trudoviks and more right-wingers. With Stolypin firmly in the saddle, and his controversial land bill introduced under the emergency Article 87 of the Fundamental Laws and now before the Duma for confirmation, there was much less chance of success for the Second Duma than the First. Again there was some talk of a party-based ministry, but it had come to nothing by the time that Stolypin used the refusal of the Duma to surrender the immunity of its S.D. members to dissolve it on 3 June. On the same day new electoral arrangements were announced which restricted the popular vote and led to the election of the much more compliant Third and Fourth Dumas.

From 3 June 1907 to the outbreak of war Russian political life experienced what Soviet historians call a Bonapartist phase, the Bonaparte in this case being P. A. Stolypin. Perhaps the most interesting discussion of the phase is by A. Ia. Avrekh, who begins one of his books on the subject with a discussion of what he calls the Stolypin Terror.[20] In 1908, he claims, there were in tsarist jails more than 200,000 inmates, twice the number of places available. Many were tortured, and more than 5000 death sentences were passed for political offences between 1907 and 1909. No fewer than one and a half million people were affected by oppressions ranging from investigation to execution during the years 1904–9. In a somewhat different period, 1906–12, more than 600 unions were forced to disband and as many were refused registration. 978 newspapers and periodicals were put out of action, with 174 of them being fined a total of 112,000 roubles. Meanwhile, the government connived at the activities of the anti-Semitic Black Hundreds and corrupt elections. The tsar himself sent congratulations to the leader of the *Union of the Russian People* and both he and his son wore the badges of this organisation of the radical right, to which Church leaders also lent their support. Meanwhile, in 1909, some liberals showed their hand with their collective publication of *Vekhi*, or *Landmarks*, expressing their clear opposition to socialism. Lenin denounced *Vekhi* as the encyclopedia of liberal renegades.[21] From the other side, *Vekhi* has been defended, even praised, as a thoughtful and perspicacious series of essays.[22] Western appraisals of Stolypin have been mixed, although even those antipathetic to him have not usually been as denunciatory as those of Avrekh and his colleagues.[23] The essence of the defence of Stolypin has been that extraordinary times demand extraordinary measures. If he meted out terror, it was in response to the terror directed at him and other tsarist officials. According to government statistics, more than 1500 of them were killed by terrorists in 1906 and more than 2500 in 1907. Against a background of disturbances among the workers and peasants, a group of terrorists bombed Stolypin's summer home in the summer of 1906, killing more than thirty people and wounding more than twenty, including his son and daughter. Stolypin himself escaped unhurt, but his reprieve was temporary; he was assassinated in September 1911, probably not at the orders of the tsar, as was rumoured, but by a double agent acting on his own initiative.[24]

In the Third Duma, elected in 1907 by about 15 per cent of the population, the Octobrists replaced the Cadets as the centre party. They enjoyed no absolute majority, but could be the dominant members of two majorities, to the left with the Cadets for reform, or to the right with the conservative deputies for stabilisation. According to Avrekh, such a situation was no accident, but rather the manipulation of tsarism and its chief minister to retain power in conditions of Bonapartism. Stolypin nevertheless needed a considerable amount of skill, since he and his associates were themselves often manipulated by the real government, the court camarilla. Using the formula pacification, then reform, and making patriotic appeals such as 'no second Tsushima', Stolypin persuaded the Duma moderates to give out tens and hundreds of millions of roubles to the army and navy, the police and other organs of the state apparatus while conceding 'legislative cud' to their appetite for liberal measures. An example of such 'reforms' scornfully dismissed by Avrekh was a bill 'On the institution at the Erevan Teachers Seminary of 20 stipends for Tatar students, with the issue from the treasury of 2600 roubles a year, on the supplementary consignment of 140 roubles a year as payment for a teacher at the said seminary and on the transformation of the one-class elementary school at this seminary into a two-class structure with a supplementary consignment for his upkeep of 970 roubles a year'.[25] More meaningful measures which passed the Duma, such as some projects on religious toleration, were turned down either by the State Council or the tsar. When attempts to restrict the power of the second chamber or to assert its own power appeared to be making even the conservative Third Duma something of a real threat, Stolypin crushed such impudence with the full support of the court camarilla. In such a context, Avrekh argues, Miliukov's ideas of 'parallel activity', the struggle for democratic constitutionalism in the Duma at the same time as popular pressure outside it, acquire their real empty meaning. For Geoffrey Hosking, Stolypin's programme is best called a kind of 'constitutional nationalism', a mixture 'similar to that which Joseph Chamberlain had been preaching in Britain a few years earlier: an Empire for the common man'. Meanwhile, 'Germany was the model to which the centre and right in Russian politics tended to look as an example of the successful integration of an authoritarian monarchy, an imperial patriotism and parliamentary institutions'. In Hosking's evaluation, it was the latter right-wing Octobrist model which stood the better chance of adoption in the Third Duma, Avrekh exaggerating the importance of Miliukov and the Cadets.[26]

At the cost of his position and perhaps his life, Stolypin was able to put through the Duma much of his legislation concerning the difficult problems of the peasants, the workers and the nationalities. On the agrarian question, his formula was first the citizen, then citizenship. He secretly said to a meeting of the Council of Ministers in July 1907, 'a strong rich peasantry permeated with the idea of property serves everywhere as the best stronghold of order and quiet, and if the government manages to achieve this aim through the implementation of its land measures, there will be an end once and for all to dreams of a state and socialist revolution in Russia'.[27] After much debate and some anxiety, Stolypin received the support of the Duma for his land programme. As far as the workers were concerned, there was a considerable amount of talk and some action, on insurance projects for example, but only enough to persuade liberal members of the Duma that they were taking some steps at least to solve the growing proletarian predicament. On the nationalities question, Stolypin undoubtedly took the Great Russian point of view, but his western *zemstvo* project did not go far enough for some patriots and he was running into trouble with it from several sides at the time of his assassination.

The Fourth Duma, which first met at the end of 1912, was weaker and more to the right than its predecessor and controlled by a similarly endowed minister, V. N. Kokovtsov. As he came to power, he received advice from the royal couple. Nicholas said, 'Don't follow the example of Petr Arkadevich, who tried to overthrow me', and Alexandra said, 'You must not try to continue blindly what your predecessor had done. . . . Do not seek support in political parties; they are so insignificant with us. Depend on the trust of the sovereign.'[28] On the whole, Kokovtsov took the advice, but was removed at the beginning of 1914 for taking a stand against corruption and Rasputin. He was replaced by the ineffectual reactionary I. L. Goremykin, a seventy-five-year-old sycophant.

Bonapartism was more than a governmental system, as far as the historian Avrekh and his Soviet colleagues are concerned. To them, it also reflected the social system, the unsteady alliance between the landed aristocracy and the industrial bourgeoisie. Stolypin was able to control the Duma, to put it in an oversimplified manner, because he was able to exploit the tensions between the two classes which were demonstrated in the two majorities capable of being formed by the Octobrists. With the outbreak of the First World War, and the shift from monopoly capitalism to military state monopoly capitalism, the alliance between the aristocracy and the bourgeoisie moved into a new phase. Against such a background, the last political manoeuvres of the tsarist period were played out. Thus, the attempt of Miliukov and the Progressive Bloc to achieve 'a ministry enjoying the confidence of the public' in 1915[29] and 'the ministerial leapfrog' of 1916 (as Commander-in-Chief Nicholas at the front and the Empress Alexandra behind his back tried to find a man enjoying the confidence of their 'Friend', Rasputin), reveal tsarist society at successive stages of its dissolution.

Some Western historians would agree to some extent with the Soviet interpretation of the government and its social setting between 1905 and 1917. For example, Leopold Haimson comes close to an acceptance of the Soviet view of social stability in urban Russia from 1905 to 1917, except concerning the part played by the peasants coming into the towns and the extent to which the Bolsheviks were losing touch with the worker movement on the eve of the outbreak of war.[30] On the other hand, Miliukov's biographer, Thomas Riha, argued that Russian constitutionalism had several solid achievements to its credit and weathered the storm well until 1914.[31]

While the Duma debated, the revolutionary movement was quiet from 1907 until 1910. Resistance to tsarism was passive on the whole, one of the most evident forms that it took being emigration. Between the beginning of the century and 1910, roughly a million and a half people went from the towns and villages of European Russia, the Ukraine, Belorussia, Poland, Lithuania, Latvia and the Jewish Pale to the New World. Between 1896 and 1914, about three and a half million colonists moved from these older areas of settlement to Siberia. But the 'safety-valve' of the domestic and transoceanic frontier was not enough to relieve the Empire's social tensions. A new strike movement gathered momentum in 1911 and moved on to a new level after the massacre in April 1912 of more than 250 strikers at the Lena Goldfields in Siberia. There were sympathy strikes in Moscow and St Petersburg, the Ukraine and the Baltic provinces, and in towns along the Volga. And then in 1913, 250,000 workers came out to press for the reprieve of some revolutionary sailors who had been condemned to death for plotting an abortive uprising in the fleet. 40,000 people demonstrated over the Beilis Affair, the apparently rigged trial of a Jew for the ritual murder of a young Russian. Altogether, there were nearly 1,000,000 strikers in 1912, 1,270,000 in 1913 and 1,300,000 in the first six months of 1914.[32]

A new revolution was in the air, in the towns if not in the countryside. The outbreak of war brought tsarism some respite, with only a handful of demonstrators incurring the wrath of Russian patriots, but a new upsurge set in early in 1915 and continued, albeit with some fluctuation, right up to the February Revolution. The biggest outbreak of violence was in central Asia, where a revolt by the inhabitants against their mobilisation in 1916 cost the tsarist army more casualties than the entire conquest of Turkestan.[33]

The internal collapse of the Empire was inextricably connected with the failure of its foreign policy to avoid war. Stolypin had realised clearly enough that Russia could deteriorate in such a manner. 'Our internal situation does not permit us to pursue an aggressive foreign policy', he once declared. 'Peace at any price' was his motto. A reactionary adviser of the tsar, P. N. Durnovo, argued in a memorandum of early 1914 that Russia's probable defeat in a European war would fling the Empire into 'hopeless anarchy, the issue of which cannot be foreseen'. A voice even closer to the tsar's ear, that of Rasputin, proclaimed that 'with the war will come the end of Russia'.[34] Why was it then that Russia became involved in the first World War?

The answer to this vexed question does not lie in the Far East, except in the negative sense that *rapprochement* with Japan after 1905 allowed tsarist ministers to concentrate their attentions elsewhere. In the Middle East and Central Asia, there was further tension with Britain before, and, to a lesser extent, after the Anglo-Russian Agreement of 1907, which divided Persia into spheres of influence. But tension did not lead to crisis and Russia, already tied to France, joined the Entente Cordiale between France and Britain as the European situation deteriorated. As the weakest of the imperialist powers, Russia was obliged to follow the lead of its stronger partners; in the last resort, the decision for war would be taken in London, Paris or Berlin. But we cannot evade the question of Russia's involvement. Why was it that Russia was sucked into the vortex by way of the Balkans? Was her rivalry with Austria–Hungary and Germany so great that skilled diplomats such as Izvolskii and Sazonov could not avoid the ultimate confrontation?

At times, it appeared that the Three Emperors' League would be revived to supplant the Triple Entente. Germanophilia possessed an influential group of reactionary landowners and some members of the court camarilla. The tsar himself was very fond of the kaiser, and embarrassed his ministers by signing a bilateral treaty with Wilhelm at Björkö in the summer of 1905 while the two Emperors were cruising together on the Baltic in their yachts. And then, at the very brink, the 'dear cousins' exchanged an unsuccessful series of telegrams. However, the circumstances making for war were bigger than both of them.

If A. J. P. Taylor is justified in calling the dénouement of 1914 'war by timetable',[35] there were still necessary great powers keen to abide by the schedule. As far as Germany is concerned, Fritz Fischer has most thoroughly documented its grasp at world power. In his view, the generals and their allies in business and government were aiming at a huge empire stretching from Hamburg to Constantinople.[36] At the very least, as even Fischer's critics would concede, a line of defence would be drawn to the east of Germany's frontiers and large parts of Eastern Europe looked upon as a sphere of German commercial and diplomatic influence.[37] As for the Russians, far from wanting to accede to the reduction of their Empire and interest without a fight, many of them harboured dreams of expansionism hardly less ambitious than those of their German counterparts. According to such Soviet analysts as I .V. Bestuzhev, a powerful segment of bourgeois-landlord opinion was in favour of the firm protection of Russia's power and of its extension too. They increased their demands through the series of Balkan crises until they were making loud cries for a showdown in the summer of 1914. L. C. F. Turner sees the Russian mobilisation of July 1914 as the decisive moment.[38] More generally, with his emphasis on socio-economic factors, Bestuzhev claims that the July crisis was 'not an accidental catastrophe, but the consequence that was bound to follow from the objective conditions reflected in the policies of the imperialist powers'.[39]

In the early days of the war, German pressure on Paris was very great indeed, and the Russians were asked to afford relief by attacking from the east. The Russians took the French chestnuts out of the fire, but at the cost of putting their own in it. As Smirnov puts it, 'The famous Battle of the Marne, that saved Paris, was won at the cost of the blood of Russian soldiers in East Prussia'.[40] Those not killed, wounded or captured were exhausted and wretchedly supplied. Little resistance was offered to a determined attack by the Central Powers in 1915 as the original plan of campaign, named after Schlieffen and concentrating on the Western front, was reversed. By the end of that year, all of Poland and Lithuania had been lost, as well as part of Latvia and Belorussia. Many important economic resources were no longer available to the Russians. Moreover, their total losses in manpower, including prisoners, were nearly three and a half millions. In March 1916 the Russians again attacked to relieve pressure on the Western front, this time on Verdun. Losses were as high as before. Then in May an army under General Brusilov attacked the Austro-Hungarians on the south-western front and advanced all summer, thus keeping beleaguered Italy in the war and virtually knocking the Habsburg Empire out of it. But the success was not followed up on other fronts, nor was Nicholas II encouraged by Rasputin and the Empress to pursue it. In any case, the Russian forces were by now thoroughly weak. By the end of 1916 the Russian Empire's western flank was almost as fragile as its insides.

In return for its efforts in the war, which included some successful operations and some failures in minor theatres such as Transcaucasia, Russia received large amounts of aid from the Allies and the U.S.A. Because of inadequate transport facilities and sometimes because of the reluctance of businessmen to support a bad risk, by no means all the aid promised to Russia reached it or was even sent. Moreover, the tsarist régime found itself increasingly treated as a junior partner of the Entente, with its place at the conference tables by no means secure. In such a manner, a military and diplomatic legacy was built up too heavy for its successor to bear. The war broke President Kerensky as surely as it had broken Tsar Nicholas.

Economic

At the turn of the century, Russia was an inseparable part of the world capitalist economy. She shared in the prosperity of the later 1890s, in the crisis which struck about 1900, and to a lesser extent in recovery from 1904 to 1907. Set back by another depression in 1907, she moved on from 1909 to 1913 to a new and greater recovery. The dislocation brought about by the First World War was greater for the Russian imperial economy than elsewhere, and it succumbed in 1917.

Before we take a closer look at this process, we must briefly consider the demographic trends of the period, as previously promised. This may conveniently be done by first looking at the following analysis of the class composition of the population in 1913 compared with that in 1897 and set out in tabular form, putting urban and rural dwellers together:

	Whole population: Both sexes in millions		Proportion in percentages	
	1897	1913	1897	1913
Large-scale bourgeoisie, landlords, higher officials	3·0	4·1	2·4	2·5
Wealthy small proprietors	23·1	31·5	18·4	19·0
Poor small proprietors	35·8	42·0	28·5	25·3
Semi-proletariat	41·7	55·6	33·2	33·6
Proletariat	22·0	32·5	17·5	19·6
Total	125·6	165·7	100·0	100·0

Secondly, as far as native language indicated, in 1897, nearly 45 per cent were Great Russians, 18 per cent Ukrainians and 11 per cent Turkic peoples. Of the hundreds of other peoples who went to make up the polyglot Empire, the largest single group was the Jews, just over 4 per cent of the total. Thirdly, the urban population was about 17 millions in 1897 and grew by 1914 to about 22 millions, by 1916 to about 28 millions. Both St Petersburg and Moscow had over 2 million inhabitants by 1917. The urban proletariat, which was to have a significance far beyond its members, increased from $1\frac{1}{2}$ millions in 1897 to nearly $4\frac{1}{4}$ millions in 1913, over half of the workers being employed in large-scale enterprises.[41]

Although the most significant features of the Russian economy from the imperialistic point of view may be found in the industrial sector, we can readily see that most of the people were still involved in agriculture, and the most influential class in late tsarist society was the landed nobility. Grain was by far the most important export at the beginning of the twentieth century, and the Stolypin land reforms are often considered by 'optimists' and even by 'pessimists' to have been the basis for Russia's best chance of achieving a peaceful path to modernisation.

While the landlords sold nearly 27 million acres of land through the Peasant Bank in the years 1906–16, and nearly as much more was mortgaged through the Noble Bank in the same period, there were still in existence on the eve of the February Revolution more than 75,000 estates of the nobility covering more than 7 million hectares (about 19 million acres), with less than 10,000 of the estates accounting for more than half the area. Just before the First World War broke out, from a total grain production of more than 80 million metric tons, about 12 per cent of the total still came from the estates of the landlords. Nearly 50 per cent of the landlords' wholesale grain production was sold in the market, and landlords were also very busy with the manufacture on their estates of sugar, vodka and flour. On the whole, the profitability of their agriculture was higher than that of the peasants.

This comparative prosperity was achieved through the maintenance of the backward semi-serf labour system of agriculture known as *otrabotka*. Even when not subjected to a landlord, peasant farming was often held back by the stranglehold of the commune and the persistence of strip farming. Discussions of reform did not get very far before the Revolution of 1905, but, with provisions made in November of that year for the cancellation of the redemption payments, the way was now open for reforms such as those envisaged by Stolypin. More than two

million individual farmsteads had been set up by 1915. Whereas to
Mosse, the success of the Stolypin reform was greatest where it was
least needed, and the programme of the Socialist Revolutionary Party
posed a far greater threat to Lenin's chances of success, Tokmakoff
quotes with approval a Soviet verdict that, with the reform, 'the Russian
pre-revolutionary village considerably moved forward on the road of a
rapidly developing capitalism'.[42]

Soviet historians generally note the boost that the reforms of 1906
and 1910 gave to capitalist farming, but also stress that the rural proletariat rose in numbers to reach four and a half millions by 1913. They
also point out that, while co-operative farms increased eighteen times
from 1900 to a figure of 23,841 in 1915 and the gross annual harvest
rose by about two-fifths in roughly the same period, more than half the
peasant farms still used primitive ploughs at the time of the February
Revolution. To show the relative backwardness of Russian agriculture
as a whole, they present such statistics as, for example, the ratio in 1914
between population and head of cattle – 1000:293 in Russia, 1000:622
in the U.S.A. and 1000:888 in Denmark.

For an industrial revolution to succeed without foreign assistance,
indigenous capital must come ultimately from the rural sector of the
economy. This was the necessity which drove the Soviet government
towards collectivisation. In the pre-1917 case, the foreign capital was
forthcoming, and so the need was not so great. Of importance here
was the work of Sergei Witte, Minister of Finance from 1892 to 1903.
To T. H. Von Laue, Witte was a far-sighted, energetic statesman trying
'to rally both government and people to one common, almost super-
human effort'. For Smirnov, he was 'a militant monarchist'.[43] Certainly,
by the time that the Stolypin reform was under way, a considerable
capital base had already been formed in the Empire, and so the pressure
was not on it for immediate success. At the commencement of the advance of 1909–13, there was twice as much railroad as in 1893, when the
previous leap forward had occurred. The railroads were still insufficient
for Russia's industrialising needs, as we shall see below, but, coupled
with such increases as a doubling of heavy industrial production and a
50 per cent rise in the number of workers during the same period, they
provided a more substantial foundation for growth than there had been
at the beginning of Nicholas II's reign. A further advance could now
take place towards monopoly capitalism.

During the years 1909–13, the annual growth rate of Russian industry
was about 8.8 per cent per annum as opposed to 9 per cent per annum
in the years 1893–1900. This rate was broadly similar to that of other

industrialising countries during the same years. Although the Russian tempi were sometimes higher than the Western (for example, world production of cast-iron, 1909–13, up by 32 per cent: U.S.A. up by 20 per cent; Germany up by 50 per cent: Russia up by 64 per cent), Russia produced fewer machines than the U.S.A., Germany or Japan, if more than France. As a consequence of this, in 1912 the import of industrial machinery equalled domestic production, while that of agricultural machinery exceeded it. While capital also came from abroad (about 126 million roubles per annum on average from 1908 to 1913), domestic investment now rose above foreign (225 million roubles per annum on average in the same period).[44]

The industrial advance in the years leading up to the First World War took place for the most part in six regions: the central in and around Moscow; the north-west in and around St Petersburg; the Baltic in Riga, Tallin and other towns; the southern in the Donbas and Krivoi Rog; the Polish at Dombrova and elsewhere; and the Urals. In 1911 more than 75 per cent of all wholesale production took place in these regions, and nearly 80 per cent of all large-scale enterprise workers were employed in them. In the comparatively new southern region alone, more than 80 per cent of Russia's coal and more than 70 per cent of her cast-iron were produced. Baku on the Caspian, the most important centre for oil, was the only town not in the six regions that could properly be called industrial. The advance was strictly regional, then, and so it was possible to visit the Empire in 1913, as it still was possible to visit the Soviet Union sixty years later, without noticing the level to which industrialisation had climbed. But in 1912 there were more than 250 metallurgical works and in 1911 more than 550 coal mines. In 1913 there were nearly 850 cotton factories, with 9 million spindles and more than 200,000 looms. By 1914 $4\frac{1}{2}$ million horse-power was being applied in industry by machines, a rise from something over 2 million horse-power in 1908. For each worker, there was now $1\frac{1}{2}$ horse-power, as opposed to less than 1 horse-power per worker earlier.

For all this advance, the structure of Russian industry in the period of imperialism was very different from that of other advancing countries. In 1913 more than 40 per cent of Russian workers were in textiles and food processing, while about 35 per cent of them were in the mines, metal extraction and smelting or machine-making. In Germany the comparable figures were something less than 25 per cent and something more than 40 per cent respectively. True, in concentration of industry, Russia out-stripped Germany and the other developed countries, but this was a reflection of the insufficiently intensive industrial development of the Empire as a whole, and was for the most part accompanied by a lower level of specialisation and less technical equipment.

Growth in large-scale industry was accompanied by growth in the small-scale and peasant sectors. On the eve of the war, out of a grand total of about 800,000 such enterprises, there were about 150,000 of them with 2–15 workers in each. There were also about 600,000 small tradesmen working by themselves or with one worker. Meanwhile, peasant crafts supplemented the income of up to 4 million semi-proletarianised tradesmen during the winter months. In underdeveloped regions workers employed in small-scale industry outnumbered those in large-scale concerns. On the whole, however, Soviet historians say that after 1900 the part played by large-scale industry became marked. It 'determined the level of industrialisation of the country at large and could serve as the material-productive basis for the transition to socialism'.[45]

Such a basis could have been more substantial if there had been a commensurate expansion of communications and transport. But between 1908 and 1913, railroad construction reached its lowest level since the 1880s: about 4500 kilometres of track being added to those already in existence to produce a grand total of about 65,000 kilometres. Even in European Russia, the railways were considerably less widespread than in Western Europe or the U.S.A. The state continued to dominate this principal artery of communications and transport, along with six large private companies in the 1890s. It was government policy, then, for railroad construction to be curtailed, for reasons that will be considered below. Even those lines already in existence were not adequately kept up, and about 40 per cent of the Empire's locomotives were out of date in 1913. The average freight carried by a Russian wagon was about 15 metric tons while a German wagon could carry up to 50 metric tons. Moreover, the government's priorities, partly at the bidding of its foreign creditors, were military and strategic rather than commercial. Perhaps the most noteworthy of those enlargements of the system that did manage to be achieved during the last years of tsarism resulted in the extension of the Trans-Siberian Railway to Vladivostok in 1916.

A sizeable amount of inland freight was carried by waterways, particularly the Volga network, which accounted for about 60 per cent of all waterborne traffic. There were more than 30,000 river-boats in operation in 1912, including more than 5500 steamboats. Telegraph and telephones were other forms of communication to show some advance from 1900 onwards. However, there were very few properly metalled roads, and the cart was the standard means of transport along most of them. Baedeker's *Handbook for Travellers* in Russia for 1914 advises motorists: 'The great national highroads connecting St Petersburg, Moscow, Warsaw, and Kiev are admirably adapted for motoring and are kept in good condition. . . . The roads maintained by the provincial authorities are of a very different character, and the traveller is advised not to try any of them until he has made enquiries at a local motor club'.[46] Except for oil freighters on the landlocked Caspian Sea, Russia's mercantile marine was negligible in size.

Foreign ships, then, carried most of her growing external commerce. By 1913 this had doubled from the 1890s, and was now worth more than 2·5 billion roubles.* But her share of the world's trade had not grown nearly as much, from about 4 per cent at the end of the nineteenth century to 4·25 per cent in 1913. This was about half France's share, twice that of Japan at the time. Unlike the more developed countries, Russia continued to export grain and other agricultural produce, and to import mainly industrial goods. By 1913 grain exports had risen one and a half times in quantity and twice in value from the 1890s, and most of the other exports by at least as much, butter, eggs and timber by three or even four times. During the years leading up to the war, Russia's annual exports were valued at 1·5 billion roubles per annum, of which grain comprised 44 per cent, and cattle and forest products 22 per cent. Industrial exports did not reach 10 per cent, and nearly all of them went east to Asia. Imports also doubled during the same period, reaching an average annual value of 1·2 billion roubles from 1909 to 1913. The principal items of import were textile raw materials – cotton, wool and silk, coal for the north-west and Baltic industrial regions, chemicals and non-ferrous metals, machines and technical equipment, tea and luxuries for the consumption of the ruling classes. While the balance of trade was favourable to Russia, her balance of payments was under strain from the burden of the payment of percentages and dividends on foreign debts and investments, and from the considerable expenditures of prosperous Russians travelling abroad. Germany continued to take first place in Russia's foreign trade – 30 per cent of exports and 50 per cent of imports in 1913, Great Britain was second and France a long way behind in third position.

The internal trade was much more valuable than the foreign, reaching a total of 18 billion roubles in 1913, which was one and a half times the 1900 level. According to Soviet calculation, her internal trade network

* Billion here and elsewhere expresses a thousand million, nor a million million.

consisted of 1,118,000 units in 1913 compared with 854,000 in 1900. Among them were 183,000 wholesale and large retail firms, and more than 1·2 million shopkeepers, stallholders, traders and distributors. With hired workers added, the total number of people involved in domestic commerce approached 2 millions. Their activities were partly capitalist, partly pre-capitalist. They were distinguished by a strong seasonal and fluctuating character because of their agricultural emphasis. Although in decline, fairs were still important. The standards of internal trade were low. Payments were often late, contracts poorly observed and specialisation lacking. Russian backwardness was clearly demonstrated in her grain trade. There were not many elevators or proper collection points. Conditions at the ports were bad, and much grain was spoiled. Large-scale operations were few, and credit facilities undeveloped, constant peasant indebtedness causing perpetual troubles.

Nevertheless, trade as a whole was more profitable than industry, accruing 788 million roubles in 1913 as opposed to 510 millions from large-scale industry and 142 millions from small-scale industry. And so commercial-mercantile capital, based mostly on Moscow, was very important during the imperialist period. The growth of capitalist enterprise in general was reflected in the expansion of the banking system. Not only did the State Bank and the joint-stock commercial banks mainly centred on St Petersburg increase their operations during the period under discussion, local banks also were either founded, or expanded their already existing business. From 1908 to 1913 the resources of all commercial banks grew two and a half times to 7 billion roubles, and their active operations expanded in approximately the same degree. The State Bank was the central issue bank, looking after the gold reserves, regulating the circulation of money and putting out gold-backed notes ever since 1897 when Witte put Russia on the Gold Standard. It also kept the state income, which was the basis of its loan operations. The State Bank of Russia was distinguished from that of most other countries through its close connection with the state budget and the Ministry of Finance. It was thus able to keep a close watch on the financial operations of the Empire as a whole. Mutual credit and co-operative banks expanded in number and activity in the pre-war years, and the Land Bank system was still in active use. In 1914 the Land Banks had a total capital of 5·3 billion roubles, of which just under a third belonged to the bourgeoisie. Even in *Junker*-bourgeois Germany, the urban share in such mortgage operations was considerably more than twice that of rural proprietors. Here, as elsewhere, comparative Russian backwardness was clearly revealed.

Such backwardness was to an appreciable extent the result of the government's priority of financial stability. It saw railroad construction as the basic lever of economic growth, but restricted it to keep the budget steady. It favoured the protection and expansion of industry, but the latter only at a moderate pace. Thus, having approached the economic level of other countries in the 1890s, Russia fell behind in the early twentieth century. The budget was balanced, but at great cost, particularly since it included a state debt increasing from 7·9 billion roubles in 1900 to 12·7 billion roubles in 1913. 5·4 billion of the latter figure were of foreign origin, and 400 million roubles had to be sent to France and elsewhere every year to repay the debts of the state and of private commerce. Tsarist Russia was the greatest international debtor in the world. For this reason, taxes had to be squeezed as much as possible out of a recalcitrant public, more than a quarter of the state's income actually coming from the state's monopoly on spirits.

Backward though it was in some aspects of its financial arrangements, Russia was very advanced in others. By the outbreak of the war, its economy had entered the stage of monopoly capitalism. The stock exchange, which had previously been used mostly for the floating of state and land loans, was now very much interested in industrial stock, particularly in St Petersburg, where it was dominated by the large banks. The joint-stock capital of all companies, including non-industrial enterprises and banks, had grown to 2·1 billion roubles, of which 64 per cent was floated in Russia itself, and most invested in heavy industry. While the first monopolistic amalgamations had been brought about in the late nineteenth century, and a second group of them achieved during the crisis at the beginning of the twentieth century, the third and most decisive stage took place in the immediate pre-war years, when a wide range of trusts, cartels and syndicates was set up. Glass, cable and agricultural machinery were just three of the items covered by the new organisations, which spread throughout the provinces as well as expanding their activities in the capitals. For example, *Prodamet*, which had been originally set up in 1902 to manage the all-Russian sale of ferrous metals, came by 1912 to control 76 per cent of the Empire's rails and 95 per cent of her girders. In 1910 *Prodamet* consisted of about 30 enterprises, including 16 to the south, 8 in Poland, 3 by the Baltic, and 1 each in the centre, the Urals and along the Volga. The syndicate had a complex accounting and distributive network, with central and provincial branches. It would undercut competitors and compensate by high prices where no competition existed.

The banks played an important part in *Prodamet* and other syndicates, and were extending their operations to the peripheral regions of the Empire. The railway was reaching into Central Asia and Siberia, too, and Russians were going to live there in increasing numbers. Colonies of the settlement type, similar to Canada and Australia, were being formed in Siberia and Kazakhstan, while subject colonies, similar to India and Algeria, were being developed in Uzbekistan and Trans-caucasia. About four million Russians moved into the new lands be-tween 1896 and 1916, and many raw materials were produced by them. For example, cotton production rose from about a quarter of a million metric tons in 1907 to a figure approaching half a million metric tons in 1914. About a third of the total requirements of Russian industry were supplied from such a source in 1900, more than a half by 1913.

On the eve of the war, then, the Russian Empire possessed the most advanced form of financial-industrial management on the one hand and primitive nomadic forms of economic organisation on the other. As a whole, it was a country of middle-level economic development, its means of production having risen sevenfold from 1890 to 1913. In the latter year, Russia was fifth overall in world industrial production, in some branches fourth. However, as far as her share was concerned, it amount-ed to only 4·2 per cent of the world's total. Russia was in an advancing but precarious international position, then, when the war broke out.[47]

The immediate impact on Russia of the war was tremendous. The cornerstone of her financial policy, the Gold Standard, was abandoned almost immediately. Without gold backing for its notes, the currency was undermined by rampant paper inflation. Foreign loans increased to a level which meant more than 6 billion roubles going on repayment and relevant orders just before the February Revolution. Even more than before, Russia had become the client of foreign powers, Britain, France, the United States, Japan and Italy in descending order of im-portance. An additional burden was placed on the Empire's strained financial resources by the introduction of prohibition. Moreover, the break with Germany meant the loss of Russia's major trading partner. While the decline was not always immediate or continuous, crises had set in by 1916 in transport, metallurgy, fuel, and other branches of in-dustry as well as in agriculture.[48] Social dislocation had been brought into the city and the village.

On the other hand, the concentration of the economy brought about by the war had moved it into a new and higher stage, that of military-state monopoly capitalism. War Industrial Committees and Special Consultative Councils for defence, fuel, supply and transport, brought government and business closer together. There are two ways of looking at this development, as there are of considering Russian economic progress during the age of imperialism as a whole. Von Laue, Carr and other 'pessimists' in the West join Soviet historians to assert that it was making revolution more unavoidable. Gerschenkron is perhaps the most ingenious exponent of the 'optimistic' point of view, which argues that Russia was moving towards the pattern of the Western industrialising powers, and nearing the point when revolution would have been superfluous.[49] Even most 'optimists', however, find it difficult to persist in their argument when considering the years after 1914.

Cultural

'Not only the body but the soul of Russia as well was growing stronger and healthier during the decade which preceded the World War', argued the émigré Michael Karpovich, finding striking progress in cultural activity as well as in the economy.[50] In his view, education took important strides forward. With a relaxation of censorship, the daily press, including opposition newspapers, came to occupy a significant position in Russian life, and religious toleration grew, even though the Orthodox Church remained a central part of the tsarist establishment. Now that the Duma was an outlet for political expression, many intellectuals were able to turn more exclusively to the sciences or the arts, to both of which Russians made exciting new contributions. In the Soviet view, on the other hand, while many of the artistic and scientific achievements are to be celebrated, other developments reveal the sickness of a society on the point of collapse. Above all, this was the period which saw the formation of the revolutionary and post-revolutionary outlook. As S. S. Dmitriev puts it:

> Russian culture of the epoch of imperialism is not only our yesterday, but also something of today. The ideas of Lenin illuminate the world. They are the zenith of Russian culture at the beginning of our century. The literature and art of socialist realism were born in our country in the years of the first Russian revolution, and developed in the difficult time between the two revolutions. Many achievements of contemporary science are rooted at the beginning of our century. The war of ideas by Marxists for progress in science, against decadence in literature and art, for the correct understanding of national pride and respect for the revolutionary and democratic traditions, campaigns against apostasy, for socialist optimism, for a scientifically based belief in a bright future are still timely and instructive.[51]

While recognising the cultural progress of the other nationalities soon to be members of the Soviet Union as well as the Russian move forward, Dmitriev notes the opposition of Lenin to the bourgeois, often Black Hundred clerical slogan of 'national culture' and his substitution for it of the international culture of the democratic movement of the workers of the world.

In our discussion of these 'optimistic' and 'pessimistic' appraisals of the last stage of tsarist culture, we may make a division, as in our political discussion, between a pre-1905 and a post-1905 period. We may also notice that during this period Russia was not unaffected by new phenomena which were beginning to fill the earth and sky – the train, the automobile and the aeroplane. On 27 August 1913 N. N. Nesterov revealed a previously unrealised aspect of the potential of the aeroplane by performing the first loop-the-loop in the history of mankind, Dmitriev proudly tells us. Before the outbreak of the war, both the army and the navy were using radio. By that time too, there were nearly 1500 cinemas in Russian towns, of which both St Petersburg and Moscow as well as others such as Kiev, Odessa, Riga and Tiflis, were taking on all aspects of a modern shape. Baedeker's *Handbook for Travellers* in Russia for 1914, for example, gives information on the electric tramways as well as on the horsedrawn vehicles in all these cities, among others.[52] Even the appearance of many villages was changing, with the replacement of at least some wooden buildings by stone.

According to some 'optimists', Imperial Russia was at last in sight of a solution to the age-old problem of illiteracy by the time of its collapse. A growing debate in the 1890s, intensified by the revelation of the 1897 census that barely a fifth of those for whom information had been gathered could read and write, and given new emphasis by the Revolution of 1905, led to the law of 3 May 1908. While more progressive legislation was turned down by the State Council, the Duma believed that through this law it was still making provision for the complete application by 1922 of compulsory education to all children between the ages of eight and eleven. The problem was barely half solved for such children by 1914, and is made to appear much more formidable if a wider age bracket is considered or a more regional emphasis is given. In such a case, the problem would be more like a bare quarter on the way to solution. Nevertheless, progress was marked from 65,000 primary schools (including church schools) with about $3\frac{1}{2}$ million pupils in 1896 to 122,000 schools with more than 8 million pupils in 1915. State appropriations for these schools increased from just over 3 million roubles in 1900 to more than ten times that amount by 1914, while *zemstvo* expenditure on education rose about eight times by 1914 from an 1891 figure of rather more than 5 million roubles. Even though they concede that the target for 1922 was unlikely to be reached even if the war and the revolutions had not intervened, the 'optimists' consider that the delay would not have been great. On the other hand, Lenin declaimed in the pre-war period that 'Such a savage country, in which the mass of the people are so robbed in the sense of education, enlightenment and knowledge, – there is no such country in Europe as Russia'.[53]

Such an assertion could be supported to some extent at the secondary school level by the comparative ratio of students to population for a number of modernising countries halfway through the 1890s: U.S.A. 1 : 83; Prussia 1 : 122; England 1 : 202; France 1 : 300; and Russia 1 : 564. To this, an 'optimist' would point out that by 1914 figures for secondary schools of all types and students of both sexes had approximately doubled from the beginning of the reign of Nicholas II, when they had been about 900 and 225,000 respectively. The number of university students also at least doubled between 1900 and 1913, reaching approximately 36,000 in the latter year, even though only one new university – at Saratov in 1909 – was founded during the period. If higher institutions of education as a whole are taken, that is, if engineering and technical colleges and the like are included, the total enrolment increases from just under 30,000 in the mid-1890s to a figure variously estimated from 90,000 to 150,000.[54]

If the educational advance, according to some figures at least, appears greatest at the highest level, it was also here that the tensions between the government and those involved in the educational process showed themselves to be most strained. After a series of troubles at the turn of the century, including the first all-Russian University strike in 1899, more than 340 academics in a *Memorandum on the Needs of Education* produced for the one hundred and fiftieth anniversary jubilee of Moscow University on 12 January 1905 declared: 'The threatening condition of enlightenment in the fatherland does not allow us to remain inactive and forces us to express our deep conviction that the contemporary state order of Russia is not compatible with academic freedom. For its achievement partial corrections of the existing order are insufficient, and its complete and thorough reformation are necessary'.[55] During the ensuing Revolution of 1905, the tsarist régime relaxed somewhat its regulations of 1884–5 and restored a certain amount of self-government to the universities. But more disturbances in 1910–11 led to several 'undesirable' staff members of Moscow University being driven from their posts. More of their colleagues resigned in protest, including

the historians Kizevetter, Kliuchevskii and Vinogradov. Relations between the universities and the government remained strained up to the
outbreak of war, and to some extent up to 1917.

Somehow, through all these tribulations, not only the historians just
mentioned but also their colleagues in their own and other fields managed to produce work of the highest quality, both in institutions of
higher learning and outside them. A just roll of honour would be long
and contain many names that should be better known in the West. But
since they would mean little without a full explanation of their contributions, just a few representatives must be chosen here: Petr Lebedev, a
great physicist; Nikolai Zhukovskii, the mechanical mathematician,
whom Lenin called 'the father of Russian aviation'; Konstantin Tsiol-
kovskii, expert on rocketry, who predicted space travel; and Ivan Pavlov,
continuing his outstanding work in physiology.

Open lectures managed to communicate some of the achievements of
Russian savants to the public, who were also able to read about them and
everything else in a growing number of books, journals and newspapers.
In 1913 in the Russian language alone, more than 100 million copies of
books to a value of more than 40 million roubles were sold. Two-thirds
of them were produced in Moscow and St Petersburg, where the first
millionaire publishers based their activities, but the provinces were also
becoming more active, both in Russian and regional languages. In 1912
of the more than 2000 registered periodicals well over half were in
Russian, but the rest were divided among thirty-two different languages.
Among all these publications, many were political, even revolutionary in tone. Lenin wrote that after the Revolution of 1905, 'Millions
of cheap editions on political themes were read by people, by the masses,
by the crowd, by the "lower orders" more greedily than ever before in
Russia. . . . Merchants stopped dealing in oats and began a more profitable trade – the popular cheap pamphlet. Popular books became a
market product.' Among the newspapers were those of the Mensheviks
and Bolsheviks, about which a member of the Cadet Party commented
respectively: '*Luch* (The Ray of Light) and *Pravda* (the Truth) are
powerful not because they write about workers and for workers, but
because in them workers write about themselves. No other party could
achieve this, not from the right, or the left.'[56] It was also during the
reign of the last tsar that Lenin, in exile and out of it, wrote some of his
most solid works, notably *What Is To Be Done?*, *The Development of
Capitalism in Russia*, and *Imperialism, the Highest Stage of Capitalism*.
Lunacharsky and Plekhanov were others among a growing number of
socialist critics and analysts.

Even those writers with more purely literary intentions, if such existed, found it difficult to avoid politics completely in this turbulent period. The patriarchal Tolstoy increasingly turned from realism to didactic preaching, determined to drive as many people as possible from the evils of tobacco, alcohol and sex back to the simplicities of the life of the commune, where, as Tolstoy must have known, there was in fact as much smoking, drinking and fornicating as in other sections of society. Of his later large-scale works, perhaps the novel *Resurrection* most completely exercises his genius. Although no supporter of the new parties, the ex-communicated Tolstoy was a sympathetic figure to young radicals, and the neglectful reception of his death by officialdom did much to promote the university disturbances of 1910–11.

Anton Chekhov, critical of Tolstoy's lack of understanding of scientific and other forms of progress, was broadly liberal rather than specifically committed to any political programme. Although he broke with a patron over the Dreyfus affair, Chekhov even denied that he was a liberal. Such commitment he rejected as likely to damage the artistic creativity which he prized above everything else and which he believed could be kept apart, or perhaps rather above. Western critics would therefore argue that Soviet commentators have exaggerated Chekhov's progressive beliefs, and that the alienation and melancholy of his short stories and plays are a reflection on the human condition in general rather than a condemnation of tsarist society in particular.

About Aleksei Peshkov, that is Maxim Gorky, there can be less dispute. A man of the people, Gorky writes about the men and women from *The Lower Depths* in a manner which starkly lays bare the life of the poor along the Volga and in St Petersburg. Among other prose writers, V. G. Korolenko, A. I. Kuprin, Leonid Andreev and Ivan Bunin have met with lasting critical approval from Western and Marxist critics alike, albeit with different emphasis from each side. What can be seen as a new approach from the one point of view might be looked upon as a blind alley from the other. On the whole, the Western estimate of this period sees it as one of interesting experiment, of renaissance, a Silver Age or even a Second Golden Age.[57] From the Soviet side, A.Ia. Avrekh talks of a decadent literature being produced around 1910 and after, its main themes being death, disintegration, eroticism and individualism.[58] Similarly, the two attitudes differ to the principal poetic movements of the period, symbolism and futurism. Soviet critics are less happy about the stamp of 'symbolist mysticism' on Aleksandr Blok, Andrei Belii, Valerii Briusov and others, regret that Vladimir Maiakovskii (Mayakovsky) started his career in the escapist world of futurism, and are much happier when 'motifs of social and civic significance' appear in their work in a reasonably straightforward manner.[59]

Both the symbolist and futurist movements were influenced by developments in France, Italy and elsewhere. They also partly stemmed from the group centred around the review *Mir iskusstva,* or *World of Art,* which was published between the years 1898 and 1904 and edited by A. N. Benua (Alexander Benois) and Sergei Diagilev. The group was agreed on total commitment to creation, but realised their commitment in ways which differed considerably. Issak Levitan, an impressionist, has been called 'the poet of the Russian landscape'. Valentin Serov was perhaps the best portraitist of the modern school. M. Larionov and N. Goncharova became well known abroad as cubists and then as futurists. More radical movements developed in the second decade of the twentieth century, taking such names as *Knave of Diamonds* and *Ass's Tail* and including such abstract painters as V. Kandinskii (Kandinsky) and K. Malevich. A combination of styles received distinctive treatment at the hands of Marc Chagal. The sculptors and architects of the period made far less of an impact.[60]

The last years of tsarism were great years for Russian performing artists. The plays of Chekhov, Gorky and others received the best possible production at the Moscow Arts Theatre from the method of Konstantin Stanislavskii (Stanislavsky). But these names are only the best known of a large number of talented people working in the drama, as Pavlova, Nidzhinskii (or Nijinsky) and Diagilev are the most famous of those who made Russian ballet known throughout the world. Shaliapin and others did almost the same for Russian opera. Obviously in such a period, there were many opportunities for musical composers to apply their talents, although the work of Rimsky-Korsakov, Glazunov, Rakhmaninov, Skriabin, Stravinskii (Stravinsky) and Prokofev (Prokofiev) often goes far beyond the simple needs of orchestral accompaniment.

All the new developments in the arts passed by the majority of the people, whose tastes were more traditional. Folk motifs from all parts of the Empire were used by the artists, but the exchange was hardly mutual. In the pre-revolutionary period, the gap did not worry those who were interested in art for art's stake. After the Revolutions of 1917, it would become a problem of considerable dimensions.

Part Three

Contemporary Russia: The Soviet Union

Introduction

The First World War acted as a mighty accelerator of many historical processes: it contributed to the decline of the empires of the European powers while giving a tremendous boost to the influence of the United States of America; it was a major factor in the overthrow of Russian tsarism and the institution of the Soviet Union. Secondly, the latter event, which was the result of the Russian Revolution of 1917, made a profound impact throughout the whole of the terrestrial globe. Few Western historians would deny this, although not many of them would choose to agree with their Soviet colleagues that 'The Great October Socialist Revolution inaugurated a new era in the history of the Soviet peoples and of all mankind, and marked the beginning of the transition from the old, exploiter society, to the new, socialist system'.[1]

The Union of Soviet Socialist Republics was the first major society to announce its creation according to a coherent ideology. Since 1917, the claims of this ideology – Marxism–Leninism – to be not only a scientific, global and progressive explanation of history but also a guide to its transformation have come to be widely accepted in the Second and Third Worlds and to a considerable extent in the First. The events of 1917 and subsequent years have therefore been a subject of great controversy among both supporters and opponents of Marxism–Leninism. The account of those momentous events that follows here will probably not be welcomed by either side, since it borrows arguments from both of

3 Contemporary Russia

them. While based on the fundamental proposition that the Revolution of 1917 was part of the organic evolution of Russian history and in no sense an unfortunate accident or avoidable tragedy, it will seek to demonstrate that the modern and even the medieval periods of development weighed very heavily upon the new society and prevented it from fully realising the great hopes laid upon it. Steering a middle course between savage condemnation and lyrical glorification of the U.S.S.R., this explanation is aimed not at feeble compromise but at a balanced appraisal of the part played by the Soviet Union in the contemporary phase of world history. Here, as in the medieval and modern sections, objectivity will be pursued partly by considering the Soviet experience in a comparative light.

An analysis of the February and October Revolutions of 1917 and the Civil War and Intervention that formed their sequel is the subject of Chapter 10, opening this contemporary section. Chapter 11 covers the period 1917–29, during which, the energy of the government was concentrated on the consolidation of the Soviet Union in a largely unsympathetic international atmosphere. By 1929, after tremendous effort and bracing experimentation, little more had been accomplished than the approximate restoration of the economic level of 1914, the establishment of political unity at home and credibility abroad, and the near conquest of illiteracy. Between 1929 and 1941 (the terminal dates of Chapter 12), the construction was achieved at enormous cost of Soviet socialism, a variant of the species so mutated that some analysts believe that it is better called state capitalism. Although many terrible events occurred during the 1930s, the advances that were made in an international atmosphere even more hostile than that of the preceding decade were solid enough for the U.S.S.R. to triumph in the Second World War. The Second World War and its sequel, the Cold War (1941–53) are the central events of Chapter 13, which also discusses the arduous process of reconstruction. Chapter 14, covering the period 1953–64, considers the establishment of Soviet superpower, which made the presence of the U.S.S.R. felt not only throughout the world but also in space. In Chapter 15, concluding the book, a brief analysis is made of policies and progress since 1964, and some attention is given to the direction that Soviet civilisation could take in the future. Throughout Part Three, some evaluation is made of the parts played by Lenin, Stalin, Khrushchev, Brezhnev and other outstanding figures. Nevertheless, although the terminal dates of a given chapter often coincide with phases of their periods in power, history will not be personalised and simplified to the extent that Soviet successes and failures will be attributed to them alone.

10   The Russian Revolution, 1917–1921

I   The February Revolution

A Soviet critic, G. Z. Ioffe, attributes the five following faults to Western bourgeois writing on the February Revolution:

1. It gives far too much emphasis to the possibility of the avoidance of revolution through the peaceful modernisation of the Empire. Too much blame is attributed to the incompetence of the tsar and his entourage and to the burdens imposed by the war.

2. On the immediate origins and course of the February Revolution, it wrongly stresses the degradation and collapse of tsarism, thus talking of the fall of Nicholas rather than his forcible overthrow.

3. Discussing the motive forces of the Revolution, it gives an erroneous impression of the unanimity of all classes, of all social groups.

4. Analysing the nature of the Revolution, it is guilty of distortion through typifying the events as anarchistic and spontaneous and underestimating the role played by the Bolsheviks.

5. Comparing the significance of the February and October Revolutions, it talks of the democratic gains of February being liquidated by a totalitarian October, when in fact the two Revolutions are complementary rather than antagonistic.[1]

For their part, Western critics charge Soviet writing with an overschematic approach to February, making it appear an inevitable moment in the relentless march of the proletariat to power rather than a few days of confusion and surprise whose outcome hung for some time in the most delicate of balances.[2]

In a real sense, the events of 1917 had been prepared by the whole previous course of Russian history, and to emphasise out of proportion 'turning points' at which tsarism could have righted itself is to distort that course. The accidents of history, such as the haemophilia of the tsarevich, may delay or advance the arrival of a crisis, but they cannot completely avert it. If this were not the case, then the study of history could not be attempted in any rational manner, since random events would assume such importance that explanation would be rendered impossible. On this premise, which will by no means satisfy everybody, we shall now proceed to an examination of the February Revolution.[3]

After an intensification of the burdens of the war had led to a wave of strikes in October 1916 and January 1917, the government made a number of arrests and separated the Petrograd military region from the Northern front as a whole, hoping to isolate any threat posed in the capital by the internal enemies of the state. The Petrograd garrison commander, S. Khabalov, prepared his plans, placing his trust for the suppression of any serious disturbances in the police and the Cossacks. While Miliukov and most of the future members of the Provisional Government attempted to retain the Duma as the chief vehicle of opposition and protest, left-wing politicians and the workers were thinking more in terms of demonstrations in the factories and on the streets.

Such demonstrations led to the outbreak of the Revolution on Thursday 23 February (8 March New Style). The initiators of the movement in many cases were the women who had particularly suffered from the hardships imposed on their families by the bread shortage – appropriately enough, 23 February was International Woman's Day. The movement quickly spread to the Vyborg working-class district in the north-east of the city and to the Putilov metalworks in the south-west, where a lockout had already brought about a critical situation. While the radical leadership gave no clear directive, rank-and-file Bolsheviks, Mensheviks and S. R.s undoubtedly played an energetic part in organising bands of demonstrators in the various localities. Moreover, the boiling over of dissatisfaction into revolution must at least to some extent be seen as the result of years of propaganda and political education. The radical workers, many of them already on strike, were the heart of the movement.

Crowds poured on to the Nevsky Prospect, the traditional assembly place for demonstrations. When the police closed the main bridge from the Vyborg side, the insurgents came over the ice. Well over 100,000 people appear to have joined in. There were many meetings throughout the capital. Many of the slogans were still moderate; there were clashes with the police, but only a score or so of arrests and few casualties. The government was surprised by the demonstration and by its size, but was not unduly downhearted on the evening of 23 February. For their part, many members of the Duma believed that it would still be possible to make some accommodation that would avert revolution. Meanwhile, educated by their experiences and discussions since 1905, the workers and the radical politicians were beginning to realise that they were on the brink of the final showdown with tsarism.

On Friday 24 February the number of striking demonstrators grew to about 200,000 and the clashes with the authorities became more intense. Crowds sang the *Marseillaise* and cries of 'Give us bread!' were mixed with 'Down with the tsar!' and 'Down with the government!' By Saturday 25 February, another 100,000 had joined the movement, and the police, Cossacks and dragoons became more irritable. The number of casualties and arrests mounted. But the demonstrators grew bolder and freed some of those arrested. While the Duma leaders still talked of action within the law, and the government was still not unduly alarmed with Nicholas at Army Headquarters believing that the worst was over, revolutionary leaflets circulated around the capital and revolutionary politicians discussed how best to achieve the disaffection from tsarism of the troops.

This central question was largely decided on 26 February, one of history's many Bloody Sundays. During the night more than a hundred members of radical parties were arrested, but all was relatively quiet in Petrograd during the morning. But this was the proverbial lull before the storm, for the crowds were gathering in the working-class districts, and poured into the Nevsky Prospect in the early afternoon. The clashes with the troops were even sharper, and scores of demonstrators were shot, machine guns being used as well as rifles. Pressed by complaints from some members of the Duma, the president M. V. Rodzianko suggested that the fire brigade's hoses be directed against the insurgents. Khabalov rejected the suggestion as more likely to inflame the crowd than to pacify it. At the same time, Rodzianko still believed that, if only the tsar would create a 'ministry of trust', all could be well. As for the workers and the students and their other supporters, their resolution was increased by the bloodshed. The revolutionary parties intensified their activity. And most significant of all, soldiers from the reserve battalion of the Pavlovsky Guards Regiment started to defect.

On Monday 27 February this trickle became a flood, particularly after the shooting of an unpopular officer, and many soldiers of the capital's garrison deserted the cause of tsarism. Among the exceptions was a battalion of bicyclists, who after all had more to lose than their chains; but even those who did not defect no longer actively supported the government. Encouraged by their successes and by more revolutionary leaflets, the crowd stormed the Bastilles of Petrograd, and freed thousands of prisoners. Khabalov was becoming powerless, and his urgent telegrams to tsarist headquarters met with no response. Considerably to their surprise, the Duma leaders at the Taurida Palace found themselves being hailed as the prospective revolutionary government. The reasons for this are difficult to isolate, but have been said to include the following circumstances. Firstly, the Duma had just been prorogued by the tsarist Council of Ministers, and by deciding in some confusion to stay in session informally, had moved however gently to the side of illegality. Secondly, the soldiers who had broken their oath of loyalty were looking for a new source of authority. Thirdly, while the Bolshevik and other revolutionary leaders hesitated, orators such as Kerensky of the Socialist Revolutionary Party and Chkheidze, the Menshevik, were doing all they could to get mass support for the Duma. Fourthly, the Revolution, like most of its predecessors, had to pass through a moderate phase before it became radical, in this case through a bourgeois phase before it could become proletarian. And so, the provisional committee of the conservative Fourth Duma was inching its way towards becoming the Provisional Government of the Russian Revolution.

But already Miliukov noted that the Duma members felt that they were not alone in the Taurida Palace, that they were already not complete masters of it. There were in fact squatters in the Palace, the members of a Soviet or Council similar to that created in 1905. Labour leaders and revolutionary intellectuals and politicians, some of them just freed from jail, gathered together from 24 February and on the afternoon of 27 February elected a Provisional Executive Committee of the Soviet at the Taurida Palace. N. Chkheidze was elected chairman and A. Kerensky (strictly Kerenskii) one of the vice-chairmen. Two Bolsheviks were in the Committee – A. Shliapnikov and P. Zalutskii – but the membership consisted predominantly of their Menshevik opponents. Immediately, the Committee began to consider the important questions of the war and supply, of Soviet and militia organisation. The decision was taken to publish the newspaper *Izvestiia* daily. At the same time, the moderate leadership of the Committee, supported by some elements in the rank and file, was deferentially seeking a compromise with the Provisional Committee of the Duma, of which Chkheidze and Kerensky were also members. When a plenary session of the Soviet obliged the Executive Committee to pass on 2 March a resolution forbidding socialists to be members of a future bourgeois cabinet, Chkheidze obeyed. But Kerensky became Minister of Justice and the only link between the Soviet and the provisional Government.

On the same day the citizens of Petrograd were informed that 'the Provisional Executive Committee of the members of the Duma, with the aid and support of the garrison of the capital and its inhabitants, has triumphed over the dark forces of the Old Regime to such an extent as to enable it to organise a more stable executive power'.[4] Some of the limitations on the accuracy of this declaration we have already seen. It is also true that, before triumphing over the dark forces of the Old Régime, the Duma leaders made some last-ditch attempts to come to terms with them.

Tsarism was still not completely lost by 28 February. As his ministers were being arrested in Petrograd, the tsar finally decided to yield to the entreaties of Rodzianko and others and to return to the capital. But he found his way blocked and his train diverted to Pskov. There he spent a couple of days giving impotent orders for the suppression of the Revolution and discussing the question of his abdication with his generals. The Soviet stopped Rodzianko from going to Pskov, but two other emissaries did manage to get through to the tsar. Nicholas was finally persuaded that his departure from the throne might save it for his son or his brother, and he abdicated on 2 March, first to Alexis and then to the Grand Duke Michael. After talking the matter over with the Duma leaders, Michael said that he would accept the crown only if it were offered to him by a Constituent Assembly and if his personal safety could be guaranteed. And so, like a good old soldier, the monarchy did not die but rather faded away. The constitutional framework of Russia, if that were of any importance in a time of complete upheaval, passed into an uncertain limbo until Kerensky belatedly declared it to be a republic on 1 September. Even then, the objection was put forward that Kerensky was arrogating to himself the powers of the Constituent Assembly, the convocation of which was widely looked upon in 1917, as it had been in 1905, as a matter of central importance.

The form of political organisation that in fact emerged from the February Revolution is best described as the 'dual power' of the Provisional Government and the Soviet. On the one hand, the leading members of the Duma and a few outsiders such as Kerensky strove for the 'legitimate' succession. The first president of the Provisional Government, Prince G. E. Lvov, was a rich but liberal landowner, who expressed his estimate of the extent of his administration's control over events towards the end of April in the statement: 'We are tossed about like flotsam on a stormy sea.'[5] He resigned in July. Made of sterner stuff, but for that reason remaining in office for an even shorter period were P. N. Miliukov, leader of the Cadets, and A. I. Guchkov, leader of the Octobrists. Having been alone in urging Michael to take the crown, they were now the most uncompromising ministers in their dealings with the Soviet and in their conduct of the policies put to their charge, foreign affairs and the army and navy respectively. A much more adaptable minister, an eloquent and impassioned piece of flotsam, was A. F. Kerensky, who declared himself 'sent by the revolution'.[6]

By the middle of March, the other component of the 'dual power', the Petrograd Soviet of Workers' and Soldiers' Deputies, as it had come to be called, numbered about 3000, the soldiers outnumbering the workers by more than two to one. Since the soldiers tended to be less extreme in their political outlook than the workers, the Soviet was weighted against revolutionary policies, a trend reinforced by the lack of radical resolution on the part of its leaders. Moreover, the Soviet was a somewhat undisciplined and vacillating body, and would have made it difficult for the Executive Committee to carry out consistent policies even if the leaders had attempted to do so. Nevertheless, the cry 'All power to the Soviets!' was already heard in early March, albeit soon to die down for several months. The number of such bodies grew by the end of March to nearly a hundred and by the end of the summer to about six hundred in many parts of the former Empire, and so there was an enormous amount of potential waiting to be tapped when the cry rose up again.

During the first two months of its existence, the 'dual power' already showed signs of breakdown. While the Provisional Government put through such liberal measures as civil rights and set up committees to consider such important problems as land reform, the Soviet at times moved in a more radical direction. This was particularly so with Order No. 1, which Trotsky called 'the single worthy document of the February revolution'.[7] Published on 2 March in *Izvestiia*, the order declared that committees should be elected in every army unit and that deputies to the Soviet should be elected by all regiments. These and other concessions to the new democratic spirit began to undermine the army discipline that was already shaky enough. Guchkov and the Provisional Government attempted to make further limitations on the order which the Executive Committee of the Soviet itself imposed, but the damage was done.

Even more serious disruption of the 'dual power' was caused by disagreements about the conduct of foreign policy. By and large, Miliukov and the Provisional Government attempted at the outset to continue the foreign policy of tsarism, the prosecution of the war to a 'victorious conclusion'. Miliukov argued that the February Revolution had excited Russia's fighting spirit rather than revealing its complete exhaustion, and that the army could now press on to the realisation of historic objectives such as the annexation of Constantinople. Meanwhile, the Soviet called for war 'without annexations or indemnities', for a defensive war which would result in a democratic peace and the establishment of international unity. The Provisional Government declared its acceptance of such a policy, but Miliukov still talked of the necessity of the pursuit of decisive victory and of adherence to wartime agreements with the Allies. Demonstrations against Miliukov led to his resignation and that of Guchkov around the end of April.[8] At the same time, the Executive Committee of the Soviet agreed to let its members join the Provisional Government, and a coalition set up on 5 May deceptively appeared to make for a new stability. In fact, nothing had been gained except a short breathing space.

For the coalition to succeed, it would need either to solve or appear to be solving the severe problems which faced Russia in the spring and summer of 1917. The greatest of these, which permeated all the others, was the war. The depth of feeling on this subject has just been hinted at; if peace were not established, then fresh purpose would have to be injected into the prosecution of hostilities. Hardly less vital to the continuance of the coalition than the support or at least acquiescence of the army was that of the peasants and the workers. Something had to be done about the hunger for land of the rural inhabitants and the hunger for bread of those who lived in the towns. A further difficulty for the government was the control of the centrifugal forces which were threatening to get out of hand in many of the peripheral regions of the former Empire. A solution real or apparent to these problems would call for a correct analysis of them and for the highest political skill and will-power. In the end, such desiderata could be supplied from one source only.

II   The October Revolution

On 3 April 1917 Lenin arrived at the Finland Station in the Vyborg working-class district of Petrograd. A large crowd greeted him, and Chkheidze the chairman of the Executive Committee of the Soviet delivered an address of welcome. Then Lenin spoke. A sympathetic eye-witness later recollected that Lenin declared that:

the workers and soldiers had heroically overthrown the autocracy and had, within a few days, turned Russia from a politically backward country into one of the freest democratic states. 'And now they want to palm off on us another tsar – capital', he continued. 'But the factories and mills must belong not to the capitalists but to you, and the land must not belong to the landowners but to the peasants.' Lenin finished his short speech with the words: 'Long live the socialist revolution!' It seemed as though the workers and soldiers were spellbound. They were not used to hearing such words. Then they broke their silence and applauded and cheered.[9]

On 7 April the Bolshevik newspaper *Pravda* published the essence of Lenin's more theoretical elaboration of the message contained in his speech at the Finland Station, the *April Theses*. They began with the argument that fraternisation with the soldiers of the Central Powers should be encouraged and that the war could be carried on only if it became a war against imperialism as the revolution was carried a stage further. The *Theses* then put forward the contention that such a development was possible, since the situation existing in Russia at that time could be characterised as 'the transition from the first stage of the Revolution, which gave power to the bourgeoisie as a result of the insufficient class consciousness and organisation of the proletariat, to its second stage, which must give power into the hands of the proletariat and the poorest classes of the peasantry'. The transition involved the 'maximum of legal toleration' and the 'absence of violence against the masses' on the part of the government and the 'ignorantly trustful attitude of the masses toward the Government of the capitalists, the worst enemies of peace and socialism' on the part of the governed. In such special conditions, the Bolsheviks must not support the Provisional Government in any way, but rather patiently work for the establishment of a revolutionary government by the Soviets. This would not be a parliamentary republic but a truly democratic polity in which the police, army and bureaucracy would be eliminated and their functions taken over by elected and removable officials from the people, none of whom would be paid more than a good worker. At the same time, the land and banks would be nationalised, while the party would change its name to become the Communist Party in order to escape the opprobrium deserved by the compromising European Social Democrats, and its programme would be changed to fit in with the new circumstances. Finally, a new revolutionary International would be created.

Lenin spelled out his views further in his most substantial work of 1917, written in hiding during the lull before October, *The State and Revolution*. Here, following Marx and Engels, he described at some length the necessity for the complete dismemberment of the old bourgeois state before the construction of the new proletarian state would be possible. While many Western analysts have seen this work as essentially visionary, Marc Ferro has suggested that the process described by Lenin was actually occurring in 1917. The peasants and workers were already governing themselves as the government lost its grip on them, and the process of disintegration had already reached an advanced stage. Thus, *The State and Revolution* was 'as much the pertinent diagnosis of the situation as the utopian exposition of a theoretician'.[10] In a more literary manner, a similar analysis is to be found in Konstantin Paustovsky's description of a young writer's account of a tour round Russia at about this time:

> He discovered the strangest, ancient, moth-eaten little towns – Khvalynsk, Sarapul, Serdobsk – so remote and so cut off from Moscow that it was hard to believe in their existence except as a myth.
>
> Russia seemed once more to be split up into small fiefs, separated by the lack of roads, the breakdown of the post and telegraph, by forests, swamps and demolished bridges, by distance grown immeasurably longer.
>
> In these God-forsaken corners of the country, autonomous republics were proclaimed and banknotes printed by the local printers (though more often postage stamps were used for money).
>
> It was all mixed up with remnants of the past – balsam in the window-boxes, bell-chimes, wedding feasts with drunken salvoes from sawn-off shotguns, and weed-choked fields of straggly corn, and talk about the end of the world when nothing would be left of Russia but 'black night and three pillars of smoke'.[11]

In such dislocated conditions, the coalition government attempted to impose some kind of order and sense of direction while the Bolsheviks and other disaffected elements sought to increase the disruption and to take advantage of it. Until the left-wing demonstrations of the July Days, which brought the first coalition to an end, and even to some extent up to the Kornilov Revolt at the end of August, many people on the right also believed 'the worse, the better', since the government would be given the excuse for crushing the revolutionary groups and parties. After the utter failure of Kornilov's attempt to institute a military dictatorship, the remnants of the right still vainly hoped that the centre could somehow hold. Thus, a renewed threat from the left, more powerful since more organised than in July, could be resisted. These phases of development were intimately linked with the rise and fall of Kerensky, and mostly centred around events taking place in Petrograd. But they will also have to be considered against the background of the problems posed more widely to the workers, peasants, nationalities and soldiers. And the general context will have to be established of Russia's continued involvement in the war and the attitudes to it of the other belligerents.

In the first coalition formed at the beginning of May Kerensky was Minister of War and Navy. The new Foreign Minister was M. I. Tereshchenko, a rich industrialist who had previously been Minister of Finance. Although Lvov remained President, the cabinet in general may be said to have taken a move to the left, with such appointments as the S. R. leader V. M. Chernov as Minister of Agriculture. Apparently at an end, the 'dual power' was soon shown to be still in existence as members of the new government and of the Soviet expressed their disagreement on a number of important issues, both foreign and domestic. At the same time, support grew for the Bolsheviks and other extremists outside the Soviet, making it possible to talk of the 'triple power'. The split between the Soviet and some of its erstwhile supporters became apparent in mid-June when the Executive Committee decided to hold a demonstration in support of the coalition as a response to an earlier march, planned but never in fact taking place, on behalf of the Bolsheviks. Participating in full force in the Soviet demonstration of 18 June, the Bolsheviks and their supporters were able to give the impression of more opposition to the policies of the coalition than support for them. But this and some other minor incidents involving anarchists were small in their significance compared with the crisis that broke out at the beginning of July.

Soldier and worker discontent which had been building up for some time came to a head on 3 July when the First Machine-Gun Regiment led an untidy march on the Taurida Palace to demand that the Executive Committee of the Soviet replace the Provisional Government. At the peak of the demonstration on 4 July, according to Miliukov, a worker shook his fist in the face of the S. R. Minister of Agriculture Chernov while screaming 'Take power, you son of a bitch, when it's given to you'. The Bolshevik leadership was divided on the response that it should make to such encouragement, Lenin believing that the time for the armed struggle for power was not yet ripe and categorising the event as 'more than a demonstration and less than a revolution'.[12] In the aftermath of the 'July Days' Lenin was forced into hiding in Finland and others such as Trotsky were temporarily arrested. The Bolsheviks in general were branded as traitors in the pay of the Germans, a charge previously levelled at the court camarilla. With the Executive Committee again expressing its confidence in the government, a new coalition was formed with Lvov resigning and Kerensky becoming Prime Minister while remaining Minister of War and Navy. Confident and rhetorical,

Kerensky moved into the Winter Palace and appealed to the Russian people to achieve 'a new, free and great Russia' through submitting themselves to an 'iron rule'.[13]

While Kerensky toyed with the idea of 'iron rule', discussing what needed to be done in small groups and large conferences, there were those who believed that it should be made an immediate reality. Among them was the commander-in-chief, General L. G. Kornilov, a man of plain speech and strong character, to his supporters, while to Trotsky a man with the heart of a lion and the brain of a sheep. Proclaiming that he wanted nothing more than the salvation of the motherland and the preservation of Great Russia, Kornilov was quite possibly using the encouragement of right-wing business and patriotic organisations to aim at the assumption of power for himself. The debate still rages about the Cossack general and his contorted relations with the Prime Minister. Two points can be made with some certainty. Firstly, when Kornilov attempted to move to Petrograd to crush Bolshevism, his troops were reluctant to follow him and in any case had their way blocked by resolute railway workers. The 'Kornilov Revolt' quickly fizzled out. Secondly, in order to avert the threat to his power that Kerensky himself had rightly or wrongly discerned, he appealed on 27 August for the support of the Bolsheviks and the workers' militia or Red Guard. Soon Trotsky and other imprisoned leaders were freed, and the right having been revealed as powerless, the left was in the ascendancy. Even Miliukov argued that the choice was between Kornilov and Lenin, and the choice had now been made.[14] Assuming yet another office, that of commander-in-chief, Kerensky appeared to be reaching a new pinnacle of power. In fact, on the crest of a wave, the biggest piece of flotsam thrown up by the February Revolution was about to be hurled to the depths.

The Provisional Government was on the point of collapse because it had been unable to solve the problems bequeathed to it by its tsarist predecessor. The attempts at solution, however unsuccessful, must briefly be considered along with the exacerbation of the problems before our consideration of the actual events of the October Revolution. To start with the centre of the revolutionary movement, the proletariat, the organisation of the workers, the extent of their demands and the seriousness of their plight all grew in the months following the February Revolution, particularly from May onwards.[15] Trade Unions and the more militant factory committees staged important strikes in the textile, leather, printing and metal industries, and in the Donets mines. While the strikes amply demonstrated that the workers would have liked more to eat, as well as higher wages and shorter working hours, the political content of their demands grew, and proposals for the introduction of labour control, limitation of profits and nationalisation of industry were now common. The government attempted to arbitrate and conciliate, and gave some support to such concessions as the widely demanded eight-hour day. But with inflation rampant and food in fluctuating supply, the workers could not be satisfied by such palliatives and turned increasingly to the parties with more radical policies while applying pressure to the Soviet for more vigorous action. Although the proletariat was small in numbers, it provided the vanguard of the Bolshevik revolutionary movement.

At the same time, the vast masses of the peasantry were to help create conditions in the provinces which would make more likely further action at the centre. Fluctuating in their intensity after February, rural disturbances reached a new climax towards October. The peasants wanted the land which they had believed to be theirs from time immemorial and which they now had the real chance of acquiring. But they were impatient with the land committees of the Provisional Government, even when Chernov tried to speed up their work and to make it more effective. Stories about the ignorance of the peasants were frequently told by the officials sent out into the countryside. A peasant was said to have cried out at an agitator: 'Hey, you! You've got such long nails, aren't you the Antichrist?' And he and his friends assaulted the man from the city to find out if he was covered in hair and had a tail. Another anecdote was that when asked to vote, the peasants whispered in hushed tones about whether to cast in favour of the tsar or the undergraduates. But the 'dark people' were making their intentions clear enough with their axes and sickles. Although some observers were too condescending or too aloof to see the point, Trotsky forcefully argued that if the peasants had not read Lenin, Lenin had clearly read the thoughts of the peasants.[16]

In the peripheral regions the problems of the peasantry were often compounded with those of centrifugal nationalism, which also exercised the local bourgeoisies and sometimes peoples at the feudal or even pre-feudal stage of development. The answer of the Provisional Government to the nationalities was roughly the same as to the workers and peasants – pending the decisions of the Constituent Assembly or the government chosen by that Assembly, nothing much could be done except to collect preliminary information. But often they were not prepared to wait. The Finns argued that their ties had been with the tsar, the Grand Duke of Finland, and that if he had gone, so could they. Sometimes they were not allowed to wait. Particularly was this the case with the Ukraine, where the Central Council or Rada was forced into a separatist position. In some instances the question was at least temporarily solved in fact by the invasion of the armies of the Central Powers, for example into Poland and the Baltic States. In a few of the outlying areas, it is true, 1917 was a comparatively quiet year. The Armenians in Transcaucasia, their brethren across the border massacred by the Turks, were not keen to break away from Russia at that time. In other Asian areas, however, there was considerable violence. As Richard Pipes puts it: 'In the second half of the year, while a class struggle was taking place in Russia proper, an equally savage national conflict developed in the vast eastern borderlands of the Empire: Chechen and Ingush against Russian and Cossack; Kazakh-Kirghiz against the Russian and Ukrainian colonist; Bashkir against the Russian and Tatar.' Sometimes, strong Muslim feeling revealed itself in the borderlands, a leader in the eastern Caucasus declaring: 'I am spinning a rope with which to hang all engineers, students and in general all those who write from left to right.' Many years would pass before such turbulent areas would be brought back to a condition of quietude.[17]

A further problem that could not be left unsolved for so long was that of the soldiers, two million of whom deserted in 1917, voting for peace, as Lenin put it, with their feet. However, the picture presented by the army during the inter-revolutionary months was not one of complete disintegration. On the whole in the region near the theatre of war, the further west and south a unit was from turbulent Petrograd, the greater was its stability, and the further north and east from the front, the more complete was its demoralisation. But such a picture has to be built up from reports given by various observers ranging from members of the government and the generals to members of the rank and file and political agitators, and not all of these described exactly what they saw. For example, while an ex-general, Golovine, talks of official optimism as a result of a fear of pessimism being looked upon as defeatism, Trotsky argues that the highest officers sometimes exaggerated the signs of demoralisation among the troops in order to provoke some decisive action from the government against agitators.[18] Certainly, although there were many incidents of fraternisation, some of the generals were still confident that the morale of the troops, at least at the front, was sufficiently high for a new offensive, which would not only drive the Germans and the Austrians back, but also raise the spirits of the army, possibly those of the navy also, and of the people as a whole.[19]

A new offensive might be additionally welcomed by the Provisional Government as a means of keeping faith with the Allies and retaining their support. By no means a client of the Allies, often indeed demonstrating irritation at the neglect of Russian interests in strategic decisions and at the reluctance to discuss with the Russians the aims for which the war was being fought, the Provisional Government nevertheless was as fundamentally loyal to the cause of the Allies under Tereshchenko as it had been under Miliukov. The difference was that the cause was for a just peace rather than for imperial expansion. In such a spirit a new offensive was launched in mid-June, Kerensky having talked himself to new heights of patriotism and having even aroused some of the soldiers. But the offensive soon collapsed, and the disillusionment of the army in its aftermath had some influence on the nature of the July days. The restoration of the death penalty and of military tribunals, far from restoring anything like good order or military discipline, accelerated new collapse and the army fought no more. Although the Americans made some efforts to restore morale, the Allies in general were soon virtually writing the Russians off.

American dollars came too late to save the Provisional Government, German marks (if they ever came, and it has not been conclusively proven that they did come) were unnecessary to ensure the success of the Bolsheviks.[20] The day after the Kornilov Revolt was crushed, the Petrograd Soviet passed its first Bolshevik resolution. On 5 September the Moscow Soviet followed suit, and during the course of that month, Bolshevik majorities were achieved in a considerable number of Soviets, mainly in towns and industrial areas. The cry 'All Power to the Soviets!' was raised with new fervour and with unprecedented coherence. In desperation, Kerensky rushed forward the elections to the Constituent Assembly which he had previously been delaying.[21] He called together a 'Democratic Conference' which in turn produced a 'Council of the Republic'. But all to no purpose. Lenin decided that the moment had come for the Red Guards, who had been building up their strength since the Kornilov Revolt, and other Bolshevik supporters to be led into armed insurrection. With some reluctance, the Party's central committee came round to agree with him.

The final victory of the October Revolution was achieved with surprising ease. It was at first led largely by Trotsky, who was chairman of both the Petrograd Soviet and the Military Revolutionary Committee, which had been set up in early October for the revolutionary defence of Petrograd against any surviving Kornilovists and the advancing Germans. Lenin returned from hiding on the evening of 24 October, and assumed command for the overthrow of the Provisional Government. During the night of 24–5 October, insurgents took such important points as bridges, railways and the telephone exchange. The Winter Palace had not fallen, but Kerensky could see that his hour had come, and made a getaway escorted by an American Embassy car. Ostensibly he was looking for support, but in fact making his final exit. After a blank shell had been fired at it by the cruiser *Aurora* and some real shells fired at it from the fortress of Peter and Paul, the Winter Palace was deserted by the Cossacks and army cadets who had been acting in its defence and a stubborn women's battalion then decided to surrender. The remaining members of the Provisional Government were arrested. With far less bloodshed than the February Revolution, the October Revolution had triumphed.

But bloodshed is not the only indicator of the significance of a revolution. The influence of October was to be felt on a very wide scale indeed, and John Reed was quite correct to celebrate it as *Ten Days that Shook the World*. Of course, as with all revolutions, October soon acquired its own mythology and distortions. A decade later, Lenin had already been made a revolutionary saint, and Eisenshtein's cinematic celebration of October 1917 was in some ways more epic than the event itself. More seriously, the factional disputes of the Communist Party in the twenties and thirties resulted in the exaggeration of the part played by Stalin and the virtual suppression of the part played by Trotsky and some of the other leading Bolsheviks.

Nevertheless, those who argue that the October Revolution was no more than a coup or that it can in no proper sense be said to have followed the Marxist pattern are demonstrably incorrect. If the February Revolution was in any sense bourgeois, there was nothing unorthodox about a proletarian sequel following hard on its heels. In *The Communist Manifesto*, Marx and Engels had written:

> The Communists turn their attention chiefly to Germany, because that country is on the eve of a bourgeois revolution that is bound to be carried out under more advanced conditions of European civilisation and with a much more developed proletariat than that of England was in the seventeenth, and of France in the eighteenth century, and because the bourgeois revolution in Germany will be but the prelude to an immediately following proletarian revolution.

While the eyes of Communists were still very much on Germany in 1917 and the years immediately following, there was an argument in this passage about the accelerated process of revolution that could be applied to Russia as well. Such an application was indeed made by Marx and

Engels themselves to the Russian edition of *The Communist Manifesto* in 1882, in the preface to which they said that a Russian revolution could become 'the signal for a proletarian revolution in the West'.[22] This is what Lenin and his supporters fervently believed in the aftermath of October, and many people since have come to see October as a signal for both West and East. In the short run, such an attitude was to have an influence of no small significance on both the Civil War and the Allied Intervention.

III The Civil War and Intervention

October was not the end to the Russian Revolution, in some ways it was more of a beginning. True, there was immediate celebration, tumultuous applause for Lenin when he made his first public appearance since July at the All-Russian Congress of the Soviets which had just convened. However, when Lenin declared: 'We shall now proceed to construct the socialist order!',[23] few of his supporters could have realised, as they renewed their roars of approval, how painful a process that construction was going to be. The ease with which the takeover of power had been accomplished in Petrograd was deceptive. Almost immediately, the Bolsheviks were under attack from domestic opponents – the Whites and dissident S.R.s – aided by foreign interventionists. Several years were to elapse before the attack was fully overcome, and the Soviet Union could be constituted.

The White forces took on embryonic shape after the collapse of the Kornilov Revolt, imprisoned officers and others looking for an opportunity to crush the radical left as soon as possible. Kerensky aroused no enthusiasm among them, it is true, and an attempt at a Cossack counterattack against the Bolsheviks under General Krasnov got nowhere. But a group including Kornilov (who was soon to be killed by a shell while sitting in his headquarters) were released from prison by General Dukhonin who assumed the position of commander-in-chief after Kerensky's departure. Dukhonin was killed by infuriated soldiers; the others escaped to the Don where they were joined by Krasnov and began to organise from various disaffected elements a counter-revolutionary Volunteer Army. In loose alliance with this first nucleus of the White opposition were the Cossacks – for the most part unattracted to the new régime. Springing up in European Russia and Siberia were various large and small groups of brigands and partisans who sometimes supported the Whites and sometimes opposed them.

At the beginning of 1918, Red forces established themselves in the

Ukraine and drove the Whites from the Don. But their victory was short-lived since the Treaty of Brest-Litovsk transformed the Baltic provinces and Ukraine into German satellites in March. By May the Finns had achieved their independence, with German assistance, and German troops had reached the Don, protecting the Whites as they prepared themselves for further action. At the same time, with support from the British, French and particularly the Japanese, General Semenov was initiating anti-Communist action in the Far East. About 40,000 Czech prisoners being shuttled along the Trans-Siberian Railway revolted. Their action encouraged the S.R.s to form two régimes in June, one at Samara and the other at Omsk. In June, too, Allied forces were established at Murmansk to the north and a revolt against the Tashkent Soviet broke out in Central Asia. Throughout the summer of 1918, the Reds found it difficult to contain such opposition, which showed itself in the capitals as well as the periphery. The Czechs and S.R.s advanced into the Urals and along the Volga, capturing Kazan. The Communists were driven from Archangel, and Allied forces occupied it. Japanese troops in Vladivostok were joined by Americans after Woodrow Wilson overcame some initial hesitancy, and along with the Czechs and Semenov's followers they together drove the Reds from the Far East and Siberia. British assistance came to the aid of the Central Asian insurgents, F. D. Volkov asserting that General Malleson was aiming there at the establishment of a Turkestan Republic which would be a British colony.[24] The British presence was so well imposed upon Transcaucasia that several street signs in Baku were in English. A short-lived commune in that city was liquidated in September.[25] The Volunteer Army began to move forward from the Don. The outlook for the Communists was gloomy.

But then from the autumn of 1918 to the spring of 1919 the Red fortunes revived. At the end of the First World War the Germans left the Ukraine and the Communist forces moved in, although Odessa was taken over by an Allied detachment under French control. Kazan was recaptured and the Communists advanced on Siberia. True, a new leader arose in Siberia, Admiral Kolchak, who made himself Supreme Ruler of the region and inflicted reverses on the Reds. Moreover, the Volunteer Army in the Causasus recouped some of its losses. But the secret decision taken by the Allies in March 1919 to withdraw their troops meant that the complete defeat of the Whites could only be a matter of time.

To take the various sectors in turn, the British left Murmansk and Archangel by September after a limited offensive to cover their evacuation in the late summer. The situation was more serious in the Baltic region, where troops of various nationalities took Riga in May. They neared Petrograd by October with the assistance of British naval detachments, although they were soon repelled. In the south Red hopes were high in the spring after the French had left Odessa and Bela Kun had carried out a Communist coup in Hungary. They even began to contemplate a revolutionary drive into south-east Europe, but defections and squabbles with a local peasant guerrilla army under the anarchist Nestor Makhno caused them to change their minds. Moreover, White forces under Denikin launched a major offensive from the south which approached Moscow in the late summer. But the Whites had over-extended themselves and were in confused retreat by November. On the lesser Transcaspian and Transcaucasian fronts, the Reds encountered no great difficulty, while in the east Kolchak fell back after some initial successes and was executed by the Czechs in Irkutsk. At the beginning of 1920, after months of anxiety and near-crisis, all seemed to be over, but then at the end of April without much warning the Poles launched an invasion reaching Kiev by early May, and the Volunteer Army now under Baron Wrangel broke out from the Crimea in June. After fluctuating fortunes, and more thoughts about extending the revolutions particularly into Germany the Reds agreed with the Poles on an armistice in the Treaty of Riga of October and the Whites evacuated the Crimea in November. The Far East remained a problem until 1922, when the Japanese finally left Vladivostok, the Americans having done so in 1920. To most intents and purposes, however, the Civil War and Intervention were over by the winter of 1920–21, even though they left wounds which would take many years to heal and whose scars still show.

Our brief survey of the campaigns of 1918–21 completed, we may now turn to some analysis of them in order to discover the reasons for the Red victory and the nature of their legacy. The first question is the less difficult to answer. The Reds possessed certain strategic and ideological advantages. They had the active sympathy of most towns and at least the indifference of the peasantry, possibly the balance of their support. They were able to exploit the inner lines of the battle fronts, and gained much material and moral benefit from their possession of Petrograd and Moscow. Moreover, although there was undoubtedly dissension among the Red leaders about plans for defence and attack, the direction of their war effort was both more-co-ordinated and more efficient than that of the Whites. Lenin, in this sphere as in every other, was at the centre – 'a one-man political-military staff' in Louis Fischer's apt phrase.[26] A keen student of Clausewitz, Lenin discarded much but always retained the view that 'war is politics continued by other means'. His first object was therefore to preserve and extend the revolution, by any means that came to be necessary. Such a policy involved departures from traditional means of making war on the one hand and theoretical orthodoxy on the other. A good example is the organisation of the Red Army. In the beginning, Lenin believed that a militia of workers and peasants would be the best force for fighting the Civil War, but he soon came round to the recognition that a regular conscript army had to be created. 'Bourgeois specialists', particularly former tsarist officers, would have to be used, and at critical moments, more general use was made of members of the middle class as cannon fodder for the workers and peasants. At the same time, more than customary attention was paid to the upkeep of revolutionary morale and political orthodoxy.[27] An indispensable figure here was Trotsky, dashing everywhere in his armoured train to encourage and instruct Red Army units. At a lower level, there were many dedicated commissars and ordinary soldiers. More than for any other reason, the Reds won the Civil War because they believed in their cause.

For their part, the Whites had no concerted drive or clear positive purpose. True, they mostly aspired to the overthrow of the Communist régime and the institutions of a military dictatorship, but they could not agree about who should be dictator and what policies he should pursue. Even towards the conclusion of hostilities, Wrangel had arrived at no clearer ideology than that contained in the following declaration of June 1920:

Hear me, Russian People! For What Are We Fighting?
For violated faith and desecrated shrines.
For the liberation of the Russian people from the yoke of the Communists, tramps and criminals, who have completely ruined Holy Russia.
For the cessation of civil war.
So that the peasant, who has acquired the land which he farms as his own property, may engage in peaceful labour.
So that the honest worker may be assured bread in his old age.
So that real freedom and justice may rule in Russia.
So that the Russian people may choose for itself a *master*.
Help me, Russian people, to save the Motherland.[28]

Bravely and well though White units often fought, they rarely persisted sufficiently to drive home the initiative. And they were at least as much harmed as helped by the fitful nature of the Allied intervention.

Lloyd George, as ignorant as most Western politicians about the realities of the Russian situation (for example, referring at one point to the town of Kharkov as one of the revolutionary leaders) was at least shrewd enough to observe that to make war on Lenin was to play into his hands. The error of intervention was compounded by the half-hearted nature of its commission. At least as confused as the Whites about their motives for sending men and materials to aid the anti-Communist cause, the Allies agreed that Communism was an evil influence. But they had no idea what they would do if the White cause should turn out to be victorious, and did far too little anyway to ensure such an eventuality.

The principal legacy of the years of Civil War and Intervention was harmful to the cause of national and international harmony. The Russian traditions of xenophobia and security mania became intensified, while the Russophobia of foreigners took on a more virulent and widespread form as fear and hatred of Communism. Separatist nationalism in such areas as the Ukraine and Transcaucasia was as exploited by the enemies of the Soviet Union as it was feared by the Communists.[29] Moreover, the declared aims of world revolution on the one hand and of the suppression of that revolution on the other could hardly lead to immediate amity between the Bolsheviks and capitalist governments. True, by 1921 these aims were recognised as incapable of immediate realisation. But the experiences of the years 1917–21 were to give the antagonism between the Soviet Union and the ex-interventionist powers an intensity that was to blind both sides to some of the realities of the situation that developed in the ensuing decades.

11 The Consolidation of the Soviet Union, 1917–1929

After the October Revolution, Lenin pointed out that the new order would have to be constructed from the bricks of the old. If the tsarist government had condoned primitive savagery, the Communist successor which he now headed could not immediately enjoy completely civilised brotherhood. Many concessions would have to be made to the inertia of the past. The transformation was made even more difficult through the circumstance that the embryonic Soviet Union found itself continually surrounded by hostile powers which wished its great experiment no success at all. And so, while it never forgot the major cause of the international revolution, Lenin's government was mortally afraid for its own survival and brought the historic Russian concern for security to a high pitch of intensity. Moreover, since the Civil War and Intervention weakened the proletariat before it was able fully to establish its dictatorship, the Communist Party found itself increasingly bound to act as a substitute for it. In this substitution, as well as in the later neglect of the international revolution, many critics find the beginning of the bureaucratisation which was in their view completely to negate the dictatorship of the proletariat in favour of the Party and then of a single individual, Stalin.

In this chapter, we shall consider the first two phases of Soviet history which brought about the consolidation of the U.S.S.R.: War Communism and the New Economic Policy, or N.E.P. We shall see how, with a mixture of experiment and improvisation, the economic, political and cultural policies of the Communist government took shape. For the first half of the period, Lenin was in control. Before his death at the beginning of 1924, he undoubtedly discovered that to lead a revolution, difficult enough though that was, could hardly be considered more of an exertion than to administer the state that emerged from it.

The central figure is still the subject of heated controversy. Anathema to those who dislike him, Lenin for others comes as near to deity as it is possible for adherents of dialectical materialism to allow. Before any attempt at assessment here, an outline of his earlier career needs to be given. Vladimir Ilich Ulianov was born on 22 April 1870 in the small, provincial town of Simbirsk on the Volga. He was the second son in a family of six children, his mother being a doctor's daughter and his father the local school inspector. Lenin's childhood and early adolescence were free from any obvious trouble and the Ulianov family life was boisterous but on the whole harmonious. But then, in 1886, the father died and in 1887 the eldest son Alexander was executed after an attempt on the life of Tsar Alexander III. Far from deterring Lenin from a revolutionary course, his brother's execution appears to have placed him more firmly on it. Graduating top of his class from Simbirsk gymnasium a month after that shocking event, Lenin was able to use a favourable reference from the gymnasium's director whom his father had designated as the family guardian (by a coincidence stranger than fiction the father of Kerensky) to gain entrance to the nearby University of Kazan. Almost at once, however, he was drawn into political activity and expelled. At his mother's intercession, Lenin was allowed to take an external law degree from St Petersburg University, but while reading for the bar was also reading Marx and organising clandestine political discussions. Passing his examinations with honours in 1891, he devoted more and more time to political activity in the provinces, being particularly enraged by a famine which swept along the Volga in 1892. He then moved to the capital in 1893. In St Petersburg Lenin quickly became a member and then the leader of a secret Social Democratic circle known later as the Elders. Deeply involved in revolutionary agitation and writing, Lenin was arrested at the end of 1895 after his return from a visit to Western Europe where he had met and talked with Plekhanov. From prison he went to exile in Siberia, where he vigorously continued his publicist work and took his revolutionary pseudonym from the river Lena. There too he married Nadezhda Krupskaia who was to be his closest collaborator until his death. The principal events in his life from the end of the Siberian exile in 1900 sufficiently belong to history for them to have been recorded in earlier chapters.

One of the best portraits of Lenin after October 1917 was drawn by Arthur Ransome, most remembered for the stories he wrote for children after his return from Soviet Russia where he was correspondent for the *Manchester Guardian* in 1919. Ransome later remembered a meeting with Lenin in the following manner:

More than ever, Lenin struck me as a happy man. Walking home from the Kremlin, I tried to think of any other man of his calibre who had a similar joyous temperament. I could think of none. This little, bald-headed, wrinkled man, who tilts his chair this way and that, laughing over one thing or another, ready any minute to give serious advice to any who interrupt him to ask for it, advice so well reasoned that it is to his followers far more compelling than any command, every one of his wrinkles is a wrinkle of laughter, not of worry. I think the reason must be that he is the first great leader who utterly discounts the value of his own personality. He is quite without personal ambition. More than that, he believes, as a Marxist, in the movement of the masses which, with or without him, would still move. His whole faith is in the elemental forces that move people, his faith in himself is merely his belief that he justly estimates the direction of those forces. He does not believe that any man could make or stop the revolution which he thinks inevitable. If the Russian revolution fails, according to him, it fails only temporarily, and because of forces beyond any man's control. He is consequently free with a freedom no other great man has ever had. It is not so much what he says that inspires confidence in him. It is this sensible freedom, this obvious detachment. With his philosophy he cannot for a moment believe that one man's mistake might ruin all. He is, for himself at any rate, the exponent, not the cause, of the events that will be for ever linked with his name.[1]

Here, we shall adhere to this view of Lenin as 'the exponent, not the cause', a view which is not shared either by Lenin's critics or by his admirers. Among the kinder and more scholarly of the critics, Leonard Schapiro writes of him in the aftermath of October: 'A great revolutionary, he had not managed to develop the qualities required of a statesman . . . his obsessional character must then also be seen as one of the elements which led to the chaos of 1917 out of which bolshevik victory emerged; and it must be seen in the aftermath of 1921, from which, whatever the future may hold, so many consequences disastrous for Russia have flowed.'[2]

From the other side, Academician I. I. Mints writes that in the years of the Civil War and Intervention, 'Lenin showed himself to be not only a wise political leader and statesman but also a strategist of genius. . . . Under the control of V. I. Lenin the Party demonstrated the flexibility, patience and skill to wait and prepare for a change in the attitude of the broad masses.'[3]

During much of the rest of this chapter, we shall be noting the policies which Lenin advocated and the recommendations which he left at his death. Towards the end of the 1920s, another leader arose in the shape of Joseph Stalin. We shall leave to Chapter 12 a description and appraisal of this even more controversial figure.

Political

When Lenin and the Bolsheviks came to power, they saw the need, not only to conquer practical difficulties, but also to solve through action theoretical problems, too. A long tradition stretching back to the early Christian philosophers had looked upon the state as a necessary evil, and such an attitude became more pronounced with the development of socialist materialism in the nineteenth century. Marx and Engels shared the anti-state views of their predecessors, arguing that the state was the result of class conflict and implying that it would become redundant with the establishment of the dictatorship of the proletariat and the elimination of the bourgeoisie. Marx was not very explicit about this, but Engels wrote: 'With the disappearance of classes the state will inevitably disappear. Society, which will organise production anew on the basis of a free and equal association of producers, will send the whole state machine to the place where it will then belong: to the museum of antiquities, along with the spinning-wheel and the bronze axe.' With the dictatorship of the proletariat, which could be detected in foetal form in the abortive Paris Commune, Engels believed that there would be 'a blowing up of the old state power and its replacement by a new, truly democratic power'. (See note 4.) After the death of the Commune, the ideas of Marx and Engels were rejected by some socialists, anarchists and syndicalists who did not want to wait for the withering away of the state and some social-democrats who had come to believe that the state could be transformed into a proletarian-democratic institution. It was against these two deviations that Lenin directed much of the attack of his major work of 1917, *The State and Revolution*.

While, as we have seen, *The State and Revolution* contains a view of Russia in 1917 that is in many ways realistic, its vision of the future undoubtedly possesses elements of wishful thinking. Lenin does not foresee the replacement of the government by another similar to it in any basic way: while the withering away of the state is not to be immediate, it will be progressive and continuous, and while it will have to be strong enough to repress the old order, no special machinery will be necessary, rather just the simple organisation of the masses. No bureaucracy or army in the traditional sense will be needed, and the Soviets will provide whatever new apparatus is called for. In production and distribution too, the people will take over. Lenin declares:

> Thus, when *all* learn to administer and in fact independently administer socialised production, and independently carry out the checking and control of the boneheads, lordlings, sharpers and such like 'defenders of the capitalist tradition', then evasion of this checking and control by the whole people will inevitably become so immeasurably difficult, so rare an exception, and will in all probability be visited by such swift and condign punishment (since the armed workers are practical people and not sentimental intellectuals, and will not allow themselves to be trifled with), that the *necessity* of observing the uncomplicated fundamental rules of very human society will soon become a *habit*. (See note 4.)

According to E. H. Carr, whose theoretical survey has been closely followed here: 'Lenin's theory of the state reflected the dichotomy in Marxist thought, which combined a highly realist and relativist analysis of the historical process with an uncompromisingly absolute vision of the ultimate goal, and strove to bridge the gap between them by a chain of causal development.' Lenin himself was able to bridge this gap for the most part, although subject to some doubts and fears about the future towards the end of his life. He argued that the state could hardly be expected to wither away while the Soviet Union was under attack from hostile internal and foreign forces. Moreover, although the dictatorship of the proletariat had been established, the working class was weakened by the extraordinary efforts that it had been called upon to make during the troubled times from 1917 to 1921, and the Communist Party would therefore have to substitute for it. At the same time, bourgeois engineers, bureaucrats, army officers and other experts would have to be used in the struggle to build up the economy, the administration and the armed forces. Far from being persuaded that such developments necessitated a considerable change in his aims, Lenin considered that they made it all the more urgent to train all citizens, so that the 'government of men' could be transformed into an 'administration of things'.[4] In Lenin's tradition, Soviet ideologists assert that there has been no compromise with the fundamental aims of the Communist Party and that the nature of Communist society itself has none of the utopian elements ascribed to it by E. H. Carr. Carr, Lenin and Lenin's self-appointed heirs at least share the view that revolutionary theory was much more than a superficial frivolity during the 1920s; that the debates that took place then involved far more than a naked struggle for power.

Lenin's active life in government falls into two main periods, from October to the adoption of N.E.P. in the spring of 1921, and from then up to his final incapacitation two years later. In the succession crises that followed, policy and personality were both involved. By 1926 fundamental decisions had been taken about the planned economy and the government that was to carry it through, and these were elaborated and confirmed up to 1929 when a shattering dénouement took place. Let us consider each of these phases in turn.

The Decree on Peace of 26 October 1917 abolished secret diplomacy, annulled annexations, declared an armistice and called on the workers of Great Britain, France and Germany to support the movement for peace. Its influence spread across the Atlantic to the United States, where Woodrow Wilson had it in mind when composing his Fourteen Points. However, if the Decree on Peace had certain bourgeois-democratic overtones, the first People's Commissar for Foreign Affairs had none. Describing his policy as 'active internationalism', Leon Trotsky announced: 'I will issue a few revolutionary proclamations to the peoples of the world and then shut up shop.'[5] And Trotsky was not alone in his uncompromising attitude towards the continuance of the war in conjunction with the Allies, while they in their turn would have little to do with the peace feelers put out by the Soviet government at the end of 1917 and the beginning of 1918.

With one nation, however, business had to be done. This was with Germany, which was bearing down upon the new and fragile state arising from the wreck of its erstwhile tsarist enemy. Protracted negotiations between the imperialists and the Communists took place at Brest-Litovsk. The Russian delegation argued among itself about what to wear, how to deal with its token peasant representative who spent more of the time under the table than round it, and, much more seriously, whether or not to accept the extremely harsh terms demanded by Germany. Some delegates agreed with Bukharin's demand for a 'revolutionary war'; others supported Trotsky's formula of 'neither war nor peace'; Lenin argued for acceptance of the terms as an appalling necessity. After much inter-party and intra-party dispute and threats of resignation from Lenin, the Treaty of Brest-Litovsk was finally signed on 3 March 1918 and then ratified at an emergency Party Congress.[6] Poland and the Ukraine had been lost as well as the Baltic States and Finland. The isolation and weakness of the Red position was felt all the more keenly as appeals for support from the workers of other lands were not answered nearly as much as hoped for, although the response was by no means negligible.

Meanwhile, the government moved to Moscow in mid-March, its dynamic force acquiring a new name – the Communist Party – to dissociate it from the renegade social democrats of Western Europe, and its time-scale being adjusted – to gain thirteen days – in order to catch up with the modern calendar. While the Red Army was being organised to fight the military opposition, the All-Russian Extraordinary Commission for the Suppression of Counter-Revolution, Sabotage and Profiteering (*Cheka*) had been set up in December 1917 under Feliks Dzerzhinskii to deal with civil enemies. These probably became more numerous after the government dissolved the Constituent Assembly with its Socialist-Revolutionary majority after a single session on 5 January 1918, Lenin putting forward the argument that 'a republic of Soviets is a higher form of the democratic principle than the customary bourgeois republic with its constituent assembly'.[7] On 10 July the creation of the R.S.F.S.R. (Russian Soviet Federated Socialist Republic) was the first step in the new direction. Meanwhile, dissident S.R.s and their allies attempted through political murder and insurrection to oust the Communists, and the summer of 1918 was tense. The assassination of the German ambassador, Mirbach, brought about a diplomatic crisis, and Lenin himself was seriously wounded. However, by the autumn of 1918, the immediate danger was past and the Red Terror was in full swing. Many of the S.R.s and Mensheviks who had first been adherents of Lenin's government were now removed from power; some went into exile, others went over to the Bolsheviks.

As the Civil War was being won, and peripheral regions were being occupied, decisions about self-determination had to be taken. Many Ukrainians were hoping that they would be able to govern themselves, but the option was not given to them. Transcaucasians had a brief experience of separate government, but they were harshly disciplined by Stalin. Among the Muslim and other peoples of Central Asia and Siberia, there was some desire for independence, although often of a prenationalistic variety. To encompass such a wide variety of race, creed and level of civilisation within his ideas on the dictatorship of the proletariat was a difficult task for Lenin, but he just about succeeded. Broadly speaking, his pre-October argument was that bourgeois nationalism or even more rudimentary centrifugal force was progressive because it weakened the rule of the tsar or of Kerensky. But after October all such threats to social cohesion became reactionary, as educated workers would realise. Since educated workers in the peripheral regions were few and usually Russian, there were dangers in Lenin's argument – of Great Russian chauvinism and 'substitutional' bureaucratisation – that he himself was worried about before his death.[8]

Nearer the centre, a clear focus for many of the government's problems towards the end of the Civil War was the Kronstadt Revolt of March 1921. Peasants were already in revolt in the provinces and workers already on strike in Petrograd factories when the Kronstadt sailors petitioned for re-elections to the Soviets and relaxation of many of the controls that had been introduced during the years of fighting. Their revolt was ruthlessly suppressed, the workers' opposition and peasant insurgency overcome. And so, as the compromise policies of N.E.P. were being introduced at the Tenth Party Congress, Party controls were being tightened.[9]

Lenin argued that the true meaning of the Kronstadt Revolt was to be seen in the nature of its support from abroad. If enemies of the October Revolution were in favour of the sailors, the sailors were wrong. If their 'petty-bourgeois anarchist' ideology triumphed, the Russian Revolution would go the way of the French Revolution, and Russia would be given over to capitalism like France before it.[10] While clearly still determined to work for the world socialist revolution and to judge everything in that perspective, Lenin was nevertheless coming to realise by 1921 that some form of compromise was necessary in the international as well as in the internal sphere. From the other side, there was the beginning of the realisation that some form of *rapprochement* was possible now that the German revolts of 1918–20 had come to nothing and the *cordon sanitaire* against the spread of Bolshevism created at Versailles appeared to be holding fast.[11] And so, while the flag of international revolution was kept flying by the Third International set up in 1919, the Soviet Union and other powers were developing something like normal relations. A trade agreement with Great Britain in March 1921 was followed by similar deals with other bourgeois nations, and the opportunity was taken during the Genoa Conference on European problems in April 1922 to arrange a *rapprochement* with Germany at nearby Rapallo. And so the powers excluded from Versailles came together. Treaties with Turkey, Iran, Afghanistan and Mongolia in 1921 showed that the Soviet government was taking a considerable interest in the affairs of the Near and Far East.

Before the onset of his final illness (which was largely the result of the wounds inflicted on him in 1918), Lenin was able on 30 December 1922, to supervise the official creation of the Union of Soviet Socialist Republics, which replaced the Russian Soviet Federated Socialist Republic. The original federation of Russia, the Ukraine, Belorussia and Transcaucasia was later joined in 1925 by the Turkmen and Uzbek republics and in 1929 by the Tadzhik republic of Central Asia. Among his last instructions, Lenin stressed the necessity of the democratic treatment of all nationalities within the Soviet Union.

Another prime concern for Lenin was the cohesion of the Communist Party which was to continue to be the motor of government in the U.S.S.R. as it had been in the R.S.F.S.R. Before his death, Lenin suggested enlarging the size of the Central Committee to include a hundred members. Such a measure would serve 'to raise the prestige of the Central Committee, to do a thorough job of improving our administrative machinery and to prevent conflicts between small sections of the Central Committee from acquiring excessive importance for the future of the Party'. Among those chosen to enlarge the Central Committee should be rank-and-file workers who by attending all its meetings and reading all its documents, as well as going to sessions of the supreme Party body (the Politbureau), could constitute 'a cadre that would be loyal to the Soviet system and able, firstly, to impart stability to the Central Committee itself and, secondly, really work on renewing and improving the apparatus'.[12] As W. E. Mosse has pointed out, the early Party leadership was predominantly middle class and highly educated, with proportionately many members of non-Russian origin. But if those born between 1868 and 1874 are compared to those born between 1883 and 1891, a process of democratisation can be detected, the younger men tending to be provincial Russians from the lower classes.[13] And so there was some reason for thinking that the new blood coming into the Party leadership would provide the anti-bureaucratic transfusion that Lenin believed to be necessary. Ironically, the leadership of the younger men was to go to a non-Russian born in 1879, Iosif Vissarionovich Dzhugashvili, alias Stalin.

Recognising the rising power of Stalin, the dying Lenin was not happy about it, writing:

Comrade Stalin, having become General Secretary, has concentrated boundless authority in his hands, and I am not sure whether he will always be capable of using that authority with sufficient caution. . . . Stalin is too rude and this defect, although quite tolerable in our midst and in dealings among us Communists, becomes intolerable in a General Secretary. That is why I suggested that the comrades think about a way of removing Stalin from that post and appointing somebody else differing in all other respects from Comrade Stalin solely in the degree of being more tolerant, more loyal, more polite and more considerate to the comrades, less capricious etc.[14]

Lenin's warning was read out at a restricted Party meeting before the Thirteenth Congress of May 1924, and Stalin confessed his faults and promised to correct them. The delegates gave him a vote of confidence, looking upon Trotsky and 'petty-bourgeois deviation' as the greatest threats to Party unity. A believer in 'the natural selection of accidents' in the great process of historical evolution, Trotsky had already lost ground to his opponents after catching a fever at an important moment in the autumn of 1923. As he put it in his autobiography, 'one can foresee a revolution or a war, but it is impossible to foresee the consequences of an autumn shooting-trip for wild ducks'. Accident though this may have been, its importance became magnified as Trotsky employed faulty tactics in the period following Lenin's death.[15] Meanwhile, with quiet cunning, Stalin was making his bid for the succession. The flavour of his approach was revealed in an oration on the death of Lenin in January 1924. While others talked in the usual Bolshevik manner, Stalin introduced a quasi-religious tone, putting his remarks in the form of Leninist precepts and liturgical responses, the first of which was 'leaving us, comrade Lenin enjoined on us to hold high and keep pure the great calling of member of the party. We vow to thee, comrade Lenin, that we will fulfil this thy commandment.' As the mummified body of Lenin was moved to its mausoleum under the Kremlin wall, those observers who detected neo-Slavophile elements in the Soviet outlook must have received encouragement for their views. Undoubtedly, Stalin was attuned to the cultural wavelength of many of the Party members.[16]

Moreover, Stalin was able to make use of his position as General Secretary to gauge the mood of the Party and to manipulate it through appeals to its loyalty as his opponents were outmanoeuvred in the great debate whose main contours we have already sketched. Trotsky and the pro-permanent revolution left opposition were thrown out of the Party in 1927 after some street demonstrations in their favour, and Trotsky was banished to Alma Ata, and as far as Soviet chronicles are concerned, to the 'dustbin of history'. Trotsky's recent allies Zinovev and Kamenev recanted and lived to be purged another day. Before being with Trotsky they had been against him, and with a similar change of attitude, Bukharin, who had been the most radical of the Bolsheviks after October, now led the right-wing opposition in its campaign for the continuance of N.E.P. Increasingly expounding his concept of 'socialism in one country', Stalin finally overcame Bukharin and his associates by the spring of 1929. Although the debate naturally centred around personalities, its theme transcended them, as we shall see in the next chapter.

In the international sphere, the early years of 'socialism in one country' meant the comparative neglect of the world revolution, arguably its betrayal. G. Chicherin, who was chief Foreign Commissar from Trotsky's resignation after Brest-Litovsk in 1918 to his own virtual replacement by M. Litvinov in 1928, brought about to a considerable degree the normalisation of relations with foreign powers. Great Britain's recognition of the Soviet Union in 1924 was followed by that of most other Western states, the most important exception being the U.S.A. At the same time, the Third International or Comintern was pursuing a 'united front' policy of infiltration rather than confrontation. This policy led to some curious episodes. In 1924, for example, the first Macdonald administration was brought down soon after its recognition of the U.S.S.R. at least partly by the Zinovev letter, a forgery urging British Communists to work for the forcible overthrow of the government and thus helping to achieve the objective of whoever wrote it in a peaceful manner. The Comintern's attitude to the British General Strike in 1926 amply demonstrated that its bark was far worse than its bite. Nevertheless, mutual suspicions were still great enough in 1927 for Anglo-Soviet commercial relations to be broken off and the threat of war to arise. At the same time, the Soviet Union was subscribing to the principles of the Kellog–Briand Pact renouncing war as a means of settling international differences.

Soviet policy towards what was to become known as the 'Third World' continued throughout the 1920s to involve compromise with bourgeois nationalism, much to Trotsky's disgust. To take China as an example, the Soviet government co-operated from 1923 onwards with Chiang Kai Shek, a course of action which led in 1927 to the slaughter of the Chinese Communists. Relations with Japan were stabilised in 1925, and further treaties established with states in the Middle East.

Support for bourgeois nationalism abroad was combined with ruthless suppression of the same phenomenon at home. As Commissar for Nationalities, Stalin demonstrated unwonted severity towards his native Georgia in 1921 and his dislike of counter-currents to the consolidation of the Soviet Union was hardly milder towards the end of the decade.

Economic

From the economic point of view, Roger Portal believes that 'the October Revolution marked a complete break with the past'. Although the fact that many of the basic conditions had not changed suggests 'a natural continuity between the Russia of 1914 and the Russia of the

First Five-Year Plan', appearances are deceptive since 'this continuity did not extend to forms of organisation, or to the structure of industrial life, or to the working of the system'. It is true that Sergei Witte had written in his secret memorandum of 1899 that 'Every measure of the government in regard to trade and industry now affects almost the entire economic organism and influences the course of its further development', and that he had argued from such premises that governmental policy for trade and industry be carried out 'according to a definite plan, with strict system and continuity'. It is also true that measures taken under the pressure of war by the tsarist government, and then under the pressure of war and revolution by the Provisional Government, appeared to be along the road mapped out, if not for the most part actually constructed, by Witte. Moreover, even before Witte, the tradition was well established in Imperial Russia of the state playing an important part in economic life. But the virtual disappearance from the scene of large-scale private capital, of huge foreign loans and of the landlord and bourgeois classes combined with the arrival of a much stronger belief in planning, aimed this time at the creation of socialism, to produce a clear break in continuity.[17]

And so after December 1917 the Provisional Government's Economic Council, which had never been very active and was now moribund, was finally killed off. In its place, the Supreme Council of the National Economy (*Vesenkha*) was set up to supervise in general and to give special attention to industrial development. *Vesenkha* became the keystone of War Communism, the title which somewhat flattered the hand-to-mouth policy of the government during the critical days of the Civil War and Intervention. By the summer of 1918, most branches of industry and the banks had been nationalised, forced labour introduced, and private trade largely replaced by government-supervised rationing. The land, which had been socialised in February, was expected to be used by the peasants for the general benefit. Compulsion was soon brought into agriculture as well as into industry, and a food levy obliged farmers to hand over almost all their produce to the hungry workers and soldiers. What had been intended to be fraternal co-operation and mutual sustenance soon degenerated under the pressure of events into severe control. This is not to say that there were fewer examples of selfless heroism than of vicious egocentricity during these dark days. And the government survived.

Scientific organisation of the country's economy continued to be the aspiration, and the Ninth Party Congress in the spring of 1920 supported the principle of a single unified plan. Provisions were to be made in it for the restoration of the transport system and the collection of reserves of grain, fuel and raw materials. Heavy industry was to be developed first, then light industry, with comprehensive electrification as the fundamental guarantor of success. It was towards the end of 1920 that Lenin made his famous pronouncement that 'Communism is Soviet power plus electrification of the whole country'.[18]

After a considerable amount of debate about the optimum extent of planning, the General Commission on State Planning (*Gosplan*) was set up by a decree of 22 February 1921. According to Portal, for the first few years *Gosplan* was 'little more than a consultative organisation on the economic problems of the moment. It did, however, collect studies and statistics, in 1925 began to publish its "control figures", and in 1926 was instructed to work out a "long-term" plan for five years.'[19] But before the Herculean efforts of the Five-Year Plans, a breathing space was necessary.

Just after the creation of *Gosplan*, in the spring of 1921, the Tenth Party Congress accepted the decision to adopt N.E.P. in place of War Communism. Lenin and his colleagues had little choice, in face of the desperate situation which confronted them as the Civil War and Intervention drew to a close, but to push through the N.E.P. Industrial output had fallen to less than 20 per cent, possibly less than 15 per cent of its pre-First-World-War level, with the metal, fuel and textiles sectors all nearly destroyed. The number of workers in large-scale industry had dropped from more than $2\frac{1}{2}$ millions in 1913 to just over $2\frac{1}{4}$ millions, with the loss in skill and leadership being greater than the figures suggest. In agriculture, cultivated land had shrunk to less than two-thirds of the pre-First-World-War acreage, and the harvest yield to little above a third of the contemporaneous total. Two roubles could be exchanged for an American dollar in 1914, now 1200 roubles were necessary. Territorial and demographic losses in general had been great. Finland, the Baltic Provinces and Poland had gone. About twenty million people had died through starvation, epidemic, war and Terror, Red and White, before the end of 1921. Small wonder that from September 1920 onwards peasant and worker unrest grew as the army began to demobilise, and tens, even hundreds, of thousands of ex-soldiers were turning to banditry. And then, to confirm to the Tenth Party Congress the need for N.E.P., the Kronstadt Revolt broke out soon after its assembly.

In his speech to Tenth Congress recommending the adoption of N.E.P., Lenin reiterated an argument that he had advanced as long before as 1905. In a country like Russia, where well over 80 per cent of the population were peasants, socialist revolution would be successful only on two conditions: support from further socialist revolution in other countries; and a compromise between the proletariat and the peasant majority. Although Lenin did not specifically say so, the emphasis in the world situation of 1921 would obviously have to be on the second condition, or thus it was soon claimed by the advocates of 'socialism in one country'. At the time, the essence of N.E.P. was put succinctly by the Communist theoretician Riazanov who called it 'a peasant Brest': a forced withdrawal in face of economic problems reminiscent of the military pressure of 1918.[20] The main feature of N.E.P. was the reduction of the compulsory deliveries of grain by the peasants from the whole of their surplus to a fixed quantity paid as a tax. The balance could be sold on the open market, and even the compulsory deliveries were later commuted to a tax in money rather than in kind. Small-scale industry as well as small-scale trade was less tightly controlled, although the government was to retain the 'commanding heights' of the economy, that is large-scale industry and trade, including foreign trade, modern transportation and finance. The currency, which some Communist economists thought had gone for good with War Communism, was now stabilised as the lubricator of the partly capitalist, partly socialist 'transitional mixed system' as Lenin called it; for a brief period, as a symbol of new directions, there was an attempt to introduce a new monetary unit – the *chervonets*.

In the short run, N.E.P. made little impact. The year 1921 brought harvest failure and terrible starvation, which would have been far worse if it had not been for the work of the American Relief Administration; then the situation took a turn for the better in 1922. However, Lenin declared in 1922 that:

> Russia cannot be saved only by a good harvest in a peasant economy – that is not enough – or only by the good condition of light industry which supplies articles of consumption to the peasantry – that also is not enough; *heavy* industry is also indispensable. Heavy industry needs state subsidies. Unless we find them we are lost as a civilised state – let alone, as a socialist state.[21]

While economic recovery continued throughout the mid-1920s, the problem of heavy industry remained unsolved. Moreover, in 1923 the 'scissors' revealed themselves in high manufacturing and low agricultural prices, and the blades were closed by state order in 1924, continuing that way until the end of N.E.P. Here obviously were trends that a government committed to socialist industrialisation could not accept.

A great debate took place among the Party leadership about what needed to be done. On the right, there was Bukharin, who argued that the Soviet Union should ride to socialism on the back of the peasant donkey or proceed in the same direction with the steps of the tortoise, i.e. continue N.E.P. Another spokesman of a similar point of view was the neo-populist A. V. Chayanov, whose work on peasant farm organisation published in 1925 put forward the thesis that the individual family should remain the basic unit in the countryside.[22] On the left there was Trotsky, giving strong emphasis to the need to continue the international revolution and to press forward more quickly towards industrialisation. On this side of the debate, although not in agreement with Trotsky, was E. I. Preobrazhenskii, whose book *The New Economics* came out in 1926 to stress that 'primitive socialist accumulation' could only be carried out through peasant investment in the socialised sector of the economy.[23] In the middle of the argument, as we shall see below, was Stalin.

In 1927 an American delegation which included such future New Dealers as R. G. Tugwell visited the Soviet Union and found a peaceful but poor community that was beginning to conquer its difficulties and establish a new civilisation. Industry was back to the pre-First-World-War level and agriculture had surpassed it. Little sense of urgency or impending crisis was detected.[24] But the government was not happy that the 'Nepmen' had taken three-quarters of retail trade into their private hands and that the 'capitalist kulaks' should be enriching themselves from the proceeds of agriculture while the co-operative, socialist sectors of the economy were enjoying less prosperity. Exports of grain, oil, timber and other resources were not earning enough capital for full industrialisation, and dependence on foreign assistance was too great.[25] For a complex mixture of motives, which we shall be examining in Chapter 12, the First Five-Year Plan and the attack on the kulaks were launched in 1928 and then intensified in 1929. Thus came the end of the New Economic Policy and the beginning of a period of Soviet history that nobody in the government or outside it appears to have foreseen.

Cultural

Cultural revolution was a constituent part of Communist ideology, entailing the creation of a new co-operative outlook among men. In Lenin's view, the cultural revolution was to be closely linked with that in political and economic life. To maintain the connection between factory, farm and school, for example, education would be polytechnical. But 'to pay the cultural debt of many centuries', as he put it, would perhaps take longer than was first thought by those celebrating the October Revolution or by those who later believed that they had found much progress where there was little. With Stalin in mind, Lenin said in late 1922: 'People dilate at great length and very flippantly on the notion of "proletarian culture". We would be satisfied with real bourgeois culture for a start, and would be glad if we could dispense with the cruder types of bourgeois culture, such as bureaucratic or serf culture.'[26]

Among the obstacles to be overcome was religion. Before the people could properly imbibe the new culture, they would have to stop taking the old opium. If further excuse for its persecution were needed, the Orthodox Church gave the new régime plenty. Already upset by such moves from the Kerensky government as the secularisation of the parish schools, the Church leaders were incensed by the Soviet confirmation of this move, as well as by the nationalisation of church lands, removal of financial support and introduction of civil registration of births and marriages. Separated from the state that had for so long been its chief bastion, the newly reformed Patriarchate moved into the counter-attack under Tikhon. Tikhon condemned the Bolsheviks and called on the faithful to resist them. Encouraging those who appeared in mass demonstrations in Petrograd and Moscow towards the end of January 1918, the Church in Council declared: 'It is better to shed one's blood and win a martyr's crown, than to abandon the Orthodox faith to be abused by the enemy. Take heart, Holy Russia. Go to thy Calvary!'[27]

The Communist Party was not slow to respond to the challenge, its atheism made all the more energetic by the Patriarch's dismissal of Brest-Litovsk as a 'shameful peace' and the open support of many church leaders for the White cause in the Civil War. While some party members remained clandestine believers and the Central Committee adopted a policy of at least limited toleration, others wanted to take the fight for scientific materialism against superstitious idolatry in a more positive direction. Although Tikhon and some of his followers made an accommodation with the government, others sought and suffered martyrdom, thus further encouraging persecution. A vehicle for such activity was the League of The Godless formed in 1925, becoming the League of the Militant Godless in 1929. Propaganda from this and other organisations through their journals and campaigns made some headway, but surveys towards the end of the 1920s amply demonstrated that religion was still deeply entrenched. For example, graduates of atheist schools were said to be in attendance at church services, and it was alleged that monasteries were continuing their existence under the guise of 'collective farms'.

The principal positive means of spreading secular enlightenment during the first years of Soviet power was through educational advance. Nothing seems to have struck foreign visitors so forcibly in these early days as the struggle to teach everybody to at least read and write. Two by no means completely sympathetic Canadians wrote:

Nobody could be ten days in Russia, if he were really listening, and not sense how keen the people are for education. They are just like a people who have long had an intense craving, and suddenly have found the means of slaking their thirst. It comes out at every turn. . . . They have a phrase constantly on their lips – 'the liquidation of illiteracy'. At first it seemed to be humorous, but soon it took on another colour as one sensed the eager effort behind it.[28]

Progress was difficult at first; in the schools, the factories and the huts, teachers and teaching materials were hard to find. A decree of 26 December 1919 declared that all citizens between eight and fifty years of age should be obliged to learn to read and write either in Russian or their native language, but the difficulty of implementing the decree was clearly shown in a manual published in the same year containing a section 'how to make do without paper, pen, ink and pencils' – pieces of wood, glass and coal were among the substitutes recommended. A further contemporary illustration may be taken from the memoirs of a young woman teaching soldiers on the southern front how to read. On hearing the first phrase from an old primer, 'Masha ate her kasha', a loud mocking voice shouted out, 'We had kasha, and we had Masha, but now we don't have kasha and we don't have Masha.' But the young woman did not lose her grip; her training as a political agitator did not let her down. Before the laughter died away, she sternly said: 'Please answer for me the questions, why in our country, which occupies one-sixth of the world's land surface, is there no kasha? Why do your mothers, wives, sweethearts, sisters lead such a miserable life alone? Why aren't you doing peacetime work? What are you fighting for now in the front lines of the Civil War?' Silent seriousness returned to the soldiers as one of them answered that if they did not carry on the fight, the landlords and the capitalists would come back and make the peasants slaves again, but they were not slaves. And so the young woman started to compose a new primer beginning with the words 'We are not slaves, we shall overcome'. Filled with such ideas, the primer was printed on wrapping paper by the press of the political department of the southern front.[29]

Towards the end of 1919, there were nearly 4000 schools for Red

Army soldiers. With these and other special institutions for workers and peasants, some eight million adults were taught to read and write in the first ten years of Soviet power. But the U.S.S.R. was still in nineteenth place for literacy among the nations of Europe. Moreover, although just over half the people as a whole were literate, the figure for the peasantry was less than 50 per cent and for the outlying region of Tadzhikistan less than 4 per cent.

In the basic schools there were more than ten million children at primary and secondary level in the academic year 1925–6 as opposed to less than eight million just before the outbreak of the First World War. In the cities there was a considerable amount of exciting experiment with new curricula, student participation in the administration of the schools and co-education. But complaints developed about the anarchism growing up in the reformed schools, and the Young Communist organisation, the *Komsomol*, was increasingly taken over by the Party to maintain political conformity. In the villages teaching and learning were often carried out in the most primitive of conditions where there could be little thought of progressive experimentation. At the higher level of education, there were in 1925 145 universities and institutes with 167,000 students, compared to less than 100 and 120,000 respectively in 1914. In 1923 nearly a half of the intake into higher education was of peasant or worker origin. Some of these students became distinguished scholars, and they largely compensated for the losses brought about by emigration.[30]

During these early years, the writing of history became dominated by M. N. Pokrovskii (Pokrovsky), who defined his craft as 'politics projected into the past', and who reduced Russia before the Revolution to a somewhat schematic arena for the class struggle.[31] The break with tradition was not so noticeable in the field of the natural sciences, where outstanding work was done by such men as the biologist Ivan Michurin, the metallographer Dmitrii Chernov and the still-active physiologist Ivan Pavlov. In the world of learning, as elsewhere, Lenin was anxious to see the Soviet Union taking the proper path: one of his last polemics was against a deviating historian; as early as April 1918 he had prepared a scientific and technical plan linking research closely to production needs so that natural resources could be properly exploited.

A large part of the cultural revolution was the discovery of literary and art forms which would properly represent Soviet man and his aspirations at the same time as being comprehensible to him. Lenin made clear his views on the subject in an interview with Klara Zetkin, stressing that a proletarian culture would take a long time to develop. Although he pointed out that efforts were being made to take enlightenment to the provinces, he also made the observation that 'at the very time when here in Moscow a few tens of thousands of people are enjoying a brilliant theatrical performance, throughout the country millions are still striving to spell their names, and have to be told that the earth is not flat but round and that the world is governed by the laws of nature instead of by witches and sorcerers jointly with the Heavenly Father'. At the same time Lenin confessed that he himself had little appreciation for some of the newer forms of expression and declared himself a barbarian. Nevertheless, Lenin did not interfere very much with artistic freedom, as Stalin was to do. As for Trotsky, he went even further than Lenin, pointing out that since bourgeois culture required no less than five centuries for its creation, the proletariat would have to follow the one possible path of apprenticeship for many years to come, concentrating the bulk of its immediate energy on the proletarian world revolution. Meanwhile the leading members of the class could not through 'laboratory methods' build the proletarian culture by themselves.[32]

Such good sense as this was too sober for writers and artists wishing to celebrate the arrival of the Revolution. The poet Vladimir Mayakovsky proclaimed: 'Only the proletariat will create new things, and we, the Futurists, are the only ones to follow in the footsteps of the proletariat.' Fellow futurists declared that bourgeois artists had concentrated their attention on subjects such as landscapes of which the reality far surpassed the imitation. With the Revolution, 'Factories, mills, and workshops are waiting for artists to appear and supply them with new models of objects never seen before'. His eye roving wider, Mayakovsky cried 'Streets are our brushes, squares our palettes', and some of his colleagues forcefully expressed their agreement with him. For one celebration, all the grass, trees and flowers in front of the Bolshoi Theatre in Moscow were painted red and purple. Streets, trams and buildings were also covered in dazzling geometrical patterns of paint. In something like the same spirit, the architect Tatlin proposed the following plan for the 'dynamomonumental' building of the Third International in Petrograd. As Miliukov describes this huge edifice, it was to consist of:

> three stories built in the shape of a cube, a pyramid, and a cylinder, each in turn to revolve perpetually, yearly, monthly, and daily. The ground floor was intended for meetings of legislative institutions and congresses of the Comintern, the second for executive agencies, and the third for press and propaganda. Double walls were to provide even temperature. A gigantic spiral, which coiled round the entire

building, was the symbol of the new spirit of Communist dynamics in contrast to the bourgeois horizontal, which was the symbol of the spirit of greed. Steel and glass, materials created by fire, symbolised the power of a sea of flame.

With similar exuberance, musical works such as *Engine c 15* and *Komsomol Leap Frog* attempted to catch the new spirit. So did a symphony orchestra, formed in 1922 without a conductor, who they believed would restrict their freedom of expression.[33]

During the first years of Soviet power, a thousand flowers bloomed, including some that were not revolutionary but produced through the spirit of 'art for art's sake'. Among the more perennial of the flowers of the Revolution have been the poems of Blok, Esenin and Mayakovsky, the prose writings of Maxim Gorky, Nikolai Ostrovskii, Isaak Babel, Mikhail Bulgakov and Evgenii Zamiatin. The satirists Mikhail Zoshchenko and Ilf and Petrov persuaded people to laugh at the mistakes and shortages of the N.E.P. period. Miaskovskii was the most successful musical composer of the time. The cinema, called 'the most important of all the arts' by Lenin, made a wider impact than the theatre, with directors such as Pudovkin, Dovzhenko and above all Eisenshtein making films of high excellence. Special trains became a mobile cinema for the provinces. Experimental movements involving the drama and all the arts, such as Constructivism (of which it was said that 'it must not reflect, imagine or interpret, but really build'), flourished for some years. But at the same time a beginning was made to the creation of the heroic-revolutionary style of Stalinist times, and of its more sinister rigid controls.[34]

And so in the U.S.S.R. during the 1920s there was on the one hand an attempt to create a new culture worthy of the proletarian revolution, on the other a realisation that even the basis for such a culture–consisting of literacy and the eradication of superstition – had still to be constructed. In its social aspect, Alexandra Kollontai was calling for the abolition of the family and the emancipation of women at a time when the reality throughout most of the Soviet Union was a household ruled by a stern and even cruel husband and father.[35] Some people would take a step in the fresh direction by choosing a revolutionary name – Vladlen, Diamat, Oktiabrina or Elektrifikatsiia – for their children, but even this move would make them worry about incurring the wrath of the Church at a time when a large number of Soviet citizens would agree with the peasant who said that 'Religion is your only comfort: you tell yourself that only God knows what is good and bad, and that is some consolation'.[36] Much of the peasant belief would still be pre-Christian, the world full of evil spirits and demons. The predicament was neatly set out by the ex-shepherd Esenin who not long before committing suicide confessed 'I am not a New Man. With one foot in the past, I try to catch up with the army of steel but I stumble and fall.' Something similar to what happened to Esenin in particular in 1925 was to occur in rural Russia as a whole in 1929.

12 The Construction of Soviet Socialism, 1929–1941

'The spring of 1929 is a terminal landmark for the historian of the Soviet Union', says E. H. Carr, adding the explanation that:

> Down to that time, debates were conducted in the leading party organs on major issues of policy; and, though the free expression of opinions hostile to the party was increasingly restricted, the historian has no great difficulty in unravelling the issues at stake, in appreciating the arguments advanced on either side, or in knowing, by and large, who advanced them. This – almost suddenly – ceases to be true after the spring of 1929. Though we understand well enough the pressures which led to the decision at the end of that year to embark upon the forced collectivisation of agriculture, we know little of the discussions in the inner counsels of the party which must have preceded the decision, or of the view taken by any leading Soviet politician other than Stalin. Later, the fog becomes thicker still, and, in spite of a few piecemeal revelations, envelops all Soviet policy in the nineteen-thirties'.[1]

Along with the fog, there comes a large amount of social disruption involving the loss of life on a scale unsurpassed in contemporary European history and not often approached in the recent development of other continents. For these reasons, the period 1929–41 makes great demands on Carr's assertion that the historian should not make moral judgements. Most Western analysts of the period have been far away from such a standard of objectivity, many of them over-simplifying it with explanations centring around the characterisation of Stalin as an omnipotent dictator, enslaving millions of people to satisfy his own persecution mania and sadistic perversity. However, as the period has receded in time, some of them have managed to play the part of the historian as described by Carr, and look for explanations of its principal developments beyond the 'cult of personality', as well as giving proper weight to its more constructive aspects. Nevertheless, hardly anybody would yet choose to make an assessment more neutral than Carr's own, that 'seldom perhaps in history has so monstrous a price been paid for so monumental an achievement'.[2]

For their part, the Soviet commentators who first used the term 'cult of personality' have not succeeded forty years on in giving a fully Marxist interpretation of the significant events of the 1930s. To attribute all the errors to Stalin alone is unsatisfactory; to go further than that might implicate some of the individuals who are still in power and could even involve some fundamental criticism of the whole Soviet system. One worthy attempt at a balanced objectivity is made by the 'unofficial' Soviet historian Roy Medvedev in his *Let History Judge*.[3] Trotsky's conclusion was that 'the crushing of Soviet democracy by an all-powerful bureaucracy and the extermination of bourgeois democracy by fascism were produced by one and the same cause: the dilatoriness of the world proletariat in solving the problems set for it by history. Stalinism and fascism, in spite of a deep difference in social foundations, are symmetrical phenomena. In many of their features they show a deadly similarity.' Nevertheless, Trotsky emphasised that Soviet Russia even under Stalin was separated from Hitler's Germany and Mussolini's Italy by 'the difference between a workers' state and a capitalist state'.[4]

Before describing the period during which Stalinism arose, we must pay some lip-service to the 'cult of personality' by saying something about the early career of the man who came to embody it. Iosif Visarionovich Dzhugashvili was born in 1879, the son of a Georgian shoemaker and his young wife Ekaterina. Both parents were of serf origin, and living in poor circumstances in the town of Gori, about a hundred kilometres from Tbilisi (Tiflis). Iosif or Joseph was their fourth child, but the first to survive infancy. Even he had smallpox at the age of six or seven, which made him pock-marked for life, and he later suffered a serious blood infection of the left arm, which he could thereafter never properly bend. The father had to go off to work in Tiflis and died there when his son was eleven, leaving the mother to care for him while working as a washerwoman. Hard-working and deeply religious, Ekaterina struggled to keep her son at the ecclesiastical academy at Gori, to which she had first sent him at the age of nine. A precocious pupil, Joseph was able to move on in 1894 to the Theological Seminary in Tiflis, and he remained a student there until the spring of 1899. Even in the barrack-like atmosphere of the Seminary, Joseph picked up extracurricular reading such as Darwin and Hugo and developed a social conscience as well as Georgian patriotism. A combination of these influences took him into an underground local political party in 1898, and out of the Seminary in disgrace a few months later. Soon a full-time political agitator, he took the pseudonym Koba, the name of a legendary outlaw. A few months' work in the oil town of Batumi gained for Koba his first jail sentence.

In the 'university' of prison and Siberian exile, Koba developed his political consciousness, becoming a Bolshevik in a predominantly Menshevik area soon after his return to Tiflis in 1904. During the Revolution of 1905, he was an energetic and loyal advocate of Lenin's standpoint and thus first came to the Bolshevik leader's attention. Congresses in Finland, Stockholm and London put Koba more in the wider limelight, although most of his attention was given to activities in Georgia, including liaison work with local 'fighting squads' who raised funds for the party by robbing banks. Leadership of strikes in the oil-fields around Baku took Koba back to jail in 1907 and then to exile in European Russia. He escaped for a time, but was then recaptured and sent back to complete his sentence. On his release in 1911 he did not go back to the Caucasus, but still directed his energies towards the revolutionary end nearer the centre of the movement. There has been some allegation that at about this time he was working as a double agent, undermining the socialist cause as he worked for it. But the evidence here is inconclusive. By the beginning of 1913, he had acquired a new revolutionary pseudonym – Stalin, taken further 'business trips' abroad to Krakow and Vienna, written a paper on the nationalities and helped to edit *Pravda*. For such activities, he gained another sentence to Siberian exile, in which he appears to have spent some comparatively idle years until the February Revolution of 1917 brought him back to Petrograd. Compared to Lenin and Trotsky, Stalin played a minor part in the events of 1917, devoting himself mostly to further editorial and propagandistic activity. During the Civil War, he ruthlessly held Tsaritsyn, the important town on the Volga which was later named after him and then after the river on which it stood. (Tsaritsyn – Stalingrad – Volgograd: an interesting discussion of Soviet history could be based on these changes alone.) Stalin's official posts in these early years included Commissar for Nationalities after October, Commissar of the Workers' and Peasants' Inspectorate in 1919, and General Secretary of the Party in 1922. For all its modest title, this last position more than any other was to carry him to power.

Before 1929 Stalin had already shown the psychological traits that were to be more fully exhibited during the next quarter-century. As well as demonstrating considerable capacity for leadership and administration, he had also revealed those negative characteristics that Lenin complained of in his 'last testament'. But from 1929 onwards, both sides of Stalin were to be forgotten in the Soviet Union as he became elevated into the super-human titan of the 'cult of personality'. Already in a party journal in December of that year, he was referred to as Lenin's 'most outstanding disciple and comrade-in-arms' who as far back as the pre-October period had 'stressed and defended the Leninist principles of the possibility of building socialism in one single, backward country'. Stalin was the 'only theoretician' apart from Lenin and 'the great strategist of the Leninist school', 'the perfect prototype' of the leader who 'combines Russian revolutionary fervour with American efficiency'.[5]

We shall return to the problem of the explanation of the 'cult of personality' after an examination of the period in which it became firmly established. For the moment, the final emphasis in these introductory remarks must be given to the major achievement of the 1930s which the 'cult' must not be allowed to overshadow, the construction of Soviet socialism. Such a concept would itself appear a reckless distortion to those who prefer to describe the Soviet system as state capitalism. Undoubtedly, the crude compromises that were made between aspiration and reality produced a society that few of those who died in the struggles of the post-revolutionary years would recognise as that for which they had made their final sacrifice. Moreover, there is no doubt that the Soviet Union borrowed heavily from the experiences of those capitalist societies which had undergone the process of industrialisation before it. Nevertheless, experimentation was to more than a sufficiently high degree and on more than an adequate scale for it to deserve a title which differentiates it from anything that had gone before.

Political

The years of the first Five-Year Plans are most commemorated in the West for the not unrelated developments of the final imposition of Stalin's dictatorship and the elimination of the opposition to it, both real and imagined. Let us begin then with the familiar, and the alternative explanations of it that have been put forward in the Soviet Union and abroad.

In the first place, there was the official pronouncement given at the time, that various opponents of Leninism – Trotskyists, Zinovievites, Bukharinists and others – were agents of the international bourgeoisie and had to be destroyed if the world's first socialist state was to survive.

Hardly anybody would now fully accept such an assertion, although to many it was acceptable enough at the time. Rather more plausible is the account given by Khrushchev at the Twentieth Party Congress in 1956. Allowing some part of the persecution to be right and necessary, Khrushchev condemned Stalin for excesses committed in the cause of guaranteeing and boosting his own security and power. A Soviet general history argues that 'the fact that people had faith in Stalin made it difficult to struggle against illegality and arbitrary rule. Any acts against him were not supported by the people and were regarded as acts against socialist construction'.[6] While there is obviously something in both Khrushchev's and the textbook's accounts, neither of them comes near to a full explanation from a Marxist or any other point of view.

More satisfying is the analysis made by Isaac Deutscher, which merits considerable attention. Beginning with one of his illuminating comparisons between the courses of the French and Russian Revolutions, Deutscher observes that Robespierre's 'reign of terror' was much closer to the commencement of the Revolution than Stalin's, that it lasted for a much shorter time, and ended with the execution of its leading instigator, while Stalin survived. The Russian revolutionaries constantly had in mind French precedents, and were anxious to avoid those that appeared less agreeable, particularly Thermidorean reaction and Bonapartism.[7] And so at first many oppositionists, including Trotsky, were allowed to emigrate, although the 1920s were not completely bloodless.

In exile Trotsky published tracts which contained much inside information about developments in Soviet Russia and exerted some influence there, his avid readers probably including Stalin himself. Suspected of adhering to the Trotskyist or lesser branches of opposition, hundreds of thousands of members were thrown out of the Party during the early 1930s. According to Deutscher, the opposition now disagreed among itself about the response to be made to this early purge, one of the clearest cleavages of opinion reflecting the generation gap. While the old men grumbled, sometimes arguing that a change in the system was more important than the persecution of individuals and that such a change could perhaps be achieved in co-operation with Stalin, the young thought of the terrorist heroes of the nineteenth century and how to act in such a tradition. One of them named Nikolaev assassinated Sergei Kirov in Leningrad on 1 December 1934.

Kirov was immensely popular in the Party, and some observers have believed that his assassination was instigated by Stalin, as anxious as ever to remove a potential rival.[8] The ruthless Andrei Zhdanov was appointed in Kirov's place, and tens of thousands of Party members, old and young, were deported to Siberia from Leningrad and other cities. There they were joined in the spring of 1935 by about forty members of the Leader's own bodyguard, two of whom were executed. In Siberia 'Kirov's assassins', as the Leningrad contingent was called, and the other political prisoners found themselves subjected to a harsh régime aimed at rendering impossible the revival of the practice of tsarist times for prisons and places of exile to be used as 'universities' of the opposition.

Further explanation of this excessive retaliation, and of the even greater political purges which followed it, is to be found in Russia's previous history. As Deutscher puts it, 'the cruelty with which the past oppressed the present was proportionate to the determination with which the revolution had set out to repudiate the past'. In the construction of socialism, a new aim, the Soviet government was obliged to resort to an old method, coercion from above. And so Deutscher sees Stalin as part Nicholas I, part Alexander I, part Peter the Great and part Ivan the Terrible, and the Leader himself appears to have concurred with the second pair of comparisons, if not the first pair.[9] Stalin put the predicament of the U.S.S.R. in historical perspective in a famous speech made on 5 February 1931:

To slacken the tempo would mean falling behind. And those who fall behind get beaten. But we do not want to get beaten. No, we refuse to be beaten! One feature of the history of the old Russia was the continual beatings she suffered because of her backwardness. She was beaten by the Mongol khans. She was beaten by the Turkish beys. She was beaten by the Swedish feudal lords. She was beaten by the Polish and Lithuanian gentry. She was beaten by the British and French capitalists. She was beaten by the Japanese barons. All beat her – because of her backwardness, because of her military backwardness, cultural backwardness, industrial backwardness, agricultural backwardness. They beat her because to do so was profitable and and could be done with impunity. You remember the words of the pre-revolutionary poet: 'You are poor and abundant, mighty and impotent, Mother Russia.' These gentlemen were quite familiar with the verses of the old poet. They beat her, saying: 'You are abundant', so one can enrich oneself at your expense. They beat her, saying: 'You are poor and impotent', so you can be beaten and plundered with impunity. Such is the law of exploiters – to beat the backward, and the weak. It's the jungle law of capitalism. You are backward, you are weak – and therefore you are wrong; hence you can be beaten and enslaved. You are mighty – therefore you are right; hence we must be wary of you. . . . We are fifty or a hundred years behind the advanced countries. We must make good this distance in ten years. Either we do it, or we shall go under.[10]

The style of the speech itself, as well as the content, is a mixture of nationalist and socialist rhetoric. Containing a digest of Russian history which is in some ways inaccurate – more battles were won than lost between Poltava in 1709 and the Crimean War of 1854 – the speech is still a powerful argument for the patriotic necessity of forcing the pace.

From coercion to persecution had always been and was still now a small step, and there were several additional reasons for taking it in the 1930s. Scapegoats could be found for errors and excesses in the implementation of the Five-Year Plans. In the increasingly unstable international atmosphere of the period, enemy agents were feared to have permeated even the innermost ranks of the Party. There were old scores to settle from the infighting of the 1920s. Such thoughts did not occur to Stalin alone.

In the second half of 1935 and the first half of 1936, the situation was fairly peaceful as a new Constitution was inaugurated with much ceremony, Stalin collecting bouquets and distributing kisses and giving every semblance of quiet contentment. Under the surface, however, all was far from well. It was at about this time that Trotsky claimed that his Fourth International – founded in 1933 – already possessed 'its strongest, most numerous and most hardened branch in the U.S.S.R.'.[11] *Pravda* and *Izvestiia* were publishing stories about clandestine opposition groups and about 'sabotage' and wilful resistance to the introduction of new production methods. The outbreak of the Spanish Civil War, Hitler's move into the Rhineland, and the conclusion of the Nazi–Japanese Anti-Comintern Pact were giving rise to concern. In such an atmosphere, the great purges began.

There were four major trials: of the 'sixteen', Zinovev, Kamenev and others, in August 1936; of the 'seventeen', including Piatakov and Radek, in January 1937; of the 'twenty-one', among whom were Rykov, Bukharin and Yagoda, in March 1938; and (in secret and very summary fashion, if at all a 'trial') of Marshal Tukhachevskii and a group of the highest generals in the Red Army in June 1937. Among those arraigned were every member of Lenin's Politbureau except Stalin and Trotsky, two heads of the political police department, ambassadors, generals and other high functionaries. All were accused of attempting to assassinate Stalin and wreck the Soviet Union in collusion with various foreign powers. While none of the charges were substantiated, the defendants without exception pleaded guilty. Some appear to have seen their false confession as a last service to the Party for which they had worked for much of their lives, others might have been more concerned to save their wives and families. Certainly, the recantations became as much a part of the ritual of the trials as the denunciation made by the chief prosecutor Andrei Vishinskii, 'Shoot the mad dogs!'. At the lower Party levels, and outside the Party, millions of others were purged, often without ceremony. J. Berger, E. S. Ginzburg, A. V. Gorbatov and N. Ia. Mandelshtam were among those who lived through the harrowing experiences of the period to tell the sorry tale of its less famous victims. No level of society or area of the Soviet Union was left untouched, and, according to various calculations, from four to sixteen million people died, and at least as many more were kept in concentration camps.

Stalin and many of his entourage were themselves able to survive the firing squad or the concentration camp largely because they themselves believed and were able to persuade others to believe that their course of action was one of the harsh necessities on the road to the establishment of 'socialism in one country'. Savage means were justified by the glorious end, in the way of which neither internal nor external opposition must be allowed to stand. The unity of the Party and of its allies abroad thus gained its rationale, and would be the basis for all branches of domestic and foreign policy. Moreover, the new élite, which included the secret police, often had a vested interest of a more personal kind in the maintenance of the régime. Not that individuals were safe even there, as the personal histories of two heads of the secret police, Iagoda and Ezhev show.

As a centre piece or symbol of the order that was being created, a formal framework for it was set up in the mid-1930s. A Soviet history describes the process in the following manner:

The time had now come when it became possible to lift all limitations to Soviet, socialist democracy.

A decision to draft a new Constitution was passed at the Seventh All-Union Congress of Soviets in 1935. In 1936, it was published in the press for nation-wide discussion.

Nearly half of the adult population took part in the discussion.

The new Constitution was adopted in November 1936 by the Eighth Extraordinary Congress of Soviets of the U.S.S.R. in Moscow.

It recorded the triumph of socialism and provided the foundation for broad socialist democracy, stating that a socialist economic system and ownership of the means of production were the economic basis of the Soviet Union, while the Soviets of Working People's Deputies were its political foundation. It removed the remaining restrictions in elections to the Soviets, replaced multi-stage elections by direct elections and established the election of all Soviets on the basis of universal, equal and direct suffrage by secret ballot. Citizens of the U.S.S.R. received equal rights to elect and be elected to the Soviets.[12]

While many foreign analysts and Soviet dissidents have seen the Constitution of 1936 as little more than an empty propaganda gesture, pointing out that in fact it receives very little mention of either a direct or an indirect kind in later legislation, some of them also put the argument that it performs the vital function of giving the Soviet Union a considerable amount of social cohesion. In such a case, there was at least a grain of truth in Stalin's claim that it was a legislative embodiment of what had already been achieved. Furthermore, what was established for the Soviet peoples in general was particularly granted to those of Kazakhstan and Kirgizia, which became Union republics, and for the members of the Transcaucasian Federation, which was now split into three – Armenia, Georgia and Azerbaidzhan. The constituent parts of the Soviet Union were thereby increased from seven to eleven. The addition of Moldavia and the Baltic States in 1940 brought the number of republics up to fifteen. Undoubtedly this process was attended, for the individuals and groups involved, by extreme discomfiture, the nature and intensity of which possessed features peculiar to the larger process of the construction of Soviet socialism. At the same time, it is worth recording that industrialising societies everywhere show little mercy to those who stand in their path. Thus, some of the tribesmen of Central Asia and the Caucasus who were overcome at this time might be compared to the Indians of North and South America. Returning to the Constitution but retaining the same area for analogy, we could point out that the Federal Constitution of the United States is broadly comparable with that of the Soviet Union in this one respect, that its cohesive influence has often been greater than its literal interpretation.

Moreover, if the Soviet Constitution is criticised for stating that the government is carried on by the ministries and Soviets and neglecting to stress its real motor, the Communist Party, something similar could again be said about the Federal Constitution of the U.S.A., which makes no reference to party at all. This is not to suggest that constitutional comparisons can be taken anywhere near the point of identity or to deny that the specific historical conditions obtaining in the Soviet Union were a major influence on the development of the C.P.S.U. during the 1930s. Throughout the course of that momentous decade, there were significant changes in the Communist Party both quantitative and qualitative. As far as the numbers were concerned, the total rose from just over 1 million to nearly 2¼ millions in the first hectic years of the Stalinist forced pace from 1929 to 1933. From 1933, there was an annual decline down to about 1½ millions in the later years of the decade, the total climbing again to almost 2½ millions by 1941. Such fluctuations in the figures were attended by variations in age and occupation. The official intention was that workers should provide the bulk of the party membership, and indeed they did so, although from the ranks of those who were classified as workers there were many who were employed in the office rather than on the factory floor. The new intelligentsia was a vital constituent of the Party. Other distinguishing characteristics of the Communists of the 1930s were their comparatively youthful age and their male sex.[13]

Apart from the Party, another major constituent part of the Soviet polity was the army, something over half of whose officers in the 1930s were members of the C.P.S.U. The general tendency of the decade was towards the professionalisation of the army, while keeping it under strict political control. This involved the restoration of ranks and of privileges which had at first been abolished after the October Revolution. In such a manner, military developments paralleled those in many other spheres of the national life.[14] At the same time, the armed forces were being mechanised. The outstanding figure of the period was Marshal Tukhachevskii, whose purge along with many other senior and junior officers has been held partly responsible for the initial poor performance of the Red Army after the outbreak of war in 1941.

Before 1941, the Red Army had been involved in little action since the end of the Civil War. Although the threat of international conflict had been constant, the only actual fighting of any consequence was in the Far East, where in 1938–9 the Japanese were engaged on a fairly large scale near the Soviet borders. This area had been causing concern ever since the Japanese moved into Manchuria in 1931, and the U.S.S.R. attempted to guarantee its security there through treaties with both Mongolia and China. The second of these two treaties implied the continued neglect of the Chinese Communists led by Mao Tse-tung. The signing of the Anti-Comintern pact by Japan and Nazi Germany in 1936 amply demonstrated that there could be no clear distinction between East and West, and revived old fears of trouble on two fronts or even something approaching virtual encirclement. Such fears were intensified as the Anti-Comintern pact was joined by Italy in 1937 and by Spain in 1939.

They constitute much of the explanation of the Soviet foreign policy in the 1930s.

For these and other reasons, the Soviet Union's chief Foreign Commissar, Maxim Litvinov, played a vigorous part in international attempts to secure disarmament and collective security. But the efforts of Litvinov and his associates met with little success. For example, at the World Conference on the Reduction and Restriction of Armaments at Geneva in 1932, the Soviet proposals for the partial and then complete destruction of the weapons of war were welcomed by the major Western powers no more than the Soviet delegates looked with approval upon the Western suggestions. However, the U.S.S.R. had now shown itself to be an important enough force for the U.S.A. to recognise it in 1933 and for the League of Nations to invite it to become a member in 1934.

The principal Soviet aim in the mid-1930s was the transformation of this recognition into an alliance against Fascism, to the rising threat of which the U.S.S.R. itself had mistakenly made a contribution by discouraging early opposition to Hitler. Non-aggression treaties with most of the states of Eastern Europe were consolidated by 1934, and mutual defence treaties albeit of a limited nature were arranged with Czechoslovakia and France in 1935. Italy's aggression against Ethiopia in 1935–6 was condemned by the Soviet government, which also gave republican Spain some if by no means enough moral and material support after it had been attacked in 1936 by Franco with the encouragement and *de facto* intervention of both Italy and Germany. The Western Allies could not agree to any firm stand against Fascism, and then appeared to be making every attempt to conciliate it in the Munich agreement of 1938. The Soviet interpretation of this appeasement is based on the by no means unsupportable hypothesis that the French and British governments were assuming that the major Fascist strike would be to the east against Communism and for *Lebensraum*.

In the aftermath of Munich, the U.S.S.R. made its last desperate attempts at securing collective security. Firstly, it did everything possible to arouse public opinion abroad through its policy of reducing the emphasis on the Third International and increasing its encouragement for the 'popular front', without any great degree of success. Secondly, after the Nazi takeover of the whole of Czechoslovakia in early 1939, it initiated talks with the French and British governments on the question of concerted action against any further Nazi moves. But the Western Allies treated the question with little urgency, sending low-rank missions in a tardy manner, and in desperation the Soviet government, in the person of a new Foreign Commissar, Molotov, turned to Germany (with whom discussions had been in progress for some time, albeit in secret), and signed a non-aggression pact with its chief potential adversary in August 1939. Like the Tilsit Peace with Napoleon more than two hundred years previously and Brest-Litovsk in 1918, the pact was recognised by both sides as nothing more than a breathing space. Taking as full advantage as possible, the Red Army moved into areas contiguous to the Soviet Union, incorporating much of the Baltic provinces, Moldavia and parts of Poland as the Nazi Army invaded Poland on 1 September to start the Second World War. But Finland was not prepared to make concessions to her powerful neighbour and the Winter War of 1939–40 which brought about these concessions by force inflicted both military and diplomatic reverses on the Soviet Union. The Western Allies were completely alienated by the Soviet non-aggression pact with Hitler and the attack on Finland, and for more than a year there seemed even less prospect of an anti-Fascist coalition than in 1938–9. However, the speedy successes of the German armed forces in western and central Europe throughout the year 1940 encouraged Hitler to turn to his major purpose of the defeat of the Soviet Union and persuaded the remnants of the Western Allies to be less fastidious about the political philosophy of potential anti-German friends. Meanwhile the Soviet government made sure that its eastern flank was reasonably secure by concluding a neutrality pact with Japan in April 1941.

The debate still continues about the errors and miscalculations of international diplomacy in the years leading up to 1941 and the entry of the Soviet Union into the Second World War. Munich of course has become a notorious example of appeasement, although Soviet analysts may be forgiven for complaining that the later reputation of Chamberlain's fateful step has been used against the Soviet Union almost as much as the step itself. On the other hand, so some arguments run, Stalin and his advisers should have been able to see that their best interests lay in declaring at an earlier stage that they wholeheartedly wished to work for an anti-Fascist alliance and even as late as 1939 in engaging the German forces on the eastern European front at the same time as France and Great Britain moved in from the west. Either of these commitments would have necessitated a degree of trust considerably higher than the Soviet experience since 1917 was capable of achieving.

Economic

The economic construction of Soviet socialism consisted basically of two interconnected processes: the development of heavy industry and the collectivisation of agriculture. The first of these measures was carefully prepared, the second hastily improvised; both of them produced severe dislocation, but could be said to have met with striking success by the time of the Soviet entry into the Second World War in 1941.

The First Five-Year Plan was launched in 1928 after some years of debate and preliminary calculation. Samsonov's Soviet textbook describes its aims in the following manner:

> The overall target of the First Five-Year Plan was to modernise industry, turn the Soviet Union from an agrarian into a powerful industrial country that would be economically independent of the capitalist states, and strengthen its defence potential.
>
> The socio-economic relations in the country had to be changed, industry and agriculture had to be developed on a single socialist foundation, and a considerable proportion of small peasant farms had to be merged into socialist, collective farms. It was planned to draw some 4–5 million peasants into collective farms and enlarge their crop area in the country. It was planned to improve the standard of living, introduce universal elementary education, and so forth.[15]

Immediately after the commencement of the implementation of the plan, trouble arose in the agricultural sector. Already in the winter of 1927–8 there had been a grain crisis with deliveries by the peasants to the towns falling short of expectation if not of absolute need. The refusal of some farmers – particularly the well-to-do kulaks – to sell their surpluses at reasonable prices at last stung the government into action, and what started off as an attempt at the forced collection of grain became an all-out war on the kulak and a drive to solve Russia's age-old farming problems once and for all.

The reasons for this change of tack are still hotly debated. Certainly, it was annoying for a government embarking on the construction of a modern planned economy to have to worry about inadequate or even critically short food supplies, for the new socialist administration to be hampered by the kind of difficulty which most capitalist societies had long overcome. Moreover, as revolutionaries steeled in the harrowing experiences of the years following October, who had not hesitated to introduce the rigorous controls of War Communism, Stalin and his associates would not stop short of further compulsory measures where necessary. Since the link between the proletariat and the peasantry seemed to be breaking down in the relaxed conditions of N.E.P., the only course now open was the forcible re-establishment of the link.

Socialist industry and capitalist agriculture could no longer co-exist. Proper socialist planning required scientific arrangement of all branches of economy.

Encouraged by early sucesses, the government had swung into a programme of full collectivisation by late 1929. Isaac Deutscher graphically describes the painful sequel:

> Within a short time rural Russia became pandemonium. The overwhelming majority of the peasantry confronted the government with desperate opposition. Collectivisation degenerated into a military operation, a cruel civil war. Rebellious villages were surrounded by machine-guns and forced to surrender. Masses of *kulaks* were deported to remote unpopulated lands in Siberia. Their houses, barns, and farm implements were turned over to the collective farms – Stalin himself put the value of their property so transferred at over 400 million roubles. The bulk of the peasants decided to bring in as little as possible of their property to the collective farms which they imagined to be state-owned factories, in which they themselves would become mere factory hands. In desperation they slaughtered their cattle, smashed implements, and burned crops. This was the muzhik's great Luddite-like rebellion.[16]

The scale of the process is indicated by the fact that the number of households in collective farms rose from 1 million at the beginning of July to nearly 5 millions at the end of December 1929 and to almost 15 millions by the beginning of March 1930. In some areas, almost all the households were collectivised. Stalin attempted to exculpate himself in a speech of 2 March 1930 entitled 'Dizzy with success'. He complained about 'excesses', and suggested that further introduction of the new system be carried out in a more moderate manner, with the peasants being allowed to choose for themselves. Within a few weeks, the level of collectivisation fell from nearly 60 per cent to less than 25 per cent; more than 10 million households had left the collectives by the autumn of 1930. With less crippling but still powerful pressure being re-applied to the peasants, about 14 million households (that is 75 per cent approximately of the total), were in the system by the end of the First Five-Year Plan.

Most of these belonged to the type of organisation known as *kolkhoz*, that is a collective farm owned by its members, who were jointly responsible for the delivery of certain quotas but who were allowed to spend the rest of their time on their own small private plots. Some worked for wages in the other basic form of arrangement called *sovkhoz*, or state farm. During the 1930s, a number of attempts were made to raise incentives in agriculture. Another important ingredient in farming progress was its modernisation. To transform rural Russia into a part of the economy worthy of inclusion in the Five-Year Plans, it would have to be mechanised. The focus of the effort in this direction was the M.T.S. or Machine-Tractor Station, which was looked upon not only as an accelerator of such processes as ploughing and harvesting but also a means of maintaining party discipline and promoting cultural enlightenment. But since there were only a few thousand M.T.S.s and about a quarter of a million collectives, the hopes held out for them could not be realised, and the problem of bringing rural Russia up to date was to remain with the Soviet government long after the initial difficulties of setting up heavy industry had been overcome.[17]

By the end of 1932 the First Five-Year Plan was proclaimed as completed in four years and three months. The major emphasis had been on heavy industry, about 85 per cent of all industrial investment going in that direction, and now some 1500 new large-scale enterprises had been completed. New branches of industry – machine, chemical, electrical – were now set up, and new towns built as centres of industrial activity. Describing the construction of a metalworks at Kuznetsk in Siberia, an eye-witness wrote:

> People streamed to us from all parts of the country. In addition to Russians and Ukrainians there were Kazakhs and Kirghizes. These formerly illiterate people who had never seen a real factory in their lives performed incredible exploits. Instead of their quota of 150 mixes, the concrete-mixers produced 408. . . . The rivetters drove 266 rivets home during a shift instead of their quota of 105. The navvies sometimes fulfilled ten quotas during a single shift. YCL members braved temperatures of –50c to continue rivetting at a great height. Bricklayers each laid up to 15 tons of refractory brick during a shift. Nothing, neither snowstorm nor rain, could dampen the labour enthusiasm of the builders.[18]

An American at Magnitogorsk in the Urals compared his experiences there to a battle involving more casualties than some of the engagements of the First World War.[19] Undoubtedly, the great progress was achieved at enormous sacrifice, much of which was voluntary, some of which was enforced. A great amount of assistance, voluntary and purchased, came from abroad: not only were bourgeois specialists of various kinds employed,[20] about 17,300 million roubles worth of capital and other goods were imported.[21]

Dependence on such outside sources declined during the Second Five-Year Plan from 1933 to 1937 and the initial stages of the Third Five-Year Plan from 1938 onwards. Progress during the 1930s set the seal on the construction of a self-reliant modernised economy. In comparison with the level reached in 1913, production in heavy industry grew twelve times, in machines and metal thirty-five times and in electricity twenty-five times. Some 9000 new enterprises were in operation and the Soviet Union was now the first industrial power in Europe and second only to the United States in the world. Not all targets were reached but even agriculture which remained a problem managed finally to surpass the 1913 grain totals in 1940.

A necessary component of the great transformation was a steep rise in the mileage of communications, particularly railroads. The most solid achievement of the First Five-Year Plan was the completion of the Turksib Railway, nearly 1500 kilometres of track bringing Central Asia firmly into the Union network. Altogether about 5500 kilometres of track were laid during the period, and transport by rail nearly doubled. Advances of a smaller kind occurred in the minor Soviet sectors of road and water transport. Such growth continued if more slowly during the Second Five-Year Plan, with the emphasis still being given to the eastern regions. A consequence of such concentration was the creation of a unified Soviet economy which at last began to make real use of vast natural and human resources.

The staggering costs of all the agricultural and industrial enterprises were met internally, by socialist accumulation which by 1941 had ceased to be primitive even if it was by no means refined. From 1930 onwards the turnover tax – a mixture of excise, purchase and processing tax – was the major source of state income. In theory equitable, the burden of the turnover tax fell mainly on the peasants. The state budget ran into increasing difficulty as expenditure on rearmaments necessarily but unexpectedly increased in the years immediately preceeding the Second World War.

The social dislocation involved in the fulfilment of the First and Second Five-Year Plans was tremendous. From 1926 to 1940 the urban population increased in size from something over 25 millions to nearly 60 millions, that is roughly from less than 20 per cent to more than 30 per cent of a total climbing from just under 150 to about 170 millions. The number of towns grew from just over 700 in 1926 to more than 1200 in 1940. During the same period, the rural population – about 115 millions in 1940 – fell from more than 80 per cent to less than 70 per cent of the total. The blood, sweat, toil and tears involved in these statistics would be hard to convey. A widely celebrated 'peak of labour heroism' was said to have been reached on 31 August 1935 when a miner named Aleksei Stakhanov allegedly cut more than 100 metric tons of coal in one shift, thus overfulfilling his quota by 1300 per cent. Stakhanovites, 'shock' workers and forced labour using machines and bare hands maintained productive and statistical output in sufficient flow for the Soviet Union to withstand many if not all the blows of the Nazi invasion of 1941 on its own resources. But before 1941 Soviet citizens had not experienced much of the fruits of the modernised economy in the shape of good housing and ample consumer goods. Queues and the black market were much in evidence in peacetime and were to become even more so after the outbreak of war.

Cultural

An integral part of Stalinism although one of its often neglected aspects is the cultural revolution which took place during the 1930s. Accompanying the forced pace of the industrialisation programme and the imposition of strict political controls, this cultural revolution most clearly marked the painful reconciliation between socialism and Russian tradition which is the most characteristic feature of the period as a whole. So great was the incubus of the past that progress in several directions was restricted enough for cultural counter-revolution rather than revolution to the appropriate designation. Nowhere was this more the case than in the field of religion, although appearances were at first deceptive. As Fainsod describes the initial process:

> The abandonment of the N.E.P. marked a new turn in Soviet policy towards religious organisations. In the eyes of the regime the church interposed an obstacle to the successful fulfilment of the new programme of collectivisation and rapid industrialisation, and a frontal assault was launched to diminish the power and influence of all forms of religious organisation. The campaign took the form of discriminatory penalties against the clergy, of tightening restrictions on religious activity, and, most important, of the closing of churches on a mass scale.[22]

Jews, Muslims and Buddhists fared no better than Christians, in fact probably worse, as the campaign mounted.

The Second Universal Congress of Atheists, which met in June 1929, heard from one of its speakers that no more than 250 out of 600,000 members of the Union of Atheists came from rural areas, and that therefore a long and bitter struggle would be necessary before the Union's aims were achieved. Even in the towns, religion was in no more than a slow decline, as the Smolensk archives examined by Fainsod tell us. In 1930 the members of a Party cell in a Smolensk factory shop were revealed by an investigation to be far from atheistic in their outlook: 70 per cent still hung icons in their homes, and more than 10 per cent had children who were baptised after their fathers had joined the Party, one of the baptisms taking place in celebration of the father's survival of a purge. In 1937 a census taken of the people as a whole was widely believed to reveal that 40 per cent of them were still religious in their outlook, even after years of much propaganda, some persecution and not a little announcement of positive progress towards atheism. For example, the local Soviet of Iaroslavl claimed in 1930 that it had abolished the ringing of church bells at the request of 80,000 people.[23]

These and other impressive statistics could not disguise the persistence of religion, in recognition of which the government moved, not without some backtracking, towards partial accommodation. Demonstrations against the celebration of Christmas and Easter were curtailed in the mid-1930s, although clergymen and some of their charges fell in the purges of 1937–8. The additional circumstances of a deteriorating international situation appears to have contributed to the introduction at the beginning of 1939 of a new general religious policy. Not only did the government now admit that its attempts at the liquidation of religion had been over-zealous, it also argued that it was wrong to condemn religion as being solely an instrument of class oppression. Christianity, for example, helped to preserve the family and boost morality. Its historic significance had at times been progressive, too. Commenting on the absence of the Orthodox Church from the film *Alexander Nevsky*, the League of Militant Atheists declared that there was 'no reason to be afraid of objectively showing the role of the Church in Russian history. Anti-religious propaganda is permissible in films of this kind; however, it must be directed not against the Orthodox clergy but against Catholic monks and the Roman Pope.'[24] Such evidence of accommodation with Orthodoxy was to become much more marked after the Nazi attack on the Soviet Union in 1941.

Compromise between aspiration and reality was noticeable at an earlier stage in education. While the persistence of prayer did not necessarily interfere with the realisation of the Five-Year Plans, lack of skill and knowledge often did present obstacles, as other industrialising societies had discovered previously. And so the tendency away from experimentation and improvisation towards regularised inculcation of basic skills, already noticeable in the mid-1920s, now became much more pronounced. A decree of 5 September 1931 pointed out, as a basic defect of the current system, 'the fact that school instruction fails to give a sufficient body of general knowledge'. Thus, there was a dearth at the higher educational level of 'fully literate people with a good command of the basic sciences'. Although the decree did not cease to emphasise the importance of the polytechnical approach, at the same time it stressed the fact that 'Every attempt to separate the polytechnisation of the school from a systematic and firm mastery of the sciences and of physics, chemistry, and mathematics in particular . . . constitutes the most flagrant perversion of the ideas of the polytechnical school.' To ensure that future progress would be along the correct lines, such lines were to be clearly drawn. By 1 January 1932 the educational authorities in the constituent republics of the Soviet Union were to work out and implement revised programmes which would ensure the inculcation of 'a strictly defined body of systematic knowledge (native language, mathematics, physics, chemistry, geography, history)'. Such a curriculum was to be uniform for virtually all children undergoing the first ten years of education. Moreover, teaching methods were to be characterised by 'decisive warfare against irresponsible projectorising and the introduction on a mass scale of methods untested in practice', although 'attempts to go back to the bourgeois school' were to be resisted at the same time as 'extreme left tendencies'.[25] A further series of decrees restored traditional methods of discipline and assessment, while textbooks were reintroduced in contradiction to the assertion of Krupskaia and other early Soviet educators that 'life must be the textbook'.

Against such a background, numerical advances were clearly made. While the final conquest over illiteracy was brought several stages nearer, from the beginning of the 1930s, four-year primary education was made compulsory for all young Soviet citizens, seven-year for those living in towns, these figures being increased to seven and ten respectively by 1941. At the outbreak of war, there were more than 35 million pupils being taught in Soviet schools by nearly 1,250,000 teachers. At university level, there were more than 800,000 students, at least half of whom were women.

The rise in the general educational level was reflected in the fact that there were more than 70,000 public libraries in existence by the late 1930s. In 1937 the total of books published in the Soviet Union approached 700 millions in at least a hundred different languages. Of course, it goes almost without saying that most if not all of this reading matter was subject to a severe censorship before publication and that the breadth of choice open to library users was strictly limited. Somehow, in spite of similar difficulties and under the almost constant threat of the purges, Soviet scholars managed to continue to produce work of real worth. For example, among outstanding scientists, the mathematician I. M. Vinogradov developed a new analytical method for the theory of numbers; the physicist P. A. Cherenkov discovered an aspect of the luminosity of liquids under the action of gamma-rays; and the chemist N. N. Semenov devised a theory of chemical chain reactions. In biology progress was retarded by the official support given to the genetic views of T. D. Lysenko.[26] Arctic and other scientific expeditions continued to provide useful information for many branches of natural science.

Historians such as B. D. Grekov and M. N. Tikhomirov made research advances and fresh syntheses in Russian medieval history, while E. A. Kosminskii did the same for the medieval history of England. But both history and other social sciences were held back by the dead hand of institutionalised error. Pokrovsky's views of the past were renounced, and a Soviet patriotic interpretation, reviving some of the pre-revolutionary glories, was put in their place. In no field perhaps was rigidity so ruinous as in linguistic theory where the crude assertions of N. Ia. Marr were enthroned with the approval of Stalin.

A similar bureaucratic degeneration occurred in literature and the arts. During the 1930s the unions for writers, musicians and other artists increasingly imposed their control over the creative output of their members, many of whom disappeared temporarily or for ever during the purges. Somehow or other, even in such straitened circumstances as these, work of real merit was produced. Leaving aside for other fuller discussions the question of what exactly constitutes real merit in a culture dedicated to the basic principle of socialist realism, even readers untutored in theory as most of us are have been impressed by such works as Mikhail Sholokhov's *And Quiet Flows the Don* and *Virgin Soil Upturned*; Nikolai Ostrovskii's *How the Steel Was Tempered*, Valentin Kataev's *Time Advance!* or *Lone White Sail*; and Leonid Leonov's *Soviet River*. While these novels dealt with twentieth-century subjects, others which went much further back in history also achieved considerable popularity. Among these were Viacheslav Shishkov's *Emelian Pugachev* and Aleksei Tolstoy's *Peter I*. This list could be extended without much difficulty. At the same time, although nothing of commensurate length could be written about contemporary painters, sculptors and architects, such directors as Eisenshtein, Dovzhenko and Kosintsev were continuing to produce remarkable films, if by no means so many as in the 1920s. Composers such as Prokofiev, Shostakovich, Miaskovskii, Kabalevskii and Khachaturian were composing some memorable music as well as some that might be best forgotten. In music, as well as in the other arts, it might be said that creativity flourished best when untrammelled by pressure or directives from the union's bureaucrats. For example, we do not hear so much today of pieces written specifically to commemorate various aspects of the Five-Year Plans as of those written to a less specific order, although some of them such as Mossolov's *Symphony of Machines* make an undoubted impact.

But such an argument would take us back to the consciously abandoned 'art for art's sake' position, which no Soviet worker in any creative field was allowed to adopt in the 1930s. Granted that the emergence of a proletarian culture could not be much more apparent than in the previous decade, most of the novelists, film directors and musical composers who have been mentioned here as representative distinguished figures would inevitably be responding in part to the growth of a larger audience brought up to at least some appreciation of that culture's distinguishing features. It could be argued that such interaction impeded these artists from moving down some of the blinder alleys of arid experimentation. True, this possibly beneficial effect would be counterweighed by the oppressions of untalented bureaucrats and by the imposition of the 'cult of personality'.

The Soviet Union had set out to construct socialism with hope and vision. The spirit of the times was caught in a primer written near the beginning of the Five-Year Plans for the illiterate of all ages: 'We must root out uncouthness and ignorance, we must change ourselves, we must become worthy of a better life. And this better life will not come as a miracle: we ourselves must create it. But to create it we need knowledge: we need strong hands, yes, but we also need strong minds.' [27]

A decade later, much of the spirit had been dashed, but the material task was nearly completed.

13 War and Reconstruction, 1941–1953

The dominant theme of Soviet history from 1941 to 1953 is war. By far the most bloody battles of the Great Patriotic War, as the Second World War is known in the U.S.S.R. were fought on Russian soil and over twenty million soldiers and civilians lost their lives. And then, soon after the return of peace, the Cold War arose to make the task of reconstruction an even more painful task than it already would have been. At the death of Stalin in 1953, the Soviet Union was struggling to fulfil the difficult roles of the world's second super-power and the titular leader of international socialism.

During this period, Stalin took on the guise of a firm if unemotional leader of the Soviet peoples in the fight against Fascism. In 1943 he became Marshal Stalin, and donned the uniform that became his most remembered attire and which, in its dress form, recalled the splendour of pre-revolutionary days. Such a reversion was soon apparent in his speech, too. On 6 November 1941 at the meeting to commemorate the Revolution held in the Mayakovsky metro station, Stalin appealed to the soldiers not only to recapture the spirit of the dark times of the Civil War when 'three quarters of our country was in the hands of foreign interventionists' but also to fight with the spirit of the heroes of modern and medieval Russia. He declared: 'Let the manly images of our great ancestors – Alexander Nevsky, Dimitry Donskoy, Kuzma Minin, Dimitry Pozharsky, Alexander Suvorov and Mikhail Kutuzov – inspire you in this war!'[1] And so the collision of tradition and socialism that had brought much of the suffering of the 1930s as well as their triumph now emerged at a time of greater crisis in a clearer form.

Stalin was both a figurehead and something more. Although he never personally visited the front line, the image of the leader watching over the people from the Kremlin helped to boost an often flagging morale and was still strong enough at the beginning of the seventies to draw spontaneous applause from cinema audiences of the war epic '*Liberation*'. Moreover, although caught napping at the beginning of the war, Stalin became something of a strategist as well as a manager while the fighting progressed. At the same time, his energies were mostly directed towards logistical problems.

With the arrival of peace, Stalin appears to have degenerated into a tired tyrant driven mostly by a powerful persecution mania. Purges and other forms of oppression again became a common feature of Soviet daily life. However, even in his final phase, the leader reflected something of a wider mood as well as his own psychopathology. Now as before, the 'cult of personality' possessed sociological as well as personal characteristics, and therefore needs to be seen against the background of contemporaneous political, economic and cultural developments.

Political

At the beginning of the period, Nazi Germany launched its attack on the U.S.S.R. Stalin was taken by surprise and the Soviet peoples as a a whole were improperly prepared. Some analysts believe that Stalin trusted Hitler too much and the Western Allies not enough. In a Soviet evaluation:

> The country's poor preparedness was due to grave errors of judgement made by Stalin in evaluating the general strategic situation and in his estimates of the probable time the war would break out. Stalin dismissed information coming in from various quarters about Germany's preparing to attack the U.S.S.R. as a provocation devised by the foreign press to create trouble between the U.S.S.R. and Germany.[2]

Premature from the Soviet point of view, the German attack may well have been too late from that of the Nazis. If Stalin has been blamed for thinking that the invasion came too soon, Hitler has been blamed for not launching it soon enough. But the extent of the delay caused by action in the Balkans has probably been exaggerated as well as that resulting from the eccentricity of the Führer; probably it was physically impossible for the German war machine to mobilise the necessary huge army of more than 150 divisions much before the fatal day of 22 June 1941 whatever the other circumstances. Even so, the German generals were gambling on a quick end to hostilities.[3]

Plan Barbarossa entailed a three-pronged offensive against Leningrad, Moscow and Kiev. The Nazi forces were most successful in the south:

Kiev managed to hold out for nearly three months, but the Soviet army then fell back towards the Don. Neither Moscow nor Leningrad fell in 1941, or indeed at any time. Perhaps the war was already lost as the policy of *Blitzkrieg* failed for the first time, but a great amount of effort would be expended before that possibility was made certain.

In 1942 the Nazis increased their strength on the Russian front to 266 divisions of which 193 were German. (The relative importance of this theatre of war at the time was reflected in the fact that there were no more than 4 German and 11 Italian divisions in North Africa.) Stalin believed that the main drive would be made for Moscow and made provision accordingly, but Hitler decided rather to strike for the Volga and the Caucasus, where he would be able to acquire much-needed oil supplies. By the end of July Rostov-on-Don had fallen and the approaches to Stalingrad on the Volga were under attack; by mid-September the outskirts of Stalingrad were occupied and the Caucasus threatened. But neither the river nor the mountains were taken in the end. The holding of the Volga line through the heroic defence of Stalingrad was one of the great epics of the war, with such individuals as Sergeant Pavlov and the small detachment who held out in a single building becoming justly famous. Sticking to his task at the insistence of his High Command, Field-Marshal Paulus and nearly 100,000 men were forced to surrender in February 1943. In January of that year the appalling blockade of Leningrad, during which as many as a million people died of starvation, was finally broken, and the spring saw the Soviet troops pushing back the Germans on all fronts while partisans harried the enemy rear. In July a large-scale counter-offensive was mounted by the Germans with tanks and self-propelled guns in the Kursk region; once this was broken, the enemy moved back towards the Dnepr, harried by partisans.

All was not yet over, for 70 per cent of the German forces were still on the eastern front, while the Western Allies pushing up through Italy rejected as impracticable the Soviet pressure for the opening of a second front through the invasion of France. Soviet historians argue that the D-Day operation was finally undertaken on 6 June 1944 mainly because the Allies were becoming alarmed at the speed of the Red Army's success in eastern Europe at the beginning of that year, a spring offensive clearing the Crimea and the Western Ukraine and considerable advances taking place in most sectors.

With further successes achieved in the summer and autumn of 1944, everything was ready for the European war's final phase. In January 1945 a large-scale winter offensive was undertaken at the request of the

Western Allies, hard pressed in the Ardennes by German forces whose government was hoping to secure a negotiated peace before being driven to the point of unconditional surrender. The Red Army moved forward on a wide front extending from Prussia to the Carpathians to liberate the whole of eastern Europe. Many émigrés and others would, of course, argue that this last advance was actually to subject a large part of the continent to a new and more terrible occupation. To take the Polish case as an example, a passionate argument has been put forward that the Red Army had massacred the Polish officer corps at Katyn in 1941, and now deliberately delayed the recapture of Warsaw in 1945 until the partisans involved in the uprising had been wiped out by the Germans.

Charges still fly in the other direction, since Soviet historians argue that the Allies were acting in an unfriendly manner before the end of hostilities and that the part played by the Soviet forces in the final phase of the war both in Europe and Asia has been misunderstood. One of the allegations is that the Western Allies made a point of destroying cities previously assigned to the care of the Red Army – among them Dresden. Another is that the entry of the U.S.S.R. into the fight against Japan has been misrepresented; it is claimed that the promise was made to effect this entry three months after Victory-in-Europe Day, and then scrupulously carried out. V.E. Day was 9 May 1945, and the declaration of war against Japan was made on 8 August. Red forces attacked the Japanese in the Transbaikal, Amur and Maritime regions, adding to the predicament that was already critical enough with the dropping of atom-bombs on Hiroshima and Nagasaki on 6 and 9 August respectively.

These terrible events have been looked upon as not so much the final blows against Imperial Japan as the first blows against the Soviet Union in what has become known as the Cold War. Further early evidence is sought in the exclusion of the U.S.S.R. from the peace negotiations with Japan, even though Japan's long-held aggressive intentions towards the Soviet Union, the Red Army's involvement in the Asiatic war and Allied agreements concerning its outcome all pointed to the U.S.S.R.'s inclusion. While the Red Army remained in Sakhalin and the Kurile islands, great pressure was exerted to push it back from Manchuria.

To understand fully the Cold War, some observers have argued that it is necessary to commence discussion, not with the varied interpretations of the events of 1945, but with an analysis of the Russian Revolution and the Allied Intervention.[4] In a sense, the whole of Russian and American history needs to be studied as a prerequisite for a proper appreciation of the Cold War. Here, while there is no need to retrace ground already covered, it is indeed necessary to glance back at the conferences held during the war, which developed the policy of unconditional surrender and unwittingly, or at most semi-consciously, prepared the ground for later disagreement and severe tension.

The most celebrated or most notorious of these conferences was that held at Yalta in the Crimea in February 1945. An essential insight was revealed about the agreement reached there by Roosevelt's chief of staff, Admiral Leahy, when he observed that it was 'so elastic that the Russians can stretch it all the way from Yalta to Washington without ever technically breaking it'.[5] Moreover, the sad fact needs to be recalled that in the international sphere of law as in most others possession comprises nine-tenths of the whole. Furthermore, having experienced two German invasions in less than a half century, the Soviet government could hardly be blamed for wanting to ensure security in eastern Europe. Its response to the situation at the end of the Second World War would have been one of criminal folly if it had not largely consisted of the attempt to erect as strong a barrier as possible against any future *Drang nach Osten*. Any analysis which takes no account of factors such as these may be dismissed as worthless.

This is not to accept the more extreme version of the revisionist thesis which attaches all the responsibility for the Cold War to the United States and its European allies.[6] Few conflicts where the participants are of roughly comparable strength can be attributed solely or even predominantly to one of them, although as the stronger power, in this case the United States had at its disposal more of the initiative.

A year of great significance was 1947, which saw the launching of the Truman Doctrine and of the Marshall Plan. Both these measures are usually interpreted in the West as counters to the ringing down of the 'Iron Curtain', first named by the Nazi propagandist Goebbels after Yalta and then again by Churchill in his Fulton speech of 5 March 1946. The Truman Doctrine aimed at the protection from subversion by Communism of any government accessible to American aid, the first two recipients being Turkey and Greece. As Walter Lippmann and other distinguished commentators pointed out at the time, such a choice was not made because Turkey and Greece were shining examples of democracy but rather because of their strategic position by the Black Sea and in the Balkans.[7] The Marshall Plan, for its part, was advertised as a selfless gesture of assistance to war-torn Europe in its enormous task of reconstruction. While an element of idealism was almost certainly present in the minds of those who conceived it, the Plan could hardly avoid increasing the strength of the donor power which already controlled something like two-thirds of the world's industrial capacity. Although they took a close look at the offer, Stalin and his entourage came to believe that acceptance of the Plan would place the Soviet Union and the rest of Eastern Europe in a client relationship to the United States and that the only alternative open to them was a return to 'socialism in one country' which could now at least be extended to several countries. Left to themselves, the other governments of Eastern Europe might well have decided to accept the American offer, but in the atmosphere that the Truman Doctrine reflected and intensified, their choice became increasingly restricted to the extremity of non-existence. In September 1947 the Cominform was created to replace the Third International, and the satellites were all brought into closer orbit to the Red Star. In 1949 the Council for Mutual Economic Aid, or Comecon, was set up as an alternative to the American-dominated Western European arrangement.

In 1948, the split between East and West widened, the Communist coup in Czechoslovakia reflecting and intensifying the division of Europe. The conflict between the Soviet Union and Yugoslavia increased the suspicion of both sides. A more serious conflict arose over Berlin. The agreements made about Germany at the Yalta conference and at the Potsdam conference which followed it never worked smoothly, and discussions about a more permanent settlement ended in deadlock, each side blaming the other. Again a similar background of mutual recrimination, the Soviet government impeded access to Berlin, arguing that a unilateral devaluation of the mark by the Western powers was undermining the East German economy. As a response, the Western powers organised the 'air lift'. In May 1949 freer access to Berlin was restored, but the division of Germany had by this time become solidified, both Republics – the Federal (Western) and Democratic (Eastern) – being created in that year. In 1949, too, NATO was founded just in time to counter the ending of the Western monopoly of atomic weapons.

1949 also brought a victorious end to Mao's long struggle for power with the proclamation on 1 October of the People's Republic of China. Although the fact that Soviet assistance to the Chinese Communists was never anything like wholehearted had already sowed some of the seeds of later dissension, at the time it appeared that a vast Red monolith of 800 million people had been created. Concern about this new combined threat led to the American-sponsored intervention in Korea in June 1950. The war widened with the injection into it at the end of 1950 of Chinese troops. World conflict again appeared possible, and the Korean War was not brought to its untidy halt until some months after Stalin's death in 1953. Elsewhere in Asia the Vietnam War was a minor but persistent cause of international tension, the French forces becoming more and more bogged down in their attempt to retain a hold on this outpost of empire.

By 1953 not only Europe and Asia were caught up in the global rivalry of Soviet socialism and American capitalism; all parts of every continent were affected. The influence of the Cold War became inextricably involved with the process of decolonisation that was dismantling the old empires of Europe and encouraging the growth of the spheres of influence of the new superpowers peripheral to it. Many of the new leaders of the Third World proclaimed themselves socialist, although their views and policies would often be more accurately characterised as 'bourgeois nationalist'; ironically, even Ho Chi Minh in Vietnam at first modelled his ideology on the American and French Revolutions rather than on Marxism–Leninism. While concentrating its major energies on domestic reconstruction and European security, the Soviet government found itself increasingly concerned with developments from Indonesia to Iceland.[8]

The 'cult of personality' in the war and post-war years was in some ways a more, in others a less, baneful influence on Soviet political life than in the pre-war period. The greatest improvement in the situation was the cessation of mass purges, even though the brink of such a horror seemed to be near in 1949 and 1953. During the Second World War, while Beria and the N.K.V.D. were far from unemployed, their major attentions appear to have been directed less towards dissident Party members and Great Russians than to centrifugal nationalities. The Crimean Tatars, the Kalmyks, Karachai-Balkars and Chechen-Ingush from the Caucasus region, and the Germans from the Volga were all deported to Central Asia, the Far North or Siberia, and many of them were executed. A similar fate might have been meted out to the Ukrainians if there had not been so many of them.

As far as all Soviet citizens were concerned, there was a reaction almost immediately after the war under the slogan 'back to class vigilance'. Rigid adherence to Party orthodoxy was restored under A. A. Zhdanov, who had been governor of Leningrad during the siege and was now to give his name to the repressions of the years 1946 to 1948. After his death, many of his associates fell from power; the so-called 'Leningrad case', involving allegations of intrigue with Yugoslavia and other crimes, accounted for most of them. At about the same time, an anti-Semitic tinge became apparent in Soviet political persecution, charges of Zionism being widely flung after the creation of Israel in 1948, for which the U.S.S.R. had nevertheless been a sponsor. Many of those arrested in the 'doctors' plot' which was 'discovered' by Stalin as an attempt to murder him in 1953 were Jewish. Not only Jewish doctors, but also several Gentile members of the Politburo were more than apprehensive about their future at the time of Stalin's death.

A convenient focus for a discussion of developments in party and government in the last years of Stalin is the Nineteenth Party Congress which met in 1952 nearly fourteen years after the previous congress, a delay infringing party rules. Between 1939 and 1952 the membership had nearly trebled from less than $2\frac{1}{2}$ millions to more than $6\frac{3}{4}$ millions. But greater size did not necessarily mean more mobility; particularly at the higher levels, there does not appear to have been much change in personnel in the years leading up to 1952. At the same time party and government were coming even closer together than before, with the dominance of the former being clearly marked. In other words, the terror of continuous purges was already ceasing to be the main motor of political progress before the death of Stalin. A somewhat more stable life for top Soviet politicians was taking shape, even though not yet discernible either to the individuals concerned or to foreign observers. The arrival of the new phase was to some extent symbolised by the change in nomenclature from the All-Union Communist Party (Bolsheviks) to the Communist Party of the Soviet Union.

Economic

Although the launching of the Nazi plan Barbarossa came as a surprise, the U.S.S.R. was able to adapt itself with considerable speed. A Soviet account declares that 'The conversion of the Soviet Union into a close-knit military camp and the phenomenal rate at which the economy was reshaped along wartime lines laid the foundation for ultimate victory.'[9] During the first three months of hostilities, more than 1500 enterprises were moved to safe regions behind the lines. On the other hand, many important natural resources and some of the industrial plant that could not be moved were soon lost to the invading forces.

To supervise the migration of industry and to solve all the problems posed by the war, a State Committee of Defence was set up. By the spring of 1942 the monthly production of artillery weapons had risen to 6000, of tanks to 1690, and of aeroplanes to 1650. Most of these figures were achieved in the Urals and Western Siberia, some of them in Central Asia. New sources of raw materials were exploited in these regions, and better assembly procedures and techniques were used. By a decree of 26 December 1941, labour was mobilised to an unprecedented degree, with forced overtime and directed employment; productivity rose by 19 per cent in 1942 and 7 per cent in 1943. And so the workers made an enormous contribution to the war effort. With recaptured areas being brought quickly back into action, annual production rose to 120,000 artillery weapons, 30,000 tanks and armoured cars, and 40,000 aeroplanes. Such totals were supplemented by Allied Lend-Lease. (On 11 June 1944 *Pravda* acknowledged the receipt of nearly 9000 aircraft, more than 3000 tanks and over 3700 anti-aircraft guns.) In addition, large supplies of food and clothing were delivered by the Allies, whose part in the Soviet economic offensive has been evaluated by G. Warren Nutter as one-third of the value of Soviet pre-war industrial production.[10] Soviet estimates would be considerably lower than this.

Transport was severely hit by the Nazi attack, 15,000 locomotives and 400,000 wagons being destroyed during the war and railroad use in general falling by 40 per cent before the beginning of 1943. Yet 10,000 kilometres of track were constructed on average during each wartime year, mostly in the east, and many important lines were kept open through the great heroism of the railroadmen, for example at Stalingrad. Sea and river traffic was also as active as possible, and the 'road of life' brought about 350,000 tons of truck-borne cargo to Leningrad during the winter of 1941–2. On the other hand, chaos was endemic in all forms of transport, and supplies were by no means distributed in the most rational manner.

Such dislocation was intensified through the loss in the first year or so of the war of 40 per cent of the pre-war sown area. More than a hundred thousand tractors were put out of action and millions of cattle and pigs were killed. But decline in production was halted to some extent in various ways: collective farm-workers reported for duty on about 350 days in 1942 as opposed to 250 days in 1940; new regions were opened up behind the lines, in Siberia, Central Asia and the Far East; and women and young people were mobilised as labourers and mechanics. Such measures, combined with strict rationing and price control, wide use of kitchen gardens and small plots, ensured something like a reasonable supply for most of the people most of the time. And as occupied regions were retaken, they were quickly brought back into production, thus alleviating the problem still further.

Like any other wartime economy, that of the Soviet Union could not dispense with a budget. Soviet historians argue that, whereas the tsarist government needed to resort to large foreign loans and rapid paper inflation to acquire the money to fight the First World War, the Communist government was much more self-reliant and self-controlled during the Second. Roughly a half of the necessary income came from the turnover tax and socialist profits; new taxes were levied and much money contributed in loans and collections by the people. In the years 1941–5, expenditure amounted to 1,146 billion roubles,* of which 582 billion were devoted to military expenditure, but an increasing percentage devoted to social and economic purposes. At the same time, the value of money fell, although Soviet historians claim that the inflationary rate was still lower than in the First World War, even after it had been accelerated by the Fascist injection of forgeries.[11] Western historians tend to take less sanguine a view, but few war histories of any origin manage to escape entirely a patriotic bias.

Nobody could deny that Soviet losses during the war were enormous; the most tragic of them was in population – more than twenty millions were lost. Such mortality defies the imagination. Material losses were correspondingly enormous, including thousands of large and small settlements and millions of buildings. Soviet calculations claim that one-half the destruction in Europe during the war years was suffered by the U.S.S.R.[12]

The daunting task of reconstruction was tackled by the Fourth and Fifth Five-Year Plans. The aim of the Fourth Plan was to restore and surpass pre-war levels of production during the years 1946 to 1950. The emphasis was to be on heavy industry, but it was not intended to neglect either light industry or agriculture. Current Soviet appraisal of the degree of success is mixed. Undoubtedly, big steps forward were taken in heavy industry. For example, by 1950 iron smelting was up to 19·2 million tons and steel smelting up to 27·3 million tons, 29 per cent and 49 per cent more respectively than the totals for 1940. Coal and oil were also being produced in larger quantities than ever before, and electric power nearly doubled the rate for 1940. New regions had been opened up and new methods brought into use. However, the timber and construction industries lagged behind, the latter reaching little more than half of its target increase. Labour productivity in general barely reached its expected level.

Light and food industries grew comparatively slowly. Clothing and footwear were in desperately short supply. The food problem was exacerbated by the fact that the plan for agriculture was fulfilled in non-comestible production only. While rationing was abolished after a bad harvest in 1946 had caused some delay, a decree of that year made no secret of the failures of collective farming: improper adherence to working hours; neglect of collective fields in favour of private plots; abuse of collective property; and 'destruction of the democratic bases of collec-

* As notified earlier, billion here expresses a thousand million.

tive government' or maladministration. Additional problems recognised during the course of the Fourth Five-Year Plan were: the inadequate fixing of prices; the improper arrangement of incentives; and insufficient application of mineral fertilisers. To combat these huge difficulties, the average size of collective farms was increased and the system of collective farming was introduced into new areas; some special attention was paid to each of the specific problems. A rise in tractor and other machine production was of some benefit to the farmers. But neither the Fourth Plan nor the first years of the Fifth came near to achieving for agriculture the degree of success attained by heavy industry. Such a disparity was to contribute to the rise of Nikita Khrushchev. Before the death of Stalin, trade was mainly restricted to the Eastern bloc.

Transport in the post-war period faced a problem whose size is reflected in such data as the destruction of some 13,000 bridges and the disablement of 26 railway lines. As early as 1944, however, 60 per cent of the disabled lines were restored, and the task of the reconstruction of the railroads was wholly completed in the three years after 1945. By 1950 railroad capacity was 44 per cent up over 1940, with several new lines being built in Siberia and Soviet Asia. Twelve times the number of pre-war diesel trains were brought into use, but both diesel and electric trains were still much less in operation than steam trains. Other forms of locomotion were of little significance; although both water and road transport increased in size, the latter accounted in 1950 for no more than 2·8 per cent of the total.

A final economic aspect of consideration for the period of Stalin's last years is the financial. Of central importance here was the monetary reform of December 1947, by which ten old roubles were to be exchanged for one new rouble. The measure was aimed at the inflation of the war and post-war years and at the black-market and other speculators who had been exploiting it. Savings of up to 3000 roubles were exchanged one for one, with a declining rate for larger sums. The government's aims were by no means completely realised since, even with the new rate, retail prices of 1950 were 86 per cent above those of 1940. In the same ten-year period, the national income went up by 64 per cent more than half the total coming from the turnover tax, while the national expenditure included 38 per cent spent on the economy and 24 per cent on defence. These figures would be disputed by many Western economists, who would also dispute the general Soviet assertion that international socialism prospered as international capitalism weakened. The revaluation of the rouble against the dollar is seen by them as a meaningless gesture.

Cultural

Under the pressure of the Second World War, several traits of cultural development now became more marked. Such a tendency is discernible in all three of the major areas of our consideration, religion, education, and literature and the arts. Broadly speaking, the tendency may be characterised as the further reconciliation of the weight of Russian tradition to the new impetus of Soviet socialism.

In the previous chapter it was noted that the 'new religious policy' launched in 1939 had very much reduced the militancy of the drive towards atheism. This relaxation paid dividends during the war, since the Church was able to play something like its pre-revolutionary part in assisting social cohesion. On the very first day, 22 June 1941, the Acting Patriarch condemned the 'Fascist bandits' and blessed the people 'with heavenly grace for their heroic battle'. On 26 June a 'Te Deum' was sung for the victory of the Soviet Union at the Cathedral of the Epiphany in Moscow with an estimated congregation of 12,000 in attendance. On 8 August the Metropolitan Nikolai spoke about 'the well-known fact that Hitler brings with him his atheist world view and his cult of the pagan god Wotan', and on 14 October the Acting Patriarch complained that some Orthodox clergy were enrolling 'under the shadow of the pagan swastika instead of the holy cross'.[13]

These last remarks were a prelude to one of the most important activities of the Orthodox Church during the war years. Its officials continued to condemn those who had gone over to the other side and to make appeals to the faithful not only within the borders of the Soviet Union but as far away as Greece and Yugoslavia. As the occupied lands were retaken, the Church hierarchy assisted the task of sorting out the faithful from the treacherous.

Meanwhile, the Church was carrying further its reconciliation with the Soviet state. On 5 January 1943 Stalin thanked it for arranging among its congregations the collection of money to pay for a column of tanks to be named after the medieval hero-saint, Dmitri Donskoi. This, Fireside says, was the first official communication to the Church since the Revolution of 1917. In August 1943 the Church leaders met Stalin and were allowed to elect a new Patriarch. And then, on 14 September an official Council for the Affairs of the Russian Orthodox Church was set up under an atheist chairman who was soon dubbed 'Narkombog' and 'Narkomopium' (People's Commissar for God or Opium). During the war as a whole, according to an eye-witness, Alexander Werth, a considerable religious revival occurred in the Soviet Union, and for some people the Church became the centre of the Russian national consciousness.[14]

At the end of the war, the Church called Stalin a 'God-given leader' and proceeded to help him consolidate the control over Eastern Europe while participating energetically in the various congresses and appeals for peace. At his death, the Church lamented his passing and talked of his 'eternal memory'.[15] Quite clearly, in carrying out such policies, the Church hierarchy was torn between spiritual duty and political pragmatism, as it had been for centuries. Some believers considered that the compromise had gone too far and sought outlets for their belief in sectarianism. Age-old and new elements were inextricably linked in certain policies: for example, the continuance of the attack on Roman Catholicism and on the Vatican in particular for their toleration and even alleged support of Fascism; and the proposition of the argument that bourgeois religion in general was to be condemned, while a newer, more enlightened religion could take an undisturbed place in a Communist society. Even Party members, including possibly Stalin himself, still retained something of a religious belief, and the less elevated of them could exercise it fairly freely until the revival of positive if not quite militant atheism in 1954.

A similar mixture of the traditional and the innovatory can be detected in the educational history of the years 1941–5. Already before the outbreak of the Second World War, one of the chief tasks of the schools had become the inculcation of Soviet patriotism. While this was not supposed to involve nationalism in the usual sense but rather more the brotherhood of peoples with a common Communist aim, a Great Russian element certainly crept in. With medieval as well as modern history summoned to help in the process, the emphasis was placed on the central development from Kiev through Muscovy to the Empire.

After the beginning of the war, new ingredients more directly connected with the fighting were brought into the curriculum. The youngest children were evacuated whenever possible, and taught the dangers of the times through rhymes and riddles. A special effort had to be made to stop their older brothers and sisters from losing all interest in school subjects in the midst of so much turmoil. This problem often ceased at the age of fourteen, for then many adolescents, particularly boys, were drafted into industrial or agricultural work. Polytechnical ideas were therefore brought into practice in a very real way indeed, even if much of the earlier experimental theory was by this time left far behind.

During the war, the move towards traditional methods and organisation begun in the 1930s now became more pronounced. From 1943 onwards, boys and girls were increasingly catered for in separate classes, and earlier methods of examination including the five-point scale were adopted still more widely.[16]

A great problem of reconstruction confronted the Soviet government at the end of the Second World War. The official estimate was that 84,000 schools and colleges had been destroyed as well as 43,000 public libraries with 110 million volumes. Thousands of teachers had been killed, and all kinds of disruption created problems. Nevertheless, the Fourth Five-Year Plan aimed at consolidating the primary base and extending secondary education by 1950. Samsonov tells us that:

> Between 1946 and 1950, inclusive, the nation built 18,500 schools seating 2,500,000 pupils, including premises for 1,300,000 pupils partially or wholly built on money contributed by the collective farms. In the first ten years after the war the country built or restored more than 30,000 educational establishments, with accommodation for 5,000,000. Obligatory seven-year schooling was enforced throughout the country in 1949 and the stage was set for universal ten-year education in the capitals of Union republics and the big cities. In the early 1950s all children of school age regained the opportunity to go to school. By 1952 the Soviet Union had, in the main, enforced universal, free seven-year schooling.[17]

The polytechnical approach was encouraged, if by no means as much as it would be during the Khrushchev years; there were still complaints about the divorce between practical life and communicated knowledge. Additional criticisms included the weak training of teachers; the deficient nature of curricula and textbooks; and the pursuit of formal achievement at the expense of general education.

At the highest level, too, all was not well with the programme, even though more than half a million students were being catered for by 1950. Great difficulties lay in the way both of inculcating and, even more, of advancing learning during the last years of Stalin. After the Second World War, Party control became more rigid rather than less, and the whole range of academic disciplines was at least partially crippled by directives which were often impossible to fulfil. Most notorious were the fields of biology and philology, where the dominant figures were Lysenko and Marr. Lysenko argued that acquired characteristics could be passed on genetically, a suggestion useful for the development of Communist society but of great harm to scientific research. Stalin personally sided with Lysenko when argument broke out in 1948. Marr had died in 1934, but his views about the origin of languages and their future direction lingered on long after him. Stalin intervened in 1950 to denounce Marr's interpretation but to substitute his own. As Deutscher puts it: 'Stalin, uninhibited by the scantiness of his own knowledge – he had only the rudiments of one foreign language – expatiated on the philosophy of linguistics, the relationship between language, slang, and dialect, the thought processes of the deaf and dumb, and the single world language that would come into being in a remote future, when mankind would be united in communism.'[18]

In a less optimistic manner, Stalin gave warning in his *Economic Problems of Socialism in the U.S.S.R.*, published in 1952, that there were limits to the transformation that could be carried out from above, that in particular the slow development of Soviet agriculture was acting as a brake on the progress of the economy, and that problems would take a long time to solve. While there were some pieces of common sense in these and other propositions, Stalinism in its last phase continued on the whole to act as a cruel and clumsy clamp on creative work in the natural and social sciences, and in party ideology. With Einstein still denounced as 'petty bourgeois', with no official admittance of cybernetics and other new concepts, fertilising ideas from home or abroad were severely curtailed.

A similar kind of straitjacket was imposed upon artistic creativity during the *Zhdanovshchina* and afterwards, although controls were to some extent relaxed during the Second World War. Then it was possible to forget for a while the strict tenets of socialist realism in favour of passionate declamations of love of country and family, of hatred for the Nazi enemy, even of hatred for the German race as a whole. Literature produced in such a framework certainly fulfilled its temporary purpose, but little of it would receive a very high critical evaluation today. Many of the writers of the period became simply war correspondents, putting the bravest face possible on the retreats and celebrating in triumphant tones the advances. Ilya Erenburg was a popular practitioner of the genre, particularly adept at denouncing the invaders. Konstantin Simonov made an impact in a number of different literary fields: his sentimental poem 'Wait for Me' was very widely known; his plays on war themes caught the attention at the time; and his novel *The Living and the Dead* published in the early 1960s was welcomed for saying something about the darker 'cult of personality' side of the fight against the Nazis as well as about its heroism. The enthusiasm of the 'common man' was perhaps most aroused by Aleksandr Tvardovskii's creation Vasilii Terkin. Other noteworthy prose writers of the time include

Vasilii Grossman and Leonid Leonov. Much emphasis was placed on the great writers of the past, Pushkin, Tolstoy, Chekhov and Gorky, names to inspire the soldier at the front and the civilian behind the lines.

But after the war was over reaction set in. Writers came in again for Party criticism; some of them were expelled from the Union of Soviet Writers in 1946. Among them were Anna Akhmatova, denounced by Zhdanov for dividing her interests between 'the drawing room, bedroom and chapel', and Mikhail Zoshchenko, held guilty of abandoned satire and pathological introversion. Formalism, aestheticism, and cosmopolitanism all came under attack during the following years, and few writers could successfully avoid these pitfalls at the same time as reconciling the demands for socialist realism with the necessities of the 'cult of personality'. Much of the worthwhile literature of the period came from the pens of Konstantin Paustovskii, Petr Pavlenko and Konstantin Fedin. A sure route to success for lesser men was the vilification of debased foreign bourgeois cultures and the proclamation of the superiority of the exalted Soviet socialist culture. The United States and its unreformed citizens were favourite targets of attack, much praised works including a play about the evils of Harry S. Truman entitled *The Ill-Fated Haberdasher*.

Other creative artists had even less to show for the period 1941–53 than the writers. Shostakovich's poignant Seventh Symphony written during the Leningrad siege was among the musical exceptions, but they were drowned in a brash and vacuous march towards victory and the reconstruction of socialism. Even more tedious to foreign eyes are most of the stilted Stalinist paintings, sculptures and buildings of the period.

To sum up, the 'cult of personality' probably exerted an even more harmful influence on scientific and artistic creativity after 1945 than it had before 1941. To some observers, the cumulative damage inflicted by the years of Stalinism was revealed as irreparable in the years following his death. To others, the rising educational levels contributed to the development of both the imagination and the power to appreciate what the imagination produced.

14 The Establishment of Soviet Superpower, 1953–1964

In the years following the death of Stalin, the Soviet Union reached a new peak of confidence as the world was astonished by the launching of the first earth satellite in October 1957 and a further row of space successes culminating in the first manned orbital flight by Iurii or Yury Gagarin in April 1961. Years of anti-Soviet propaganda about technological backwardness and inefficiency now met with a triumphant response. Less spectacular successes in the economy encouraged the government to talk of the completion of the construction of socialism and a move forward towards the full-scale building of Communism. In such an atmosphere, the severe cultural controls of the previous period were to some extent relaxed, although it was not at all difficult for individual artists to find themselves in disgrace for taking the process of thaw too far. In the governmental organisation, there was an immediate return from the 'cult of personality' to collective leadership, although a new less powerful cult arose from it in turn. In the international sphere, the Soviet Union showed its self-possession by talking less of a final showdown between socialism and capitalism and more of the peaceful coexistence between the two systems. But this did not mean that the world rivalry would be discontinued, only that it would not have to be solved by military means; this was a point made completely clear in one of the best-remembered Soviet utterances of the time, 'We shall bury you'.

This phrase, as well as many other colourful statements of the time, came from the mouth of Nikita Sergeevich Khrushchev, whose rise and fall are demarcated by the dates 1953–64. Some would say that Khrushchev's own peculiar version of the 'cult of personality' was one of the many justifications for the observation of Karl Marx that history does repeat itself, first as tragedy, then as farce. But such an assertion would be to mistake appearance for reality; Khrushchev's period in power possessed its own deep significance, and the man himself was much more than a clodhopping clown. A brief survey of his career will readily show that he had necessarily developed political skills of a very high order indeed.

Khrushchev was born in 1894 in a small village in Kursk province near the Ukraine. His father was a poor peasant making seasonal journeys to earn money in the coalfields of the Donets Basin, some three hundred miles to the south. Khrushchev himself followed this pattern in adolescence, having picked up a rudimentary education at a local school. Quite soon, although in a minor capacity, Khrushchev was involved in the working-class movement. Avoiding war service in 1914 as a skilled worker, he joined the local Soviet and Military-Revolutionary Committee at the time of the Revolution of 1917, although he did not become a Bolshevik until the Civil War was well under way in 1918. This decision, like many others later, appears to have been taken for practical rather than theoretical reasons -- Lenin's party stood out to him as the most likely victor over the Whites and Interventionists.

During the Civil War, Khrushchev was a junior commissar, working at the maintenance of the cohesion of various Red Army units. He returned to the mines during the terrible famine of 1921, which took from him his first wife and left him with a young son and daughter. In 1922 he was sent to a local technical college, where he became party secretary and listened to lessons that, according to his own later account, made him think that Karl Marx had been at the mine where his father and he had worked. In 1924, just before leaving the college, he married his second wife Nina, who was to play an important part in his life beyond presenting him with two more daughters and one more son.

Khrushchev rose with Stalin through a connection with Lazar Kaganovich, who was made Ukrainian Party Leader in 1925. With Kaganovich, Khrushchev went to Moscow in 1929 and by 1934 became the Moscow Party leader. He spent a large amount of time and energy on the detailed and resourceful modernisation of the capital city, particularly on the Metro underground railway, which was seen as a showpiece of the potential of socialism. He survived the purges in the same way as most other survivors, by praising Stalin, abusing Stalin's enemies and hoping for the best. In 1938 he was sent to the Ukraine with the dual mission of purging the Party of nationalism and other deviations and getting the economy moving more rapidly. He quickly succeeded in earning one of his nicknames – 'butcher of the Ukraine' – and was well on the way to deserving another of them – 'Nikita Kukuruznik' (Man of Corn or

Maize) – when the crisis leading up to the Second World War captured his major attentions.

During the war, Khrushchev retreated from Kiev to Stalingrad and then went back again to Kiev via Kursk. As always he played his part with great vigour, although some of his exploits as political adviser to the army were somewhat romanticised during his period of power. Returned to the Ukraine, he started where he had left off, keeping the Party 'clean' and cajoling workers and particularly peasants into higher production. His situation was very precarious during the disastrous harvest failure of 1946, but he negotiated this and more than one later hazard to be back in Moscow from 1949 well placed for the succession after the death of Stalin.

The differences between Khrushchev's style and Stalin's were well caught by Milovan Djilas: 'Unlike Stalin's humour, which was predominantly intellectual and, as such, cynical, Khrushchev's humour was typically folksy and thus often almost crude, but it was lively and inexhaustible.' Djilas considered that the clichés of Khrushchev's conversation were 'the expression of both real ignorance and Marxist maxims learned by rote'. Nevertheless, Djilas believed, 'He was the only one of the Soviet leaders who delved into details, into the daily life of the Communist rank and file and the ordinary people.' Moreover, 'he did not do this with the aim of changing the system, but of strengthening and improving things under the existing system. He did look into matters and remedy them, while others issued orders from offices and received reports.'[1]

A more succinct characterisation of Khrushchev would be that of a vigorous N.C.O. who increasingly while in power devised policies as well as trying to make sure that they were carried out. In such a manner, although he was clearly a man of strong personality and individual character, he was also very much the representative of a generation or even of a wider group of Soviet citizens. His career reflected the common experience of many who had moved from peasant agriculture to proletarian industry, through wars and purges to responsible Party positions. Thus he was well fitted to play the part called for when the death of Stalin left such a void in the political consciousness of the people at large. As J. P. Nettl aptly puts it:

Khrushchev represented the often inchoate wishes and sentiments of the Soviet population and particularly of the Party. The new contact with the outside world, even with the arch-imperialist United States, was genuinely welcomed everywhere. The doctrine of peaceful co-existence, according to which communism would succeed by demonstration of superiority instead of the revolutionary or military destruction of its opponents, was only a theoretical justification for the determination of the newly educated and professional groups in positions of power not to live any longer in an inbred, isolated world of their own. The incessant call for reform and modernisation, for the exploitation of the enormous industrial potential of the Soviet Union, struck a deep chord among all these groups. Above all, the self-confident articulation of Soviet power challenging American technological and political domination contrasted favourably with the fearful and defensive isolationism of Stalin. In all these directions Khrushchev represented the future, and had the support of the most progressive groups in Soviet society.[2]

However, in the Soviet Union as in other societies, political survival depended on the maintenance of the support of the centre, and Khrushchev therefore found it necessary to change his tack more than once while in power. What finally brought him down appears to have been the loss of support on all sides through the over-hurried pursuit of easy palliatives and solutions for ills and problems which were in fact of some seriousness and complexity.

Political

Peaceful coexistence in the foreign sphere directly depended on domestic stability and development. In a rapidly changing and shrinking world, such interconnection was more clearly pronounced than in any previous period of history. Successes in both major sectors brought him to power, and failures in both of them removed him from it. However, for the sake of convenience and clarity, we shall consider his rise and fall first from the internal, secondly from the international, point of view.

At the death of Stalin, according to several accounts, Khrushchev wept. As Averell Harriman reports his words, Khrushchev explained his tears in the following manner. 'After all, we were his pupils and owed him everything. Like Peter the Great, Stalin fought barbarism with barbarism but he was a great man.'[3] Undoubtedly, a huge gap had been left, and now the pupils had to decide among themselves who was going to fill it. The heir apparent was Georgii Malenkov, who at first assumed the leading role in a restored collective leadership without very much obvious difficulty.

The only immediate obstacle to temporary fraternal harmony was

Lavrentii Beria, Stalin's last secret police chief and, according to his daughter Svetlana, the source of many of the Soviet leader's woes.[4] Beria was now continuing to make full use of the apparatus at his disposal, and was conceivably making a bid for the supreme power. But in June 1953 he was arrested and, after interrogation at a special meeting of the Presidium, was shot, possibly at the meeting itself.

The removal from power of Malenkov took place rather more gradually, and appears to have occurred for three main reasons. Firstly, the very fact that he had been assigned the succession by Stalin told against him. Secondly, he concentrated on the governmental side of the Soviet power base to the comparative neglect of the more important Party side. Thirdly, his over-optimistic assessment of the agricultural situation and his emphasis on consumer goods production aroused the opposition of many of his colleagues in the Presidium. At the beginning of 1955, Malenkov resigned from his post of Chairman of the Council of Ministers, which was now filled for a short period by Nikolai Bulganin.

Meanwhile, Khrushchev had become Party Secretary in 1953, and, like Stalin before him, had built up a considerable network of patronage. He was now poised for the final assumption of power, and fully seized the opportunity presented to him by the Twentieth Party Congress at the beginning of 1956. This Congress is best remembered, of course, for the attack launched at it by Khrushchev and others on the Stalin cult. Samsonov puts it this way:

> The Central Committee exposed the gross violations of socialist legality and abuses of power that occurred in Stalin's time, and decided to tell the Party and the people about them from the rostrum of the Twentieth Congress. It knew that this might create bitterness, even some discontent, among a certain section of people. It knew too that its candid criticism of errors may be used by enemies for anti-Soviet ends. But it had no choice, because it had to eliminate the conditions in which violations of democracy and of the principles of collective leadership, the abuses of power and other acts alien to Soviet society had been possible. Valid guarantees had to be created that such things would never recur within the Party and the country.
>
> While criticising the errors and distortions made by Stalin, the Party gave him due credit for his previous services to the country and the international working-class movement. The Twentieth Congress produced a model of Party criticism, whose ultimate goal was to strengthen socialism and encourage the creative initiative of the masses in communist construction.[5]

Foreign observers to both left and right of the political spectrum would agree to reject such an explanation as a weak excuse; Soviet apologists would argue that those who were actually faced with the task of running the government had to live with their own past and could not therefore reject it as being completely worthless. While some foreign socialists remained fervid supporters of Stalin, many others believed that the attack on him had not gone far enough and that it was a monstrous distortion to talk of the architect of socialism in one country as a performer of creditable services to the international working-class movement. Stronger talk than this would be necessary to return the Soviet Union to the true Leninist path. For their part Kremlinologists argued that Khrushchev was primarily anxious to save his own face at the same time as isolating his opponents in the Presidium who were about to be unmasked as an anti-Party group. As a further explanation which leads on to a more complete exculpation, adherents to the Party's general line would claim not only that to condemn Stalin unreservedly would be to deny the achievements of the years during which he was in power, but also that those who saw the Twentieth Party Congress solely in terms of Stalin were helping to perpetuate the cult rather than dismantle it. They are anxious to point out that great efforts were made at it to consolidate the restoration of Party democracy at all levels.

Some support for the latter argument could be gained from the manner of the overthrow of the anti-Party group in 1957. Defeated in the Presidium by the votes of Malenkov, Molotov, Bulganin, Kaganovich and others, Khrushchev appealed to the Party Central Committee of some three hundred members for support. With the assistance of Marshal Zhukov, who brought members to Moscow from all parts of the Soviet Union in military aircraft, Khrushchev won a vote of confidence. He then proceeded to remove his opponents from power, completing the process by his own replacement of Bulganin as Chairman of the Council of Ministers in March 1958. By this time, Zhukov had also been demoted. However, the point must be emphasised that it would be wrong to see the political events of 1956–8 solely as a struggle between the individuals just mentioned. They also marked an increased trend towards the professionalisation of the Party at the top and its democratisation at lower levels. About two-thirds of the members of the new Presidium were full-time Party secretaries; worker recruitment increased proportionately as the Party expanded in size.[6]

After the extraordinary Twenty-First Party Congress which met in early 1959 to endorse the Seven-Year Plan, the Twenty-Second Party Congress was convened towards the end of 1961. Given the unofficial title of the 'Congress of the Builders of Communism', the meeting addressed itself to the consideration of a New Party Programme, to replace the second Programme, whose prime aim of the construction of socialist society was now considered to have been completed. The new Programme therefore mapped out the course that was to take the Soviet people to Communism within a generation. Khrushchev concluded the Congress by declaring:

> Comrades, never before have our forces, the forces of world socialism, been as great as they are today. The new Programme opens before the Party and the people the most radiant, breath-taking vistas. The sun of communism is rising over our country. Let us do everything to hasten, by our tireless labour, the day when this sun will flood with its light the boundless spaces of our wonderful country! Let us devote all our forces, all our Bolshevik energy, to the triumph of communism! Under the leadership of the glorious Leninist Party – forward to the victory of communism! [7]

For some sceptics, the sun would rise over an horizon defined as a vague and indistinct line which retreated as it was approached. These would include dissidents from the nationalities and elsewhere.[8] Others were fired with enthusiasm.

For Khrushchev in particular the Congress should have meant the seal on his triumph. De-Stalinisation was taken further with the removal of the Leader's body from the Lenin Mausoleum in Red Square, while the words of the First Secretary and Chairman were frequently and widely quoted. In fact, however, Khrushchev's power was already on the wane. His division of the Party according to the 'production principle' in 1962 increased the awareness of his waywardness and lack of ideological sophistication. His promises were becoming bigger and his delivery of the goods smaller. Both the Presidium and the Central Committee were alienated, and Khrushchev was unable to outmanoeuvre the opposition when it moved against him in October 1964. In a sense, as Mark Frankland says, Khrushchev's dismissal 'was his finest hour: ten years earlier no one would ever have imagined that Stalin's successor would be removed by so simple and gentle a process as a vote'.[9]

Khrushchev's rise and fall may be traced through international as well as internal developments. In these as well as in the others, however, the ebullience of the dynamic protagonist must not blind us to the significance of the general shifts in the position of the Soviet Union which occurred during the years 1953–64. In a longer perspective than we have at our disposal, the most important theme may well appear to be not the split with China or the crisis over Cuba which made the greatest impact at the time, but the Soviet contribution to the formation of what has become known as the 'Third World'. At the same time, we must recognise that, if peaceful coexistence had not been firmly established as a policy, there would never be a perspective in which such an observation could be made. We must also recognise that, without armed forces equipped for the deadly game of nuclear rocket strategy, the Soviet Union could not establish itself as a great world power.[10]

Soon after the death of Stalin, the first steps were taken in such a direction in the shape of *rapprochement* with Turkey, Iran, Afghanistan and India. An armistice was finally reached in Korea during the summer of 1953, with the Soviet Union giving its support to North Korea and China. Nearer home, there was trouble in the shape of riots in Czechoslovakia and East Berlin, all of which were nipped in the bud through the uncompromising intervention of the Red Army. Such irksome embarrassments were forgotten as Soviet diplomacy moved back to the wider stage in an attempt to solve general European and Asiatic problems.

The foreign ministers of the U.S.S.R., U.S.A., Great Britain and France met in Berlin at the beginning of 1954 and vainly tried to come to some agreement about the Vietnamese and European security problems. Transferring to Geneva and joined by China in the spring, the foreign ministers appeared to set some way nearer agreement on Vietnam, but unwittingly prepared the way for later troubles in South-East Asia. As far as Europe was concerned, late 1954 and early 1955 was a period of retrogression rather than progress. From the Soviet point of view, the most unwelcome developments were the Paris agreements of October 1954 on a Western Alliance including the Federal Republic of Germany and the commencement in 1955 of the build-up of the armed forces in the Federal Republic, which joined NATO in May. A countermove in the same month was the Warsaw Pact, which committed the states of Eastern Europe to a twenty-year term of 'Friendship, Co-operation and Mutual Assistance'. In the same month the situation took a turn for the better with the agreement on the evacuation and neutralisation of Austria. In July 1955 the 'Big Four' met in Geneva at a summit conference, which was conducted in a friendly atmosphere and did much to indicate the real possibilities of peaceful coexistence even though nothing like a concrete agreement was reached. In August the Soviet government stated that it was reducing its armed forces by more than half a million men, and in September a friendship treaty with Finland was signed. At about the same time, however, a further meeting of foreign ministers confirmed the impossibility of the major powers coming to any firm arrangement about the vexed questions which divided them.

During the winter of 1955 the first of the 'B and K.' visits beyond Eastern Europe took place, on this occasion to India. Apart from the rich pabulum that Bulganin and especially Khrushchev supplied for the news media, the visit clearly indicated the new attitudes that had developed in the Soviet Union towards the Third World. Stalin travelled little abroad and was suspicious of 'bourgeois nationalists' everywhere. Khrushchev and his advisers clearly believed that the experience of the world's first socialist state could be fruitfully passed on to emerging 'bourgeois nationalist' states along with certain amounts of material aid. Later trips by Soviet emissaries took in several other Asian, African and Latin American states, and were reciprocated by the journeys of a considerable number of Third World visitors to Moscow. (It was partly in response to such a widening of Soviet vistas that the South-East Asia Treaty Organisation was created by the Manila Pact of September 1954 and the Central Treaty Organisation was set up soon afterwards to guarantee the collective security of a large part of the Middle East.) China was a special case. While the Soviet Union supported Mao's government over the issue of the off-shore islands of Quemoy and Matsu, which flared up in the winter of 1954–5, and provided aid in technical expertise and material goods, the fraternal relations between the two greatest socialist powers were already by no means completely harmonious. Among the reasons for this was Chou En-lai's bid for Chinese leadership of the Third World at the Bandung Conference in April 1955.

Troubles back in the 'Second World' pre-empted much of the Soviet Government's attentions during the year 1956. A limited *rapprochement* which was gradually being arranged with Yugoslavia and the dissolution of the Cominform in April seemed to be the prologue to some relaxation of Soviet control over Eastern Europe. While such was certainly the long-term trend, the immediate direction was in reverse owing to outbreaks of violence in Poland and Hungary. Scores of Poles were killed in the riots which broke out in Poznan in June, and thousands of Hungarians fell in the uprising which commenced in Budapest in October. Severe repression was the order of the day in both cases, although in the aftermath the Gomulka régime in Poland and the Kadar régime in Hungary necessarily resorted to some concessions in order to restore the greatest possible approach to harmony. Luckily for Khrushchev, the West was busy with the Suez Crisis at the time.

There were echoes of the disturbing events of 1956 after the celebration of the fortieth anniversary of the October Revolution in 1957. Communist leaders from more than sixty countries came to a conference in Moscow, which appeared to confirm the U.S.S.R.'s leadership of the worldwide movement and to condemn 'polycentrism'. But cracks in the monolith soon began to show themselves again, particularly in Chinese policy. Differences of attitude to Middle Eastern and Far Eastern crises could be discerned in 1958, with China taking a less compromising, harder line than the Soviet Union. A meeting between Khrushchev and Mao in the summer of that year did little if anything to iron out these differences. In 1959 they became wider as Khrushchev's famous visit to the U.S.A. increased Chinese suspicion that the U.S.S.R. was going soft on capitalism, particularly after the friendly exchanges between Krushchev and Eisenhower at Camp David.

Détente with America and alienation from China looked even more likely as another summit meeting was arranged for the summer of 1960 in Paris. Although the shooting down of the U-2 reconnaissance plane and the capture of the pilot Gary Powers gave Khrushchev little alternative but to break off the meeting before it had really begun, the immediate aftermath to the disruption, as well as the meeting with Kennedy and the proclamations of the Twenty-Second Party Congress in 1961, demonstrated that the Soviet government was still firmly committed to the policy of peaceful coexistence with the capitalist states of the West. Meanwhile the withdrawal of Soviet experts from China and the increasingly sharp words exchanged between the Soviet and Chinese leaders revealed that the split of the two great Communist states was near completion.

Such a trend continued throughout the last few years of Khrushchev's power, for all the many appearances to the contrary. The two most important events were the crises over Berlin and Cuba of 1961 and 1962 respectively. The Soviet version of the first crisis is that the Western powers had rejected all attempts to settle the question of Germany in general and of Berlin in particular, while transforming the former capital into 'a nest of spies and the seat of subversive activities'. And so, on 13 August 1961, the wall was hastily constructed to impede such contamination. The Western response of 'war hysteria' was countered with firm resolution.[11] It goes almost without saying that such an account would appear ridiculous to most Western observers, who believe rather that the Communist governments simply could no longer bear the embarrassment of the juxtaposition of an outpost of freedom and prosperity on the one hand and a citadel of captivity and exploitation on the other.

What could be noted with certainty is that this storm was weathered somewhat more easily than its predecessors. By any standards, the Cuba incident of October 1962 was more serious. Again, the Soviet interpretation was in almost diametrical contradiction to the Western: rockets were sent to the Caribbean not for offensive purposes, but to defend Cuba against the repetition of any invasion such as that in the Bay of Pigs. And then, although the rockets were withdrawn to avert the threat of war, the Soviet action had secured from the American government a guarantee that it would cease its 'export of counter-revolution' and therefore abandon the 'gunboat diplomacy' traditional to imperialist powers for more than a century. For their part, Western analysts talked of Khrushchev's reckless adventurism and saw the removal of the rockets as a setback for him.[12]

In international relations as in domestic politics, a year can be a long time, and August 1963 saw the representatives of the Soviet Union, United States and Great Britain signing the nuclear test ban treaty in Moscow; but further discussions on disarmament were getting nowhere because of disagreement about what constituted adequate safeguards. China (like France) would not sign the treaty, and there were those in the Soviet government who believed that Khrushchev was taking peaceful coexistence with the Western capitalist bloc too far. On the whole, however, as far as their international aspects were concerned, probably the increasingly individualistic manner of Khrushchev's policies rather than their essential content led to his downfall. Changes of emphasis rather than direction were most noticeable after 1964.

Economic

At the death of Stalin, according to a Soviet view, a high-enough level of economic development had been reached for new methods to be tried by a restored collective leadership. Since socialism was now moving beyond one country towards a world scale, this new phase was to assume a very wide significance indeed. The opportunities presented by it were considerably restricted, however, by the harmful effects of the 'cult of personality' on the economy, particularly on agriculture. The standard Western view would be far less sanguine, arguing that all branches of the economy showed signs of maladjustment to the stage of full industrialisation, and in its extreme version, suggesting that Soviet socialism had shown itself to be fundamentally unworkable.

At least, there were more people now to experience both the failures and successes of the Soviet economy. In 1956 the total population was

200,200,000, and life expectancy was approaching seventy. Between 1950 and 1954 the town population rose by 17 million, something less that a half of which was brought about by influx from rural areas. The urban population as a whole was 43·4 per cent of the total by 1956.

Undoubtedly, the problem singled out for special attention by the new administration was agriculture. Decrees of 1953 and 1954 attempted to isolate the problem and to suggest a cure for it. In 1953 a Party directive talked of the over-concentration on heavy industry as opposed to agriculture, the inadequate incentives given to farm-workers and the inferior personnel and equipment of the Machine Tractor Stations. Electrification of rural areas was proceeding too slowly. In 1954, in order to solve the central problem of grain production, the Party announced its decision to increase the area under the plough by up to 30 million hectares during the following two years, the figure being later raised to more than 35 million hectares. Most of this new area was to be in previously uncultivated regions in Kazakhstan, Siberia, the Northern Caucasus and the Urals. The 'virgin lands' scheme was supported by a large amount of propaganda. Young Communists and others were exhorted to lend a hand to the land, and more than 350,000 of them were already on the job by the summer of 1954. More than 200,000 tractors were injected into the new scheme, too. Agriculture as a whole was given a boost through the improvement of technical standards; the Machine Tractor Stations were dismantled and replaced by Repair Technical Stations, with individual collective farms assuming primary mechanical responsibility. Material incentives were raised, food prices becoming higher to cover the necessary costs. Undoubtedly, there were considerable successes resulting from the new arrangements. Between 1953 and 1958, grain production went up by more than 70 per cent. Dairy produce did not achieve the same spectacular results, but Khrushchev was sufficiently encouraged to talk of catching up and overtaking American agriculture.

During the last years of the Fifth Five-Year Plan and the first years of the Sixth Five-Year Plan (which was later withdrawn to accommodate newly discovered mineral resources and to scale down some over-optimistic targets), industry also moved forward, albeit in a somewhat more moderate manner. The emphasis here was still on the side of heavy industry, of course, and many of its sectors steadily continued their advance. However, the Twentieth Party Congress of 1956 noted that some items such as cast-iron, certain non-ferrous metals and gas had not reached their expected levels, and that productivity had climbed by 44 per cent rather than by the envisaged 50 per cent. Consumer goods output was even more disappointing. While 3000 kilometres of railroad were constructed between 1953 and 1958, and there was a large growth in rail transport, conversion to electric and diesel power was slow. Transport by sea still accounted for only 6·6 per cent of the total and by river for about 5·3 per cent, that by road being little more than negligible.

In response to economic disappointments, the Twentieth Party Congress decided on a decentralisation of the administration. A law passed in 1957 largely replaced the central ministry organisation by regional councils. Individual republics played a large part in the reorganisation, and an Economic Commission was formed in which they would all co-ordinate their activities.

The Twenty-First Party Congress of 1959 confirmed the tasks of the next period which were to be carried out in a Seven-Year Plan running from 1959 to 1965. These were: to create the material–technical basis of Communism; to develop and complete socialist productive relations; and to educate Soviet citizens in the spirit of Communism. In practice, the emphases were much as before. With priority being given to heavy industry, industrial output by 1965 was to be 80 per cent greater than in 1958. Some stress was to be put on the growth of the chemical industry, particularly on polymer-plastic materials. Electrification of the economy was to near completion, and the transport network was to be consolidated. Agricultural and consumer goods production were to rise by up to 70 per cent.[13]

The Twenty-Second Party Congress of 1961 was informed in the Report of the Central Committee that all was going well. Khrushchev triumphantly declared: 'Let those who prophesied the failure of our plans think of a way out of the bog into which they have floundered, that is not our headache.' Claiming that production in the U.S.S.R. now amounted to more than 60 per cent of that in the U.S.A., he went on to say:

I would remind you that a mere ten or eleven years ago Soviet industrial output was less than 30 per cent that of the U.S.A. At the present time the U.S.S.R. has already outstripped the United States in the extraction of iron ore and coal, the production of coke, prefabricated concrete elements, heavy diesel and electric locomotives, sawn timber, woollen textiles, sugar, butter, fish, and a number of other items.

Our country now accounts for almost a fifth of the world's industrial output, or more than Britain, France, Italy, Canada, Japan, Belgium and the Netherlands combined. Yet these are all highly-developed countries with a total population of 280,000,000. The fact that our country with a population of 220,000,000 has surpassed them in total volume of industrial production shows how swiftly and surely socialist economy is progressing.

The implementation of the Seven-Year Plan will bring our country up to such a level that little more time will be required to outstrip the United States economically. By fulfilling this basic economic task the Soviet Union will achieve an historic victory in the peaceful competition with the United States of America.[14]

This was Khrushchev at his most confident, but in fact the situation was not nearly as happy as he claimed. Those foreign analysts who accepted his quantitative claims could point out that many of the items which the Soviet Union was now producing at a greater rate than the United States were no longer priorities in the American economy. After the fall of Khrushchev, the following inadequacies in industrial production were noticed by Soviet critics: plan targets were not being reached in electricity and gas, plastics, turbines, diesel engines and some consumer goods; light industry in general was progressing more slowly than heavy; and productivity, planning and technical progress were insufficient in both sectors. For such reasons, even before 1964, the decentralisation policy inaugurated in 1957 was severely modified.[15]

Life for the average Soviet citizen undoubtedly improved during the years 1953–64. From 1959 to 1962 alone, wage rates rose by 18 per cent, and income tax (never an important feature of the Soviet system admittedly) fell. A six- or seven-hour day became standard, and housing and consumer conditions were to some extent eased. In a sense, it was possible to interpret complaints about houses and consumer goods as a reflection of the rising expectations that the improvement was bringing about. On the other hand, prices were rising as well as expectations, although a new monetary reform of 1961 exchanged ten old roubles for one new rouble (without any real devaluation, or so it was officially claimed). High prices and shortages were noticed particularly in agricultural produce.[16]

Khrushchev's agricultural policy had undoubtedly brought about a rise in production, but 80 per cent of this had come from the extension of the area under cultivation rather than intensification. The Soviet Union produced only one-third as much wheat per hectare as Western Germany, for example. While the mechanisation of Soviet agriculture was reasonably well advanced, the plan of replacing the M.T.S. by the R.T.S. had proved a failure. Fertilisation, particularly by chemicals, was still at an abysmally low level. The incentives to collective farm-workers and the administration of collective farms continued to be inadequate.

Khrushchev's response to such problems was as varied and pragmatic as ever. His agro-town project which was to give farm-workers a proper social centre was not forgotten. A campaign was launched against private plots which still produced more efficiently than the collective fields. Meat and milk prices were raised; fertilisers were produced and stronger efforts made to get them used. And Nikita Kukuruznik persisted in his belief that the answer to many of the Soviet Union's problems was a development of corn (maize) growing. So important was the agricultural sector to Khrushchev that he attempted to divide the Party into two halves, one to deal with industry and one with farming. And so, as we have seen, his economic policies were inextricably connected with his political programme, and with his downfall.

Cultural

The word most used to describe cultural developments between 1953 and 1964 is 'thaw'. While certainly not inapplicable, the word needs to be used with care; indeed, at some times and from some points of view, the temperature went down rather than up. Moreover, there is no point in applying somewhat idealised Western standards to the concrete Soviet situation.

Governmental policy towards religion is an apt example here. In the summer of 1954, after a brief lull, the campaign against the Church was stepped up. Then, militancy was reduced, some observers believing that this was because of Khrushchev's intervention, others claiming that it was the result of the fact that Khrushchev was not yet completely his own master and could not therefore continue the campaign as he would have liked. Certainly, towards the end of the 1950s atheistic propaganda resumed an intense form. To quote an American authority on the subject, 'by 1960 this modest beginning had spread over into the antireligious campaign which was to become the dominant feature in the lives of all denominations, legal and illegal, throughout the succeeding decade'.[17]

In 1960 the Party Central Committee declared that anti-religious propaganda should be intensified. Both G. G. Karpov, who had been chairman of the Council for the Affairs of the Russian Orthodox Church since its creation and the Metropolitan Nikolai, his contemporary, were removed from their posts. And then at the Twenty-Second Congress in 1961 Khrushchev observed that the battle with survivals of capitalism in the consciousness of the people, the changing by the cultural revolution of the habits and customs of millions of people built up over the centuries, would be a prolonged and not a simple matter. 'Survivals of the past are a terrible power that weigh on the minds of people', he declared. 'Communist education implies the emancipation of the mind from religious prejudices and superstitions, which still prevent some Soviet people from displaying their creative ability to the full.' [18] In other words, with the return to the Leninist path, the transition from socialism towards Communism and the creation of the 'new Soviet man' required the more energetic extirpation of the old morality and more positive inculcation of the new.

Under various kinds of direct and indirect pressure, the number of active monasteries appears to have declined from about seventy to just over thirty, and the number of churches certainly dropped steeply, although estimates of the exact figure vary widely. Known believers were harried and sometimes found it difficult to find employment or entrance to educational institutions. While baptism by immersion was discouraged through a decree making it illegal to jeopardise health in the name of religion, a Communist 'baptism' ceremony was encouraged which gave the child a 'commemorative certificate' to read and follow on growing up. Among the injunctions was 'Walk firmly on the path of life indicated by the great Lenin. Be honourable, diligent, and orderly in great and small matters. Respect parents and elders.' Also during the early 1960s, the first 'palaces of marriage' were set up to compete with the impressive church ceremonies. Films, radio and television contributed to the campaign. At work and at school, Soviet citizens found themselves confronted with various programmes of 'scientific atheism'. Many special texts were prepared, including some providing expressly atheistic methods of teaching such subjects as agriculture and algebra.[19]

But the creation of the 'new Soviet man' involved more than the injection of atheism. Khrushchev himself placed heavy emphasis on the polytechnical aspects of education, his own experience obviously influencing his attitude to a considerable extent. Reflecting such an attitude, which was at the same time very much in the Soviet socialist tradition, the new Party programme of 1961 asserted that:

The system of public education is so organised as to ensure that the instruction and education of the rising generation are closely bound up with life and productive labour, and that the adult population can combine work in the sphere of production with further training and education in keeping with their vocations and the requirements of society. Public education along these lines will make for the moulding of harmoniously developed members of communist society and for the solution of a cardinal social problem, namely, the elimination of substantial distinctions between mental and physical labour.[20]

Some analysts believed that the vocational training given to students who were attempting to concentrate on more theoretical or academic subjects impaired their scholastic progress at the same time as doing little to create unity between hand and brain. Partly for this reason, the polytechnical element in education was somewhat reduced after the fall of Khrushchev, although by no means abolished.

While the qualitative nature of some aspects of Soviet education is debatable, there can be no argument about its quantitative advance. By the mid-1960s there were more than 20 million students at each of the first two levels, primary and junior high. High school attendance was approaching the 10 million mark, and about 6·5 million students were undergoing higher education, nearly half of them at university or advanced institutes. Such figures put the Soviet Union near the top of the international comparative education table. Moreover, as always, the Soviet Union had at least its fair share of outstanding scientists. Such engineers as Sergei Lebedev, such physicists as Igor Kurchatov and such mathematicians as Ivan Vinogradov, to name just a few, achieved a wide international reputation. Historians like P. A. Zaionchkovskii and B. F. Porshnev impressed their foreign colleagues, while Pokrovsky was to some extent rehabilitated. But the difficulties experienced by the editorial board of the periodical *Problems of History* during the mid-1950s were just one example of the limited nature of the 'thaw' in the intellectual world.

The Thaw was the title of a novel by Ilya Erenburg, the first part of which was published in 1954, and gained for its author a reprimand from the Writers' Union. The Twentieth Party Congress rehabilitated some writers and subjected others to attack, Mikhail Sholokhov declaring that 'the last twenty years had produced no more than a handful of good books'. In the eight years after the Congress, that handful hardly increased to a huge pile, partly because the 'thaw' was so limited and partly because there was not a large number of talented writers around. From the point of view of the Western reader, appreciation of Soviet literature was restricted by the circumstances that novels and poems were examined more for their political message than for their artistic value. Thus it was that good writers such as Konstantin Paustovskii and Vladimir Soloukhin were little known abroad while the most famous works of the period included Vladimir Dudintsev's *Not By Bread Alone* (1956), Boris Pasternak's *Doctor Zhivago* (1957) and Alexander Solzhenitsyn's *One Day in the Life of Ivan Denisovich* (1962). The first of these was noted for its attacks on the bureaucracy and the somewhat woolly-minded idealism of its hero, the inventor Lopatkin. *Doctor Zhivago,* which needs no introduction, was published in the West, not the Soviet Union, and gained for its author the Nobel Prize, a distinction which not every Western critic believes to have been deserved by literary merit alone.[21] An interesting point about *One Day,* which also needs no introduction, is that Khrushchev himself gave its publication his support. Soon afterwards, the Chairman appears to have realised that he had gone too far in relaxing controls and made his celebrated remark at a Moscow Art Exhibition about certain modernistic paintings looking like the product of a donkey's rear end.

Even this would have been a welcome change to most of the 'official' art and architecture produced at the time. The cinema, theatre and ballet all produced at least some worthwhile works, however, and Soviet performers impressed foreign audiences throughout the world. In this respect as in others, the Soviet Union was moving out from the Eurasian heartland into all quarters of the globe.

Tremendous progress had been made by 1964. The Soviet Union was now the only state which could qualify along with the United States as a superpower. Soviet rockets could not only move out into space but also deliver nuclear bombs throughout the earth in sufficient numbers to destroy mankind. Fortunately for us all, the transformation had been completed without the terrifying destructive capability being put to use.

15 Problems of Coexistence, Competition and Convergence since 1964

Soon after the removal from power of Khrushchev in October 1964, two new leaders emerged in the shape of L. I. Brezhnev and A. N. Kosygin. Their order or precedence soon turned out to be more than alphabetical (unlike the earlier B. and K.), and a new if minor 'cult of personality' was erected round the substantial figure of Mr Brezhnev. Having occurred once as tragedy with Stalin and once as farce with Khrushchev, the 'cult of personality' now appeared to be making a bid to become a long-running serial. Such facetiousness needs to be qualified by the observation that the 'cult of personality' surrounding Mr Brezhnev was in its own way no greater than that connected with many other world leaders. Allowing for differences in personal and national background, some commentators might place them all in the category of skilful but not very colourful bureaucrats, men with 'grey flannel faces' to use one of the current labels. Mr Brezhnev's lack of flamboyance could well be one of the reasons for the decline in 'kremlinology', the attempt to understand the policies of the Soviet government through analysis of its leadership. Another, and probably more important reason for the rejection by professional investigators of the 'kremlinological' approach has been the realisation that, whatever changes occur in the leadership, certain problems persist. This is not to deny the importance of the Russian Revolution, and certainly not to accept equations of the Union of Soviet Socialist Republics with the empire of the tsars.

The basic problem has remained what it has always been for every human society, that of security, compounded in the Russian case by its difficult geographical situation. English-speaking peoples in the British Isles, Western Hemisphere and Antipodes have enjoyed a high degree of immunity from invasion, owing to the seas that surround them and their remoteness from potential aggressors. As they all know, it is not their moral superiority which has freed their soil almost entirely from international hostilities, while the Soviet peoples have undergone centuries of invasion and destruction, culminating in the agonies of the two World Wars. The continued allusions to the Second and more ruinous of the World Wars that confront visitors to the U.S.S.R. are not therefore a morbid self-indulgence on the part of Soviet citizens but the expression of a still lively apprehension.

True, in these days of global nuclear strategy, the U.S.S.R.'s fundamental lack of immunity is shared by all human societies. Moreover, deprived though they are of the bases around the world which their American counterparts and their allies enjoy, the Soviet armed forces can now gain some positive advantage from what throughout the medieval and modern periods has mostly been a handicap. Bestriding one-sixth of the earth's land surface through Europe and Asia, the Soviet armies are deployed from Vladivostok to Berlin, and dominate what students of geopolitics are accustomed to call the 'heartland'. At the same time, the Soviet navy is to be found on all the major waterways of the world, and under them, too. If an enemy should threaten first strike to incapacitate the Soviet Union and its surface-launched rockets, submarines would constitute a most effective, virtually indestructible counterweight in the continuing rehearsals for annihilation.

Meanwhile, at the conference tables, Soviet and American negotiators have made some progress with their Strategic Arms Limitation Talks, although many complex technicalities remain to be settled. Probably, the differential calculus of nuclear and conventional disarmament will never be resolved until compounded by a higher degree of mutual understanding and trust. And the longer the solution is delayed, the more the problem of security proliferates, for the two original superpowers are becoming increasingly aware that their number may one day increase. The day is not all that near, for among the candidates for inclusion, Japan lacks the strategic credibility, China the industrial strength and Western Europe the political cohesion. However, in the interim, the length of which nobody can calculate, each of the present superpowers could effectively alter the power balance by making a closer alliance with the lesser great powers. If détente between the United States and China were taken further and added to the strength of Western Europe and a fully rearmed Japan, traditional Soviet fears of encirclement would reach a new pitch of intensity. And so the Soviet government has been conducting negotiations with all these powers at the same time as those with the U.S.A. The most likely source of conflict, with China over the boundary dispute, was brought nearer an end in 1973. Renewed attempts were being made to reduce tensions between Eastern and

Western Europe, while discussions aimed at co-operation in Siberia and the Pacific Far East were being carried on with Japan.

While working for its policy of 'peaceful coexistence' with the world's great powers, the Soviet Union has not neglected the not so great. Its apologists would claim that it has contributed to some kind of equilibrium throughout the Third World, including the most troubled regions such as South-East Asia, the Indian sub-continent and the Middle East, at the same time as continuing to promote the cause of decolonisation in certain areas, Portuguese Africa, for example. Allegedly, it has given protection and support to various societies attempting the difficult task of modernisation, among others Cuba in Latin America, India and Afghanistan in Asia and Somalia in Africa. From the left, such a description of Soviet policies would seem empty when compared with their original aim of global revolution. From the right, it would appear to constitute unbridled flattery of uncompromising diplomacy and energetic subversion.

Even some of those observers who would accept the description of the apologists as accurate might want to point out that it needs to be seen against a background of the Soviet Union's ruthless suppression of independence within its own special sphere of influence in Eastern Europe and within its own boundaries. Undoubtedly, there are Czechs, Poles, Rumanians and Hungarians, among others in Eastern Europe, who would like to enjoy complete national sovereignty, and Ukrainians, Transcaucasians, Central Asians and Balts, among others in the Soviet Union, who would like to loosen or even sever ties with Moscow. Such aspirations have their nobler and more realistic aspects, but have not always been totally admirable. Few governments in Eastern Europe were models of democracy between the two World Wars, and there were many niggling disputes in the territories between the Soviet Union and Nazi Germany which are still not forgotten today. In other words, the situation would not be immeasurably improved if Soviet controls were relaxed. Moreover, nationalistic yearnings must be examined in the context of superpowers, multinational corporations and the 'global village', where no society can exercise complete sovereignty.

All this is not to ignore the imprisonment and persecution of political dissidence within the Soviet Union and without, or to forget such outrages as the invasion of Czechoslovakia in 1968. But to understand such miserable occurrences, we cannot consider them solely in isolation; unfortunately, they are not confined to the Second World, the First and Third have experienced them all too frequently as well. There are at least as many Latin Americans alienated from the hegemony of the

United States as there are Eastern Europeans opposed to that of the Soviet Union, for example. Commentators all over the world have stressed the essential similarity between the overthrow of Allende's Chile and Dubcek's Czechoslovakia. And everybody knows that there are at least some citizens of the U.S.A. who do not fully share the rights and freedoms of that citizenship. Throughout history, empires have dealt ruthlessly with subject peoples in the periphery and with at least some of the inhabitants of the metropolis. The new heirs to the old empires, the superpowers, have not shown exceptional forbearance.

The United States and the Soviet Union differ from their imperialist predecessors in the universal application of their ideologies (and cynics would say in the thoroughness of the hypocrisy with which they have failed to pursue their avowed hopes and aims). The Declaration of Independence and many other announcements of the Founding Fathers are as stirring in their own way as are some of the first decrees of the Soviet government and post-October pronouncements of Lenin and his colleagues. The democratic revolution of the eighteenth century was as progressive in its motivation as the proletarian revolution of the twentieth century, and the United States and the Soviet Union remain their principal embodiments. It would be wonderful if their respective hopes for individual human beings and the collective hopes of humanity could be realised.

The real world of 1973 approximated less to the realisation of such a dream than to the nightmarish fulfilment of prophecies of doom. Systems of government throughout the world appeared incapable of executing their appointed tasks, and some of them seemed to have exhausted their fair share of opportunity to make such an attempt. The government of the U.S.S.R. is no exception to what comes near to being a rule. In theory, it should function smoothly according to the principles of democratic centralism. That is, all matters arising would be fully discussed at all levels and the appropriate decision then taken at the top by a committee fully apprised of all the relevant information and arguments. In practice, the leaders promulgate their decrees without full consultation of their lesser colleagues in the Communist Party, the Soviets or the administration. The extent to which they exercise complete autocracy is debatable, however. The label 'totalitarian', which has been widely applied for decades, is at last being abandoned by some Western social scientists, who realise its inappropriateness, in a manner broadly similar to that in which investigators into earlier periods have recognised the necessity to examine the actions of government as something much more than the self-willed volition of princes or tsars. While Western social scientists have not gone so far as to apply the label 'pluralist' to the Soviet system, they are to an increasing extent accepting the fact that the process of socialist modernisation has created interest groups and strata which make their impact felt in the conduct of both foreign and domestic problems. Moreover, they are paying ever closer attention to the concept expressed by an anonymous member of their gild to the effect that: ' "No critical evaluation without international comparison!" should be the watchword of the prudent Western Sovietologist!'[1]

Such exhortation loses none of its relevance as we turn to consider the second of our problems, that of competition, within the narrower focus of the economy. Here, we would have the tacit support of the Soviet government itself, which with varying emphasis has for some time proclaimed its belief that socialism, particularly as practised in the Soviet Union, will catch up with and then overtake capitalism, particularly as practised in the United States. Indeed, as noted above, Khrushchev in his more expansive moments announced that the process of overtaking had already in some important respects occurred. At the same time as expressing his belief in peaceful coexistence, he was sure that competition between the two forms of economy would result in the burial of capitalism. With the Dnepr and the Volga no less polluted than the Hudson and the Mississippi, an equally valid forecast might now be that both the Soviet Union and the United States will soon disappear in a self-dug grave of industrial filth.

Looking at the problem in the more traditional manner, some Western economists assert that the Soviet Union is finding it very difficult to adjust to the demands made upon it once the initial task of achieving quantity has been completed. The command techniques which were sufficient for dragooning peasants and workers through the arduous labours of the first Five-Year Plans can no longer be attuned to the more refined adjustments necessary for the attainment of quality at a higher level than was necessary in the pre-war pioneering days.[2] In other words, what is the point of producing more and more steel if you cannot manufacture a reliable transistor radio? And if, at the same time as still devoting a large part of your energies to the implementation of the orders of the armed forces, you are becoming more responsive to the wants of your individual consumers, can you still set up reliable production targets? Can any of your aims for industry be attained when your agricultural sector is still incapable of satisfying your basic food needs?

From the Soviet side, there is no denial that the economy has encountered serious weaknesses and problems. The newspapers and periodicals are full of complaints about machinery that does not work, out-of-fashion clothes that nobody wants to buy, and about periodic shortages of meat, fruit and vegetables. At such times as the disastrous harvest of 1972, there can be no disguising the necessity for using up valuable foreign exchange on the import of grain and other comestibles. But these admissions are not accompanied by acceptance of Western suggestions for improvement. In the first place, so the counter-argument runs, nothing much can be done to effect radical climatic change. Bad summers will for the foreseeable future be bad summers. Meanwhile, agronomists are doing all they can to improve productivity in marginal areas and administrators encouraging the peasants to make full use of fertilisers and the latest techniques. Market gardening and some other activities can be left in the private sector, and socialist profits and incentives might well be raised. But this does not mean that there should be anything like a return to N.E.P., still less to full-scale capitalism. On the contrary, with greater application of the computer, planning can be extended rather than reduced. Faults in the consumer sector can be rectified without recourse to the advertising mania, artificial creation of concupiscence and planned obsolescence of advanced capitalism. Pollution can the more readily be suppressed and limits more easily be applied to growth.

The debate transcends national boundaries, with the Eastern European Comecon ranged against the western European Common Market,[3] and the Soviet experience widely recommended as a model for emulation to developing countries throughout the Third World. To the charge that Comecon is nothing more than a cover for the exploitation of its neighbours by the more powerful but less advanced Soviet Union, the response can be made that such can hardly be the case when the average standard of living in most of the client states remains higher than that of the patron. As far as the Third World is concerned, Western critics argue that Soviet altruism is transparent from both quantitative and qualitative points of view. They calculate Soviet foreign aid as less than one-tenth of that of the Western powers. They contend that its aim is to drive a wedge into the developing states, promoting the selfish ends of the U.S.S.R.[4] Here the reply would be, what is wrong with the dissemination of socialism, the system which holds out the best hope for mankind?

Some of those who see man's salvation by the more traditional means of worldwide conversion to Christianity attack the Soviet Union even more virulently for the persecution of the Orthodox, Roman Catholics and Protestants within its own borders. Among the more oecumenical of these critics, there are strong protests on behalf of Soviet Jews, Muslims and Buddhists, too. In this instance, the explanation is given that believers are given the same basic rights as the irreligious and are punished only when they abuse those rights and break the law. While this explanation does not always seem to be supported by the evidence, it is more clearly the case that, if churches, chapels, synagogues, mosques and temples are being closed in the Soviet Union, their number is diminishing elsewhere. Secular culture is in the ascendancy in many other countries, both socialist and non-socialist.

While there is some, although by no means conclusive, evidence that the process of industrialisation has been an encouragement everywhere to the decline in religious faith, there can be no doubt at all that in the Soviet Union the decline has been accelerated by the positive inculcation of atheism. With primary education given to all, secondary education to most and higher education to at least some even in those republics where illiteracy was almost complete at the time of the Revolution, it is claimed that a true proletarian culture, atheistic, rational and comprehensive, is being created. Many Western critics are far from convinced by such an assertion, pointing to the wide difference in outlook between white-collar and blue-collar workers and the even greater gap between all town dwellers and the peasants.

This and other evidence has encouraged social scientists to detect in operation the convergence of capitalism and socialism. It appears to them that the creation of an industrial society forces states with differing backgrounds into similar moulds. For further consideration of this phenomenon, let us put ourselves in the expert hands of A. G. Meyer, who writes of the greatest capitalist and socialist powers that there are:

> three theories of convergence, one that posits the development of both Soviet and American societies within the framework of democratic socialism, a model similar to the Swedish system. The basic assumption here is that a pluralistic society will be able to govern itself only with the help of a democratic, participatory, pluralistic political system based on a civic culture of mutual toleration. A second theory of convergence regards the same social pluralism as the basis for a political order modelled rather on the modern corporation or perhaps on the company town – an order stressing hierarchy, coordination, structured communications, rational elite recruitment, and the like. Hence this is convergence on a bureaucratized polity. Finally, we have

an apocalyptic theory of convergence in a new fascist-like totalitarianism engendered by the psychological cost of modernization and the resulting crisis of political rule. The model here would be the Third Reich. Some would add a fourth theory forecasting the end of both the Soviet Union and the United States in their present forms in a revolution, followed by the thorough restructuring of both polities according to anarcho-syndicalist or socialist ideals. I have not considered this last possibility because it is not, strictly speaking, a theory of convergence, and it is in my view the least likely of all the possible alternatives'.[5]

These different theories, which may conveniently be identified by colour – pink, grey, black and green or red – obviously vary in their appeal. Social scientists can be as guilty of wishful thinking and of unwarranted gloom as their fellow human beings,[6] and none of them can yet forecast what will happen with any certainty. Some would want to reject the concept of convergence entirely, believing that capitalism and socialism will always remain apart, and that their principal champions, the United States and the Soviet Union, will conserve the principal features of their systems in something like their original form. Among those who have accepted the convergence concept, perhaps the noblest version was put more than a hundred years ago by Alexander Herzen:

> The North-American States and Russia represent two solutions which are opposite but incomplete, and which therefore complement rather than exclude each other. A contradiction which is full of life and development, which is open-ended, without finality, without physiological discord – that is not a challenge to enmity and combat, not a basis for an attitude of unsympathetic indifference, but a basis for efforts to remove this formal contradiction with the help of something broader – if only through mutual understanding and recognition'.[7]

Historians analyse the development of the Soviet Union according to their own world outlook. Worthwhile work can be produced by the devoutly religious and the militantly atheistic, the most stubborn conservative and the most dedicated progressive.[8] But this does not mean that historical analysis is a completely random activity. Apart from accepted conventions of scholarship, which enforce their own demanding restrictions, and the guiding principles of whatever philosophy possesses the researcher, there is the relentless governor of time itself. As far as has been possible, this book has attempted to be consistent with the canons of scholarship and with the definition of history offered by E. H. Carr: 'History is the long struggle of man, by the exercise of his reason, to understand his environment and to act upon it.'[9] As to the value of this definition, as to the accuracy of its application here, time alone will tell.

Select Bibliography

I General Guide to Further Study

For those readers who wish to find out about the resources of LIBRARIES and ARCHIVES, a fundamental work is J. S. G. Simmons, *Russian Bibliography: Libraries and Archives – A Selective List of Bibliographical References for Students of Russian History, Literature, Political, Social and Philosophical Thought, Theology and Linguistics* (A. C. Hall, 30 Staines Road, Twickenham, Middlesex, England, 1973). This magnificent bibliography, at the bargain price of £1.00 thanks to the generosity and industry of Mr Simmons, lists items in Russian, English and other languages. For researchers in the United Kingdom, a valuable guide is G. P. M. Walker *et al.* (eds), *Directory of Libraries and Special Collections on Eastern Europe* (London, 1971); those in the United States will find assistance in M. J. Ruggles and V. Mostecky, *Russian and East European Publications in the United States* (New York, 1960).

For the resources of European libraries, see Simmons, *Russian Bibliography* (cited above). The Helsinki University Library has an outstanding collection of materials, a legacy of its Russian imperial past. Prospective visitors to the Soviet Union should consult P. K. Grimsted, *Archives and Manuscript Repositories in the USSR: Moscow and Leningrad* (Princeton, N.J., 1972), and three of Grimsted's articles: 'Archives in the Soviet Union: Their Organisation and the Problem of Access', *American Archivist*, vol. 34 (1971); 'Soviet Archives and Manuscript Collections: A Bibliographical Introduction', *Slavic Review*, vol. 24 (1965); and 'Regional State Archives in the USSR: Some Notes and a Bibliography of Published Guides', *Slavic Review*, vol. 28 (1969). Also to be consulted is G. A. Hosking, 'Libraries and Archives: 4. Russia', *History*, vol. 55 (1970).

For BOOKS and ARTICLES, see K. Maichel, *Guide to Russian Reference Books*, vol. 1– (Stanford, Calif. 1962–   ): to be completed. Volume 1 comprises general bibliographies and reference books; volume 2 concentrates on history, ethnography and geography. A starting point for those who do not read Russian is P. L. Horecky, *Russia and the Soviet Union: A Bibliographical Guide to Western-Language Publications* (Chicago, Ill. 1965). P. A. Crowther, *A Bibliography of Works in English on Russian History to 1800* (Oxford and New York, 1969) was comprehensive at the time of its publication. Still most useful, though less complete because of its earlier publication date and because of the much greater amount of available published material, is David Shapiro, *A Select Bibliography of Works in English on Russian History, 1801–1917* (Oxford, 1962). There is nothing of comparable utility for the contemporary period, although assistance can certainly be gained from P. Grierson, *Books on Soviet Russia, 1917–1942* (London, 1943), W. Kolarz, *Books on Communism* (London, 1963), and P. H. Vigor, *Books on Communism* (London, 1971).

For current publications in English, see: *American Bibliography of Russian and East European Studies* (Bloomington, Ind. and Columbus, Ohio, 1956–); 'Soviet, East European and Slavonic Studies in Britain, 1971– : A Bibliography', in *ABSEES: Soviet and East European Abstracts* series (Glasgow 1971) – this is preceded by 'Information Bulletin', in Soviet Studies in *Soviet Studies* (1966–70) – and *Historical Abstracts, 1775–1914* (Vienna, Munich and Santa Barbara, Calif., 1955–). On unpublished theses in the field, see J. J. Dossick, *Doctoral Research on Russia and the Soviet Union* (New York, 1960), with annual supplements in *Slavic Review*, vol. 23– (1964–).

Most worthwhile books are reviewed in the major periodicals. Specialised journals in the field include *Slavic Review, Slavonic Review* (full title: *Slavonic and East European Review*), *Russian Review, Soviet Studies* and *Canadian-American Slavic Studies*. Translations of Soviet articles are published in *Soviet Studies in History*, and longer reviews of Soviet books are given in *Kritika*.

On HISTORIOGRAPHY and METHODOLOGY, there are several books critical of the Soviet approach. These include C. E. Black (ed.), *Rewriting Russian History: Soviet Interpretations of Russia's Past* (New York, 1956; London, 1957); N. W. Heer, *Politics and History in the Soviet Union* (Cambridge, Mass., 1971); J. L. H. Keep and L. Bratby, *Contemporary History in the Soviet Mirror* (London, 1964); A. G. Mazour, *Modern Russian Historiography* (New York, 1958), and the same author's *The Writing of History in the Soviet Union* (Stanford, Calif., 1971); and K. F. Shteppa, *Russian Historians and the Soviet State* (New Brunswick, N.J., 1962). Acquaintance with the Soviet approach can be gained from A. P. Mendel, 'Current Soviet Theory of History: New Trends or Old?' *American Historical Review*, vol. 72 (1966), and from answers to a questionnaire sent to Moscow by A. P. Mendel, M. Gefter and V. Malkov, 'A Reply to an American Scholar', *Soviet Studies in History*, vol. 5 (1966–7).

Marxist 'classics' on history which would not now be completely accepted in the U.S.S.R. include works by Plekhanov and Bukharin. Available translations include: G. V. Plekhanov, *In Defence of Materialism: The Development of the Monist View of History* (London, 1947), and N. I. Bukharin, *Historical Materialism: A System of Sociology* (Ann Arbor, Mich., 1969). For more recent analysis, see for example D. I. Chesnokov, *Historical Materialism* (Moscow, 1969). A stimulating brief examination of problems of history written by a scholar whose major work is concerned with the first years of the Soviet Union is E. H. Carr's *What Is History?* (London and New York, 1961)

On GEOGRAPHY, see:
J. P. Cole and F. C. German, *A Geography of the USSR: The Background to a Planned Economy* (London, 1970; Totowa, N.J., 1971).
P. E. Lydolph, *Geography of the USSR* (New York, 1970).
R. E. H. Mellor, *Geography of the U.S.S.R.* (London and New York, 1964).
W. H. Parker, *An Historical Geography of Russia* (London, 1968; Chicago, 1969).

Collections of MAPS include:
A. E. Adams, *An Atlas of Russian and East European History* (London and New York, 1967).
A. F. Chew, *An Atlas of Russian History* (New Haven, Conn., 1967).
H. Fullard, *Soviet Union in Maps: Its Origin and Development* (London, 1961).
M. Gilbert, *Russian History Atlas* (London and New York, 1972).

There are some worthwhile REFERENCE WORKS, including:
M. T. Florinsky, *Encyclopaedia of Russia and the Soviet Union* (New York, 1961).
R. Maxwell, *Information USSR* (Oxford, 1962).
S. V. Utechin, *Everyman's Concise Encyclopaedia of Russia* (London and New York, 1961).

ANTHOLOGIES and COLLECTIONS OF READINGS and DOCUMENTS include:
B. Dmytryshyn (ed.) *Medieval Russia: A Source Book* (New York, 1967).
B. Dmytryshyn (ed.), *Modern Russia: A Source Book* (New York, 1967).
J. M. Edie (ed.), *Russian Philosophy*, 3 vols (Chicago, Ill., and London, 1965).
G. P. Fedotov (ed.), *A Treasury of Russian Spirituality* (New York, 1948; London, 1950).
S. S. Harcave (ed.), *Readings in Russian History*, 2 vols (New York, 1962).
M. Raeff (ed.), *Russian Intellectual History: An Anthology* (New York, 1966).
T. Riha (ed.), *Readings in Russian Civilization*, 3 vols in one (Chicago, Ill., 1964).
A. E. Senn (ed.), *Readings in Russian Political and Diplomatic History*, 2 vols (Homewood, Ill., 1966).
G. V. Vernadsky et al. (eds), *A Source Book for Russian History from Early Times to 1917*, 3 vols (New Haven, Conn., and London, 1972).
W. B. Walsh (ed.), *Readings in Russian History*, 3 vols (Syracuse, N.Y., 1963).

As stated in the Preface, there have been hundreds of GENERAL HISTORIES of Russia, many of them excellent of their kind. Only a few can be listed here:
J. D. Clarkson, *A History of Russia from the Ninth Century* (New York, 1961).
H. J. Ellison, *History of Russia* (New York, 1964).
M. T. Florinsky, *Russia: A History and An Interpretation*, 2 vols (London and New York, 1953).
L. Kochan, *The Making of Modern Russia* (London, 1962; Baltimore, 1963).

B. Pares, *A History of Russia* (London and New York, 1960).
N. V. Riasanovsky, *A History of Russia* (New York, 1969).
B. H. Sumner, *Survey of Russian History* (London, 1964).
G. V. Vernadsky, *A History of Russia* (New Haven, Conn., 1961).
R. Wittram, *Russia and Europe* (London and New York, 1973).

TRANSLATIONS from the Russian include:
V. O. Kliuchevskii (rendered as V. O. Kluchevsky), *A History of Russia*, 5 vols (New York, 1960). This is a reprint of C. J. Hogarth's translation, rightly criticised for its incompleteness and inaccuracies, but better than no translation at all. Superior translations of individual volumes of this work are listed below.
S. F. Platonov, *A History of Russia* (London and New York, 1925).
M. N. Pokrovsky, *Brief History of Russia*, 2 vols (London and New York, 1933).
I. I. Smirnov and A. Samsonov, chief editors, *A Short History of the USSR*, 2 vols (Moscow, 1965). In internal references to this work in the present book, volume 1 is ascribed to Smirnov and volume 2 to Samsonov.

The following is a short list of REGIONAL HISTORIES:
W. E. D. Allen, *A History of the Georgian People from the Beginning Down to the Russian Conquest in the Nineteenth Century* (London, 1932; New York, 1971).
W. E. D. Allen, *The Ukraine: A History* (Cambridge, 1940).
A. Bilmanis, *The History of Latvia* (Princeton, N.J., 1951).
A. Gieysztor *et al.*, *History of Poland* (Warsaw, 1968).
O. Halecki, *Borderlands of Western Civilisation: A History of East Central Europe* (New York and London, 1952).
G. Hambly (ed.), *Central Asia* (London, 1969).
M. S. Hrushevsky, *A History of the Ukraine* (New Haven, Conn., and London, 1941).
D. M. Lang, *A Modern History of Georgia* (London and New York, 1962).
G. A. Lensen, *Russia's Eastward Expansion* (New York, 1964).
A. Lobanov-Rostovsky, *Russia and Asia* (New York, 1933).
P. Longworth, *The Cossacks* (London and New York, 1969).
W. H. McNeill, *Europe's Steppe Frontier* (Chicago, Ill., 1964).
B. Nolde, *La formation de l'empire russe* (Paris, 1952–3).
W. F. Reddaway *et al.*, *Cambridge History of Poland*, 2 vols (Cambridge and New York, 1941).
H. Schreiber, *Teuton and Slav: The Struggle for Central Europe* (London, 1965).
H. Schwartz, *Tsars, Mandarins and Commissars: A History of Chinese-Russian Relations* (London and Philadelphia, Penn., 1964).
A. E. Senn, *The Emergence of Modern Lithuania* (New York, 1959).
E. Uustalu, *The History of Estonian People* (London, 1952).
N. P. Vakar, *Belorussia: The Making of a Nation* (Cambridge, Mass., 1956).
J. H. Wuorinen, *A History of Finland* (New York, 1965).

Most general histories are political and diplomatic in emphasis. Perhaps for that reason there are no histories exclusively devoted to these themes.

There are, however, several works concentrating on ECONOMIC and CULTURAL DEVELOPMENT, although few of them consider all three major periods.

Economic

V. T. Bill, *The Forgotten Class: The Russian Bourgeoisie from the Earliest Beginnings to 1900* (New York, 1959).

J. G. Blum, *Lord and Peasant in Russia from the Ninth to the Nineteenth Century* (Princeton, N.J., 1961).

P. I. Lyashchenko, *History of the National Economy of Russia to the 1917 Revolution* (New York, 1949).

J. Mavor, *An Economic History of Russia* (London and New York, 1925).

M. Mitchell, *The Maritime History of Russia, 848–1948* (London, 1949; New York, 1950).

A. I. Pashkov (ed.), *A History of Russian Economic Thought: Ninth through Nineteenth Centuries* (Berkeley, Calif., 1964).

Cultural

T. Anderson, *Russian Political Thought: An Introduction* (Ithaca, N.Y., 1967).

J. H. Billington, *The Icon and the Axe: An Interpretative History of Russian Culture* (London, 1966; New York, 1966, 1970).

M. Cherniavsky, *Tsar and People: Studies in Russian Myths* (New Haven, Conn., 1961).

G. H. Hamilton, *The Art and Architecture of Russia* (Harmondsworth and Baltimore, Maryland, 1954).

R. A. Leonard, *A History of Russian Music* (London and New York, 1956).

N. O. Lossky, *History of Russian Philosophy* (New York, 1951).

T. G. Masaryk, *The Spirit of Russia*, 2 vols (London and New York, 1955).

P. N. Miliukov, *Outlines of Russian Culture: Religion and the Church – Architecture, Painting and Music*, 3 vols (New York, 1943).

T. T. Rice, *A Concise History of Russian Art* (London and New York, 1963).

G. Seaman, *History of Russian Music*, vol. 1–   (Oxford, 1967–   ; New York, 1968).

M. Slonim, *An Outline of Russian Literature* (Oxford, 1958).

Y. M. Sokolov, *Russian Folklore* (London and New York, 1950).

S. V. Utechin, *Russian Political Thought* (New York, 1963; London, 1964).

A. Vucinich, *Science in Russian Culture: A History to 1860* (Stanford, Calif., 1963; London, 1965).

A. Vucinich, *Science in Russian Culture: 1861–1917* (Stanford, Calif., 1970).

V. V. Zenkovsky, *A History of Russian Philosophy*, 2 vols (London and New York, 1953).

N. Zernov, *The Russians and their Church* (London and New York, 1945).

The principal GENERAL WORKS IN RUSSIAN are:

V. O. Kliuchevskii, *Sochineniia*, 8 vols (Moscow, 1956–9).

V. N. Pomomarev *et al.* (eds.), *Istoriia SSSR*, 12 vols in two series (Moscow, 1967–   ). In internal references to this work in the present book, each volume is ascribed to its main editors.

S. M. Solovev, *Istoriia Rossii*, 15 vols (Moscow 1962–6).

II   Part and Chapter Bibliographies

Part One   Medieval Russia: Kiev to Moscow

Political

R. Coulburn (ed.), *Feudalism in History* (Princeton, N.J., 1956), including M. Szeftel, 'Aspects of Feudalism in Russian History'.

R. Hellie (ed.), *Readings for Introduction to Russian Civilization: Muscovite Society* (Chicago, Ill., 1967).

W. Philipp, 'Russia's Position in Medieval Europe', *Russia: Essays in History and Literature*, ed. L. H. Legters (Leyden, 1972).

Economic

J. G. Blum, 'The Rise of Serfdom in Eastern Europe', *American Historical Review*, vol. 62 (1956–7).

W. Kirchner, *Commercial Relations between Russia and Europe, 1400–1800: Collected Essays* (Bloomington, Ind., 1966).

R. E. F. Smith, *The Enserfment of the Russian Peasantry* (Cambridge, 1968).

Cultural

N. Andreyev, *Studies in Muscovy: Western Influences and Byzantine Inheritance* (London, 1970).

'The Problem of Old Russian Culture', a discussion in *Slavic Review*, vols 21, 22 (1962–3) with contributions from N. Andreyev, J. H. Billington, G. Florovsky and D. S. Likhachev.

S. A. Zenkovsky, *Medieval Russia's Epics, Chronicles and Tales* (New York, 1963).

Ch. 1   The Construction and Collapse of Kiev, 882–1240

S. H. Cross (trans. and ed.), *The Russian Primary Chronicle* (Cambridge, Mass., 1953).

G. P. Fedotov, *The Russian Religious Mind*: vol. 1, *Kievan Christianity, The Tenth to the Thirteenth Centuries* (Cambridge, Mass., 1966).

B. D. Grekov, *Kiev Rus* (Moscow, 1959).

D. Obolensky, *Byzantium and the Slavs: Collected Studies* (London, 1971).

B. A. Rybakov, *Early Centuries of Russian History* (Moscow, 1965).

M. N. Tikhomirov, *The Towns of Ancient Rus* (Moscow, 1959).

G. V. Vernadsky, *Kievan Russia* (New Haven, Conn. and London, 1948).

Ch. 2   Invasion and Disunity, 1240–1462

G. P. Fedotov, *The Russian Religious Mind*: vol. 2, *The Middle Ages, the Thirteenth to Fifteenth Centuries* (Cambridge, Mass., 1966).

J. L. I. Fennell, *The Emergence of Moscow, 1304–1359* (London and Berkeley, Calif., 1968).

R. C. Howes (ed.), *The Testaments of the Grand Princes of Moscow* (Ithaca, N.Y., 1967).

A. E. Presniakov, *The Formation of the Great Russian State: A Study of Russian History in the Thirteenth to Fifteenth Centuries*, trans. A. E. Moorhouse, intro. A. J. Rieber (Chicago, Ill., 1970).

J. J. Saunders, *The History of the Mongol Conquest* (London and Boston, 1971).

B. Spuler, *History of the Mongols, Based on Eastern and Western Accounts of the Thirteenth and Fourteenth Centuries* (London and New York, 1972).

G. V. Vernadsky, *The Mongols and Russia* (New Haven, Conn. and London, 1953).

Ch. 3 Consolidation under Moscow, 1462–1645

J. L. I. Fennell, *Ivan the Great of Moscow* (London and New York, 1961).

I. Grey, *Ivan III and the Unification of Russia* (London, 1964).

I. Grey, *Ivan the Terrible* (London, 1964; New York, 1964, 1967).

B. Nørretranders, *The Shaping of Tsardom under Ivan Groznyi* (Copenhagen, 1964).

S. F. Platonov, (ed.), and trans. L. R. Pyles, with intro. by J. T. Alexander, *Boris Gudunov: Tsar of Russia* (Gulf Breeze, Flo., 1972).

S. F. Platonov, (ed.), and trans. J. L. Wieczynski, *Moscow and the West* (Gulf Breeze, Flo., 197   ).

S. F. Platonov, trans. J. T. Alexander, *The Time of Troubles: A Historical Study of the Internal Crisis and Social Struggle in Sixteenth- and Seventeenth-Century Muscovy* (Lawrence and London, 1970).

G. V. Vernadsky, *Russia at the Dawn of the Modern Age* (New Haven and London, 1959).

G. V. Varnadsky, *The Tsardom of Muscovy, 1547–1682*, vol. 1 (New Haven and London, 1969).

Contemporary writings include:

L. E. Berry and R. O. Crummey (eds.), *Rude and Barbarous Kingdom: Russia in the Accounts of Sixteenth-Century English Voyagers* (London and Madison, Wis., 1968).

J. L. I. Fennell (trans. and ed.), *The Correspondence between Prince A. M. Kurbsky and Tsar Ivan IV of Russia* (Cambridge, 1955).

Baron von Herberstein, trans. and ed. R. H. Major, *Notes upon Russia: Being a Translation of the Earliest Account of that Country, Entitled: 'Rerum Muscoviticarum Commentarii'*, Hakluyt Society, series 1, vols 10 and 12 (London 1851–2).

H. von Staden, trans. and ed. T. Esper, *The Land and Government of Muscovy: A Sixteenth-Century Account* (Stanford, Calif., 1967).

Part Two   Modern Russia: The Tsarist Empire

General Histories

V. V. Kallash (ed.), *Tri veka: Rossiia ot smuty do nashego vremeni*, 6 vols (Moscow, 1912–13).

M. Karpovich, *Imperial Russia, 1801–1917* (New York, 1932).

A. A. Kornilov, *Modern Russian History from the Age of Catherine the Great to the End of the Nineteenth Century*, 2 vols in 1, reprint (London and New York, 1970).

S. G. Pusharev, *The Emergence of Modern Russia, 1801–1917* (New York, 1963).

M. Raeff, *Imperial Russia, 1682–1825* (New York, 1971).
G. H. N. Seton-Watson, *The Russian Empire, 1801–1917* (Oxford, 1971).

Political

E. Amburger, *Geschichte der Behördenorganisation Russlands von Peter dem Grossen bis 1917* (Leyden, 1966).
J. A. Armstrong, *The European Administrative Elite* (Princeton, 1973).
B. Jelavich, *A Century of Russian Foreign Policy, 1814–1914* (Philadelphia, Penn., and New York, 1964).
V. Leontovitsch, *Geschichte des Liberalismus in Russland* (Frankfurt-on-Main, 1957).
M. Raeff, *Plans for Political Reform in Imperial Russia, 1730–1905* (Englewood Cliffs, N.J., 1966).
M. Raeff, 'The Russian Aristocracy and its Officials', in *Readings*, vol. 1, ed. Harcave.

Economic

A. Baykov, 'The Economic Development of Russia', *Economic History Review*, series 2, vol. 7 (1954).
H. J. Ellison, 'Economic Modernisation in Imperial Russia', *J. of Economic History*, vol. 25 (1965).
M. E. Falkus, *The Industrialisation of Russia before 1914* (London, 1972).
A. Gerschenkron, *Economic Backwardness in Historical Perspective* (Cambridge, Mass., 1962).
A. Gerschenkron, *Europe in the Russian Mirror: Four Lectures in Economic History* (Cambridge, 1970).
Paul Gregory, 'Economic Growth and Structural Change in Tsarist Russia: A Case of Modern Economic Growth', *Soviet Studies*, vol. 23 (1971–2).
A. Kahan, 'Government Policies and the Industrialisation of Russia', *J. of Economic History*, vol. 27 (1967).
R. Portal, 'The Problem of an Industrial Revolution in Russia in the Nineteenth Century', in *Readings*, ed. Harcave, vol. 2.

Cultural

P. L. Alston, *Education and the State in Tsarist Russia* (Stanford, Calif., 1969).
N. A. Hans, *A History of Russian Educational Policy, 1701–1917* (London, 1931).
N. A. Hans, *The Russian Tradition in Education* (London and Westport, Conn., 1963).
W. E. Johnson, *Russia's Educational Heritage* (Pittsburgh, Penn., 1950).
D. S. Mirsky, *A History of Russian Literature* (London and New York, 1949).
M. Slonim, *The Epic of Russian Literature from its Origins to Tolstoy* (Oxford, 1950).
M. Slonim, *Modern Russian Literature from Chekhov to the Revolution* (Oxford, 1962).

Ch. 4   The Foundation of the Russian Empire, 1645–1698

R. N. Bain, *The First Romanovs, 1613–1725: A History of Muscovite Civilisation and the Rise of Modern Russia under Peter the Great and his Forerunners* (London, 1905).

Richard Hellie, *Enserfment and Military Change in Muscovy* (London and Chicago, Ill., 1971).

V. O. Kliuchevskii (styled Klyuchevsky), trans. and intro. L. Archibald, *The Rise of the Romonovs* (London, 1970); the same work published in the United States as V. O. Kliuchevsky, trans. N. Duddington, *Course in Russian History: The Seventeenth Century* (New York, 1968).

C. B. O'Brien, *Russia under Two Tsars, 1682–1689: The Regency of Sophia Alekseevna*, University of California Publications in History, vol. 42 (1952).

Z. Schakovskoy, *Precursors of Peter the Great: The Reign of Tsar Alexis, Peter the Great's Father, and the Young Peter's Struggle against the Regent Sophia for the Mastery of Russia*, trans. from French (London, 1964).

G. V. Vernadsky, *The Tsardom of Muscovy, 1547–1682*, 2 vols (London and New Haven, Conn., 1969).

Among the contemporary accounts are:

S. Collins, *The Present State of Russia* (London, 1671).

Foy de la Neuville, *Relation curieuse et nouvelle de Moscovie* (The Hague, 1699).

P. Gordon, *Passages from the Diary of General Patrick Gordon of Auchleuchries in the Years 1635–1699* (Aberdeen, 1859; reprinted London, 1968).

Olearius (trans., ed. and intro. S. H. Baron), *The Travels of Olearius in Seventeenth-Century Russia* (Stanford, Calif., 1967).

Ch. 5   The Completion of the Structure, 1698–1761

M. S. Anderson, *Peter the Great*, Historical Association Pamphlet, General Series no. 71 (London, 1969).

R. N. Bain, *The Daughter of Peter the Great: A History of Russian Diplomacy and the Russian Court under the Empress Elizabeth Petrovna, 1741–1762* (London, 1899).

R. N. Bain, *Peter III: Emperor of Russia* (London, 1902).

J. Cracraft, *The Church Reform of Peter the Great* (London and Stanford, 1971).

V. O. Kliuchevskii (trans. L. Archibald) styled Klyuchevsky, *Peter the Great* (London, 1958).

P. Longworth, *The Three Empresses: Catherine I, Anne and Elizabeth of Russia* (London, 1972; New York, 1973).

M. Raeff, *Origins of the Russian Intelligentsia: The Eighteenth-Century Nobility* (New York, 1966).

M. Raeff (ed. and intro.), *Peter the Great: Reformer or Revolutionary?* (Boston, Mass., 1963).

B. H. Sumner, *Peter the Great and the Emergence of Russia* (London, 1951; New York, 1962).

R. Wittram, *Peter I, Czar und Kaiser*, 2 vols (Göttingen, 1964).
There are a vast number of contemporary accounts for this and all succeeding periods. Among those for this period are:

P. H. Bruce, *Memoirs of . . . a Military Officer in the Services of Prussia, Russia and Great Britain* (London, 1782).

A. Gordon, *History of Peter the Great, Emperor of Russia*, 2 vols (Aberdeen, 1755).

C. H. von Manstein, *Contemporary Memoirs of Russia: Historical, Political and Military from the Year 1727 to 1744* (London, 1856).

F. C. Weber, *The Present State of Russia . . . 1714 to 1720*, 2 vols (London, 1722-3).

Ch. 6   Enlightened Absolutism, 1761–1801

J. T. Alexander, *Autocratic Politics in a National Crisis: The Imperial Russian Government and Pugachev's Revolt, 1773–1775* (Bloomington, Ind., and London, 1969).

'The Reign of Catherine II', *Canadian-American Slavic Studies*, vol. 4, no. 3 (1970).

'The Reign of Paul I', *Canadian-American Slavic Studies*, vol. 7, no. 1 (1973).

P. Dukes, *Catherine the Great and the Russian Nobility* (Cambridge, 1967).

M. Kochan, *Life in Russia under Catherine the Great* (London and New York, 1969).

D. M. Lang, *The First Russian Radical: Alexander Radishchev, 1749–1802* (London, 1959).

A. McConnell, *A Russian Philosophe: Alexander Radishchev* (The Hague, 1964).

M. Raeff (ed.), *Catherine the Great: A Profile* (London and New York, 1972).

Contemporary commentaries include:

E. D. Clarke, *Travels in Various Countries of Europe, Asia and Africa . . .,* part I (London, 1810).

W. Coxe, *Travels into Poland, Russia, Sweden and Denmark . . .,* vol. 2 (London, 1803).

G. Macartney, *An Account of Russia, 1767* (London, 1768).

W. Richardson, *Anecdotes of the Russian Empire . . .* (London, 1784).

On the literature of the period, see:

H. B. Segel (trans. and ed.), *The Literature of Eighteenth-Century Russia: An Anthology*, 2 vols (New York, 1967).

Ch. 7   Russian Nationalism, 1801–1855

W. L. Blackwell, *The Beginnings of Russian Industrialization, 1800–1860* (Princeton, N.J., 1968).

J. S. Curtiss, *The Russian Army under Nicholas I, 1822–1855* (Durham, N.Ca, 1965).

A. McConnell, *Tsar Alexander I: Paternalistic Reformer* (New York, 1970).

A. G. Mazour, *The First Russian Revolution, 1825: Its Origin, Development and Significance* (Stanford, Calif., 1963).

S. Monas, *The Third Section: Police and Society in Russia under Nicholas I* (Cambridge, Mass., 1961).

W. McK. Pintner, *Russian Economic Policy under Nicholas I* (New York, 1967).

M. Raeff (ed. and intro.), *The Decembrist Movement* (Englewood Cliffs, N.J., 1966).

M. Raeff, *Michael Speransky: Statesman of Imperial Russia, 1772–1839* (The Hague, 1957).

N. V. Riasanovsky, *Russia and the West in the Teaching of the Slavophiles* (Cambridge, Mass., 1952).

N. V. Riasanovsky, *Nicholas I and Official Nationality in Russia, 1825–1855* (Berkeley, Calif., 1959).

P. S. Squire, *The Third Department: The Establishment and Practices of the Political Police in the Russia of Nicholas I* (Cambridge, 1968).

E. C. Thaden, *Conservative Nationalism in Nineteenth-Century Russia* (Seattle, Wash., 1964).

H. J. Törke, *Das russische Beamtentum in der ersten Hälfte des 19. Jahrhunderts*, Forschungen zur russishcen Geschichte, vol. 13 (Berlin, 1967).

Two 'classical' contemporary accounts are:

Marquis de Custine, *The Empire of the Czar*, 3 vols (London, 1843). See also G. F. Kennan, *The Marquis de Custine and his Russia in 1839* (Princeton, N.J., 1971, and London, 1972).

Baron A. von Haxthausen, *The Russian Empire: Its People, Institutions and Resources*, 2 vols. (London, 1856).

Ch. 8   The Emancipation, and After, 1855–1894

A. E. Adams, *Imperial Russia after 1861: Peaceful Modernization or Revolution?* (Boston, Mass., 1965).

C. E. Black (ed.), *The Transformation of Russian Society: Aspects of Social Change since 1861* (Cambridge, Mass., 1960).

R. F. Byrnes, *Pobedonostsev: His Life and Thought* (London and Bloomington, Ind., 1968).

T. Emmons (ed.), *Emancipation of the Russian Serfs* (London and New York, 1970).

T. Emmons, *The Russian Landed Gentry and the Peasant Emancipation of 1861* (Cambridge, 1968).

F. A. Miller, *Dmitrii Miliutin and the Reform Era in Russia* (Nashville, Tenn., 1968).

W. E. Mosse, *Alexander II and the Modernisation of Russia* (London and New York, 1958).

R. E. Pipes, *Social Democracy and the St Petersburg Labor Movement, 1885–1897* (Cambridge, Mass., 1963).

G. T. Robinson, *Rural Russia under the Old Regime* (New York, 1932).

S. F. Starr, *Decentralization and Self-Government in Russia, 1830–1870* (Princeton, N.J., 1972).

F. Venturi, *Roots of Revolution: A History of the Populist and Socialist Movements in Nineteenth-Century Russia* (London, 1960; New York, 1961).

R. Wortman, *The Crisis of Russian Populism* (Cambridge, 1967).

R. E. Zelnik, *Labor and Society in Tsarist Russia: The Factory Workers of St Petersburg, 1855–1870* (Stanford, Calif., 1971).
Outstanding contemporary descriptions include:
A. Leroy-Beaulieu, *The Empire of the Tsars and the Russians*, 3 vols (London and New York, 1893–6).
Stepniak (pseudonym of S. M. Kravchinskii), *The Russian Peasantry* (London, 1890).
D. Mackenzie Wallace, *Russia*, 2 vols. (London, 1877).

Ch. 9   Russian Imperialism, 1894–1917

R. Charques, *The Twilight of Imperial Russia* (London, 1958; Fairlawn, N.J., 1959).
M. T. Florinsky, *The End of the Russian Empire* (New York, 1961).
S. Galai, *The Liberation Movement in Russia, 1900–1905* (Cambridge, 1972).
L. H. Haimson, *The Russian Marxists and the Origins of Bolshevism* (Cambridge, Mass., 1955).
S. Harcave, *First Blood: The Russian Revolution of 1905* (London, 1965; New York, 1970).
G. A. Hosking, *The Russian Constitutional Experiment: Government and Duma, 1907–1914* (Cambridge, 1973).
G. Katkov et al., *Russia Enters the Twentieth Century, 1894–1917* (London, 1971).
J. L. H. Keep, *The Rise of Social Democracy in Europe* (Oxford, 1963).
R. Kindersley, *The First Russian Revisionists: A Study of Legal Marxism in Russia* (Oxford, 1962).
L. Kochan, *Russia in Revolution, 1890–1918* (London, 1966).
A. Levin, *The Second Duma: A Study of the Social-Democratic Party and the Russian Constitutional Experiment* (New Haven, Conn., 1940).
J. P. McKay, *Pioneers for Profit: Foreign Entrepreneurship and Russian Industrialization, 1885–1913*, London and Chicago, Ill., 1970).
H. D. Mehlinger and J. M. Thompson, *Count Witte and the Tsarist Government in the 1905 Revolution* (Bloomington, Ind., 1971).
A. P. Mendel, *Dilemmas of Progress in Tsarist Russia: Legal Marxism and Legal Populism* (Cambridge, Mass., 1961).
M. S. Miller, *The Economic Development of Russia, 1905–1914* (Oxford, 1926).
T. Riha, *A Russian European: Paul Miliukov in Russian Politics* (Notre Dame, Ind., 1969).
T. G. Stavrou (ed.), *Russia under the Last Tsar* (Minneapolis, Minn., 1969).
D. W. Treadgold, *Lenin and his Rivals: The Struggle for Russia's Future, 1898–1906* (London and New York, 1955).
T. H. Von Laue, *Sergei Witte and the Industrialization of Russia* (London and New York, 1963).
B. D. Wolfe, *Three Who Made a Revolution* (New York, 1948; London, 1956).
Among the many contemporary accounts, see:
G. Buchanan, *My Mission to Russia and Other Diplomatic Memories*, 2 vols (London, 1923).

S. N. Harper, *The Russia I Believe In* (Chicago, Ill., 1945).
B. Pares, *My Russian Memoirs* (London, 1931; New York, 1969).

Part Three   Contemporary Russia: The Soviet Union

General

E. H. Carr, *A History of Soviet Russia* (London and New York, 1950–   ).
B. Dmytryshyn, *USSR: A Concise History* (New York, 1972).
A. P. Nenarokov, *Russia in the Twentieth Century* (New York, 1968).
J. P. Nettl, *The Soviet Achievement* (London, 1967; New York, 1968).
G. von Rauch, *A History of Soviet Russia* (London and New York, 1967).
D. W. Treadgold, *Twentieth-Century Russia* (New York, 1959).

Political

I. Deutscher, *Trotsky*, 3 vols (London and New York, 1954–63); for Lenin and Stalin, see below.
J. Erickson, *The Soviet High Command: A Military-Political History, 1918–1941* (London and New York, 1962).
D. Lane, *Politics and Society in the USSR* (London, 1970; New York, 1971).
T. H. Rigby, *Communist Party Membership in the USSR, 1917–1967* Princeton, N.J., 1968).
L. B. Schapiro, *The Communist Party of the Soviet Union* (London and New York, 1960).
A. B. Ulam, *Expansion and Coexistence: The History of Soviet Foreign Policy, 1917–1967* (London and New York, 1968).

Economic

A. Baykov, *The Development of the Soviet Economic System* (Cambridge, 1966).
R. A. Clarke, *Soviet Economic Facts, 1917–1972* (London, 1972; New York, 1973).
M. Dobb, *An Economic History of the USSR* (London, 1969).
H. Schwartz, *Russia's Soviet Economy* (London, 1951). A. Nove, *An Economic History of the USSR* (Harmondsworth and Baltimore, 1972).

Cultural

V. Alexandrovna, *A History of Soviet Literature* (New York, 1963).
J. S. Curtiss, *The Russian Church and the Soviet State, 1917–1950* (Gloucester, Mass., 1965).
N. Grant, *Soviet Education* (London, 1964).
C. Vaughan James, *Soviet Socialist Realism: Origins and Theory* (London and New York, 1973).
D. Joravsky, *Soviet Marxism and Natural Science* (London, 1961).
W. Kolarz, *Religion in the Soviet Union* (London, 1961).
J. Leyda, *Kino: A History of the Russian and Soviet Film* (London, 1960; New York, 1973).
M. Slonim, *Soviet Russian Literature: Writers and Problems* (New York, 1966).
G. Struve, *Russian Literature under Lenin and Stalin, 1917–1953* (Norman, Okla., 1971).

Ch. 10   The Russian Revolution, 1917–1921

A. E. Adams, *The Russian Revolution and Bolshevik Victory: Why and How?* (Boston, Mass., 1960).

P. H. Avrich, *The Russian Anarchists* (Princeton, N.J., 1967).

J. Bradley, *Allied Intervention in Russia* (London, 1968).

W. H. Chamberlin, *The Russian Revolution, 1917–1921*, 2 vols (London and New York, 1935).

J. S. Curtiss, *The Russian Revolutions of 1917* (Princeton, N.J., 1957).

R. V. Daniels, *Red October: The Bolshevik Revolution of 1917* (London, 1967; New York, 1969).

M. Ferro, *The Russian Revolution of February 1917* (London and New York, 1972).

D. Footman, *Civil War in Russia* (London, 1961).

G. Katkov, *Russia 1917: The February Revolution* (London, 1967).

A. F. Kerensky, *The Kerensky Memoirs* (Oxford and New York, 1966).

S. P. Melgunov, *The Bolshevik Seizure of Power* (Berkeley, Calif., 1972).

L. A. Owen, *The Russian Peasant Movement, 1906–1917* (London and New York, 1937).

G. Pavlovsky, *Agricultural Russia on the Eve of Revolution* (London and New York, 1930).

R. W. Pethybridge, *The Spread of the Russian Revolution: Essays on 1917* (London and New York, 1972).

A. Rabinowitch, *Prelude to Revolution: The Petrograd Bolsheviks and the July 1917 Uprising* (Bloomington, Ind., 1968).

O. H. Radkey, *The Agrarian Foes of Bolshevism: Promise and Default of the Russian Socialist-Revolutionaries, February to October 1917* (New York, 1958).

T. Shanin, *The Awkward Class: Political Sociology of the Peasantry in a Developing Society, 1910–1921* (Oxford, 1972).

P. N. Sobolev, *History of the October Revolution* (Moscow, 1966).

L. D. Trotsky, *The History of the Russian Revolution* (London, 1934; Ann Arbor, Mich., 1957).

R. A. Wade, *The Russian Search for Peace, February–October 1917* (Stanford, Calif., 1969).

R. D. Warth, *The Allies and the Russian Revolution* (Durham, N. Ca, 1954).

For contemporary accounts, see:

D. von Mohrenschildt (ed.), *The Russian Revolution of 1917: Contemporary Accounts* (London and New York, 1971).

R. Pethybridge (ed.), *Witnesses to the Russian Revolution* (London, 1964; Gloucester, Mass., 1968).

N. N. Sukhanov, *The Russian Revolution, 1917: A Personal Record*, ed. and trans. J. Carmichael (London, 1955).

Ch. 11   The Consolidation of the Soviet Union, 1917–1929

P. Avrich, *Kronstadt 1921* (Princeton, N.J., 1957)

E. H. Carr, *The Bolshevik Revolution, 1917–1923*, 3 vols (London and New York, 1952–4).

E. H. Carr, *The Interregnum, 1923–24* (London and New York, 1954).

E. H. Carr, *Socialism in One Country, 1924–26*, 3 vols (London and New York, 1958–64).

E. H. Carr, *Foundations of a Planned Economy, 1926–29*, 3 vols (London and New York, 1969–   ).

R. V. Daniels, *Conscience of the Revolution: The Communist Opposition in Soviet Russia* (Cambridge, Mass., 1960).

T. Deutscher, *Not by Politics Alone: the Other Lenin* (London, 1973).

A. Erlich, *The Soviet Industrialisation Debate, 1924–1928* (Cambridge, Mass., 1951).

L. Fischer, *The Life of Lenin* (London and New York, 1965).

S. Fitzpatrick, *The Commissariat of Enlightenment* (Cambridge, 1970).

I. Getzler, *Martov: A Political Biography* (Cambridge, 1967).

M. Lewin, *Lenin's Last Struggle* (New York, 1968; London, 1969).

A. V. Lunacharsky, *Revolutionary Silhouettes* (London, 1967).

D. J. Male, *Russian Peasant Organization before Collectivization: A Study of Commune and Gathering, 1925–1930* (Cambridge, 1971).

A. J. Mayer, *Politics and Diplomacy of Peacemaking: Containment and Counter-revolution at Versailles, 1918–1919* (New York, 1967).

S. W. Page, *Lenin and the World Revolution* (New York, 1959).

R. E. Pipes, *The Formation of the Soviet Union: Communism and Nationalism, 1917–1923* (Cambridge, Mass., 1964).

L. Schapiro, *The Origin of the Communist Autocracy* (London and New York, 1955).

L. Schapiro and P. Reddaway, *Lenin: The Man, The Theorist, The Leader – A Reappraisal* (London and New York, 1967).

D. Shub, *Lenin: A Biography* (New York, 1948; Harmondsworth, 1966).

H. Shukman, *Lenin and the Russian Revolution* (London, 1966; New York, 1968).

J. M. Thompson, *Russia, Bolshevism and the Versailles Peace* (Princeton, N.J., 1966).

Among the many contemporary accounts are:

A. D. Makarenko, *The Road to Life*, 3 vols (Moscow, c. 1950).

A. Monkhouse, *Moscow, 1911–1933* (London, 1934; New York, 1970).

V. L. Serge, *Memoirs of a Revolutionary, 1901–1941* (London, 1963).

W. S. Woytinsky, *Stormy Passage* (Toronto, 1961).

Ch. 12   The Construction of Soviet Socialism, 1929–1941

A. Avtorkhanov, *Stalin and the Soviet Communist Party: A Study in the Technology of Power* (New York, 1959).

R. Conquest, *The Great Terror: Stalin's Purge of the Thirties* (London, 1968; New York, 1973).

R. V. Daniels, *The Stalin Revolution: Fulfilment or Betrayal of Communism?* (Boston, Mass., 1965).

I. Deutscher, *Stalin: A Political Biography* (Oxford and New York, 1949).

M. Fainsod, *Smolensk under Soviet Rule* (Cambridge, Mass., 1958).

G. Katkov, *The Trial of Bukharin* (London, 1969).

M. Lewin, *Russian Peasants and Soviet Power: A Study of Collectivization* (London, 1966; Evanston, Ill., 1968).

R. Medvedev, *Let History Judge: The Origins and Consequences of Stalinism* (New York, 1971; London, 1972).

T. H. Rigby (ed.), *Stalin* (Englewood Cliffs, N.J., 1966).

M. Schachtman, *Behind the Moscow Trials* (New York, 1936; London, 1971).

B. Souvarine, *Stalin: A Critical Survey of Bolshevism* (London, 1939; New York, 1972).

N. Timasheff, *The Great Retreat* (New York, 1946).

L. D. Trotsky, *Stalin* (London, 1947; New York, 1970).

Contemporary analyses include:

W. H. Chamberlin, *Russia's Iron Age* (Boston, Mass., 1937).

M. Hindus, *Humanity Uprooted* (New York, 1930).

L. D. Trotsky, *The Revolution Betrayed* (London, 1937; New York, 1973).

Ch. 13   War and Reconstruction, 1941–1953

J. A. Armstrong, *Soviet Partisans in World War II* (Madison, Wis., 1964).

A. Clark, *Barbarossa: The Russo-German Conflict, 1941–45* (London and New York, 1965).

A. Dallin, *German Rule in Russia, 1941–45* (London, 1957).

D. F. Fleming, *The Cold War and its Origins*, 2 vols (New York, 1961).

W. LaFeber, *America, Russia and the Cold War, 1945–1966* (New York, 1967).

R. Pethybridge, *A History of Post-War Russia* (London, 1966; New York, 1973).

V. Petrov, *June 22, 1941: Soviet Historians and the German Invasion* (Columbia, S.Ca., 1968).

A. Werth, *Russia at War, 1941–1945* (London and New York, 1964).

Contemporary accounts include:

S. Bialer, *Stalin and his Generals: Soviet Military Memoirs of World War Two* (Indianapolis, Ind., 1969).

M. Djilas, *Conversations with Stalin* (London and New York, 1962).

G. K. Zhukov, *Memoirs* (London and New York, 1971).

Ch. 14   The Establishment of Soviet Superpower, 1953–1964

A. Brumberg (ed.), *Russia under Khrushchev* (London, 1962).

N. DeWitt, *Education and Professional Employment in the USSR* (Washington, D.C., 1961).

M. Frankland, *Khrushchev* (Harmondsworth, 1966; New York, 1967).

M. Hayward (ed.), *Soviet Literature in the Sixties* (New York, 1964; London, 1965).

H. Schwartz, *The Soviet Economy since Stalin* (London, 1965).

The Road to Communism: Documents of the 22nd Congress of the CPSU, October 17–31, 1961 (Moscow, n.d.).

Ch. 15   Problems of Coexistence, Competition and Convergence since 1964.

A. Bergson, *Planning and Productivity under Soviet Socialism* (New York, 1968).

U. Bronfenbrenner, *Two Worlds of Childhood: USA and USSR* (New York, 1970).
A. Dallin and T. B. Larson (eds), *Soviet Politics since Khrushchev* (Engelwood Cliffs, N.J., 1968).
S. Hendel, *The Soviet Crucible, 1917–1967* (London and Princeton. N.J., 1967).
C. Johnson (ed.), *Change in Communist Systems* (Stanford, Calif., 1970).
J. W. Strong, *The Soviet Union under Brezhnev and Kosygin: The Transition Years* (London and New York, 1971).

To keep up with current developments, consult the following periodical publications:
The Annual Register, Current Digest of the Soviet Press, Problems of Communism, Russia and the Third World and *Survey.*

For the Communist viewpoint, see *International Affairs* (Moscow) – not to be confused with the useful Western periodical of the same name, published in London – and *Marxism Today.* The Trotskyist analysis will be found in *Fourth International.*

References

Full publication details, where not supplied here, will be found in the relevant sections of the Bibliography.

General Introduction

1. W. H. Parker, *The Super-Powers: The United States and the Soviet Union Compared* (London and New York, 1972), pp. 60–1.
2. Kliuchevskii, *Sochineniia*, I, p. 47.
3. R. J. Kerner, *The Urge to the Sea: The Course of Russian History – The Role of Rivers, Portages, Ostrogs, Monasteries and Furs*, reprint (New York, 1971).
4. See G. V. Vernadsky, *Ancient Russia* (London and New Haven, Conn., 1943).
5. See 'Varangian Problems', *Scando-Slavica*, Supplement 1.

Part One   Medieval Russia: Kiev to Moscow

Introduction

1. For Western views, see W. Philipp, 'Russia's Position'; M. Szeftel, 'Aspects of Feudalism'. For Soviet views, see the short summary in Hellie, *Enserfment and Military Change*, pp. 11–13; and B. A. Rybakov, in S. A. Pletneeva *et al.* (eds), *Istoriia SSSR*, pp. 1365–76.

Ch. 1   The Construction and Collapse of Kiev, 882–1240

1. Cross, *The Russian Primary Chronicle*, p. 59.
2. Grekov, *Kiev Rus*, p. 603.
3. Smirnov, *Short History*, p. 38.
4. Rybakov, *Early Centuries*, p. 4.
5. Grekov, *Kiev Rus*, p. 624.
6. Rybakov, op. cit., p. 42.
7. Vernadsky, *Kievan Russia*, pp. 73–4.
8. See, for example, A. D. Stokes, 'The Status of the Russian Church, 988–1037', *Slavonic Review*, vol. 37 (1958–9); M. N. Tikhomirov, 'The Origins of Christianity in Russia', *History*, vol. 44 (1959).

9. Grekov, op. cit., p. 644.
10. Ibid., p. 649.
11. Vernadsky, op. cit., p. 82.
12. Cross, op. cit., p. 142.
13. Ibid., p. 187.
14. Grekov, op. cit. pp. 674–6.
15. Kliuchevskii, *Sochineniia*, I, 239.
16. Kliuchevskii, quoted in Grekov, op. cit., pp. 46–7.
17. Grekov, op. cit., p. 70.
18. Vernadsky, op. cit., pp. 103–5.
19. Blum, *Lord and Peasant*, p. 25; Vernadsky, op. cit., p. 133.
20. Grekov, op. cit., p. 347.
21. Cross, op. cit., pp. 308–9.
22. Tikhomirov, *The Towns*, p. 149; B. A. Rybakov, *Remeslo drevnei Rusi* (Moscow, 1948).
23. Vernadsky, op. cit., pp. 121–30.
24. Smirnov, op. cit., p. 40.
25. Grekov, op. cit., p. 497.
26. Rybakov, *Early Centuries*, pp. 66–7.
27. Fedotov, *The Russian Religious Mind*, I, 412.
28. Fedotov, op. cit., I, 84, 94, 380–1, 244.
29. See, for example, J. L. I. Fennell, 'The Recent Controversy in the Soviet Union over the Authenticity of the *Slovo*', in *Russia: Essays in History and Literature*, ed. L. H. Legters (Leyden, 1972).
30. Smirnov, op. cit., p. 50.
31. See, for example, M. W. Thompson (comp.), *Novgorod the Great: Excavations at the Medieval City* (London, 1967).
32. Fedotov, op. cit., I, 380.
33. Seaman, *History*, p. 1.
34. V. N. Lazarev is sceptical; see his *L'Art de la Russie médiévale et L'occident: XI–XV siècles*, XIIIe Congrès International des Sciences Historiques (Moscow, 1970) pp. 21–2. See also Hamilton, *The Art*, pp. 35, 49.
35. Obolensky, *Byzantium*, p. 35.
36. Rybakov, in Pletneeva *et al.* (eds), *Istoriia SSSR*, I, 682.

Ch. 2   Invasion and Disunity, 1240–1462

1. Grekov, *Kiev Rus*, p. 642.
2. R. V. Viatkin and S. L. Tikhvinskii, 'Some Problems of Scholarship in the CPR', *Soviet Studies in History*, vol. 2, no. 4 (1963–4) p. 53.
3. Vernadsky, *The Mongols*, p. 1.
4. Fennell, *The Emergence*, pp. 9–10.
5. Zenkovsky, *Medieval Russia's Epics*, p. 18.
6. J. J. Saunders, 'Matthew Paris and the Mongols', in *Essays in Medieval History presented to Bertie Wilkinson*, ed. T. A. Sandquist and M. R. Powicke (Toronto, 1969).
7. Smirnov, *Short History*, p. 59.
8. Vernadsky, op. cit., p. 338.
9. Ibid., p. 390.

10. Smirnov, op. cit., p. 61.
11. Kliuchevskii, *Sochineniia*, II, 5–27.
12. Presniakov, *The Formation*.
13. Fennell, op. cit., p. 110.
14. A. V. Cherepnin, *Obrazovanie russkogo tsentralizovannogo gosudarstva v XIV–XV vekakh: ocherki sotsialno-ekonomicheskoi i politicheskoi istorii Rusi* (Moscow, 1960).
15. M. K. Liubavskii, *Obrazovanie osnovnoi gosudarstvennoi territorii velikorusskoi narodnosti: zaselenie i obedinenie tsentra* (Leningrad, 1929). See also O. P. Backus, 'The Problem of Feudalism in Lithuania, 1506–1548', *Slavic Review*, vol. 21 (1962); 'The Problem of Unity in the Polish-Lithuanian State', *Slavic Review*, vol. 22 (1963); and *Motives of West Russian Nobles in Deserting Lithuania for Moscow, 1377–1514* (Lawrence, Kansas, 1957).
16. Smirnov, op. cit., p. 56.
17. Vernadsky, op. cit., pp. 216–19.
18. G. E. Kochin, *Selskoe khoziaistvo na Rusi v period obrazovaniia russkogo tsentralizovannogo gosudarstva: konets XIII-nachala XVIv* (Moscow-Leningrad, 1965) p. 93.
19. Kochin, op. cit., p. 434.
20. Cherepnin, op. cit., chs 2 and 3.
21. M. N. Tikhomirov *et al.* (eds), *Istoriia SSSR*, II, 81–2.
22. Florinsky, *Russia*, p. 129.
23. Miliukov, *Outlines*, I, 10.
24. A. M. Sakharov, in *Tserkov v istorii Rossii, IXv-1917g: kriticheskie ocherki*, ed. N. A. Smirnov (Moscow, 1967) pp. 74–8.
25. Vernadsky, op. cit., p. 380.
26. V. N. Lazarev, *Andrei Rublev* (Moscow, 1960) p. 23.
27. A. A. Zimin *et al.*, in Tikhomirov *et al.*, op. cit., II, 357–8.

Ch. 3   Consolidation under Moscow, 1462–1645

1. See Parker, *An Historical Geography*, p. 17.
2. See Berry and Crummey (eds), *Rude and Barbarous Kingdom*, for this and similar descriptions.
3. H. Morley (ed.), *The Discovery of Muscovy: From the Collections of Richard Hakluyt* (London and New York, 1889), p. 109.
4. See, for example, Mazour, *The Writing of History*, p. 35; and see page 35 above.
5. Von Herberstein, *Notes*, x, 24–5.
6. M. Cherniavsky, 'Ivan the Terrible as Renaissance Prince', *Slavic Review*, vol. 27 (1968) p. 208.
7. Kliuchevskii, *Sochineniia*, III, 23.
8. Florinsky, *Russia*, p. 250.
9. Smirnov, *Short History*, p. 84.
10. G. Alef, 'Reflections on the Boyar Duma in the Reign of Ivan III', *Slavonic Review*, vol. 45 (1967) p. 108.
11. Ibid., p. 107. See also S. O. Shmidt, 'Mestnichestvo i absoliutizm: postanovka voprosa' in his *Stanovlenie rossiiskogo samoderzhavstva* (Moscow, 1973).

12. G. Alef, 'The Adoption of the Muscovite Two-Headed Eagle: A Discordant View', *Speculum*, vol. 41 (1966) argues that the Habsburg example was a more immediate influence than the Byzantine.
13. T. Esper, 'Military Self-Sufficiency and Weapons Technology in Muscovite Russia', *Slavic Review*, vol. 28 (1969) pp. 188–91.
14. A. N. Grobovsky, *The 'Chosen Council' of Ivan IV: A Reinterpretation* (Brooklyn, N.Y., 1969), believes the Council should be seen rather as an undefined moral influence.
15. Esper, art. cit., pp. 193–4.
16. R. G. Skrynnikov, 'Oprichninyi razgrom Novgoroda' in N.E. Nosov *et al* (eds), *Krestianstvo i klassovaia borba v feodalnoi Rossii* (Moscow-Leningrad, 1967) pp. 157–71. See more generally his *Nachalo oprichniny* (Leningrad, 1966), and *Oprichninyi terror* (Leningrad, 1969). A near-contemporary English visitor put the figure at 700,000; see Jerome Horsey, in *Rude and Barbarous Kingdom*, ed. Berry and Crummey, p. 269. A. A. Zimin, *Oprichnina Ivana Groznogo* (Moscow, 1964) pp. 301–2, accepts a figure of around 40,000. J. Hook, *The Sack of Rome, 1527* (London, 1972) pp. 177–80, suggests that half the population (that is, up to 30,000) were lost from Rome through death or flight. In a wider comparative light, the *oprichnina* has been compared in a textbook with the Castillian *Santa Hermandad*; see P. J. Helm, *History of Europe, 1450–1660* (London, 1961) p. 55.
17. Smirnov, op. cit., p. 104.
18. Quoted in Mazour, op. cit., pp. 68–9.
19. See, for example, S. O. Shmidt, *Stanovlenie*, pp. 129, 260–1.
20. Berry and Crummey, op. cit., pp. 140, 152–3.
21. Platonov, *The Time of Troubles*, pp. 43–4.
22. Ibid., p. 159.
23. J. L. H. Keep, 'The Regime of Filaret, 1619–1633', *Slavonic Review*, vol. 38 (1959–60).
24. Vernadsky, *The Tsardom*, pp. 745–6.
25. See, for example, A. G. Mankov, *Tseny i ikh dvizhenie v russkom gosudarstve XVI veka* (Moscow-Leningrad, 1951) p. 99.
26. Smirnov, op. cit., p. 109.
27. Zernov, *Eastern Christendom: A Study of the Origin and Development of the Eastern Orthodox Church* (London, 1961) p. 140.
28. Ibid., p. 141.
29. Platonov, *Moscow and the West*, p. 23.
30. See, for example, A. I. Klibanov, *Reformatsionnoe dvizhenie v Rossii v XIV-pervoi polovine XVIv* (Moscow, 1960).
31. D. S. Likhachev, *Chelovek v literature drevnei Rusi* (Moscow-Leningrad, 1958) p. 5.
32. Zernov, op. cit., p. 143.

Part Two   Modern Russia: The Tsarist Empire

Ch. 4   The Foundation of the Russian Empire, 1645–1698

1. See T. Aston (ed.), *Crisis in Europe, 1550–1660* (London, 1965).
2. E. N. Williams, *The Ancien Régime in Europe: Government and Society in the Major States, 1648–1789* (London and New York, 1970) p. 17. For an interesting interpretation of the Muscovite variation of this process, see J. L. H. Keep, 'The Muscovite Elite and the Approach to Pluralism', *Slavonic Review*, vol. 48 (1970).
3. V. O. Klyuchevsky, *The Rise of The Romanovs*, p. 258.
4. S. Collins, *The Present State of Russia*, p. 258; G. Miège, *A Relation of Three Embassies to the Great Duke of Muscovie* (London, 1669) pp. 290–5.
5. L. G. Beskrovnyi *et al., Istoriia SSSR*, III, 98; and see P. H. Avrich, *Russian Rebels* (New York, 1972; London, 1973) pp. 118–19.
6. T. Esper, 'Military Self-Sufficiency', pp. 204–5.
7. R. Hellie, *Enserfment and Military Change.*
8. See B. F. Porshnev, *Frantsiia, Angliiskaia Revoliutsiia i Evropeiskaia politika v seredine XVIIv* (Moscow, 1970). In the wider context, see also M. Mancall, *Russia and China: Their Diplomatic Relations to 1728* (Cambridge, Mass., 1971).
9. V. I. Lenin, *Collected Works*, I, 154–5.
10. See, for example, R. H. Fisher, *The Russian Fur Trade, 1550–1700*, University of California Publications in History, vol. 31 (1943).
11. Beskrovnyi *et al.*, op. cit., pp. 28–30.
12. Collins, op. cit., p. 60.
13. See, for example, S. H. Baron, 'The Weber Thesis and the failure of Capitalist Development in ' "Early Modern" Russia', *Jahrbücher für Geschichte Osteuropas*, Neue Folge, Band 18 (1970); R. O. Crummey, *The Old Believers and the World of Antichrist: The Vyg Community and the Russian State, 1694–1855* (Madison, Wis., and London, 1970) pp. 135–7; Gerschenkron, *Europe in the Russian Mirror*, pp. 11–47.
14. Olearius, *The Travels*, pp. 139, 159, 160.
15. Crummey, *The Old Believers*, p. 16. See also M. Cherniavsky, 'The Old Believers and the New Religion', *Slavic Review*, vol. 25 (1966).
16. Crummey, op. cit., p. 10.
17. P. Pascal, *Avvakum et les débuts du raskol* (Paris, 1938) pp. xx–xxv; C. B. H. Cant, 'The Archpriest Avvakum and his Scottish Contemporaries', *Slavonic Review*, vol. 44 (1965–6).
18. See, for example, L. W. Lewitter, 'Poland, the Ukraine and Russia in the 17th Century', *Slavonic Review*, vol. 27 (1948–9).
19. See A. M. Panchenko, *Russkaia stikhotvornaia kultura XVII veka* (Leningrad, 1973); A. N. Robinson (ed.), *Russkaia literatura na rubezhe dvukh epokh XVII-nachala XVIIIv* (Moscow, 1971).
20. Foy de la Neuville, *Relation curieuse et nouvelle de Moscovie* (The Hague, 1699) pp. 175–7.

Ch. 5   The Completion of the Structure, 1698–1761

1. See R. Zguta, 'Peter I's "Most Drunken Synod of Fools and Jesters" ', *Jahrubücher für Geschichte Osteuropas*, Band 21 (1973); Zguta believes that Peter's merry pranks should not be taken too seriously.
2. Cracraft, *The Church Reform*, pp. 14, 21.
3. Quoted in Beskrovnyi, *Istoriia SSSR*, III, 249.
4. Ibid., pp. 249–50.
5. F. M. A. de Voltaire, *The History of the Russian Empire under Peter the Great*, English trans. (London, 1837) p. 324.
6. On Menshikov's subsequent trial, see R. V. Ovchinnikov (ed.), 'Krushenie poluderzhavnogo vlastelina' (dokumenty sledstvennogo dela kniazia A. D. Menshikova), *Voprosy istorii*, no. 9 (1970).
7. For documents concerning the accession of Anna, see Raeff, *Plans*, pp. 41–52.
8. V. Ulanov, 'XVII vek i reforma Petra Velikogo', *Tri veka*, III, 14.
9. See Raeff, *Origins*, p. 42.
10. Quoted in Beskroynyi, op. cit., III, 253; see also S. M. Troitskii, 'Istoriografiia "dvortsovykh perevorotov" v Rossii XVIIIv', *Voprosy istorii*, no. 2 (1966).
11. Beskrovnyi, op. cit., III, 294. For Avrich's verdict, see *Russian Rebels*, pp. 174–7.
12. For the long process of incorporation which contributed to the rising, see A. S. Donnelly, *The Russian Conquest of Bashkiria, 1522–1740: A Case Study in Imperialism* (New Haven, Conn., 1968).
13. H. H. Kaplan, *Russia and the Outbreak of the Seven Years War* (Cambridge and Berkeley, Cal., 1968); for a patriotic Soviet view, see N. Korobkov, *Semiletniaia voina, 1756–1762gg* (Moscow, 1940).
14. R. Portal, *L'Ourale au XVIIIe siècle* (Paris, 1950); A. Kahan, 'Continuity in Economic Activity and Policy during the Post-Petrine Period in Russia', *J. of Economic History*, vol. 25 (1965); Blum, *Lord and Peasant*, p. 294.
15. Anon., 'The Interest of Great Britain in Supplying Herself with Iron', *J. of the Iron and Steel Institute*, vol. 2 (1885).
16. See D. K. Reading, *The Anglo-Russian Commercial Treaty of 1734* (London and New Haven, Conn., 1938).
17. B. B. Kafengauz, *Ocherki vnutrennego rynka Rossii pervoi poloviny XVIII veka* (Moscow, 1958).
18. See V. Boss, *Newton and Russia: The Early Influence, 1698–1796* (Cambridge, Mass., and London 1972); and, for example, D. Willemse, *Antonio Nunes Rubeiro, élève de Boerhaave, et son importance pour la Russie* (Leyden, 1966).
19. See A. D. Liublinskaia (ed.), *Russkii diplomat vo Frantsii: Zapiski Andreia Matveeva* (Leningrad, 1966).
20. Miliukov, *Outlines*, I, 130.
21. Cracraft, op. cit., p. 267.

Ch. 6   Enlightened Absolutism, 1761–1801

1. Kheraskov, quoted in Kliuchevskii, *Sochineniia*, IV, 202.
2. Catherine II, *Memoirs*, trans. K. Anthony (New York, 1935) p. 264.

3. P. Petschauer, 'Catherine the Great's Conversion of 1744', *Jahrbücher für Geschichte Osteuropas*, Band 20 (1972).
4. Kliuchevskii, *Sochineniia*, v, 309–71.
5. I. A. Fedosov, 'Prosveshchennyi absoliutizm v Rossii', *Voprosy istorii*, no. 9 (1970) p. 38.
6. Ibid., p. 52; Florinsky, *Russia*, pp. 607–13; and *Canadian-American Slavic Studies*, vol. 7 (1973).
7. R. Portal, 'The Industrialisation of Russia', in *The Cambridge Economic History of Europe*, vol. 6, ed. H. J. Habbakuk and M. Postan (1966) p. 802.
8. Kliuchevskii, op. cit., VIII, 277; M. Raeff, 'The Domestic Policies of Peter III and His Overthrow', *American Historical Review*, vol. 75 (1969–70) p. 1302.
9. Quoted in Alexander, *Autocratic Politics*, p. 89.
10. Florinsky, *Russia*, pp. 612–13.
11. Dukes, *Catherine the Great*, p. 55.
12. A. W. Fisher, *The Russian Annexation of the Crimea, 1772–1783* (Cambridge, 1970); M. S. Anderson, 'The Great Powers and the Russian Annexation of the Crimea, 1783–1784', *Slavonic Review*, vol. 37 (1958).
13. J. T. Alexander, 'Recent Soviet Historiography on the Pugachev Revolt: A Review Article', *Canadian-American Slavic Studies*, vol. 4 (1970) p. 617. See also Alexander, *Autocratic Politics*; Avrich, *Russian Rebels*, pp. 246–54; P. Longworth, 'The Last Great Cossack Rising', *J. of European Studies*, vol. 3 (1970); M. Raeff, 'Pugachev's Rebellion', in *Preconditions of Revolution in Early Modern Europe*, ed. R. Foster and J. Greene (Baltimore, Maryland, 1970). For some Soviet views, see contributions by A. L. Shapiro and A. P. Pronshtein to *Soviet Studies in History*, vols 5 and 6 (1966–8).
14. I. de Madariaga, *Britain, Russia and the Armed Neutrality of 1780: Sir James Harris's Mission to St Petersburg during the American Revolution* (New Haven, Conn., and London, 1962); N. N. Bolkhovitinov, 'Russian Diplomacy and the American War for Independence of 1775–83', *Soviet Studies in History*, vol. 3 (1964–5); D. M. Griffiths, 'Nikita Panin, Russian Diplomacy, and the American Revolution', *Slavic Review*, vol. 28 (1969).
15. See P. Longworth, *The Art of Victory: The Life and Achievements of Generalissimo Suvorov, 1729–1800* (London, 1965).
16. See H. H. Kaplan, *The First Partition of Poland* (New York, 1962); L. R. Lewitter, 'The Partitions of Poland', *New Cambridge Modern History*, vol. 8 (1965); R. H. Lord, *The Second Partition of Poland: A Study in Diplomatic History* (Cambridge, Mass., 1915); R. H. Lord, 'The Third Partition of Poland', *Slavonic Review*, vol. 3 (1924–5); Smirnov, *Short History*, p. 184.
17. N. E. Saul, *Russia and the Mediterranean, 1797–1807* (Chicago and London, 1970) pp. 32–9.
18. Dukes, op. cit., pp. 93–9.
19. See M. Confino, *Domaines et seigneurs en Russie vers la fin du XVIIIe siècle: Etude de structures agraires et de mentalités économiques* (Paris, 1963); A. Kahan, 'The Costs of Westernisation in Russia: The Gentry

and the Economy in the Eighteenth Century', *Slavic Review*, vol. 25 (1966); N. L. Rubinshtein, *Selskoe khoziaistvo Rossii vo vtoroi polovine XVIIIv* (Moscow, 1957).

20. Hansard's *Parliamentary History of England* (London, 1913) XVII, 1142, 1137. See more generally Blum, *Lord and Peasant*, pp. 293–5; Beskrovnyi, op. cit. III, pp. 407–10.
21. See A. W. Crosby Jr, *America, Russia, Hemp and Napoleon: American Trade with Russia and the Baltic, 1783–1812* (Columbus, Ohio, 1965).
22. P. N. Miliukov, *Ocherki po istorii russkoi kultury* (Paris, 1937) III, 369ff.
23. Dukes, op. cit., pp. 189–93.
24. Miliukov, *Ocherki*, II, 75–8.
25. Dukes, op. cit., pp. 241–5.
26. A. V. Kokorev, *Khrestomatiia po russkoi literature XVIII veka* (Moscow 1961).
27. M. M. Shtrange, *Demokraticheskaia intelligentsiia Rossii v XVIII veke* (Moscow, 1965).
28. McConnell, *A Russian Philosophe*, p. 208.
29. See A. Lentin (ed. and trans.), *M. M. Shcherbatov*; 'On the Corruption of Morals in Russia' (Cambridge, 1969).
30. A. G. Cross, *N. M. Karamzin: A Study of his Literary Career, 1783–1803* (Carbondale, Ill., 1971); H. M. Nebel, *N. M. Karamzin: A Russian Sentimentalist* (The Hague, 1967).
31. N. N. Bolkhovitinov, 'Beginnings of the Establishment of Scientific and Cultural Relations between America and Russia', *Soviet Studies in History*, vol. 5 (1966–7).
32. W. Guthrie, *A New System of Modern Geography* . . . (London, 1782) p. 118.
33. A. W. Fisher, 'Enlightened Despotism and Islam under Catherine II', *Slavic Review*, vol. 27 (1968); Iu. Ia. Kogan et al., in Smirnov, *Tserkov v istorii Rossii*, pp. 203–5.
34. See P. Dukes, 'Russia and the Eighteenth-Century Revolution', *History*, vol. 56 (1971); K. E. Dzhedzhula, *Rossiia i Velikaia Frantsuskaia Burzhuaznaia Revoliutsiia* (Kiev, 1973); K. A. Papmehl, *Freedom of Expression in Eighteenth-Century Russia* (The Hague, 1971).

Ch. 7   Russian Nationalism, 1801–1855

1. A. P. Bazhova et al., *Istoriia S. SSR*, IV, 11.
2. A. McConnell, 'Alexander I's Hundred Days: The Politics of a Paternalist Reformer', *Slavic Review*, vol. 28 (1969) pp. 375–6.
3. Kliuchevskii, *Sochineniia*, V, 263–4.
4. Bazhova, op. cit., IV, 259–60.
5. McConnell, *Tsar Alexander I*, p. 21.
6. Bazhova, op. cit., IV, 69.
7. Raeff, *Michael Speransky*.
8. Bazhova, op. cit., IV, 168.
9. Ibid., p. 161.
10. McConnell, *Tsar Alexander I*, p. 143.
11. Bazhova, op. cit., IV, 172. For a less critical view, see R. E. Pipes, 'The

Russian Military Colonies, 1810–1831', *J. of Modern History*, vol. 22 (1950).

12. I de Madariaga, 'Spain and the Decembrists', *European Studies Review*, vol. 3 (1973).

13. Raeff, *The Decembrist Movement*, pp. 155, 121. On Pestel, see also A. E. Adams, 'The Character of Pestel's Thought', *Slavic Review*, vol. 12 (1953); contrast catechism with page 119 above.

14. Bazhova, op. cit., IV, 216–17.

15. Ibid., p. 258.

16. H. J. Törke, 'Continuity and Change in the Relations between Bureaucracy and Society in Russia, 1613–1861', *Canadian-American Slavic Studies*, vol. 5 (1971), and in colloquium with J. Keep, vol. 6 (1972). See also W. B. Lincoln, 'The Genesis of an "Enlightened Bureaucracy" in Russia, 1825–1856', *Jahrbücher für Geschichte Osteuropas*, Band 20 (1972); J. T. Flynn, 'The Universities of the Gentry, and the Russian Imperial Services, 1815–1825', *Canadian–American Slavic Studies*, vol. 2 (1968); W. McK. Pintner, 'The Social Characteristics of the Early Nineteenth-Century Russian Bureaucracy', *Slavic Review*, vol. 29 (1970).

17. See the works by Monas and Squire listed in the Bibliography to this chapter.

18. Bazhova, op. cit., IV, 300–6.

19. Florinsky, *Russia*, pp. 851–4.

20. Curtiss, *The Russian Army*, p. 112. See more generally L. G. Beskrovnyi, *Russkaia armiia i flot v XIX veke: voenno-ekonomicheskii potentsial Rossii* (Moscow, 1973).

21. Smirnov, *Short History*, pp. 191–2.

22. See M. Raeff, *Siberia and the Reforms of 1822* (Seattle, Wash., 1956).

23. See R. F. Leslie, *Polish Politics and the Revolution of November 1830* (London, 1956; Westport, Conn., 1973).

24. See V. J. Puryear, *Napoleon and the Dardanelles* (Berkeley, Calif., 1951).

25. C. von Clausewitz, *The Campaign of 1812 in Russia* (London, 1843) p. 142.

26. B. Hollingsworth, 'The Napoleonic Invasion of Russia and Recent Soviet Historical Writing', *J. of Modern History*, vol. 38 (1966); M. Raeff, 'The 150th Anniversary of the Campaign of 1812 in Soviet Historical Writing', *Jahrbücher für Geschichte Osteuropas*, Band 16 (1964). On the burning of Moscow in particular, see V. M. Kholodovskii, 'Napoleon li podzheg Moskvu?', *Voprosy istorii*, no. 4 (1966).

27. P. K. Grimsted, *The Foreign Ministers of Alexander I: Political Attitudes and the Conduct of Russian Diplomacy, 1801–1825* (Berkeley, Calif., 1971).

28. N. S. Kiniapina, *Vneshniaia politika Rossii pervoipoloviny XIX veka* (Moscow, 1963) p. 244; qualified agreement with Kiniapina would be found in V. J. Puryear, *International Economics and Diplomacy in the Near East, 1834–53* (Stanford, Calif., 1935). For other views, see J. H. Gleason, *The Genesis of Russophobia in Great Britain: A Study of the Interaction of Policy and Opinion* (Cambridge, Mass., 1950); G. B. Henderson, *Crimean War Diplomacy and Other Historical Essays* (Glasgow, 1947; New York, 1973).

29. Quoted in Smirnov, op. cit., p. 215.
30. See W. E. Mosse, *The Rise and Fall of the Crimean System, 1855–1871* (London, 1963).
31. Blackwell, *The Beginnings*, p. 3.
32. See W. McK. Pintner, *Russian Economic Policy*, pp. 184ff.
33. See N. M. Druzhinin, *Gosudarstvennye krestiane i reforma P. D. Kiseleva*, 2 vols (Moscow-Leningrad, 1946 and 1958). Most of the figures and much of the information in this section are taken from the contributions by Druzhinin and P. G. Ryndziunskii to Bazhova, op. cit., IV.
34. Riasanovsky, *A History*, p. 399.
35. Smirnov, op. cit., p. 207.
36. R. E. McGrew, *Russia and the Cholera, 1823–32* (Madison, Wis., 1965).
37. Smirnov, op. cit., p. 207.
38. See H. E. Bowman, *Vissarion Belinsky, 1811–1848: A Study in the Origins of Social Criticism in Russia* (Cambridge, Mass., 1954); M. Malia, *Alexander Herzen and the Birth of Russian Socialism, 1812–1855* (Cambridge, Mass., 1961).
39. Bazhova, op. cit., IV, 333–8. For Western views, see Riasanovsky, *Russia and the West*; P. K. Christoff, *An Introduction to Nineteenth-Century Slavophilism: A Study of Ideas* (The Hague, 1961–   ).

Ch.8   The Emancipation, and After, 1855–1894

1. F. Venturi, *Roots of Revolution*, p. 215.
2. S. B. Okun and K. V. Sivkov (eds), *Krestianskoe dvizhenie v Rossii v 1857 – mae 1861gg: sbornik dokumentov* (Moscow, 1963) pp. 364–5.
3. Mosse, *Alexander II*, p. 34.
4. S. S. Volk *et al.*, *Istoriia SSSR*, V, 355.
5. Ibid., p. 11.
6. Mosse, op. cit., pp. 178–9. See also A. J. Rieber, 'Alexander II: A Revisionist View', *J. of Modern History*, vol. 43 (1971).
7. Cited by C. C. Adler Jr, *Canadian–American Slavic Studies*, vol. 3 (1969) p. 386.
8. Ibid., pp. 392–6.
9. Volk, op. cit., V, 95.
10. Quoted in ibid., p. 100. For George Fischer's views, see his *Russian Liberalism: From Gentry to Intelligentsia* (Cambridge, Mass., 1958); and see Starr, *Decentralization*, pp. 352–4.
11. Cited by R. Wortman, *Canadian–American Slavic Studies*, vol. 3 (1969) p. 231.
12. Riasanovsky, *A History*, p. 418.
13. Volk, op. cit., V., 108.
14. P. von Wahlde, in *Canadian–American Slavic Studies*, vol. 3 (1969) p. 132.
15. Florinsky, *Russia*, p. 909; Miller, *Dmitrii Miliutin*, p. 230.
16. Lenin, quoted in Volk, op. cit., V, 116.
17. Volk, op. cit., V. 350.
18. Ibid., p. 357.
19. Quoted by C. C. Adler Jr, op. cit., p. 398.
20. See page 151 above.

21. Volk, op. cit., v, 359.
22. Ibid., p. 360.
23. Ibid., p. 363.
24. Ibid., p. 364.
25. Florinsky, op. cit., p. 1095.
26. R. K. I. Quested, *The Expansion of Russia in East Asia, 1857–1860* (Kuala Lumpur, 1968); and see more generally Lensen, *Russia's Eastward Expansion.*
27. D. Mackenzie, *Canadian–American Slavic Studies*, vol. 3 (1969) p. 310. For fuller discussion, see S. Becker, *Russia's Protectorates in Central Asia: Bukhara and Khiva* (Cambridge, Mass., 1968); N. A. Khalfin, *Russia's Policy in Central Asia, 1857–1868* (London, 1964) – an abridged translation of a Soviet work; and R. A. Pierce, *Russian Central Asia, 1857–1917: A Study in Colonial Rule* (Berkeley, Calif., 1960).
28. *Correspondence Respecting Central Asia*, C. 704. H.M. Stationery Office (London, 1873) pp. 72–5.
29. R. F. Leslie, *Reform and Insurrection in Russian Poland, 1856–65* (London and New York, 1963).
30. Smirnov, *Short History*, p. 237; and among the many other works, see W. E. Mosse, *The Rise and Fall of the Crimean System, 1855–1871* (London, 1963); M. B. Petrovich, *The Emergence of Russian Panslavism, 1856–1870* (New York, 1956); and B. H. Sumner, *Russia and the Balkans, 1870–1880* (Oxford, 1937).
31. A. J. Rieber (ed.), *The Politics of Autocracy: Letters of Alexander II to Prince A. I. Bariatinsky, 1857–1864* (The Hague, 1964); in his introduction, Rieber argues that 'military reform provided the decisive impetus for freeing the serfs'.
32. Dmytryshyn, *Imperial Russia*, p. 225.
33. Volk, op. cit., v, 51.
34. H. Willetts, in Katkov et al., *Russia Enters the Twentieth Century*, p. 121.
35. O. H. Palmer, *Statement of the Origin, Organization and Progress of the Russian–American Telegraph Western Union Extension, Collins' Overland Line, via Behring Strait and Asiatic Russia to Europe* (Rochester, N.Y., 1866) p. 165.
36. Most of the statistics and information in this section are taken from the contributions by V. K. Iatsunskii to Volk, op. cit., v.
37. Florinsky, op. cit., pp. 1114–15.
38. A Sinel, 'Educating the Russian Peasantry: The Elementary School Reforms of Count D. Tolstoi', *Slavic Review*, vol. 27 (1968); and in *Canadian–American Slavic Studies*, vol. 3 (1969).
39. Quotations from Florinsky, op. cit., pp. 1033, 1036.
40. Smirnov, op. cit., p. 237.
41. For an introduction to these and other individuals, see A. Yarmolinsky, *Road to Revolution* (London, 1957; New York, 1959); E. Wilson, *To the Finland Station* (New York, 1940; London, 1941) and E. Lampart's two books, *Studies in Rebellion* (London and New York, 1957), and *Sons Against Fathers* (Oxford, 1965).
42. Zelnik, *Labor and Society*, p. 370.

43. See Wortman, *The Crisis of Russian Populism.*
44. Richard Pipes argues that the connection was not really made even then; see his *Social Democracy and the St Petersburg Labor Movement.* For a Soviet criticism of this book, see R. A. Kazakevich and F. M. Suslova, *Mister Paips falsifitsiruet istoriiu* (Leningrad, 1966). On Plekhanov, see the analytical biography *Plekhanov: The Father of Russian Marxism,* by S. H. Baron (London and Stanford, Calif., 1963).
45. On the liberals, see note 10 of this chapter, and J. Walkin, *The Rise of Democracy in Pre-Revolutionary Russia: Political and Social Institutions under the Last Three Tsars* (New York, 1962).
46. See the thorough study by R. F. Byrnes, *Pobedonostsev* and also K. F. Pobyedonosteff, *Reflections of a Russian Statesman* (London, 1898).
47. P. A. Zaionchkovskii, *Rossiiskoe samoderzhavie v kontse XIX stoletiia* (Moscow, 1970) pp. 435-6. For Zaionchkovskii's authoritative interpretation of this whole period, see also among his many works *Otmena krepostnogo prava v Rossii* (Moscow, 1968) and *Krizis samoderzhaviia na rubezhe 1870-1880kh godov* (Moscow, 1964).

Ch. 9   Russian Imperialism, 1894-1917

1. V. I. Lenin, *Imperialism: The Highest Stage of Capitalism* (Moscow, 1970) p. 86.
2. A. L. Sidorov *et al., Istoriia SSSR,* VI, 7-15.
3. See T. G. Stavrou's introduction to his *Russia under the Last Tsar.*
4. A most readable version of such an interpretation is R. K. Massie, *Nicholas and Alexandra* (London and New York, 1968).
5. Trotsky, *History of the Russian Revolution,* pp. 112-30.
6. Smirnov, *Short History,* p. 264.
7. For a sympathetic portrait of Rasputin, see his daughter's biography: M. Rasputin, *My Father* (London and New Hyde Park, N.Y., 1934).
8. Smirnov, op. cit., p. 326.
9. Florinsky, *Russia,* p. 1147.
10. See G. Hough, *The Fleet that Had to Die* (London and New York, 1958); and more widely J. A. White, *The Diplomacy of the Russo-Japanese War* (Princeton, N.J., 1964).
11. *The Memoirs of Count Witte* (London and New York, 1921) p. 250; considerably abridged, this version must be used with care.
12. Sidorov, op. cit., VI, 251.
13. Dmytryshyn, *Imperial Russia,* p. 309.
14. Smirnov, op. cit., p. 278.
15. Mehlinger and Thompson, *Count Witte,* pp. 32-3.
16. L. D. Trotsky, *1905* (New York, 1971; London, 1972) p. 117.
17. Florinsky, *Russia,* p. 1183; Keep, *The Rise,* p. 278; I. Spector, *The First Russian Revolution: Its Impact on Asia* (Englewood Cliffs, N.J., 1962).
18. On the right-wing radicals, see E. Oberländer, 'The All-Russian Fascist Party', *J. of Contemporary History,* vol. 1 (1966); and H. Rogger, 'Was there a Russian Fascism', *J. of Modern History,* vol. 36 (1964).
19. See R. L. Tuck, 'Paul Miliukov and the Negotiations for a Duma Ministry', *Slavic Review,* vol. 10 (1951).

H.R.—12*

20. A. Ia. Avrekh, *Stolypin i treteiunskaia sistema* (Moscow, 1966). Hosking, *The Russian Constitutional Experiment* 'has much in common with Avrekh's work' (see p. 250, from Hosking's useful 'A Note on Historiography and Sources').

21. Avrekh, op. cit., p. 14.

22. *Vekhi* has been translated in *Canadian–American Slavic Studies*, vols 2 and 3 (1968–9). For a scholarly analysis, see L. Schapiro, 'The Vekhi Group and the Mystique of Revolution', *Slavonic Review*, vol. 34 (1955).

23. Western writing on Stolypin includes M. S. Conroy, 'Stolypin's Attitude Towards Local Self-Government', *Slavonic Review*, vol. 46 (1968); G. A. Hosking, 'Stolypin and the Octobrist Party', *Slavonic Review*, vol. 47 (1969); A. Levin, 'P. A. Stolypin: A Political Reappraisal', *J. of Modern History*, vol. 37 (1965); L. I. Strakhovsky, 'The Statesmanship of Peter Stolypin: A Reappraisal', *Slavonic Review*, vol. 37 (1959); and G. Tokmakoff, 'P. A. Stolypin and the Second Duma', *Slavonic Review*, vol. 50 (1972).

24. See G. Tokmakoff, 'Stolypin's Assassin', *Slavic Review*, vol. 24 (1965). For a summary of a different verdict, see Hosking, *The Russian Constitutional Experiment*, pp. 148–9.

25. Avrekh, op. cit., pp. 38–9. See also J. F. Hutchinson, 'The Octobrists and the Future of Imperial Russia as a Great Power', *Slavonic Review*, vol. 50 (1972).

26. Avrekh, op. cit., p. 56; Hosking, op. cit., pp. 106, 113. Miliukov, whose emphasis was on the constitution rather than the nation, admired not only the British system of government, but also the American; see his *Russia and Its Crisis* (New York, 1962), a reprint of his lectures first given at the University of Chicago in 1903.

27. Avrekh, op. cit., p. 57.

28. Ibid., p. 169. See also V. N. Kokovstov, *Out of My Past* (Stanford, Calif., 1935).

29. For a Western view, see T. Riha, 'Miliukov and the Progressive Bloc in 1915: A Study in Last-Chance Politics', *J. of Modern History*, vol. 32 (1960); and see also A. N. Iakhontov, *Prologue to Revolution: Notes . . . on the Secret Meetings of the Council of Ministers, 1915*, edited by M. Cherniavsky (Englewood Cliffs, N.J., 1967).

30. L. Haimson, 'The Problem of Social Stability in Urban Russia, 1905–1917', *Slavic Review*, vols 23 and 24 (1964–5). The discussion begun by Haimson is continued by other experts.

31. See Riha's contribution to Stavrou, *Russia under the Last Tsar*.

32. Smirnov, op. cit., pp. 293–5.

33. E. D. Sokol, *The Revolt of 1916 in Russian Central Asia* (Baltimore, Maryland, 1954) p. 158.

34. Smirnov, op. cit., p. 315; Dmytryshyn, op. cit. p. 372.

35. A. J. P. Taylor, *War by Timetable* (London, 1969).

36. See the discussion in H. W. Koch (ed.), *The Origins of the First World War: Great Power Rivalry and German War Aims* (London, 1972; New York, 1973).

37. C. Jay Smith, *The Russian Struggle for Power, 1914–17: A Study of Russian Foreign Policy during the First World War* (New York, 1956); E. C. Thaden, *Russia and the Balkan Alliance of 1912* (University Park, Pa., 1965).
38. L. C. F. Turner, 'The Russian Mobilization in 1914', *J. of Contemporary History*, vol. 3 (1968).
39. I. V. Bestuzhev, 'Russian Foreign Policy, February–June 1914', *J. of Contemporary History*, vol. 1 (1966); Smirnov, op. cit., pp. 315–17.
40. Smirnov, op. cit., p. 320.
41. Sidorov, op. cit., vi, 318; P. Pipes, *The Formation of the Soviet Union, 1917–1923* (Cambridge, Mass., 1957) pp. 1–2.
42. W. E. Mosse, 'Stolypin's Villages', *Slavonic Review*, vol. 43 (1965) p. 268; G. Tokmakoff, 'Stolypin's Agrarian Reform: An Appraisal', *Russian Review*, vol. 30 (1971) p. 138.
43. Von Laue, *Sergei Witte*, p. 306; Smirnov, op. cit., p. 261.
44. Sidorov, op. cit., vi, 260–4. Using somewhat different figures, J. P. McKay, *Pioneers for Profit: Foreign Entrepreneurship and Russian Industrialization, 1885–1913* (Chicago, Ill., 1970), argues that the Russian experience proved that a developing country could surmount the problem of dependence on foreign capital. B. B. Ananich, *Rossiia i mezhdunarodnyi kapital, 1897–1914* (Leningrad, 1970) is among those who would not agree.
45. Sidorov, op. cit., vi, 269. Most of the figures and information in this section are taken from the same volume.
46. Baedeker's *Handbook for Travellers: Russia* (Leipzig, London and New York, 1914) p. xxv.
47. R. Ropponen, *Die Kraft Russlands: Wie beurteilte die politische und militärische Führung der europäischen Grossmächte in der Zeit von 1905 bis 1914 die Kraft Russlands* (Helsinki, 1968); Ropponen argues that Russia's strength appeared to her prospective allies and opponents to have recovered in several respects if by no means in all on the eve of the First World War.
48. See the contributions to the Carnegie Series on Russia in the First World War by A. N. Antsiferov, A. M. Michelson, B. E. Nolde, P. B. Struve and S. O. Zagorsky (New Haven, Conn., 1928–33).
49. See von Laue's contribution to Stavrou, op. cit.; Gerschenkron, 'Agrarian Policies and Industrialization: Russia, 1861–1917', *Cambridge Economic History of Europe*, vol. 6 (1966).
50. Karpovich, *Imperial Russia*, quoted in Adams, *Imperial Russia*, p. 87.
51. Sidorov, op. cit., vi, 717.
52. Baedeker's *Handbook*, op. cit., pp. 54, 91–2, 271–2, 377, 394, 466.
53. Sidorov, op. cit., vi, 729. Lenin's 'pessimistic' view may be placed against that of a moderate and informed optimist, T. Darlington, *Education in Russia* (London, 1909).
54. Florinsky, op. cit., p. 1233; Sidorov, op. cit., vi, 728–9.
55. Sidorov, op. cit., vi, 730.
56. Ibid., pp. 739–40.
57. See G. Struve's contribution to Stavrou, op. cit.
58. Avrekh, op. cit., p. 15.

59. Smirnov, op. cit., p. 309.
60. See C. Gray, *The Great Experiment: Russian Art, 1863–1922* (London, 1962) pp. 61–2.

Part Three   Contemporary Russia: The Soviet Union

Introduction
1. Samsonov, *Short History*, p. 7.

Ch. 10   The Russian Revolution, 1917–1921
1. G. Z. Ioffe, *Fevralskaia revoliutsiia 1917g v anglo-amerikanskoi bur-zhuanznoi istoriografii* (Moscow, 1970) p. 54. For a Western analysis, see J. H. Billington, 'Six Views of the Russian Revolution', *World Politics*, vol. 18 (1965–6); see also M. M. Karpovich, 'The Russian Revolution of 1917', *J. of Modern History*, vol. 2 (1930), and H. J. Ellison, 'Soviet Historians and the Russian Revolution', in *Russia: Essays in History and Literature*, ed. L. H. Legters (Leiden, 1972).
2. See, for example, Katkov, *Russia 1917*.
3. E. N. Burdzhalov, *Vtoraia russkaia revoliutsiia: Vosstanie v Petrograde* (Moscow, 1971), and *Vtoraia russkaia revoliutsiia: Moskva, front, periferiia* (Moscow, 1971) is the best Soviet account.
4. F. A. Golder (trans. and ed.), *Documents of Russian History, 1914–1917* (Gloucester, Mass., 1964) pp. 308–9.
5. Florinsky, *Russia*, p. 1384.
6. Ibid., p. 1387.
7. Trotsky, *The History*, p. 291. See also J. R. Boyd, 'The Origins of Order No. 1', *Soviet Studies*, vol. 19 (1967–8).
8. Wade, *The Russian Search*, pp. 47–8; V. S. Vasiukov, *Vneshniaia politika vremennogo pravitelstva* (Moscow, 1966) pp. 85–133.
9. Samsonov, *Short History*, p. 12. For the situation of the Bolsheviks before Lenin's arrival, see D. A. Longley, 'The Divisions in the Bolshevik Party in March 1917', *Soviet Studies*, vol. 24 (1972–3).
10. M. Ferro, 'Pourquoi février? Pourquoi octobre?', *Annales: économies, societés, civilisations*, no. 1 (1968) p. 47.
11. K. Paustovsky, *In That Dawn* (London, 1967) pp. 45–6.
12. Rabinowitch, *Prelude to Revolution*, p. 188; Trotsky, op. cit., p. 574. For a Soviet view, see O. N. Znamenskii, *Iulskii krizis 1917 goda* (Moscow–Leningrad, 1967).
13. Florinsky, op. cit., p. 1434.
14. Trotsky, op. cit., pp. 646–68, 711–28; H. Asher, 'The Kornilov Affair: A Reinterpretation', *Russian Review*, vol. 29 (1970); L. I. Strakhovsky, 'Was there a Kornilov Rebellion?', *Slavonic Review*, vol. 33 (1955); J. D. White, 'The Kornilov Affair: A Study in Counter-Revolution', *Soviet Studies*, vol. 20 (1968–9): J. D. White, intro. to 'A Document on the Kornilov Affair', *Soviet Studies*, vol. 25 (1973); N. Ia. Ivanov, *Kornilovshchina i ee razgrom* (Leningrad, 1965).
15. Ferro, *The Russian Revolution*, p. 271.
16. Trotsky, op. cit., p. 883. See also Owen, *The Russian Peasant Move-*

ment, p. 178; Ia. A. Iakovlev (ed.), *1917 god v derevne* (Moscow, 1967); J. Keep, 'October in the Provinces', in *Revolutionary Russia*, ed. R. E. Pipes (Cambridge, Mass., 1968).

17. Pipes, *The Formation of the Soviet Union*, pp. 51, 93–8.
18. N. N. Golovin, *The Russian Army in the World War* (New Haven, Conn., 1931) p. 262; Trotsky, op. cit., p. 282.
19. On the situation in the navy, see D. A. Longley, 'Officers and Men', *Soviet Studies*, vol. 25 (1973).
20. On marks and dollars, see E. Sissons, *100 Red Days* (New Haven, Conn., 1931). On marks, see M. Futrell, *Northern Underground: Episodes of Russian Revolutionary Transport through Scandinavia, 1863–1917* (London and West Orange, N.J., 1963); and Z. A. B. Zeman (ed.), *Germany and the Revolutions in Russia, 1915–1918: Documents from the Archives of the German Foreign Ministry* (London, 1968). The subject of German money is still controversial.
21. See also L. Kochan, 'Kadet Policy in 1917 and the Constituent Assembly', *Slavonic Review*, vol. 45 (1967).
22. K. Marx and F. Engels, *Manifesto of the Communist Party* (Moscow, 1969) pp. 96, 12.
23. John Reed, *Ten Days that Shook the World* (reprint Harmondsworth and New York, 1966) p. 129.
24. F. D. Volkov, *Krakh angliiskoi politiki interventsii i diplomaticheskoi izoliatsii sovetskogo gosudarstva, 1917–1924gg* (Moscow, 1954) pp. 39–40.
25. See R. G. Suny, *The Baku Commune, 1917–1918: Class and Nationality in the Russian Revolution* (Princeton, N.J., 1972).
26. Fischer, *The Life of Lenin*, p. 330.
27. J. Erickson, 'Lenin as Civil War Leader', in *Lenin*, ed. Schapiro and Reddaway.
28. Chamberlin, *The Russian Revolution*, II, 493.
29. See, for example, J. S. Reshetar, *The Ukrainian Revolution, 1917–1920: A Study in Nationalism* (Princeton, N.J., 1952); F. Kazamzadeh, *The Struggle for Transcaucasia, 1917–1921* (New York, 1951).

Ch. 11   The Consolidation of the Soviet Union, 1917–1929

1. A. Ransome, *Six Weeks in Russia in 1919* (London, 1919) pp. 81–2; and see W. Mandel, 'Arthur Ransome: Eyewitness in Russia, 1919', *Slavic Review*, vol. 27 (1968).
2. Schapiro and Reddaway (eds), *Lenin*, pp. 18, 20.
3. I. I. Mints *et al* (eds), *Istoriia SSSR*, VII, 709–12.
4. Carr, *The Bolshevik Revolution*, I, 238–56, including previous quotations from Engels and Lenin.
5. Ibid., III, 28.
6. See J. Wheeler-Bennett, *Brest-Litovsk: The Forgotten Peace* (London, 1934; New York, 1971).
7. Carr, op. cit., I, 123; and see page 221 above. For a different view, see O. H. Radkey, *The Election to the Russian Constituent Assembly of 1917* (Cambridge, Mass., 1950).
8. Carr, op. cit., I, 414–35.

9. See Avrich, *Kronstadt*; R. V. Daniels, 'The Kronstadt Revolt of 1921: A Study in the Dynamics of Revolution', *Slavic Review*, vol. 10 (1951); E. Mawdsley, 'The Baltic Fleet and the Kronstadt Mutiny', *Soviet Studies*, vol. 24 (1973).

10. See Lenin, *Collected Works*, XXXII, 257–82.

11. See the works by J. M. Thompson and A. J. Mayer cited in the Bibliography to this chapter.

12. Samsonov, *Short History*, p. 124.

13. W. E. Mosse, 'Makers of the Soviet Union', *Slavonic Review*, vol. 46 (1968).

14. Samsonov, op. cit., p. 125.

15. Carr, *What Is History?*, pp. 98, 102.

16. Carr, *The Interregnum*, pp. 354–5.

17. R. Portal, 'The Industrialisation of Russia', *Cambridge Economic History of Europe*, VI, 865; T. H. von Laue, 'A Secret Memorandum of Sergei Witte on the Industrialisation of Imperial Russia', *J. of Modern History*, vol. 26 (1954).

18. Carr, *Bolshevik Revolution*, II, 370.

19. Portal, op. cit., 869.

20. Carr, *Bolshevik Revolution*, II, 278.

21. Ibid., p. 315.

22. A. V. Chayanov, *The Theory of Peasant Economy*, ed. D. Thorner, B. Kerblay and R. E. F. Smith (Homewood, Ill., 1966).

23. E. Preobrazhensky, *The New Economics*, trans. B. Pearce, intro. A. Nove (Oxford, 1965).

24. S. Chase, R. Dunn and R. G. Tugwell, *Soviet Russia in the Second Decade* (New York, 1928).

25. According to A. C. Sutton, *Western Technology and Soviet Economic Development: 1917 to 1930* (Stanford, Calif., 1968), 348, at least 95 per cent of the Soviet industrial structure in the 1920s received Western, mainly German, technological assistance, but such a figure does not appear to have met with general acceptance.

26. Nettl, *The Soviet Achievement*, p. 94.

27. Miliukov, *Outlines*, I, 164.

28. R. F. and M. S. McWilliams, *Russia in 1926* (London and Toronto, 1927) pp. 75–6.

29. Mints, op. cit., VII, 686–7.

30. Iu. A. Poliakov *et al.* (eds), *Istoriia SSR*, VIII, 263–6, 273–4; and see also Fitzpatrick, *The Commissariat*, pp. 26–88.

31. H. Asher, 'The Rise, Fall and Resurrection of M. N. Pokrovsky', *Russian Review*, vol. 31 (1972).

32. Miliukov, op. cit., II, 82, 94.

33. Ibid., III, 82–3, 88, 94, 97–8, 139, 144.

34. Gray, *The Great Experiment: Russian Art, 1863–1922* (London, 1962) p. 7; 'Russian Issue', *The Drama Review*, vol. 17 (1973); Fitzpatrick, op. cit. on Proletkult and the Arts.

35. A. Kollontai, 'The New Woman', *Autobiography of a Sexually Emancipated Woman* (New York, 1971; London, 1972).

36. Lewin, *Russian Peasants*, p. 23.

Ch. 12   The Construction of Soviet Socialism, 1929–1941

1. Carr, *Foundations*, I, xii.
2. Ibid., II, 451.
3. See D. Joravsky's introduction to R. Medvedev's *Let History Judge*, pp. ix–xx.
4. Trotsky, *Stalin*, p. 336, and *The Revolution Betrayed: What Is the Soviet Union and Where Is It Going?*, quoted in Daniels, *The Stalin Revolution*, p. 103.
5. Lewin, *Russian Peasants*, pp. 450–1.
6. Samsonov, *Short History*, pp. 182–3.
7. For the beginnings of this process, see J. Keep, '1917: The Tyranny of Paris over Petrograd', *Soviet Studies*, vol. 20 (1968–9).
8. See, for example, Conquest, *The Great Terror*, pp. 72–96.
9. Deutscher, *Stalin*, pp. 356–7.
10. Stalin, *Works*, XIII, 33–4.
11. Deutscher, op. cit., p. 368.
12. Samsonov, op. cit., p. 179.
13. Rigby, *Communist Party Membership*, pp. 197–235.
14. M. Garder, *A History of the Soviet Army* (London and New York, 1966) pp. 89–92.
15. Samsonov, op. cit., pp. 150–1.
16. Deutscher, op. cit., pp. 324–5; see also M. Lewin, 'Who Was the Soviet *kulak*?', *Soviet Studies*, vol. 18 (1966–7).
17. See R. D. Laird, D. E. Sharp and R. Sturtevant *The Rise and Fall of the MTS as an Instrument of Soviet Rule* (Lawrence, Kansas, 1960).
18. Samsonov, op. cit., p. 152.
19. Deutscher, op. cit., pp. 331–2.
20. Herbert Marshall tells how he became such a specialist solely on the basis of being able to drive a car; see *The Listener*, vol. 89, no. 2295 (1973) p. 364.
21. A. C. Sutton continues to believe that such assistance was all-important, arguing that 'no major technology or major plant under construction between 1930 and 1945 has been identified as a purely Soviet effort'; see his *Western Technology and Soviet Economic Development, 1930–1945* (Stanford, Calif., 1971) p. 346. The assistance came mainly from Germany, the United States and Britain, he alleges.
22. Fainsod, *Smolensk*, p. 434.
23. Miliukov, *Outlines*, I, 202.
24. H. Fireside, *Icon and Swastika: The Russian Orthodox Church under Nazi and Soviet Control* (Cambridge, Mass., 1971) p. 168.
25. G. S. Counts, *The Challenge of Soviet Education* (New York, 1957), quoted in Daniels, *The Stalin Revolution*, pp. 60–6.
26. D. Joravsky, *The Lysenko Affair* (Cambridge, Mass., 1970).
27. M. Ilin, *Moscow Has a Plan: A Soviet Primer* (London, 1931) p. 214.

Ch. 13   War and Reconstruction, 1941–1953

1. Deutscher, *Stalin*, p. 458.

2. Samsonov, *Short History*, pp. 207-8. For a full discussion of the debate among Soviet historians on the commencement of the Second World War, see V. Petrov, *June 22, 1941: Soviet Historians and the German Invasion* (Columbia, S. Ca., 1968).
3. See M. Van Creveld, 'The German Attack on the USSR: The Destruction of a Legend', *European Studies Review*, vol. 2 (1972); B. A. Leach, *German Strategy against Russia, 1939-1941* (Oxford, 1973); B. Whaley, *Codeword Barbarossa* (Cambridge, Mass., 1972). Whaley makes interesting use of the analogy with Pearl Harbor.
4. See, for example, Fleming, *The Cold War*.
5. For a balanced assessment, see D. S. Clemens, *Yalta* (London, Oxford and New York, 1970). Quotations from Leahy, p. 278 of the paperback version.
6. W. LaFeber, *The Origins of the Cold War, 1941-1947* (London and New York, 1971) pp. 136-9; D. Horowitz, *From Yalta to Vietnam* (Harmondsworth, 1967) pp. 61-2.
7. Horowitz, op. cit., p. 99.
8. For a summary Soviet view, see Samsonov, op. cit., pp. 266-80. For a somewhat longer but still brief analysis, see N. N. Inozemtsev *et al.* (eds), *Mezhdunarodnye otnosheniia posle vtori mirovoi voiny* (Moscow, 1962) I, 571-629.
9. Samsonov, op. cit., p. 215.
10. G. W. Nutter, *The Growth of the Industrial Production in the Soviet Union* (Princeton, N.J., 1962) p. 214.
11. A. P. Pogrebinskii *et al., Istoriia narodnogo khoziaistvo* (Moscow, 1964) pp. 171-98.
12. Ibid., pp. 199-223.
13. Fireside, op. cit., pp. 172-3.
14. Werth, *Russia at War*, p. 399.
15. Fireside, op. cit., p. 183.
16. M. J. Shore, *Soviet Education: Its Psychology and Philosophy* (New York, 1967) pp. 203-18.
17. Samsonov, op. cit., pp. 374-5.
18. Deutscher, op. cit., p. 601.

Ch. 14   The Establishment of Soviet Superpower, 1953-1964

1. Djilas, *Conversations*, pp. 95-8.
2. Nettl, *The Soviet Achievement*, pp. 221-2.
3. Frankland, *Khrushchev*, p. 90.
4. S. Alliluyeva, *20 Letters to a Friend* (London and New York, 1967).
5. Samsonov, *Short History*, pp. 291-2.
6. Rigby, *Communist Party Membership*, pp. 300-6; Nettl, op. cit., pp. 218-19.
7. Khrushchev, in *The Road*, pp. 361-2.
8. See, for example, A. Inkeles, 'Soviet Nationality Policy in Perspective', in *Russia*, ed. Brumberg.
9. Frankland, op. cit., p. 206.
10. For developments in the armed forces, see Garder, *A History of the Soviet Army*, pp. 138-210.

11. Samsonov, op. cit., pp. 326–7. For a scholarly Western analysis, see R. M. Slusser, *The Berlin Crisis of 1961: Soviet-American Relations and the Struggle for Power in the Kremlin* (London and Baltimore, Maryland, 1973).
12. Samsonov, op. cit., p. 339; Ulam, *Expansion*, pp. 667–77.
13. Pogrebinskii, *Istoriia*, pp. 224–58.
14. Khruschev, in *The Road*, pp. 70–2.
15. Pogrebinskii, op. cit., pp. 258–67.
16. Ibid., pp. 267–73.
17. W. C. Fletcher, *The Russian Orthodox Church Underground, 1917–1970* (London, 1971) p. 231.
18. Khrushchev, in *The Road*, p. 154.
19. D. A. Lowrie and W. C. Fletcher, 'Khrushchev's Religious Policy, 1959–1964', in *Aspects of Religion in the Soviet Union, 1917–1967*, ed. R. H. Marshall Jr (London and Chicago, Ill., 1971) pp. 136–40.
20. *The Road*, pp. 569–70.
21. See, for example, D. P. Costello, 'Zhivago Reconsidered', *Forum for Modern Language Studies*, vol. 4 (1968).

Ch. 15   Problems of Coexistence, Competition and Convergence since 1964

1. Reviewer in *Times Literary Supplement*, 15 December 1972, of M. Matthews, *Class and Society in Soviet Russia* (Harmondsworth, 1972). Among those who have adopted the watchword are: Z. Brzezinski and S. P. Huntingdon, *Political Power: USA–USSR* (New York, 1964); J. M. Gilison, *British and Soviet Politics: Legitimacy and Convergence* (London and Baltimore, Maryland 1973); P. Hollander, *American and Soviet Society: A Reader in Comparative Sociology and Perception* (Engelwood Cliffs, N.J., 1969); W. H. Parker, *The Super-Powers: The United States and the Soviet Union Compared* (London and New York, 1972); L. Turgeon, *The Contrasting Economies: A Study of Modern Economic Systems* (Boston, Mass., 1963).

   For the breakdown of the 'totalitarian' image, see W. D. Connor, 'Dissent in a Complex Society: The Soviet Case', *Problems of Communism* (March–April 1973); J. F. Hough, 'The Soviet System: Petrification or Pluralism?', *Problems of Communism* (March–April 1972); and J. Miller and T. Rigby, *The Disintegrating Monolith: Pluralist Trends in the Communist World* (Canberra and Clifton, N.J., 1965).
2. See, for example, A. Bergson, 'Towards a New Growth Model', *Problems of Communism* (March–April 1973).
3. See, for example, M. Kaser, *Comecon: Integration Problems of the Planned Economies* (London, 1967).
4. See, for example, C. B. McLane, *Soviet-Third World Relations*, 3 vols (London and New York, 1973).
5. A. G. Meyer, 'Theories of Convergence', in *Change in Communist Systems*, ed. Johnson, pp. 336–7.
6. Some creative writers – for example, William Burroughs and Allen Ginsberg – believe that the black predictions of such novels as Zam-

iatin's *We* and Orwell's *1984* are already in process of becoming reality. Some psychologists – for example, Robert Coles, R. D. Laing and T. S. Szasz – argue that severe psychiatric treatment for social deviance is a phenomenon common to the industrialised world.

7. A. Gertsen, 'Pisma k puteshestvenniku' (1865) quoted by A. Kucherov, 'Alexander Herzen's Parallel between the United States and Russia', in *Essays in Honor of G. T. Robinson* ed. J. S. Curtiss (Leiden, 1963) p. 47. For an attempt to put the historical development of the U.S.A. and the U.S.S.R. in comparative perspective, see Dukes, *The Emergence of the Super-Powers*.

8. D. W. Treadgold, *The West in Russia and China: Religious and Secular Thought in Modern Times*, 2 vols (Cambridge, 1973) is a good example of a work governed by a religious outlook.

9. Carr, *What Is History?*, p. 134.

Index

Cracraft, J., historian 86, 101
Cross, S. H., historian 8
Crummey, R. O., historian 83
Curtiss, J. S., historian 133

Dargomyzhsky, A., composer 144, 171
Delianov, Count I. D., administrator 168
Demidov, N. I., industrialist 94; family of 98
Denikin, General A., White Leader 225
Derzhavin, G. R., writer 121
Deutscher, I., historian 253, 254, 262, 284
Diagilev, S., editor and producer 203
Dionisii, artist 64
Djilas, M., writer 288
Dmitriev, S. S., historian 198–9
Dmitrii Donskoi: as national hero 26, 33, 37, 39, 270; reign of 31
Dmitrii Ivanovich 54; impostors of 54, 55
Dostoevsky, F., writer 146, 170
Dovzhenko, A., film director 247, 269
Druzhinin, N. M., historian 125, 132, 163–4
Dudintsev, V., writer 303
Duma, Boyar 44–5, 48, 90
Duma, State 182–6, 209–12
Durnovo, P. N., diplomat 187
dvorianstvo: see nobility
Dzerzhinskii, F., head of *Cheka* 234

education: medieval 23, 38, 63–4; modern 84, 99–101, 118–19, 121, 140–2, 168–70, 199–201; contemporary, 244–5, 266–8, 282–3, 301–2, 310

Eisenhower, D. D. 295
Eisenshtein, S. M., film director 28, 50, 222, 247, 269
Elizabeth, Empress 87, 89, 95–6, 108
Engels, F.: on absolutism in East Europe 125; Catherine II 106; *Communist Manifesto* 132, 222–3; Nicholas I 125; Peter I 87; Russia 150; state 231; other references to 215
Erenburg, I., writer 284, 302
Ermak, Cossack leader 42, 53
Esenin, S., writer 247, 248
Esper, T., historian 46–7, 75
Euler, L., mathematician 121

Fadeev, A. V., historian 128
Fainsod, M., historian 265, 266
Farquharson, H., teacher and mathematician 99
Fedin, K., writer 285
Fedosov, I. A., historian 106
Fedotov, G. P. 22–3
Fennell, J., historian 27, 33
Ferro, M., historian 216
Fet, A., writer 170
feudalism 6, 12, 21, 22, 68, 123
Filaret, Patriarch 56–7, 82
finance and taxation: medieval 9, 20, 29, 30, 35, 36; modern 99, 117–18, 140, 167, 195–7; contemporary 239, 240, 241–2, 264; 278–9, 280, 299
Fireside, H., historian 281
Fischer, F., historian 188
Fischer, G., historian 152
Fischer, L., historian 225
Florinsky, M. T., historian: on land captains 158; Michael Romanov 44; Paul's political vision 111; popular indifference to religion 38